**Contemporary American
Foreign Policy**

Contemporary American Foreign Policy

Minimal Diplomacy, Defensive Strategy, and Détente Management

Lawrence L. Whetten
University of Southern California

Lexington Books
D. C. Heath and Company
Lexington, Massachusetts
Toronto   London

Library of Congress Cataloging in Publication Data

Whetten, Lawrence L
    Contemporary American foreign policy.

    1. United States—Foreign relations—1945– 2. United States—Military
policy. I. Title.
E840.W46   327.73   73-21767
ISBN 0-669-91728-1

Published simultaneously in Canada.

Printed in the United States of America.

International Standard Book Number: 0-669-91728-1.

Library of Congress Catalog Card Number: 73-21767

To Gaby

Contents

List of Abbreviations

AAM	Air-to-air missile
ABM	Antiballistic missile
ADM	Atomic demolition munitions
ARVN	Army Republic of Vietnam
ASM	Air-to-surface missile
ASW	Antisubmarine warfare
CCD	Conference of the Committee on Disarmament
CECLA	Commision Especial de coordinacion Latino-Americana
CENTO	Central Treaty Organization
CINC	Commander in Chief
CONUS	Continental United States
CSCE	Conference on Security and Cooperation in Europe
DMZ	Demilitarized zone
ECM	Electronic counter measures
EEC	European Economic Community (Common Market)
EFTA	European Free Trade Area
ENDC	Eighteen Nation Disarmament Committee
EUNUFOR	European Nuclear Force
EURATOM	European Atomic Energy Agency
FBS	Forward based systems
FEBA	Forward edge of battle area
FBMS	Fleet Ballistic Missile Submarine
FRG	Federal Republic of Germany
FROG	Soviet Tactical Rocket—range 40–50 km
GATT	General Agreement on Tariffs and Trade
GDR	German Democratic Republic—Warsaw Pact
IAEA	International Atomic Energy Agency
ICBM	Intercontinental ballistic missile
ICSC	International Commission for Supervision and Control
KGB	Soviet security forces
MBFR	Mutual balanced force reductions
MD	Strategy—maximum defense
MFR	Mutual force reduction
MIRV	Multiple independently targetable reentry vehicle
MLF	Multilateral nuclear force
MRBM	Medium range-ballistic missile
MRV	Multiple Re-entry Vehicle
MT	Megaton
NPT	Non-Proliferation Treaty
NVA	North Vietnam
OAS	Organization of American States
PCC	Political Consultation Committee

PRG	Peoples' Republic of China
QRA	Quick Reaction Alert (five-minute alert)
SACEUR	Supreme Allied Commander Europe
SALT	Strategic Arms Limitation Talks
SAM	Surface-to-air missile
SAN	Surface-to-air missile—naval
SCUD	Soviet tactical missile (140–180-mile range)
SEATO	Southeast Asian Treaty Organization
SLAM	Submerged launched air missile
SLBM	Submarine launched ballistic missile
SRAM	Short-range air-to-surface missile
SSBN	Ballistic missile submarine, nuclear
SSM	Surface-to-surface missile
SSN	Surface-to-surface missile, naval
TASS	Soviet News Agency
TOW	Anti-tank missile
USAFE	United States Air Force in Europe
VSTOL	Vertical short takeoff and landing aircraft

Preface

It has become popular to comment, as Hans Morganthau and others have, that US foreign policy has again entered another period of crisis, similar in proportion and potential consequence to those of 1898, 1914, the mid–1930s, and 1946–49. It is now in vogue among political pundits and international affairs analysts to predict an imminent retrenchment in foreign commitments and a reordering of national priorities along minimalist interests. Indeed, many American and foreign observers foresee a return to isolation (or neoisolation, as it is fashionably called), disagreeing mainly on the timing of events. What has become apparent, however, is that many have overestimated the impact of the profound national shock over the Vietnam War and too readily applied psycho-analytical analogies of reversion in direct proportion to the scope of the shock. The nation has now perceived the bewilderment and frustration of its leaders over preferred options in Southeast Asia. It also has witnessed the reluctance of the ruling circles to confide in the public because of their inability to establish consensus among themselves or to formulate a self-satisfying Grand Design. America has observed the paradox of its leaders speedily increasing its commitments to Saigon, while at the same time sharply reducing its war aims. US goals have diminished, from seeking a reunited free Vietnam, to the defeat of communism only in the South, to merely an aversion against loss of great-power prestige. The public has become gradually conditioned to the fact that whatever the terms of a final political settlement, Vietnam now represents America's worst defeat in international affairs. It was the dimensions of the presumed debacle that have led so many to forecast dire consequences for American policy—a disaster on such grand scale could only result in a slashing in US foreign interests in equal proportions.

It is the contention of this volume that while a national introspection is being conducted with a thoroughness and scope not seen since the McCarthy era, it is not likely to lead inevitably to isolation or even to a significant reduction in US foreign commitments. It is likely to produce a more definitive public and official understanding of the consequences of overengagement, the responsibilities inherent in an activist foreign policy, the constraints on great-power influences, and the limitations of the détente process. The chapters in Part I discuss the numerous crisis situations US policy-makers are dealing with in the early 1970s, and then describe the increasing momentum in US diplomacy.

The national introspection over Vietnam inevitably tried to examine the more profound casual factors for the American involvement, such as the origins of the Cold War. Because of the immediacy of the Vietnam fighting and the more abstract quality of the Cold War, people engaged in the debate over national issues tended to reduce or overlook the intensity of the latter in comparison with more vivid body counts incurred in the former. But this is a serious distortion that extracts the discussion of priorities out of the proper historic context. The Cold War was real. It was not an aberration conjured up by bureaucrats and diplomats to advance misconceived objectives. Those who lived through this period have a hard time reminding those who did not that there were real victims and body counts of enormous proportions on both sides, which were reduced in scale only by the imagined horror of a nuclear holocaust. In terms of resources expended, the Cold War was far more expensive than the Vietnamese campaign; it was one of the most costly wars ever conducted. In human indignities and injustices, the Cold War was as self-brutalizing as preceding conflicts; possibly more so, because the victimization was conducted within the respective camps rather than on the open battlefield. By these standards, then, the values and principles for which the Cold War was waged were regarded just as absolute and relevant to personal survival as those for which the sacrifices were made in earlier wars. Finally, it must be pointed out that the Cold War was a total war, as complete in its geographic commitments and longer in duration than the other two world wars—every nation was expected to take sides and to uphold its obligations indefinitely. It is intellectually irresponsible to charge that the Cold War was the product of governmental treachery, incompetence, or naiveté. An open society's participation in such intense hostilities cannot be blamed on the decisions of a few leaders. More than in either the First or Second World War, the decision for the United States to organize the·Free World into an anti-Communist campaign for the protection of the higher human values was a societal decision openly arrived at.

The controversy over the Cold War is compounded by the nature of revisionism. Revisionism that is ideologically motivated has introduced grave distortions in the debate, because of its naiveté, emotionalism, and unintentional intellectual dishonesty. Conventional historical revisionism, on the other hand, is confronted with the age-old problem pinpointed by Bernard De Voto in writing about the American Civil War. First-generation observers or analysts, those who were "there at the conception," are valuable as chroniclers of contemporary emotion and atmosphere and the most probable influences governing given decisions. But proximity and commitment tend to color objectivity. Second-generation historians have access to greater documentation, often the views of other parties, and further distance from events, providing a more reliable framework for objective analysis. In assessing a phenomenon as complex as ideological warfare, a balance between the two approaches is essential.

This book is not an attempt to analyze the origins and conduct of the Cold War. It is a collection of essays written over a four-year span focusing on the many factors that have influenced the transformation in American foreign policy. The list is far from complete; a full inventory would have to include a more comprehensive treatment of commercial and monetary considerations. Since the overriding national priority during the Cold War was defense and security problems, the chapters in Part II deal with the problems related to assessing the relative force postures of the great powers and their allies, conducting arms reductions negotiations, and providing a credible strategy for a post-SALT II and post-MFR international situation. Finally, an underlying theme throughout is the need for greater understanding of the character and scope of the détente process and the nature of normalization of adversary relations. There is inadequate historic precedent for the present transformation in the great-power relations, and there are only limited methodological tools that can accurately assess Cold War relations and their impact on "normalcy." These essays, especially those in Part III, are intended to contribute to this general discussion.

Since these essays were written over a prolonged period, minor redundancies and inconsistencies exist. They have been left in because they indicate shifts in emphasis over time. These shifts are due in large part to the efforts of others who are contributing to the ongoing discussions about these engaging problems. The author, of course, is indebted to the endeavors of those who preceded him, and in particular to the wise counsel of his colleagues, including William Van Cleave, and to Uwe Nerlich and the staff of the Stiftung fuer Politik und Wissenschaft at Ebenhausen, West Germany. My gratitude must also be expressed to James Simon, Edwin Gillis, and John Rockwell for editorial comments, and Gail Franks and Annette Reiserer for typing support.

**Contemporary American
Foreign Policy**

**Part I
The Nixon Doctrine and
Minimal Diplomacy**

Introduction

The Nixon Doctrine, as the President has let his foreign policy be called, has been intentionally designed to cope with fundamental changes in the international system. In his first Report to Congress on Foreign Policy on 18 February 1970, President Nixon declared, "The postwar period in international relations has ended."[1] This theme has been consistent throughout subsequent presidential reports to Congress. Two years later he stressed the "need to continue, with both our friends and our adversaries, to build an international system which all will work to preserve because all recognize their stake in its preservation."[2] In 1968 Henry Kissinger called for a new "world order," in which the United States would play an important role only in its organization, and the responsibilities for its perpetuation would be more equitably shared among all the major powers. "Our deepest challenge will be to evoke the creativity of a pluralistic world, to base order on political multipolarity even though the overwhelming military strength will remain with the two super-powers. . . . A more pluralistic world. . . is profoundly in our long-term interest."[3]

In defining the shape of this new world order and America's proper place in it, Richard Pipes has provided a description of the doctrine's basic parameters.

1. With regard to the Soviet Union, America's only serious military rival, "confrontation" is to give way to "negotiation." Rather than attempt at every point on the globe to match and frustrate Soviet challenges with countermoves of its own, as the theory of containment had demanded, the United States will concentrate on locating areas of agreement between the two superpowers. No matter how insignificant or even trivial these agreements may be from the politico-military point of view (so the theory runs), they create an atmosphere of mutual trust which, in time, ought to be conducive to the solution of major differences. Concurrently, through increased trade, the USSR is to be enmeshed in a "web of interests" through which it will gain a greater stake in world stability;

2. In order to make foreign policy burdens lighter and more acceptable to its public, the United States will insist on its allies and friends doing much more. Peace—and hopefully freedom—are everyone's concern. The United States will be willing to help those whose security is threatened, but it will no longer rush to bail them out. In particular, Western Europe and Japan must be weaned from their overdependence on US military strength, and invest a larger share of their national product in defense.[4]

An important adjunct for implementing this new formula was the alleged "de-ideologization" of policy and diplomacy. Nixon stated in his first report: "Then [in the postwar era] the slogans formed in the past century were the ideological accessories of the intellectual debate. Today, the 'isms' have lost their vitality."[5] The practice of diplomacy was to return to the nineteenth-century style of movement and fluidity, if not to Woodrow Wilson's notion of "open convenants openly arrived at."[6] In referring to these aspects of the new US relations with the Soviets, the second Nixon report acknowledged that it could not be ascertained at this point whether Moscow is accepting a permanent change in policy or only a passing phase concerned more with tactics than with a fundamental commitment to a stable international system. During this period of uncertainty of transition, the US would maintain communications with the USSR at various levels to prevent Moscow from careening off in dangerous directions. Specifically, the US would engage the Soviet Union in joint efforts to curb or reduce the spiraling arms race.

Implicit in the Nixon Doctrine is the notion that the US, by virtue of its international commitments, military capabilities, and universalist political philosophy, is the only true global power. Thus equipped, it is the natural leader for creating the new order. This new "American mission" would attempt to gain general acceptance of the concept of realpolitik and balance of power politics. In such a reordering of the international system there would be no real or permanent enemies, and only ad hoc adversaries and allies. Any major state could conceivably align itself with any combination of opposing states on any controversial issue for any given length of time. Explicit in this new American mission is the cautious, low-key, but deliberate abrogation of the fundamental tenets of the earlier American mission of fostering interdependence among like-minded states. Axiomatic in the former universalist conceptualization of America's role was the general belief that common principles were shared by non-Communist states and contributed to mutually accepted responsibility for the collective defense of these principles. While these responsibilities were not evenly accepted, the sense of common danger led to an interdependence that spilled over into political, economic, and cultural life. A united Free World was the philosophical goal behind the American mission in the postwar era on which a consensus of domestic support had been firmly established. The realpolitik of the new American mission intentionally undermined the belief in shared principles, interdependence, partnership, and special allied relationships. Many former political and security commitments were implicitly challenged or rendered ineffectual. A pentagonal system was called for in which a balance could be maintained between the US, USSR, China, Western Europe, and Japan. Former American obligations and responsibilities were deliberately minimized in order to stimulate greater self-reliance for Western Europe and Japan, and to secure wider latitude for the United States in dealing with China and the Soviet Union. Equilibrium of the new order was to be a function of symmetries in interests and capabilities, preserved by maintaining prescribed "distances" among all actors.

The President acknowledged the difficulty of achieving this reversed inter-dependence:

> In the nature of things, progress in all areas could not be achieved simul-taneously—and this led for a time to understandable concern that our interests in some areas were being sacrificed to the need for progress in others. Our approach to China had an impact on Japan, as did our negotiations with the Soviet Union on our friends in Western Europe. Our unilateral economic measures affected both. As a result, our relations with our allies appeared for a period of several months to be somewhat out of phase with the innovations taken in our relations with our adversaries. By the end of the year [1971], however, it was clear that our initiatives toward both our friends and our adversaries were in basic harmony.[7]

The "Nixon shocks" in 1971 served notice to the other four powers and the American public that some level of "reverse interdependence" was an indispensable ingredient for "The Emerging Structure of Peace" as conceived by the Nixon Administration. The shocks capped earlier speculation about the return of Washington to neoisolationistic policy. Allies feared a slackening of commitments and irresponsible actions, especially in security and economic matters. Domestic leaders voiced concern about the feasibility of generating a public consensus about a policy of "reversed interdependence." Most observers at home and abroad were keenly aware of the impact the Vietnam War had had on the process of reappraisal of American foreign policy; they were in large part sympathetic to the introspection and self-evaluation that took place. Many, however, were gravely alarmed about the scope and nature of "reverse interdependence" and the level of engagement and the credibility of US commitments after this process was completed. Seasoned analysts predicted that, following a series of shocks intended to uproot former ties, the US would likely pursue a policy of "minimal diplomacy:" a deliberate assessment of interests and commitments made on an ad hoc basis and related only to immediate issues, not previous sentiments, obligations, or shared principles. Thus, "partnerships" and "special relationships" would have little value in the future. The US could be expected, according to these observers, to adopt a Gaullist foreign policy based on perceived national interests and not international responsibilities. The degree of disengagement or of constraint in the use of its power would in the final analysis depend increasingly on other imperatives than the influence of the new international system Nixon sought to establish.

The essays in Part I are a related series of analyses of the application of the Nixon Doctrine during roughly the first four years. They treat the problem areas primarily on a bilateral basis and omit US-USSR dealings, which will be discussed later.

1

The Crisis in Contemporary American Foreign Policy

One school of thought about the current US crisis holds that traditionally the dominant influence in American foreign policy has been isolationism. This concept is most frequently interpreted as containing three basic features. First, stemming from the admonition in George Washington's farewell address against entanglements abroad, US isolationist tendencies have been based heavily on non-engagement. Second, isolationism prescribes a high degree of self-reliance and assured physical security. The moral superiority of republicanism was a third hallmark of isolationism. Righteous indignation expressed officially against alleged abuses of other forms of governments reflected the general public mood of confidence and superiority.

All three factors conveniently enjoyed wide latitude for development and expression, because of America's obsession during the first 170-odd years of its history with domestic problems and requirements. The necessity to expand and then consolidate, to conquer enormous physical obstacles and to assimilate a myriad of ethnic groupings, consumed the bulk of the nation's energies and imagination. There was no compelling need to alter this pattern and become engaged in international matters or challenge the existing order of foreign governments. US smugness toward the outside world was reinforced by the conviction that the nation's highest calling should be the perfection of its own society and the promotion of America as the genuine Land of Promise. During the nineteenth century, "Fortress America" remained immune from foreign attack because of the protection of the British Royal Navy and the lack of resources of other potential antagonists, rather than US defenses, reducing security requirements and the need for defensive alliances.

Roots of American Expansionism

Two exceptions to this pattern emerged, both based largely on an exaggeration of the third principle, the superiority of republicanism. The first occurred in Latin America under the aegis of the self-proclaimed right as a hemispheric guardian known as the Monroe Doctrine. Originally directed more against the unrealistic threat of Russian hegemony over northwestern North America than the prospects of further Western European colonialism in Latin America, it later became transformed into a vehicle for US intervention in domestic affairs of our southern neighbors. In most cases intervention was invoked for the protection of American commercial interests, but it has been used since World War II for the preservation of political allegiances.

The underlying ideological motive was initially genuine enough: Latin America represented the world's largest bloc of republican states and, as the wave of the future, deserved the protection of the Republican Fatherland. Belief in a common fate as the vanguard of orderly world development led to exaggerated perception of hemispheric solidarity. The right of intervention was formally renounced only in 1936. The US decision, however, was safely couched by positive demonstrations of increasing hemispheric solidarity, in the form of the Pan-American Union and other regional bodies that theoretically could reduce the need to intervene. Again under the threat of foreign subversion, the US tacitly reaffirmed and exercised its intervention rights after the development of the Cold War. Kennedy retained these rights but seized the initiative in formulating new concepts and institutions, e.g., the Alliance for Progress, for the advancement of cooperation and solidarity. The Nixon Administration is the first US government to minimize both intervention and solidarity as the axioms for hemispheric policy. A genuine transformation has apparently emerged in Washington's Latin American policy that reflects a change in America's attitude toward the preservation of republicanism and its estimate of the threat of foreign subversion. (An elaboration on these points will be made later.)

The second exception was the United States' China policy. Americans were first attracted to the Orient for reasons of romance, missionary zeal, and commercial opportunity. An important motive behind the Open Door Policy, pronounced at the turn of the century, however, was the conviction that republican democracy was more beneficial for Asian welfare than the political values being introduced by Europeans. Moreover, the Open Door Policy as envisioned by Secretary of State John Hay was to be an instrument to prevent further carving up of China into spheres of influence. While the policy was a seeming failure and had virtually no impact on the international scene, it was widely regarded in the US as a major diplomatic triumph—an American blow for an American ideal. So engrained did this notion become that it was a major contributing factor in the preferential treatment gradually afforded China in Washington's Asia policy. This legacy of political guardianship of China became a key motive in the outbreak of hostilities with Japan, and a serious obstacle in formulating an appropriate China policy after the war. Nearly all of Truman's advisers agreed on the desirability of fostering true democracy in Chiang Kai-shek's China, but when this proved utterly unfeasible they could not reach a consensus on preferred options. One of the bitterest aspects of the Chinese Communist victory was that it represented the triumph of European Marxism after over half a century of American proselyting for republicanism.

US diplomatic experience in both exceptional areas tended to confirm American beliefs in the superior virtues of its system. As a self-congratulatory and self-perpetuating experience, these exposures to the outside world also

reinforced the general condemnation of European political values and therefore justified continued nonengagement. Most Americans even today would
probably argue that the failure of Washington's Latin American and Chinese
policies was due not to the imperfection of republicanism, but to unprepared-
ness of these societies for the rigors and responsibilities for its effective application. Many liberals and conservatives alike wrongly insist that such rationale
reflects the resurrection of isolationism. But it is just the opposite. Rather than
salutation to the propagation of American political values, it registers their
limited application.

Despite the importance of the Latin American and Pacific exposures, US
foreign policy during this period was dominated by European values and
political struggles. European monarchies and then fascist regimes were regarded
as the chief threats to republicanism. Expansion of these archaic forms of
government was antithetical to the higher values of human nature. Further,
the diabolic character of these contesting forms contributed to social unrest
and political tensions that would inevitably lead to hostilities and their eventual
overthrow. As former President Herbert Hoover admonished even as late as
29 June 1941, while this process of disintegration was going on, the US must
remain aloof and uninvolved.

While the United States remained deeply suspicious of the political processes in Europe and the consequences of engagement, it believed that it could
safely influence the course of world developments as a somewhat remote balancer in the overall power equation. When the US finally felt compelled to
enter Europe in 1917, it did so not as a rejection of its traditional values, but
as a confirmation of them. Wilson had concluded that the interjection of US
political ethics at that juncture would decisively contribute to the destruction
of European political structures, and introduce a new era of republican government and open diplomacy. US rejection of the full responsibility for European
salvation and subsequent disillusionment about the durability of existing systems were critical factors in the eventual American inversion.

The interwar years were characterized by gross misperceptions, primarily
on the part of the United States. The US had aided in the defeat of Imperial
Germany, but it was Germany that had destroyed nineteenth-century Europe,
not US intervention. Britain could not retain its status as the traditional balancer in European affairs; the scepter had passed irrevocably to the United
States. Europe became increasingly unstable as its prime mover—the US—became increasingly insulated from both responsibilities and consequences of
European developments. American rejection of European values, especially
colonialism, and its failure to promote its own ideals in the chaos of the interwar period, led to the dramatic propulsion of the US in 1940 into the balancer
role it had shunned for two decades.

Ironically, the United States reluctantly assumed this burden for the
defense of policies it had despised. "Pacific first" advocates who dominated

decision-making during the immediate prewar period could not muster sufficient strength to offset the inertia of isolationism only on the issue of protecting our Open Door Policy against Japanese aggression. It was not until Japan seriously threatened the European colonies of Southeast Asia after July 1940 that the "Pacific first" school gained support from the European-oriented elements of the Establishment and allowed the Cabinet to reach a unanimous decision that if Japan moved south of the roughly present-day North Vietnam, the US would have to go to war. Once again the US abandoned under duress its preference for neutrality and isolationism and belatedly entered a world war for the preservation of Anglo-Saxon values. In the Pacific it saw the maintenance of onerous European practices as the price for the preservation of higher Western ideals.

Origins of Neo-Isolationism

The US participated in World War II with an overpowering redemption complex. Once again European duplicity had cost American lives and treasure. Positive action would now be required and dynamic leadership would be necessary to insure that the tensions and frustrations of previous eras did not return to perpetuate instability. But American leaders were torn between conflicting notions of the preferred course of future world developments and an appropriate US role. Should the US return to narrow nationalism, or project leadership in a new system of international imperialism or strive to create a world of equal opportunity? Without a clear choice, the US pursued all three simultaneously, with the obvious difficulties inherent in dividing one's resources. The US emerged from World War II with Britain's traditional charge as the guardian of the status quo, but without London's privileged position of balancer. These circumstances induced many American leaders to seek the international imperialism option under UN auspices, with the US using full participation in world bodies as the instrument for projecting balance or influence. It was widely believed that the US could use international organization to protect its interests and to mold a world safe for republicanism and democracy, those values for which it had gone to war, without becoming engaged physically abroad.

But international organizations were imperfect instruments for defending the status quo while simultaneously promoting change. How could the US seek a world of equal opportunity, requiring the destruction of imperialism, which its leaders generally advocated, and still expect British and French cooperation in reshaping Western civilization? Equally complicated, how could the US hope to gain a balancer position, that of a remote, noninvolved positive influence, in the bipolar nuclear world of the postwar period? Bipolarity eliminated the balancer role and increased immeasurably the responsibility for dynamic international leadership as the most plausible means of protecting national interests. Both factors augured against a prompt return to narrow nationalism.

These dilemmas were compounded by the unexpected persistence of imperialism, the new challenge of communism and Soviet expansion, and the difficulties of forging the UN into a body that could model the world into an American image. Because of these pressures, a new form of American isolationism developed in the period of 1946-49. The US was even more convinced than in the prewar era of the sanctity of democracy. But it experienced modifications in the other two facets of isolationism, nonengagement and self-reliance. Participation in multilateral bodies was regarded as a vicarious means of engagement, able to allow sufficient influence to alter favorably world developments without requiring physical commitments. Indeed, the UN quickly became a *substitute* for a positive US foreign policy, and American troops and foreign obligations were withdrawn or canceled with minimal regard for local conditions and without the projection of a positive alternative strategy. The Marshall Plan and Truman Aid did not mark the reentry of the US into active involvement abroad. These and similar schemes were presented to Congress as measures for self-help, incentives for the Europeans to regain their feet by themselves. They were designed explicitly to preclude the necessity for reintroducing US combat units into foreign countries. They were a distinctive feature of the postwar isolationism designed to prevent or minimize US entanglements abroad.

The US entered the postwar period confident that it was the strongest military power in history. The Soviets could claim that the Red Army had defeated the Wehrmacht. But in the era of intercontinental nuclear warfare, massive continental armies could not effectively defend the Soviet heartland from strategic destruction. This strategic imbalance gave America its first reliable sense of assured deterrence. No country could invade or conquer the Island Fortress, and now no power could dare to endanger US interests throughout the world. But Stalin recognized that the US was both unwilling and unprepared to attempt conquest of the USSR. Therefore he accepted the negligible risk of nuclear attack as the necessary price for an assertive foreign policy that would consolidate further "Socialist victories."

Practitioners of American foreign policy soon recognized that reliance on self-sufficiency was inadequate, despite the scale of absolute military power available to them. Since nuclear power could only be used for the defense of ultimate values, self-reliance now carried the implication of enforced isolation on most international issues. As the US increasingly perceived world peace as the extension of democratic values and its political competition with the USSR as mainly ideological warfare, alliances of like-minded states were sought as the most suitable means for first containing Soviet expansion, then defeating Communist ideals.

Rise of Globalism

But when the mutually perceived threat increased, both great powers adopted respective containment policies. The USSR finally dropped its schemes for cooperation with bourgeois parties and mobilized the world's revolutionary forces into an anti-imperialist front on an expanded Leninist prescription. On its part, the US tried to organize the Free World into an anti-Communist coalition that could overlook pressing local demands in order to ward off the international conspiracy. Both viewed the opponent's efforts as conspiratorial and dangerous to vital national interests, and both sought to organize their respective comparative advantages for appropriate defenses. From the American viewpoint, the Cold War developed when the US realized that its ideals were not universally applicable and that it did not have the power to preserve the Free World through the single-handed enforcement of these values. This revelation was compounded by the dual dangers of Soviet expansion and the alternative appeal of authoritarian socialism to a decolonializing Third World, which might further reduce the attraction of American ideals and increase US isolation.

The containment measures of both great powers were unique in European history. For its part, the US advocated establishment of political alliances and the retention of operational combat forces for peacetime obligations, a step followed by Moscow. For the first time in peace, both camps assumed the expediency of semiwartime conditions and prepared to adjust national priorities accordingly. This transformation of wartime requirements into peacetime conditions was a complicated undertaking. Contrary to previous collective security alliances, the creation of operational military commands in peacetime required far more detailed analyses of the national interests of allies and adversaries and the implications of compromises should challenges arise to one's own. The efforts of both adversaries to facilitate the transition to semiwar increased their mutual perception of threat and triggered a greater mutual stake in the perfection of their respective alliances and fronts. The continuing requirement for greater alliance effectiveness led inevitably to increased US engagement abroad and the gradual acceptance of coalition politics as the most durable measures for defending US national interests.

Thus the US abandoned its preference for self-reliance and nonengagement and accepted coalition politics only in the 1950s. With the aid of hindsight, it is now safe to conclude that the omissions of noninvolvement in the immediate postwar era were far more critical as contributing factors in the rise of the Cold War than the acts of commission, such as the oft-cited sellouts to the Soviets over Eastern Europe. The omissions of leadership were responsible in part for the disarray in all the American-sponsored alliances, the increasing disenchantment in the United States about nationalistic claims of many allies, and the rising concern among the smaller powers about the merits of allegiance to a great power.

Omissions in leadership also contributed to the emotional intensity of great-power competition that fostered misperceptions. US containment policy, for example, differed from a similar British nineteenth-century model, in that it relied on multilateral cooperation for enforcement and was not predicated on a strategy of reprisals but deterrence through the threat of all-out war. The totality of this concept is understandable when viewed within the context of its antecedents: unconditional surrender and Wilsonian messianism. Both implied a total acceptance of US terms for peace or normalization and progress. Adjustment was conceivable in implementations, but not on the terms as such. The alternative was total vigilance and perseverance until the forces of history would more thoroughly prepare foreign seedbeds for democracy. But the assertiveness of communism projected convincingly the impression of a worldwide assault and embattlement for democratic forces, and compelled abandonment of the more leisurely wait-and-see attitude.

US Policy in the 1960s

The Eisenhower era was a period of action and involvement. The Korean War did not produce a climate of national retrenchment, as did the Vietnam War. Rather, it stimulated containment. Washington attempted to improve the organization and cohesion of the Free World by sponsoring new collective security alliances and pressing for greater military efficiency in existing ones. The international Communist conspiracy was viewed as global in scope. It was not merely confined to the borderland of the Eurasian heartland—no region or state was immune. The US placed such a high priority on anticommunism throughout the Free World that national interests and priorities of smaller states were repeatedly, and at times systematically, ignored or neglected. In Latin America, the Middle East, and Southeast Asia the practice of coalition politics had an empty ring; it did not reflect a genuine acceptance by all parties of the legitimacy of the others' national interests. The more truculent governments were regarded as unduly influenced by nationalistic sentiments or communist propaganda.

This was the era when the US first recognized that it was engaged in an ideological war, a battle for mens' minds. The virtues of American ideals could not merely be presented rationally. They had to be graphically and dramatically presented on the spot to skeptical or indifferent audiences. On the one hand, it was argued, direct involvement in national development of Third World countries would attract the necessary public attention and illustrate the sincere generosity of the American people. On the other hand, it was theoretically possible for US military and economic aid to provide sufficient security and domestic stability for the nation-building process to establish satisfactory roots and momentum. Thus the 1950s was a decade of a sharp crescendo in American foreign aid and in the practice of becoming involved in one form or another in virtually every international crisis and in many domestic crises. Too often, however, the positive contributions of the aid program were overshadowed by the negative features of America's self-appointment as the world's policeman. The intersection of strong trends of both international and domestic opinion against the consequences of the policeman's role during the 1960s was a profound contribution to the present introspection about American foreign policy.

The Kennedy era was marked not by a reaction to American involvement overseas, but by a general expansion and invigoration of nearly every facet of US foreign policy. Because of Sputnik and the alleged missile gap, the existing US asymmetrical deterrence was increased to overkill proportions. US and NATO conventional general-purpose forces were expanded and modernized to insure the feasibility of the "less nuclear" strategy of flexible response. The Kennedy Administration sought to alter the scope, nature, and purpose of US foreign aid. The self-help feature of the Alliance for Progress is an example of the more imaginative and dynamic approach Washington introduced into its foreign aid program. But under Kennedy, the US began the slow process of assessing the risks and consequences of overengagement and the limits to beneficial commitments. Despite the euphoric blandishments of Free World solidarity, the Bay of Pigs, Berlin Wall, and Cuban missile crises, Laos and Vietnam were signposts of this reappraisal process. The United States was beginning to perceive a more precise framework for the concepts of confrontation, intervention, and limited adversary relations. The dissection of these concepts into their component parts led to a more exact calculation of risks, possible losses, and interests. Rather than perpetuating the omnipresent challenge to the Communist threat that required total allegiance to the common cause, Kennedy elected to accept the neutralization of Laos and had decided to cut US losses in Vietnam when the appropriate means could be found. The Kennedy Administration, then, began the slow recessional. The British and French anxiously pointed out that this expediency was without design or overall strategy. Moreover, the recessional was applied on an individual, *ad hoc* basis, implying no general retreat, but indicating the first signs of a gradual decoupling of crises in the international confrontation and a relaxation of the Cold War. Washington reassured its more seasoned allies the US recessional differed from theirs because it would be administered from a position of overwhelming strength.

The halt and subsequent dramatic escalation in this general process were the result of Washington's inability to establish precise objectives in Vietman and appropriate means for their attainment. No consensus could be formed among responsible American government agencies about the nature of the threat, the purpose of US intervention, or the means of terminating our commitment. Under Eisenhower, the US goal was to defeat communism and make all Vietnam free for democracy. The Kennedy Administration was not prepared to accept responsibility for the liberation of the North, and lowered its sights to merely preserving democratic rule in the South. The Johnson government avowed self-determination but informally sought withdrawal without loss of face to a great power. The Nixon Administration accelerated the withdrawal process without formulating a model mutually acceptable for the political life of Southeast Asia after the US intervention phase. Despite partisan claims to the contrary, no American government or party has yet succeeded in establishing the objectives for intervention and postintervention, or prescribed the appropriate policy instruments for their achievement. This general imprecision clouded interests, risks, and losses, and contributed more than any other factor to the protraction of the US involvement.

Viewing the 1960s in a broader context, several factors have significantly influenced the state of world developments in the 1970s. First, the détente process made clear progress in communication, comprehension, and conceptualization of great-power relations (see below). The cautious, highly circumspect détente and the accompanying strategic stability provided sufficient security for the great powers so that an altered framework for state interactions gradually emerged for other global developments. Second, the deterioration in Sino-Soviet relations was a notable new input into this altered framework that both changed the nature of Communist relations and encouraged the triangulation of global power. So far, the US-USSR dialogue exceeds the minimal contacts and communications opened between Peking and Washington. Relations among all three have reduced the dangers of hostilities but grave rivalries persist, especially in armaments. Moreover, no party is prepared to extend its services for the benefit of either of the other two. Contacts have been largely negative, i.e., to reduce the threat of war rather than construct the framework for peace. One facet of this negative communication was the establishment of mutually respected constraints on policy. For example, the great powers learned from the Korean experience—during the Vietnamese War the US kept forces away from the Chinese border and the Chinese did not intervene in a way that would directly challenge American strength.

A third factor was the erosion of Alliance cohesion in both NATO and the Warsaw Pact. French disenchantment, Greek-Turkish differences over Cyprus, the continuing military dictatorship in Athens, and persisting controversies over burden-sharing and preferred strategies have weakened the sense of common cause and interest in collective defense. This growing indifference has of course been intensified by the reduced public perception of the Soviet threat. On the other side, Rumania's Cold War with East Germany over proper relations with Bonn and with the Soviet Union over appropriate behavior for Socialist states opened the way for rapprochement with the Federal Republic, eliminating the former bogy of revanchism as the common threat. Yugoslav and Albanian defection and Rumanian defiance inscribed distinct limits to Soviet political hegemony and on the utility of the Alliance as an instrument for exercising Soviet political will. Thus, both great powers entered the 1970s with noticeable liabilities within their respective camps.

A fourth characteristic of the 1960s stemmed in part from the synthesis of the other factors: the success of Ostpolitik in stabilizing Central Europe. In essense, the Moscow and Warsaw treaties certified West German recognition of existing boundaries and renunciation of former German territories now under Czechoslovak, Polish, and Soviet rule. They also cleared the way for the codification for the first time of the Four Allied Powers' rights and obligations in Berlin, and stimulated movement toward formal normalization of relations between the two German states. These documents are milestones in the politics of conciliation. They are invaluable imperatives for fixing great-power responsibilities in a still divided Europe, and for advancing the normalization process in East-West relations. And they are already being intensely examined as precedents for modified "two states in one nation" formulae by the Chinese and Koreans. Finally, movement toward resolving differences between the two Germanys is likely to be the most important single contribution to the complex and unique problem of defining and implementing normalization among states with so many points of intense antagonism and so many opportunities for cooperation.

A fifth factor was the rise of West Germany and Japan as important and potentially dominant regional powers. Both states began competing for the role of third-ranking world industrial power, with Japan predicted to hold the lead throughout the 1970s. Japan's economic stature alone, which reached hegemonic proportions in some Asian countries, became the bulwark of its political credentials. Geography and existing power constellation in the Pacific reduced the need for Japan to seek a genuine political role based on other components of national stature, such as military prowess. West Germany, on the other hand, enjoyed a greater natural propensity for political growth, because of its location between East and West Europe. The FRG's preoccupation with its Eastern policy, which was blocked for years by Warsaw Pact solidarity, placed a firm ceiling on Bonn's political aspirations and its authority throughout Europe. It was an economic giant with a dwarf's political stature. Once Bonn adopted a genuine policy of reconciliation with the East Europeans, it lost the former constraints on its stature imposed by its demands for reunification and their charges of revanchism. By the end of the decade, Bonn was already beginning to act as the spokesman for Western Europe and as the second most authoritative power, after the USSR, in Central Europe. Unlike Japan, which began looking for a political role in an unnatural setting, the Federal Republic was emerging as the dominant European state, with many inside and outside the FRG asking how resurgent German nationalism could be assuaged.

A final characteristic of the 1960s (in a list that is certainly not exhaustive) is the changing nature of small-power influence and the relationships with the great powers. The US and USSR and the traditional powers, France and Britain, all reduced their general level of economic aid and involvement in Third World countries after the mid-1960s. Few of the developing countries could claim to be of vital importance to any of the larger powers and when they did, like possibly Afghanistan, they were recognized as such by the other states. The great powers began viewing the Third World as an arena for ad hoc influence competition, but not as a vital component in the rival's global conspiracy or an important integer in one's own defenses. A shift took place from the decade-old assumption that collective security was an indivisible seamless construction to awareness about the merits of individual crises and problems. Gradually cases were assessed on their respective merits rather than their international implications. The larger powers began to realize that they did not need the smaller states more than they needed great-power support. A growing emphasis was placed on decoupling crises from international chain reactions and on stressing local solutions to local problems whenever possible. These changes contributed to the phenomenon of vertical rather than horizontal great-power involvement in regional affairs. Both great powers became more eclectic rather than more general in their commitments. Accordingly, there were fewer instances when smaller states could demand or petition for great-power support for their respective causes. In turn, economic aid produced fewer political profits and assumed a more genuine commercial character, which Japan and West Germany rapidly seized as new opportunities for their competing industrial growth. This growing great-power indifference left the Third World still confronted with its cardinal issue: how to overcome the growing economic and technological gaps between the "have" and the "have-not" nations.

These features of the 1960s suggest that few of the problems that faced statesmen at the beginning of the decade were solved at the end. While conclusive solutions often defied political leaders, the evolution of developments sometimes reduced the intensity of the dilemma, as in SALT, or created new conditions that were more conducive to conciliation, as in Ostpolitik. The world has been made marginally safer for some people, not all, and this is no grounds for complacency or self-congratualtion. A review of the main persisting problem areas for US foreign policy in the early 1970s is warranted before implications can be analyzed and recommendations for the remainder of the decade can be proffered.

2

Washington's New Look at Latin America

In Latin America, Washington's traditional sphere of influence, the Kennedy and Johnson administrations maintained a high degree of initiative and control over events. This level of hegemony was the product of an effective carrot-and-stick policy, plus the personal attention of both presidents. Each had his own reasons for promoting the social and economic benefits of the Alliance for Progress and the political cohesion of the OAS, yet both exercised the United States' self-proclaimed right of intervention (explicitly renounced in the 1948 Bogata Declaration of the OAS) whenever local circumstances warranted. The interventions at the Bay of Pigs and in the Dominican Republic were sharp reminders to Latin Americans of the outer limits of US tolerance in security matters. But these actions were not sufficiently incongruent at the time with the national interests of other American states to promulgate the hemisphere-wide indignation over earlier intrusions. Thus benevolent presidential attention and firm reactions for infractions against hemispheric order appeased the more radical complaints of the Latin Americans, leaving them little room for disagreement among themselves and even less latitude for organizing to protect their interests.

At the Latin American Press Association meeting in October 1969, President Nixon announced a new "low-profile" policy for Latin America, a Guam doctrine of three months earlier for the southern hemisphere. The new look was based on the findings of a presidential committee known as the Plank Report. This investigation contended, with strong endorsement from Dr. Henry Kissinger, that on the basis of cost versus benefit Latin America had receded in importance to the United States. Neither strategically, economically, politically, nor ideologically could Latin America any longer be regarded as vital to US interests. Therefore a reduced US profile was both necessary and desirable. The Nixon Latin American Doctrine prescribed a diminution of US interests in Latin America's domestic affairs, an emphasis on local solutions to local problems, and a greater stress on trade than aid as the impetus for economic growth.

The Nixon Doctrine came as a profound shock in the southern hemisphere. Even responsible Latin Americans have historically taken secret pride in their ability to tweak occasionally the Great Northern Colossus by brandishing anti-Yankee propaganda and promoting antagonistic policies. Their latitude in encouraging anti-Americanism rested comfortably on the time-honored assumption

19

that Latin America collectively was more important to Washington than the US
was to any given southern country. Washington's preferential treatment for
Latin America had been confirmed for years through price bonuses and assured
markets, deferential treatment at the United Nations and other organizations,
and prestigious engratiation at the official level. So confident were Latin American leaders that they never seriously questioned Washington's presumed ideological, political, and economic dependence upon Latin America. In the final
analysis, they felt certain that they could collectively harken to the mutual
benefits of the preferential treatment as an effective counter to US actions they
jointly regarded as detrimental.

The Nixon Doctrine put Latin America on official notice that Washington's
former preferential policies could no longer be regarded as blanket privileges.
Formal indifference by the Great Colossus required urgent and radical changes
in Latin American attitudes and policies. The critical challenge was in trade and
economic aid. US dollar surpluses had increased substantially during the 1960s.
In 1960 the US trade balance with Latin America was $200 million and profit
remittances from US firms were $1070 million. In 1970 the trade balance had
reached $800 million and profit remittances neared $2500 million. By 1972,
Latin America's annual indebtedness to the United States totaled over $3.5
billion and was climbing, with the 10 percent surcharge adding $100 million
per year. This deficit was compounded by a drop in US economic aid and commercial credits. In fiscal year 1972 US bilateral assistance amounted to only
$338 million, plus $103 million aid in the Food for Peace Program and $500
million in Export-Import Bank loans and donations through international organizations—small-scale contributions compared to previous years.

Only a few months after the pronouncement on the Nixon Doctrine, concrete counteractions were taken. First, the Latin American members of the
Inter-American Economic and Social Council unanimously condemned the
newly imposed 10 percent US surcharge on trade; some members decided to
reduce active participation in the body and all agreed to the founding of a new
organization without US membership—Commisión Especial de Coordinación
Latino-Americana. The CECLA was charged specifically to coordinate regional
efforts to seek new markets and sources of supply and to cultivate alternative
sources of capital and credits, especially in Europe and Japan. (For countries
like Brazil, the CECLA quickly became more important than the OAS). In July
1970, twenty-two Latin American states formally confirmed this shift in emphasis in the Buenos Aires Declaration, which expressed "their joint determination to affirm their independence in world politics through closer links with the
European Communities." In part because of this orientation, Latin America's
total foreign exchange reserves rose in two years from $2 billion to $8.9 billion
by 1973.

Second, a new impetus was added to alter Washington's time-honored
position as the sole source of military aid and armaments. Coupled with a

genuine US desire to discourage continued purchase of expensive systems and its higher priorities for deliveries to the war zone, several Latin American countries actively explored British and French suppliers. With the purchase of French Mirage fighter-bombers, Peru opened the way for major European arms merchants in the Western Hemisphere. (The US retaliated by first condemning the sale, then suspending military aid to Peru, but finally doubling the total aid package). In 1968-72 Latin Americans spent $1.2 billion dollars on European arms, six times more than for US weapons. This figure was due to the Congress-imposed ceiling on annual arms sales to OAS countries, which was raised to $150 million in 1972. Clearly the US is losing its former sole-source position in the Latin American arms market and the battle to contain hemispheric arms escalation.

Third, in direct defiance of Washington, all Latin American states expressed support for those who had unilaterally extended the limits of their territorial waters to two hundred miles and some, such as Brazil, seized the precedent set by Ecuador and Peru to extend their limits to similar distances. The motive for these latecomers in this feud was not merely to preserve fishing grounds, but more important, to establish unequivocally national rights to sea-bed resources claimed in the Gulf of Mexico by presidents Roosevelt and Truman that are now a recurring interest in international forums.

Fourth, the unprecedented phenomenon of military and political sub-pacts emerged within the OAS. The five-nation Andean Pact became a viable grouping for the defense of regional interests with a distinct anti-American bias. Fearing isolation and growing threat along its western and southern borders, Brazil sought a political and quasi-military alignment with Argentina, designed to bolster Buenos Aires against a leftist takeover and for joint action should the guerrillas seize Uruguay. Thus ideological blocs have become an important new feature of South American politics and sources of regional tensions and counter-measures heretofore unknown.

Fifth, a new malleability in domestic politics of several Andean countries emerged that was regarded an inevitable by most and beneficial by others. Coups are endemic in Latin American politics—in 1972 only four governments had been duly elected. But juntas were gaining public support. The right-wing junta of Juan Velasco Alvarado in Peru evolved into a populist government that quickly found common cause with the hemisphere's first legally elected Socialist government in Chile. Under Torres a populist government also emerged for the first time in Bolivia. These diverse regimes had two important factors in common: they all enjoyed an unusual degree of public support and they were adopting new foreign policy measures based on a revival of nationalism.

This renewed nationalist sentiment gave rise to the final distinctive change in contemporary Latin America. A wave of expropriations of foreign commercial assets and investment restrictions aimed at the United States swept through these countries, culminating in Chile's nationalization of the US-owned copper mines. Chile's action and its subsequent decision not to reimburse Anaconda and Kennecott corporations, and to nationalize other US properties, resulted in a direct confrontation with American business interests, and the most serious challenge to US policy since the Cuban Revolution. The scope of the challenge was due in part to the antecedents provided elsewhere. In 1968 the Peruvian junta nationalized the International Petroleum Corporation and large foreign-owned estates. The right-wing regime in Ecuador has systematically seized US fishing boats violating its two hundred-mile maritime limit. The populist government of Bolivia expropriated in 1969 the Gulf Corporation's assets along with those of other US-owned mining firms. The conservative Pastrana government of Columbia signed the Andean Pact restricting foreign investments, and the Social Christian regime in Venezuela increased its oil royalties 10 percent, forced the foreign companies to accept government control, and adopted a law for the gradual expropriation of all major oil resources. Finally Argentina took over the huge Swift meat-packing facilities and signed a friendship agreement with Allende, implying support for Chile's anti-US actions and leading to speculation that further nationalization of foreign properties was possible.

With losses and restrictions of such a scale, US business circles mounted increasing pressure in Washington for positive counteractions. It was clear that Washington was no longer in control of regional developments, as it had been up to 1968. During the Johnson Administration right-wing coups in Argentina, Bolivia, and Brazil assured friendly regimes, the intervention in the Dominican Republic reasserted US privileges in Latin America. Cuba had become effectively isolated within the hemisphere, the deaths of guerrilla leaders such as Uceda, Torres, and Guevara indicated that the revolutionary threat was subsiding. And finally, US investments and dollar returns in Latin America had reached record levels. While accepting Nixon's insistence on a "low-profile" posture, Treasury officials advocated adoption of a policy of more active engagement and limited intervention to counter the adverse trend in US commercial interests.

Washington's new regional strategy centered on two basic features: strengthening Brazil as a counterrevolutionary center and possible source of military intervention, and isolating Chilean influence from neighboring Argentina, Peru, and Bolivia. Near-model relations have been cultivated with Brazil after the US dropped such grievances as the two hundred-mile maritime limit. The present government fears that in several years it may be surrounded by hostile regimes and has adopted, with strong US support, a program for constructing strategic infrastructures consisting of roads and communications with its remote frontiers. Increasing US economic aid has contributed to Brazil's surpassing Argentina as the continent's leading economic power. Brazil is now leading all its neighbors in capital formation, growth in industrial base, and progress toward modern commercial institutions. American engagement in Brazil has reached an all-time high which is likely to continue.

US efforts to isolate Allende's Chile followed a characteristic pattern. Official snubs and veiled threats were made in speeches by Rogers, Laird, and Connally. Economic aid was informally suspended and commercial credits in large part have been blocked or terminated. Most important, an effective diplomatic campaign was launched among Chile's neighbors. Two days before Chile and Bolivia were to open formal relations, the Torres government was overthrown and replaced by a right-wing military junta leader, Hugo Banzer. Bolivia was now "safe" and agreed to closer economic and political cooperation with the US and Brazil, opening a potential flank against Chile's northern border. Belatedly recognizing the urgency of foreign investment for economic development, Peru narrowed its differences with Washington and created an appropriate climate for American firms (Occidental and Union Oil Corporations are now filling the gap left by the IPC). In general, State Department officials were expressing guarded optimism about the prospects for improving relations with Lima and in creating a greater distance also in its ties with Chile.

The aim behind this dual strategy was apparently to create economic dislocations and overpressures that would demonstrate the consequences of precipitous expropriations or would discredit the government and lead to its defeat in the 1973 congressional elections. On 13 October 1971 Secretary of State Rogers issued a statement explicitly supporting the position of the US copper companies. Pressure was mounting for more effective measures to protect the over $16-billion American investment in Latin America. But Chile continued to nationalize or buy out US firms. By the end of 1971, thirty-nine major firms in all sectors of the economy with assets at a book value in 1969 of nearly $4800 million were in Chilean hands. Only eleven firms worth $75 million and producing manufactured products had not been taken over.[1] Under these circumstances, Nixon adopted a strong stand in his 19 January 1972 State of the Union Speech supporting US commercial interests. He announced the termination of loans, aid, and other economic benefits to countries that nationalize US properties, unless prompt, adequate, and effective compensation is made. In general Chile sought an amiable settlement and was prepared to meet some of the companies' terms. But a court decision that the copper companies' back taxes and other debts canceled further remunerations led to further strains, a near-total break in commercial relations, and serious domestic shortages. The food riots in August 1972 were the most severe public test the Allende government faced to that time. The subsequent protracted general strikes, the overall economic deterioration (inflation increased 180 percent in 1972), and repeated Cabinet crises did not produce marked changes in US-Chile relations.

On 12 September 1973 Salvador Allende was overthrown by a combined armed forces junta. In the presence of his captors, Allende took his own life, suicide under duress, and thereby received the beautification of the world's Leftists—Marxist martyrdom. The coup was undoubtedly the product of widespread popular discontent over worsening domestic difficulties. Washington's role in the episode remained cloudy and aroused widespread criticism, especially among European socialists. In answer to charges that the putsch was CIA engineered, a State Department spokesman told newsmen that the US knew about the coup attempt ten hours before it occurred but did not either aid the insurrectionists or warn the legitimate government. He asserted that the official US policy toward the Allende government had been one of passive resistance—intentional noncooperation because of irresponsibility toward US business interests. The aim was to use economic pressure to induce greater responsibility or accept the penalties of domestic economic hardships and dislocations. The State Department spokesman observed that it was uncertain whether US interests were best served by the putsch or by pressing the policy of passive resistance increasing the economic hardships. It was hoped that the domestic strains could convince the Chilean electorate to vote against Marxism and Allende at the next election, thus preserving both constitutionality and responsibility in government.

Thus ended the world's first and only experiment in constitutional Marxism. It was the second attempt, however, to create liberal Marxism, communism with a human face. It had complied more stringently to Anglo-Saxon principles of governmental legitimacy than the 1968 Czechoslovak experiment. The Czechoslovak reforms overthrew Anton Novotny and introduced such sweeping reforms that they too were purged, without once referring their actions to the Czechoslovak people through an election or referendum. They had acted within the bounds of party statutes, but arbitrarily as far as the public weal was concerned. Yet both the Chilean and Czechoslovak efforts to achieve national socialism were fundamentally anti-Stalinist and un-Soviet in conception. Therefore both should have been eligible for unqualified Western support. Yet Washington reacted paradoxically: with veiled euphoria and moral encouragement for the Czechoslovak reformers and with hostility and vindictiveness against Allende. Surely the US attitude toward Allende was not determined merely by the expropriation issue. The broader problem of another Communist regime in the Western Hemisphere must have been the overriding factor in the decision to oppose Allende. Whatever the motive, the overthrow of Allende was one of the best examples on record of the effective use of economic levers to achieve political goals.

A summary of four years of Nixon Doctrine was provided by the President in his May 1973 Foreign Policy Report to Congress. While stressing continued close US attention on and identification with Latin American affairs and problems, a new format and content for the relations was confirmed.

At the outset of this Administration, we surveyed the world problems that confronted us, and we made several deliberate decisions regarding our posture in Latin America. First, we resolved to avoid what we saw as the two basic flaws of past performance: taking our Latin neighbors for granted, assuming that they were irrevocably linked to us by commerce and friendship; and launching a crusade in which we would promise to lead the peoples of the hemisphere to prosperity and happiness under out guidance and our formulas. Our second decision was that, there would have to be a lessening of the dominant role the United States had previously played. Thus we deliberately reduced our visibility on the hemispheric stage, hoping that our neighbors would play more active roles. And they have—not always in perfect harmony, it is true . . . . The upsurge of national efforts to meet pressing internal problems is in part a direct result of rising nationalism. An increasing sense of national identity characterizes every one of the American states. . . . I am convinced that the low-key course we have followed over the past four years—the avoidance of slogans and gimmickry, the emphasis on Latin initiatives—has helped in an important way to provide the basis for a stronger, healthier and more realistic relationship among the members of our hemispheric community.[2]

The president concluded with a pledge of continuing interest in Latin affairs. He condemned the practice of expropriation without compensation as injurious to cooperative atmosphere and suggested that the next course of action should be the examination and perhaps overhaul of hemispheric organizations.

What conclusions can be drawn from the first four years of the Nixon Doctrine in Latin America? First, the policy of drawing down commitments is likely to be the dominant feature of long-term US objectives in the hemisphere, despite occasional alterations of emphasis. But the outer limits of US interests have been tentatively outlined mainly in the economic and commercial areas. The US will continue to place a high priority on economic stability and development, and contributions to investment and growth will come increasingly from private rather than public sources. Accordingly, Washington is likely to continue to deal firmly with policies that are detrimental to these commercial interests.

Does this not imply a return to Dollar Diplomacy of the 1920s, when governmental protection was demanded for investments abroad on the grounds that guaranteed political stability was essential for American contributions to local economies to have a satisfactory impact on national growth? Probably not, because of the continuing preference for disengagement and the Latin Americans' success in compensating for the loss of their former preferential treatment. Ideological, political, and strategic reasons were underlying factors in earlier US hemispheric intervention that have now partially declined in value, reducing the motives for engagement and hegemony. More important, the Latin Americans have achieved a high degree of unanimity through the CECLA and have been reasonably successful in exploring foreign commercial sources. One of the measures of this success is the degree of inversion Latin Americans now exercise.

For the first time, Latin Americans perceive threats to national security that are not either Yankee imperialism or Soviet expansionism. Many Latin Americans now see equally dangerous threats arising from their immediate neighbors and are organizing alliances and alignments for their protection. The new stress of local challenges and solutions reduces the need for American protection.

But the employment of political alignments along ideological lines as a solution for local problems, abetted inadvertently by Washington, may have the adverse effect of polarizing the region into contending blocs. It is conceivable that in the next four years of the Nixon Doctrine tensions among Latin Americans will actually increase to the point that the US may feel compelled to take sides for the protection of its interests. Intervention on the scale of the US occupation of Nicaragua during the 1920s will probably not take place. But sporadic and possibly intensive reengagement with all the levers of influence may be required. Thus the Nixon Doctrine was a signal and a symptom of the loss of US hegemony over Latin America and its inability to control events in the United States' only annointed sphere. But Washington's interests in Latin America will remain much higher than in any other developing region. And until a more precise formula can be devised specifying the level, scope, and means of engagement, the decline of US hegemony may contribute to regional instability that could prove more dangerous than has occurred in other troubled areas.

3 American Interests in the Middle East

It is appropriate to examine the contraction of US interests in other regions before attempting to assess the level of involvement in other areas of high priority. Washington's present interests in the Middle East are roughly fourfold: general concern for the modernization process for developing nations; containment of Soviet political influence and counteraction of the degree of military parity the Soviets have achieved in the Mediterranean; stabilization of Arab oil imports and deflation of the world energy crisis; and the resolution of the Arab-Israeli conflict as the most destabilizing factor in regional harmony. While individually important, collectively these interests do not represent the level of US involvement in the era of the Eisenhower Doctrine and the Baghdad Pact, when Washington viewed the area as an ideological battlefield and thus guaranteed the territorial integrity of *all* Middle Eastern states. Specific guarantees were subsequently issued to Jordan, Saudia Arabia, and Israel and troops were dispatched to Lebanon and the Yemeni border. Today the US probably regards the preservation of Israel as the only interest for which it would become militarily involved in the Arab world. As the last remaining vital American interest in the region, the preservation of Israel and the continuing Canal War warrant closer study.

The first four years of the Nixon Administration were marked by the opening of a unique dialogue with the Soviets and the formulation of four separate diplomatic initiatives: 28 October 1969 proposed package settlements between Israel, Jordan, and Egypt; 7 August 1970 cease-fire along the Suez Canal; March-August 1971 partial accord reopening the Canal; and proximity talks agreed to only by Israel in February 1972. These so-called repeated Rogers' peace proposals are notable indications of the progressive scaling down of Washington's interests in the five-year-old Canal War and the contribution it felt it could make to a settlement. Indeed, before the Moscow summit conference in May 1972, Rogers told Israeli Deputy Prime Minister Allon that the US had finally given up formulating comprehensive plans and accords and resigned itself to merely creating an atmosphere conducive to exchanging views between the local parties.

The reasons for this steady diminution of US interest was due to its inconsistent aims after the June War. After the Arab defeat, the USSR made one of the most significant great-power decisions since the Second World War, in agreeing to underwrite Arab rearmament. So prompt and comprehensive was the resupply operation that by the September 1967 Khartoum Conference the Arabs were assured a credible military option if political agreement could not be reached. In other words, by giving the Arabs a military choice the Soviet operation effectively denied Israel the political fruits of its military victory. When the success of the Soviet gambit was perceived, the US adopted a strategy of preserving Israeli military superiority as the best plan for reducing the chances of direct US military involvement, while holding some prospects for a local settlement. But the Soviets supported the Arabs' claims that Israeli terms for peace, inasmuch as they could be divined, were onerous and would perpetuate regional tensions. Moscow concluded the Israelis could not be allowed to deal with the Arabs from a position of overwhelming strength and decided to meet Arab demands for military parity with Israel. But each time the Arabs tried to demonstrate that parity had been attained by reopening hostilities along the Canal, Israel effectively countered by defeating Arab forces on the east bank, gaining air superiority, and finally by conducting strategic attacks against the Egyptian interior.

Soviet efforts to achieve military parity were disastrously defeated and Egypt was being attacked at will. This was almost as serious a setback for Soviet prestige as the June War itself. Moscow tried repeatedly to induce the US to restrain Israel and warned that without voluntary constraint the USSR would have to increase its commitment to Cairo. Washington rejected both the pleas and the warnings and in January 1970 Moscow agreed to participate directly in the defense of Egypt. The USSR steadily increased the scope of its commitment until the Israeli air force was fully engaged in a battle for air superiority over the east bank. During July the Israelis lost seven aircraft and admitted tacitly that it could not defeat the Soviet ground-air defenses. But before agreeing to the US-sponsored cease-fire, Israel intentionally baited Soviet interceptors and shot down four MIG-21Js. This flagrant affront to Soviet calls for restraint and obvious demonstration of Israeli determination to deal from a position of strength, even if it resulted in further Soviet involvement, confronted Moscow with more difficult choices.

The USSR had important stakes in the cease-fire and the prospect for a settlement. The basis for its strategy of involvement was that if parity was achieved and a satisfactory agreement reached, the USSR would gain credit for protecting Arab interests in both war and peace against the combined power of the US and Israel. Such results could enhance Soviet prestige and possibly provide for the first time a credible base for its influence in the Middle East. Conversely, the perpetuation of Arab inferiority and the protraction of a no-war-no-peace situation could be dangerous and counterproductive for these aims. Finally, unless the results of the Israeli attack on Soviet aircraft were redressed, the image of Moscow's military prowess would be impaired among Third World nations, at the Two-Power Talks, and in the NATO-Warsaw Pact stand-off.

Accordingly, Moscow decided to accept the onus for violating the cease-fire provisions and postponing the political talks by constructing an air-defense system along the east bank that would deter further Israeli attacks. Without degrading Warsaw Pact defenses, Moscow erected the most formidible electronic, missile, and aircraft defense system in the world. Even when turned over to the Egyptians, the new defense systems greatly increased the price to both sides for the resumption of hostilities. The Soviet decision improved the deterrence against Israel and demonstrated a greater degree of parity than existed to date. But it did not compel Israel to modify its intransigent position on a political settlement. Since it did not advance this larger Arab aim, the Egyptians began to regard the increased Soviet commitment as contributing more to the costs of defense burdens than to the promotion of their political interests. These fears were confirmed when Israel received two major consignments of US aircraft, modernizing one third of its total inventory, and more important when the US agreed in November 1971 to Israeli plans for arms self-sufficiency by agreeing to sell required licenses and manufacturing technology.

The Canal War was now stalemated and the confrontation shifted to Cairo and Moscow. In March 1971 Sadat raised new demands for "decisive" weapons that could compel Israeli moderation. Among other weapons, Sadat asked for the MIG-23, which is a superior interceptor to the F-4 and could deter Israel from strategic attacks. The Arabs' strategy was not to reconquer the Sinai but to develop a posture that would force Israel to fight on their terms, setpiece warfare where geography and numerical advantages could offset Israeli superiority in technology and mobility. Egyptian air defenses were not intended to gain air superiority, but merely to engage the Israeli air force sufficiently to deflect it from attacking the ground forces. The Egyptians could then resume systematic artillery bombardment and, if the strategic deterrent held, could deny Israel its former escalatory options. The Arabs estimated that in this scenario with limited alternatives even small casualty figures would induce flexibility among Israeli leaders. Strategic deterrence was the key element which the Soviets could not provide unless they altered the entire premise of their commitment.

In order to minimize losses in the event of unforeseen or inadvertent developments, the USSR confined its commitment to Arab military parity largely to defensive systems. Moscow apparently concluded that Washington's repeatedly stated desire for a peaceful solution and frequent calls for a ceiling in the regional arms race were sufficiently strong motives to prompt US pressure against Israel if only Soviet defensive systems were furnished. Moreover, Moscow could not supply its latest weapons without accepting the risk of grave compromises to its military stature elsewhere if they were attacked and defeated by US-supplied Israeli forces. Thus, the USSR devised a self-limiting "sufficiency" formula for its commitment to Cairo: it would provide adequate weapons to insure defensive parity without supplying offensive or strategic systems in quantities that would encourage general or total war.

Washington's position throughout the Canal War has been relatively constant. It calculated that Moscow's entire strategy was based on the assumption that the US could pressure Israel into a conciliatory stand before the escalation reached dangerous levels. If the US chose to follow this course of action even on its own merits, Moscow would emerge the prime beneficiary. There was virtual consensus among Washington agencies that the US could not press Israel until some quid pro quo could be formulated that would minimize this positive effect on Soviet influence, preferably including the reduction or elimination of the Soviet military presence in Egypt. Until a quid pro quo could be devised, the US found itself in the unwanted role of confronting the USSR, appeasing Israel, and displeasing the Arabs. The US furnished enough military aid to calm Israel's most urgent demands and fears and to infuriate and frustrate the Arabs. Yet it applied enough diplomatic pressure to antagonize the Israelis and disillusion the Arabs. However, tardily the arms consignments were distributed to Israel, Washington remained unquestionably committed to the unqualified guarantee of Israeli superiority. The US did not feel compelled to parallel the Soviets' policy of sufficiency and its guarantees to Israel compromised its credibility and claims of impartiality with the Arabs. This chain of events denied the US any prospects for mediating the dispute, especially after August 1971. Fundamental modifications were required in the positions of all players before a political settlement could be envisioned.[2]

The third US peace initiative during March-August 1971 was instructive about the political issues involved. Two cardinal questions defeated this round and remained as major obstacles to further advances: the sovereignty of the Israeli-occupied territories and the relevance of external powers to the settlement process. In February 1971 Sadat made two key concessions by agreeing to accept a peace accord with Israel and to conduct talks about an interim agreement reopening the Canal. The US was genuinely pleased and encouraged by these moves and accepted responsibility for promoting the talks. During the first exchanges and the subsequent discussions when Rogers visited the Middle East in May, Israel firmly refused to allow the return of Egyptian military units to the east bank and to territory it insisted should be demilitarized. Without a manifest Egyptian presence Sadat could not claim that the east bank had been returned to Egyptian sovereignty and therefore had no incentive to reopen the Canal. To break the deadlock, the US presented Israel with a series of detailed proposals which were regarded in Tel Aviv as an assumption by the US of a mediation role with its inherent rights of initiative. Israel's counteractions forced the US to abandon its third peace bid and to concentrate its diminishing attention in the Middle East on devising a role it could play that would be acceptable to Israel.

Tel Aviv's sharp reaction against both Rogers's and Jarring's earlier mediation attempts were projections of its basic strategy. It has consistently demanded direct negotiations with the Arabs. When denied the leverage of its military victory and superiority, it sought to construct a negotiating framework that would confine the Arabs to minimum bargaining position by denying them plausible options. Israel viewed as mandatory the necessity to preclude any external suggestions which the Arabs might use to rally international support. In other words, when unable to prescribe the terms for peace, Israel insisted upon the right to exercise control over the direction and pace of any negotiations relating to a political settlement. Confronted with this determined Israeli posture, the US concluded that its influence was limited in the crisis and would remain minimal unless it complied with Israeli terms. Washington also concluded that the crisis would remain dormant only if hostilities were not resumed. And meeting Israel's demands for weapons technologies and licenses would be the most effective means of preserving the existing cease-fire.

Cairo's options were now reduced.The elimination of external political pressure against Israel left no alternative but to shift even greater emphasis to the military aspect of the confrontation. Moreover, the US assurance of Israel's long-term arms self-sufficiency forced Sadat to devise some means to circumvent Soviet restrictions. He first tested the leniency in Soviet constraints during his October 1971 visit to Moscow by repeating requests for "decisive" weapons. Promises were made, but no deliveries. By February Sadat had decided there was no choice but to pursue a policy of Arab arms self-sufficiency, independent if necessary of Soviet aid. But as Sadat later revealed, even the threat of denying the USSR its time-honored source of influence through arms deliveries did not compel Moscow to relax its "sufficiency" formula. Sadat's next move was the expulsion in July 1972 of the Soviet advisory mission and combat units from Egypt.

Sadat's expulsion of the Soviets was the most dramatic single event in the Canal War since the Soviet decision in June 1967 to underwrite Arab rearmament. The level and form of future military cooperation between the two countries will remain the subject of protracted bargaining as both sides reassess interests and risks. Sadat's stand reflected bitterness and disappointment. He was now faced with two hard realities: the sacrifice and hardship of the long-haul, go-it-alone program, or the necessity of an even more dramatic move to shake US passivity. His harsh attacks revealed his helpless acknowledgment that ousting the Soviets had proportionally increased US authority among all four players. As Algerian President Honare Boumedienne stated in a press interview, if the US did not respond, as the only power that could now influence adjustment, Sadat's ouster of the Soviets was insignificant and may even invite military defeat. "The departure itself isn't what counts . . . . If it only means that the Russians are no longer needed to the same degree in Egypt, then it is unimportant . . . . But if it is a signal that means an eventual reorientation in US policy, then it could be a historic event."[3]

The expulsion order was a partial setback for Moscow by any standard. It had attempted to provide military parity for its sponsored state. When the upper limits of its commitments were soon reached, Israel still retained important military advantages. And when hard choices were required, Moscow had to assess the prospects of compromise to its stature in the Third World from either of two negative decisions: Either accept penalties in the eyes of other arms recipients for denying a developing nation what it regards as its ultimate security requirements, or accept the adverse consequences on the Soviet defense posture itself of a possible defeat of Moscow's sophisticated weaponry. The Kremlin chose the former alternative and accepted an inadvertantly imposed formula of "sufficiency" for Egyptian armaments.

It was Arab opposition, not American, that finally forced the Soviets to turn the corner in the Canal War. This rounding the corner, the enforcement of Moscow's sufficiency formula for Egypt and the subsequent withdrawal, highlighted Washington's failure to impose a similar sufficiency equation on Israel. But US policy in fact failed to constrain Soviet expansion; indeed, it stimulated growth in Moscow's influence. The basic premises of US policy were never really relevant, as when Dean Rusk told the US Senate in July 1967, a time of overwhelming Israeli supremacy, that American pleas for arms control were violated by Soviet arms replacements. Actual or anticipated Soviet reactions became the incremental guide for each US escalation. But Moscow's failure to secure Egyptian military parity and subsequent reluctant acceptance of sufficiency now highlights the bankruptcy of the US notion that assured Israeli supremacy would be conducive to accommodation.

The expulsion of the Soviet military forces from Egypt presented Moscow with a serious dilemma—it must either meet Cairo's demands for achieving military parity or accept a compromise in its position as the sole source for Egyptian armaments. Moscow elected to retain its position of influence in Egypt and agreed to supply the weapons necessary for a resumption of hostilities. The formula worked out between the two governments was that the Soviets would now provide a limited number of surface-to-surface missiles (SCUD B) with Soviet crews to deny Israel, by the threat of retaliation, its former option of escalating hostilities to the strategic level. Both agreed that military parity could be confined to establishing battlefield equivalence. With this agreement the rivals were prepared to resume hostilities on 6 October.

The October War, as it is now called, was one of the most intensive localized wars in modern military history. The Egyptians had erected the most formidable area air defense of any modern nation. The tank battles in the Golan Heights and Sinai were on a scale not witnessed since World War II. The equipment, training levels, and leadership on both sides had improved substantially since the June War. After hostilities broke out both great powers concurred that a political settlement could be possible only if a military stalemate was achieved. By October 22 the desired stalemate was apparent to all belligerents, with each claiming a limited tactical victory. The costs for restoring momentum in the Arab-Israeli conflict were heavy for both sides, with Israeli battle deaths proportionately equivalent to 160,000 for the US. The penalties in the October War were the most extensive of any of the previous conflicts, a fact that alone may induce greater flexibility in negotiating positions.

In the final analysis, what are the prospects for a final solution to the Arab-Israeli problem? The Canal War has provided convincing evidence that a correlation exists between military parity and political compromise among adversaries who have options other than capitulation or surrender. The degree of military parity achieved by the Arabs has now introduced a new level of fluidity into the position of all the actors. The position of the belligerents, particularly, have been eroded: they may later recalcify, but not along the former lines. The perpetuation of this new fluidity over the long term now seems probable for the axiomatic reason that the vital and important interests of all actors are closer to fulfillment than ever before.

The Arabs' sense of honor and self-esteem has now been vindicated as never before since decolonization. They have fought the "final war" of anti-imperialism-anti-Zionism and forced the traditional adversary to a standstill in a battle that necessitated using the opponent's preferred terms for conflict. When a seeming underdog can deny a formerly overwhelmingly superior adversary his announced war aims, he will inevitably claim a victory, whatever the tactical configuration at the cease-fire. This objective seems to have been the overriding Arab goal throughout the entire Canal War.

The USSR has now moved closer to its objective of gaining international recognition of its stature as a regional power than at any time in the last twenty years. The Arabs, individually or collectively, cannot grant this authority. Only the rival great power's sanction can bestow the prestige Moscow seeks. This has now been achieved by Washington's intentional exclusion of its allies, France and Britain, from the peace conference, and by its invitation to the USSR to cosponsor the gathering. Moscow's cochairmanship symbolically demonstrated American acceptance of the shared responsibility for providing the prerequisites and the long-term stability of regional adjustments. After persistently pursuing a policy of linkage between military parity and political compromise, Moscow is now enjoying its "finest hour" as a regional power protecting the rights of local states oppressed by imperialistic interests. It remains to be seen what form and role this new political splendor will take in Middle Eastern politics.

The United States is closer than ever to its goal of regional stability. Washington has consistently viewed Middle Eastern stability as requiring the curtailment or emasculation of the Soviet challenge and influence. The change in the American position acknowledged the legitimacy of Soviet presence in the Middle East. A shift also occurred in its estimation of the role of a compromise solution. The US had sought a localized solution, but had placed a higher priority on maintaining Israeli military superiority, which was self-defeating. After the October War, Washington agreed with the Soviet position that stability was a function of compromise on both the political and military planes.

Israel's vital interests in insuring its security through military superiority and adroit diplomacy has been modified to the point that it will now accept non-self-reliant mechanisms as adequate guarantees. The question of Israeli security has been and continues to be a main issue in a durable settlement. The fact that Israel entered the peace conference apparently prepared to accept some form of political guarantees to supplement its own military preparedness indicates that Tel Aviv had agreed to internationalize the issue. The internationalization of Israeli security has finally brought a solution within sight.

If it now seems plausible that the basic interests of all four actors are within reach, what will be the impact of a durable settlement on the détente process and great-power relations? A settlement is likely to have a profound impact on the detente process for several reasons:

1. It would demonstrate that the great powers could extend their collaboration, heretofore largely confined to issues of bilateral importance, to topics of vital regional necessity.
2. A settlement would serve as another precedent for guidelines in future great-power/small-power relations, with emphasis on local solutions to local problems without small-power actions that could precipitate great-power intervention.
3. If the solution holds, continuing Arab-Israeli problems would be removed from the international limelight, reducing the prospects of either great power being able to exploit any potential advantage it might gain from a settlement.
4. If the Palestinians prove to be politically mature in their quest for national rights, and if the Israelis can dissociate Palestinian justice from Israeli security, then there is a reasonable chance that future Arab-Jewish differences will revert to the issue of minority rights.
5. Finally, it remains an open question whether the precedent of great-power collaboration on Third World problems will be sufficiently durable and rewarding to provide common ground for tackling the next Middle Eastern problem—the energy crisis.

The Arab-Israeli conflict was confined largely to four actors with fairly clear national objectives. In the international energy crisis, the great powers' interests transcend prestige and influence competition to the more critical problems of national economic growth and the prosperity of one's allies. Great-power competition during the Canal War legitimized the credentials of both as Middle Eastern powers. But the cooperation involved was for the vital interests of other states, not those of either great power or of their traditional allies. The energy cirsis is likely to be a dominant international issue for the rest of the decade. For the first time in détente history, economic issues of international dimensions are likely to supersede issues that have been confined largely to political and military matters. Moreover, the energy crisis is the first instance where the initiative on major world problems has passed to developing nations. As a result, the détente process is likely to receive its most definitive test over the "have" versus "have-not" nation controversy related to future world energy needs. The SALT and MBFR talks, technically complex, are politically circumscribed to the security needs of industrial nations. The energy crisis, however, introduces a new dimension: an economic issue of vital importance for many developed and developing nations, the first serious "North-South" global crisis. The precedent of great-power collaboration on the regional issue of the Arab-Israeli conflict is not likely to provide sufficient experience and confidence for durable cooperation over the larger global problem of energy requirements. The Soviets are likely to be cautious in defining their position in the matter until Western lines are fairly well drawn. Moscow may remain confident that a side-line stance is adequate and appropriate until the issue crystallizes, then draw on its credit accrued from the Arab-Israeli conflict to support the position of the oil-producing nations. But the USSR's growing need for Arab oil and its increasing dependency upon maritime stability and its requirements for predictable economic growth will complicate the precise stand Moscow will ultimately take on the oil issue. The experience of the Canal War suggests that when Moscow has assessed the role it should play in the energy crisis it is likely to persist with even greater tenacity that it did in the Canal War—the stakes and the potential political profits are much higher. Thus, the oil issue may become the hardest test yet of détente and Moscow's policy of peaceful coexistence.

4 US Third World Politics as Mirrored in the Indian Subcontinent

Compared with the late 1950s and early 1960s, when the US was heavily engaged in the Middle East, the Congo, and Southeast Asia, the 1971 Pakistani-Indian conflict was a dramatic illustration of the decline in American public interest in the Third World. The outbreak of fighting on 3 December became a singular test of the new interpretations of US commitments. In oversimplified terms, the issues involved were relatively straightforward. Pakistan regarded the question of autonomy and civil unrest of its eastern wing as an exclusively domestic matter and would not tolerate external interference. It adopted the stand that the unrest had to be dealt with before the autonomy matter could be treated dispassionately. But the methods for suppressing the unrest were clearly excessive and exacerbated the turmoil. Wholesale arrests and mistreatment alienated the largely Bengali population and some ten million fled to neighboring India.

International concern about these outrages centered almost exclusively in India, who was forced to assume the refugee burden. Since the inconclusive 1965 conflict with Pakistan, the Indian armed forces had been reorganized and modernized and military proficiency had been restored. More important, Indian political leaders from all parties, except the extreme left, were anxious to find a final solution to the Pakistan problem—the division of a potentially hostile nation into two unconnected parts that posed threats to India on two widely separated flanks, but not necessarily by military means. The breakdown of public order in East Pakistan over the March 1971 parliamentary elections was regarded by Indian leaders as evidence of continuing instability on their southern border that should be permanently eliminated. To this end, New Delhi pursued several policies to improve its position if the situation deteriorated further. Pakistan was warned of the implications of its burtality and remonstrances were made to international bodies. The attitudes of the great powers were explored. Moscow proposed a Friendship Treaty in return for accelerated military aid and a declaratory policy that would serve to check China and isolate Pakistan should hostilities break out.

The US sought time. Washington generally accepted India's interpretation of the seriousness of the crisis but disagreed about the desirability and feasibility of external interference. Moreover, both were at odds over preferred means for resolving the dispute. The US had a formal defense agreement with Pakistan against agression by a Communist power and both states participated in regional alliances, CENTO and SEATO. Pakistan had long been regarded as a friendly but difficult state. US influence was not high since the suspension of arms deliveries after 1965 and the lack of progress registered in the Kashmir dispute with India. On the other hand, Washington had honored India's policy of non-alignment and accepted the value of a neutral state that could check Chinese expansion in exchange for massive economic aid. The Indian lobby in Washington, especially under Kennedy, had argued convincingly that when economic takeoff was achieved India could become the model democracy for Asia and an invaluable balance to the appeal of Chinese communism. Accordingly, New Delhi became a prime recipient of US economic aid. Thus the US had important interests at stake in the 1971 crisis. Not unlike the Greek-Turkish dispute over Cyprus, the 1971 crisis included only two states, friendly or allied to the US; no Communist threat was perceived and no great-power challenge existed. Again the US had to assess its interests in the dispute strictly in local terms, unrelated in general to global factors and international repercussions.

After visiting Moscow and gaining Soviet reassurances of positive neutrality in the event of hostilities, Prime Minister Indira Gandhi discussed the crisis with Nixon. A personal misunderstanding reportedly occurred. Both agreed that the matter of autonomy versus independence should be left to the various Pakistani factions, and that the best way to restore public order was to secure the release of the imprisoned Bengali leader, Sheik Moshie Raman. Mrs. Gandhi felt that the US was the only country that could wield such influence, and left Washington with the impression that Nixon would act promptly and decisively to this end. The President, apparently reassured by Gandhi's pledged restraint vis-à-vis the use of force, acted deliberately and cautiously in advising President Yahub Khan about the dangers of continuing political instability.

Washington's constraint stemmed not merely from reluctance to interfere in domestic affairs of a friendly state, or distraction with more pressing problems. Washington correctly estimated that internal pressures within Pakistan were profound and that no facile solution was at hand. The USSR was in the favorable position of being able to afford India effective aid while accepting only minimal risks. But the US could provide a tottering Pakistan the same level of aid and involvement only by taking drastic measures. The risks for the respective great powers were disproportionate because local conditions favored India to the point that the US could only hope to deter India without aiding Pakistan. The estimate proved correct. Within two weeks Pakistan collapsed, mainly from its own weight, and was dismembered, while India emerged as the second strongest Asian military power, with an enhanced political stature.

The consequence of India's deliberate aggression and dismemberment of Pakistan is likely to have far-reaching effects on US Third World policy. India was not condemned for its agression and no action was taken to redress the results of its attack by any international organization or group of states. London was unwilling and unable to mediate a dispute involving the vital interests of two Commonwealth members, signaling the further demise of this one laudable grouping. China had no formal obligations with Pakistan and provided only marginal moral support. The US aided neither side and earned the abuse of both, by dispatching a battle fleet into the Bay of Bengal when East Pakistan had virtually collapsed, and by recognizing diplomatically the fruits of aggression after only an appropriate interval.

These events caused a traumatic shock throughout Indian Ocean countries. Formerly under Western dominance for some two centuries, Indian Ocean countries were startled to witness the degree of Western indifference to local crises after only two decades of independence. Moreover, even the great powers did not exploit the crisis as before to score ideological points. One lesson for all from the East Pakistani War is that it will be increasingly difficult for Third World nations to use exclusively local crises as bait for great-power commitments. Even the threat or act of aggression will no longer assure a smaller state of the support or protection of an indignant world. In an important sense, Third World countries are finally becoming truly independent; the earlier collapse of imperialism is now being followed by the prospects of guarded erosion in the imperial will of the remaining great powers. This region is no longer the strategic unity it was under British hegemony. While increased local autonomy may raise the chances for renewed foreign manipulations, it may foster caution by external powers as well. As the stark reality of the changing circumstances is recognized, few smaller states will rejoice at the increasing burden their new responsibilities will impose. It has been several years since the call "Imperialists go home" has been heard, and it may be a few more before the cry goes out, "Please return." In the interim, the growing weight of local problems and dangers is likely to dampen further interest in the already defrocked concept of nonalignment; indeed, the incentive for alignment among smaller states may increase.

The nonalignment issue was underscored by the Soviet-Indian Friendship Treaty. India has been a champion of positive neutrality and nonalignment since its inception. Grave fears were expressed at home and abroad that the treaty compromised the virtue of this stand without affording adequate benefits. But that overstates the case. The treaty does not provide for automatic mutual defense. Nor does it authorize erection of common or operational defenses or define the presumed threat. Like other treaties granting political guarantees, e.g. the forty-two the US has signed, the Friendship Treaty provides only for consultation about joint actions in the event of a perceived threat. The danger of this approach to mutual defense is that it can afford the stronger power important, if not decisive, influence in defining the nature of the external threat, the strategic interests of both states, and appropriate countermeasures. Such leverage could spawn satellitization among weak and unresourceful states. This is not the present case with India. The degree of cooperation with the USSR or reliance on nonalignment will depend upon the level of external provocations or the assertiveness of Indian foreign policy. In any event, India will probably prefer to confine its foreign policy objectives to issues and areas that will require little Soviet attention or support.

What then is the Soviet position on the subcontinent? Moscow gained in prestige by discreetly supplying adequate aid to a friendly state during its hour of need. Indeed, India would probably not have felt sufficiently confident to attack Pakistan at that time without Soviet moral and material support. But the limits of friendship treaties as instruments of influence were demonstrated by Egypt, and Moscow wisely acted to consolidate its stature in India by reducing the need to invoke the treaty's military provisions. The USSR energetically attempted to cultivate a new "spirit of Taskhent" within the subcontinent. Within three months the leaders of India, Pakistan, and Bangladesh were invited to Moscow and encouraged to meet at the summit level to resolve outstanding differences. The Communiqué released on 17 March 1972, during Pakistani President Bhutto's visit to Moscow, implied that his urgent request for economic aid had been tied to Soviet demands for talks between the three states. Soviet motives behind this seemingly benevolent attitude were probably to further its image as the protector of the subcontinent by restoring friendly, cooperative relations as soon as possible and reducing the chances for renewed hostilities. Moscow now has a shared interest with China and the United States in insuring that New Delhi does not overreact to its new posture as Asia's second military power or adopt an assertive foreign policy on the subcontinent. The USSR can be expected to try and channel Indian military attention away from Pakistan and Bangladesh and to concentrate it on the Chinese threat.

China had deployed about 50 percent of armed forces against the US threat along its southeast border. But as the US reduced its military strength in this theater, China transferred large numbers of these units from the high-cost deployment areas in the South to the much lower-cost deployment areas in its northeast provinces, along the Soviet frontier. Thus the transfer of additional Indian divisions in the Himalayas could relieve this expected increased pressure along the Sino-Soviet frontier. In the broader context, Moscow can be expected to use its bilateral relations with New Delhi and other Indian Ocean countries to advance in a de facto manner its earlier goal of creating an anti-Chinese coalition. Moscow has apparently postponed hope for erecting a formal mutual defense pact and has confined its ambitions to cultivating an informal grouping. The Friendship Treaty and Moscow's improved posture among all three subcontinent nations are important advances in this direction.

The positions of the subcontinent nations are becoming increasingly parallel. Bangladesh had no option initially but to embrace Indian liberators and welcome Soviet aid offers. But assistance from both quarters is being increasingly condemned as niggardly, ineffective, and exploitive. Certainly the magnitude of the reconstruction task contributed to the general disillusionment and spurred the quest for sources of additional aid. Western countries and international organizations were petitioned for help, but the bloodbath inflicted on the Bihari minority for alleged complicity with the Pakistani Army dampened incentives. The euphoria, exuberance, and excesses of independence were quickly replaced by the harsh realities of nation-building in one of the world's most impoverished societies. The imperatives of survival are overcoming nationalistic sentiments, and geographic dependence on India has induced a more compliant attitude toward Pakistan and the US.

Pakistan, on its part, has shown remarkable resilience in its recovery from a humiliating defeat, loss of its richest province, and the decline of its international stature. It too felt compelled to explore all possible sources of aid and was also disappointed in the prospects for external assistance. China promised military deliveries but could not expand its economic aid, and the USSR sought regional cooperation as a by-product of new aid. Western countries were even more deliberate. President Bhutto then agreed to Mrs. Gandhi's invitation for a summit conference at Simla in the Himalayas. But only territorial adjustments were agreed upon, and the problems related to Bangladesh remained outstanding. One of the most immediate results of the East Pakistani War was to generate a decreased dependence for both Bangladesh and Pakistan on external powers, economically and politically. Neither could act truly independently of India or the USSR respectively, and it will be many years before the former degree of self-sufficiency is restored.

For its part, India was now in a position to demonstrate restraint and good will toward its neighbors. The strength of its new military posture and the anticipated Soviet resentment may dissuade India for the time being from developing a nuclear capability. Instead she is likely to strengthen cooperation with Bangladesh and to explore areas of closer identity of views with Nepal, Sri Lanka, Burma, and Afghanistan. There can be little doubt that New Delhi will use the present opportunity to seek recognition of its regional leadership and its role as the leading Indian Ocean power.

Washington's initial reactions to the establishment of Bangladesh were to encourage Pakistan to regain its feet soberly and pursue modest, nonrevanchist aspirations. It assumed a courteous stance toward India and responded promptly to New Delhi's subsequent request for a resumption of economic aid. After a respectable delay, it followed the lead of most nations and recognized Bangladesh and offered $125 million in relief assistance, plus $90 million in economic aid—more than the combined aid from the USSR and India. Secretary Laird also pledged an increased US naval presence in the Indian Ocean (temporarily postponed because of the North Vietnamese March 1972 invasion). The aims of these actions were to foster a rapid return to normalcy and a restoration of US prestige. Further, it was believed that even a modest demonstration of US interest would partially quell the shock among Indian Ocean nations and block tendencies toward "Afghanization." The sooner a degree of normalcy and cooperation was assured, the less chance there would be for aggrieved states to seek external political support, possibly resulting in regional polarization and cyclical increases in tensions. (As a long-range hedge against a great-power confrontation in this region, the US formally accepted Brezhnev's 11 June 1971 call for mutual naval reductions in the Indian Ocean. On 1 February 1972 the US announced that it had approached and held discussions with the USSR about the possibility of limitations on naval operations. There are unquestionable operational advantages for both sides in such an accord, but it will be a long time before it is reached).

This brief review of the East Pakistan War and its immediate results prompts several observations about US Third World policy. First, the United States has learned, however imperfectly, that it must painstakingly distinguish between the threatened expansion of great-power interests and the grievances of local contestants, despite the degree of overlap, complexity, or interdependence. Unless small states can convincingly demonstrate that a clear and present danger exists of great-power involvement, the US can be expected to react deliberately. The fact that Pakistan survived, however disfigured, without US intervention is compounding evidence for those who argue that civil wars as in Nigeria, Burundi, Yemen, and Indonesia can reach their own culmination without US involvement. Criteria for US involvement, its form, scope, and intensity, have not yet been devised and are likely to vary from one contingency to another. But motives for engagement will continue to reflect the merits of the respective grievances, US interests affected, risks and potential implications for alternative decisions, rather than the employment of earlier automatic leakage theories between international crises and communist conspiracies. This should not imply that Washington will not respond to future challenges from other great powers in the Third World. It merely suggests that the US, like Britain and France, will be more prudent in defining interests and challenges. The East Pakistani War should have placed the world on notice that these generalizations will be applied with rare exception among all developing nations.

5 Vietnam: Elbe or Waterloo?

Without question the strongest reagent responsible for the US contraction from its former omnipresent global commitments has been the cathartic experience of the Vietnam War. Unlike America's predicament in the East Pakistani War, there was a clear and present Communist danger in Southeast Asia which introduced an element of urgency and confirmation of the conspiratorial confrontation. In the final analysis, Vietnam may play the same role in US history as the "Suez Affair" did for France and Britain. Such a checkpoint in national development, in itself, need not be detrimental. But observers with such diverse viewpoints as Hans Morganthau and André Fontaine hold that Vietnam was a white whale that the US pursued for years without knowing why and without regard for the destruction wreaked during the chase. The obsession of the chase rendered Washington ineffectual in other theaters of action where more vital interests were at stake and forced the US to witness helplessly the devaluation of its currency from mounting foreign deficits, expropriation of business properties abroad, the decline of its international moral standing and challenges to its national virtues. This is not the place to address the accuracy of these indictments; this section will merely examine the interactions during the final stages of the war and their impact on related aspects of US foreign policy.

Origins of US Policy

The United States maintained a strong bias against French policy in Asia during the Second World War and in the immediate postwar period. It went to war partly over Japanese threats to Indochina, yet it vehemently condemned French colonial policy as a source of international tension. American motives were to defend higher European values in general. As such, it was against a restoration of the status quo ante and refused to allow France to accept the Japanese surrender or to reoccupy fully Indochina for over one year. Indeed, at one point Washington considered granting Ho Chi Minh's request for military aid and recognizing the coalition government of liberated Vietnam in which the Communists participated. Washington hesitated in part because of the uncertainty about the experimental bourgeois-communist coalition regime in Metropolitan France and the general confusion at the time about the communist threat. After the Chinese Communist victory, however, Washington shifted its support behind the French. It recognized Bao Dai and furnished aid to oppose the Viet Minh. By 1954 the US was paying $1.1 billion or 78 percent of the total French colonial war effort. This changed outlook was partly the result of the skillful efforts of French General Lattré de Tassigny, who at the time of the Korean War persuaded the US that the Indochinese conflict was the counterpart of the Korean conflict and deserved strong US assistance. Between 1950 and 1954, the US National Security Council repeatedly concluded that the Indo-chinese insurrection was detrimental to US interests. While the Geneva Confer-ence was still in progress, Washington threatened to suspend all aid to Indochina and France proper if French resistance collapsed, and introduced drafted legis-lation authorizing the commitment of US forces. In the final test at Dien Bien Phu, the US declined the request of Premier Joseph Laniel for direct involvement because other allies would not support such action. When the Geneva Accords were reached (to which the US was not a party and which were labeled a "dis-aster" by the National Security Council), Washington concentrated on aiding France in consolidating South Vietnam. When Mendès France was still Premier, General Paul Ely, CINC in Indochina, on 13 December 1954 signed a secret agreement with US General Lawton Collins violating the Geneva Agreement and transferring responsibility for South Vietnamese security matters to the US military mission. This document marked the formal beginning of eighteen years of agonizing US engagement in the security of Indochina—America's longest military operation.

Linkage with the Communist conspiracy and the inevitability of the domino theory, first coined by President Eisenhower, governed US policy during most of this period. The domino theory held that if one more state fell to com-munism in Balkanized Southeast Asia, its neighbors would soon succumb. The implementation of the theory had a Manichean attribute of black or white, a "for us or against us" quality. Threatened states were compelled to resist if their neighbors felt endangered by their inactivity. Understandably, there was a strong parallel between the operation of the domino theory in local strategy and the massive retaliation in global strategy. In both cases, the US sought to draw a line on "this far and no farther" values and to organize the most per-suasive response to any challenge. It is paradoxical that the US abandoned massive retaliation and adopted flexible response in military affairs at a time when the domino theory was being reinforced in order to preclude graduated and intermediary positions in political policy. It may be argued that the eclipse of massive retaliation generated uncertainties that indirectly strengthened the ubiquity of the domino theory.

The major constructive efforts of the Johnson Administration focused on regional integration in Southeast Asia. This undertaking was consistent with traditional American support for regionalism, but it failed for several reasons: there was a lack of ethnic, cultural or economic homegenity or compatibility;

it was initiated too late, after the integrative impulse had subsided among potentially interested states; it was clearly a mask for anti-Communist resistance, not regional development; and the total effort antagonized both China and the Soviet Union and forced them to adopt counterstrategies that contributed to the weakness of the integrative pressures. The end result was that Washington remained largely isolated in its regional policy and war efforts.

The failure of integration, however, was overshadowed by the lack of consensus in Washington about the nature of the threat, national objectives, and the utility of US intervention. Had greater unanimity prevailed, the irrelevance of the domino theory could have been exposed much earlier. But even as late as the beginning of the Nixon Administration, Washington agencies were still badly divided on virtually all aspects of the war: effectiveness of B-52 strikes, time required for pacification, Soviet and Chinese aims and future actions, infiltration rates, Vietnamization progress, and preferred US troop strengths.[1] Even after the close of Nixon's first term there was evidence of persisting cleavages at the top level.

The reasons for these differences were not merely the technical problems inherent in formulating intelligence estimates about a hostile environment. They stemmed also from fundamental philosophical issues that had plagued analysts of Communist affairs since the challenge of Stalinism and the organization of the Free World. The questions asked publicly during the anticommunism crisis of 1946-49 resemble those persisting today. Should communism be contained on a limited, temporary basis for the duration of its present assertive phase, à la Kennan, or should the inherent weaknesses of Stalinism better be exposed by engagement with the West, as Walter Lippman argued?[2] Does effective containment require the defeat locally and the rollback of communism? Is national communism, as in Yugoslavia or Cuba, a threat to a great power's vital interests? In advancing the goals of international stability and prosperity, should higher priority be placed on economic or military aid? How can the dangers be accurately forecast in linking commitments to single, potentially unpopular personalities, and where is the point of no return for ties with the Chiang Kai-sheks and the Diems? What legitimate rights should a donor state retain to insure economic and political stability? When does the exercise of these rights constitute interference in domestic affairs? When should local expediencies and demands override broader international interests; when can they be ignored and the allegiance of a smaller state still be retained? Finally, what is the anticipated impact of the continued exercise of imperial will, however benevolent, on relations with all smaller states?

These and similar questions are crucial for the effective operation of a military coalition. Yet twenty-five years of deliberation and experience have not produced pat answers that could satisfy public demands. The evasion of facile answers is also due in part to more immediate and tactical problems. For example, McGeorge Bundy has called the policy of the Johnson Administration a "model of constraint."[3] But such immaculate constraint utterly failed to achieve even its minimum goals. Rather, it strengthened North Vietnamese convictions that any US coercion could be absorbed and that the determination of the allies would be eroded before the punishment reached unacceptable levels. Further, the failure of this policy exacerbated the perennial debate between the Defense and State departments over priorities: Were security requirements prerequisites for insuring political credibility, or was the formation of a popular government the premise for effective resistance?

Continuing domestic pressure forced adoption of the political decision to withdraw without resolving these outstanding policy differences and without gaining sufficient experience for establishing conclusive precedents that could govern future commitments. Nixon made three decisions, also irrelevant to these dilemmas, but intended to buy time for the scheduled withdrawal and the pursuit of a peace settlement. He agreed to continued support of the Thieu government as the most effective, if not only reliable, resistance to the Communists; he directed the incursion into Cambodia to destroy enemy sanctuaries and logistics support; and, while the peace talks limped along, he opened a series of secret meetings between Henry Kissinger and Le Duc Tho in Paris, initially to explore the termination of the American portion of the conflict—the US presence and the prisoner return. When the secret talks proved inconclusive in the summer of 1971, North Vietnam saw no other option open except a maximum military operation including a massive and sustained invasion of the South.

North Vietnamese Military Initiative

What factors probably influenced this decision? First, the Soviet Union and China had not been able to advance Hanoi's aims at the political and diplomatic level, and an increased sense of "do it yourself" apparently emerged. Indeed, Moscow was beginning to question the utility of continued large-scale operations (every incursion at battalion or regimental level for the past two years into Military Regions I and II had been defeated). And Peking was advocating a return to guerrilla-level operations that would allow a complete US withdrawal and relaxation of tensions in the Taiwan Straits, while maintaining sufficient pressure on US taxpayers and unstable Saigon to achieve indirectly desired results. Without external aid, Hanoi had no chance of maintaining even the existing level of operations. (TASS announced on 15 March 1972 that 340 Soviet ships delivered in 1971 some one million tons of cargo to North Vietnam and that a 20-percent increase had occurred already in 1972. In 1969 Brezhnev placed the value of Soviet deliveries at approximately $1 billion.) The possible war-weariness of its prime supporters must have placed a now-or-never urgency on the decision.

A second factor, conversely, must have been the unrequited belief that North Vietnam was fighting on the frontier of revolution, the only Socialist country that was actively engaging the imperialists. Hanoi holds that this unique position in the Socialist commonwealth, a position it has consistently preserved since 1946, has earned it a privileged status with the right to demand succor from other fraternal countries. But with the alien word *détente* entering Chinese and Russian vocabularies, revolutionary fervor will become increasingly less useful as an appeal or tool for advancing Hanoi's ambitions in South Vietnam.

Third, while Kissinger was talking to Le Duc Tho, he was also chatting with Chou En-lai. The announcement on 15 July of Nixon's proposed visit must have had a major impact on Hanoi. The North Vietnamese press recovered quickly from the apparent surprise and denounced the Chinese and later the Soviet visits of Nixon in vehement terms. It was clear that Hanoi sensed a fundamental shift in the Asian power constellation upon which it had predicated its strategy for nearly thirty years. Whereas the Asian power balance had formerly rested on a reliable US-USSR-Chinese confrontation, it now consisted of an imperfect four-power rectangle including Japan that was based on limited political détente rather than ideological conflict. Moreover, like most embattled small states, North Vietnam relied heavily on international support to bolster its cause. But the political center of gravity was now shifting rapidly from Southeast to Northeast Asia, and adjustment rather than hostilities was coming into fashion. Delays in assertive action might now earn permanent international indifference. Conversely, an all-out invasion might arrest this deterioration and convince the world and its allies of Hanoi's determination to secure its objectives. At the least, it would create a situation that would augur against great-power conciliation at Hanoi's expense.

Fourth, no significant military action had taken place in South Vietnam for many months, and both the pacification and Vietnamization programs were progressing steadily. Indeed, the point had been reached that both local Communist recruitment and regimental attacks had failed. If the military option was still to be used, the intensity either had to be reduced or increased radically. And because of the progress in South Vietnamese military prowess and political stability, the delay of another inconclusive year would make a maximum invasion inevitable anyway.

Finally, the US presidential elections must have figured prominently in Hanoi's decision. But the calculated impact of war-weariness on the elections was the most risky integer in the decision. Hanoi apparently concluded that its pressure on Dien Bien Phu resulted in the resignation of the Laniel government and the appointment of a "capitulationist" government under Mendès France, and that the Tet offensive—admittedly a military defeat—was a political victory responsible for ending Johnson's political career. But would an outright invasion of the South shift alarmed sentiments of middle America to the right or the left? Moreover, if McGovern won, it would be by the narrowest margin and he might not carry either congressional house, reducing the effectiveness of his administration on such issues as Vietnam. On the other hand, the invasion would widen the distance between the two candidates and would probably favor the Nixon camp; he could rally the middle by resisting acknowledged agression. Finally, if Nixon won, there would be a strong possibility that he would carry both houses, giving him a better chance of dealing more firmly with North Vietnamese negotiators. Thus the prospects of counterproductivity had to be weighed, but they did not balance the apparent need for massive, urgent action.

The prolonged stay of Premier Le Duan in Moscow during the summer indicated the difficulties involved in planning the invasion. Moscow had devised a sufficiency formula for North Vietnam similar to the one it exercised more stringently in Egypt. It had supplied Hanoi with large numbers of antiaircraft artillery, SAM-2s and some SAM-3s, some armor and heavy artillery, and a limited number of early model MIG-21 fighters. Some of this heavy equipment could have been supplied by China, but it was not, underscoring Hanoi's single-source dependency on Moscow. Moreover, the USSR had not furnished the same level of equipment it supplied Egypt, such as the SAM-4 and 6, track-mounted 37mm AAA, and the MIG-21J, and Soviet combat crews had not participated in North Vietnamese defenses. Thus both the weapons themselves and the numbers involved reduced the probability of their being used in an offensive mode, and the USSR appeared satisfied to confine the upper level of its commitment to supplying infantry needs up to the regimental level.

There are no declaratory statements or press commentaries indicating that such a sufficiency formula actually existed. But at least three indicators point in this direction. First, the level of discrepancy between aid deliveries to Egypt and North Vietnam—who was conducting combat operations, not merely training exercises—suggests that political constraints were exercised. Subsequent deliveries of offensive level weapons demolishes the contention that operational and topographical imperatives had precluded earlier deliveries. Second, the US was not arming the ARVN forces with a capability for a sustained offensive in the North. Commando raids and regimental incursions could be made as in Laos, but the ARVN forces did not have the capability to conduct a serious invasion of the North. It appears that both the US and the USSR attached special significance to this tacit mutual constraint as a facet of the general policy of minimizing the possibility of spillover and great-power confrontation. This leads to the third indicator. When the invasion occurred, President Nixon and Secretary Laird sharply denounced the USSR for its alleged complicity to furnishing North Vietnam with an offensive capability. Responsibility for this quantum escalation was placed squarely on Moscow, suggesting that at least an informal understanding had been made on the level of constraint. The impact of the violation of its own restraints on such countries as Egypt, who had not been granted adequate weaponry for an offensive, and on its major adversaries had to be assessed before the invasion could be approved.

Moscow may have abandoned its policy of sufficiency mainly because of its assessment of China's intentions in the region. During 1966-69, China became increasingly consumed with its Cultural Revolution and as elsewhere gradually reduced its commitments to Hanoi. Soviet aid during this period took on the double aim of countering US and replacing Chinese influence. US bombing of the North was viewed by Peking and Moscow as aimed partly at undermining Soviet credibility as the protector of the Socialist Commonwealth. Moscow answered China's charges of flabbiness with claims that its strategy was a correct blend of firmness and moderation, allowing for the successful prosecution of the war while proffering hopes for political settlement. By 1971, Moscow could argue that its aid had prevented the collapse of North Vietnam and had forced the US into a military stalemate. But it had not compelled a Southern capitulation. At that juncture Moscow became instrumental in shifting greater emphasis on a political settlement.

The rise of Soviet influence in Hanoi prompted China to reexamine the dangers of a prolonged conflict, or a North Vietnamese victory and the extension of its influence throughout Indochina. The protraction of full-scale hostilities must have been viewed as an opportunity for entrenching Soviet power on its southern border—a danger that should be thwarted, even if it required adjustment with the US. For political reasons Peking had to continue nominal aid—Soviet contributions finally totaled 80 percent of the war effort, China's only 15 percent. Thus the prospects for solidifying the Soviet position in and erecting the framework for a viable anti-Chinese coalition became even more appealing when Peking opened its door to Nixon. Accordingly, Moscow apparently abandoned its former constraints and agreed to support the offensive.

Hanoi's 1972 Offensive

In meeting Le Duan's demands, it began delivery of over 2000 trucks per month, increased the inventory of T-54 tanks to over 650, and supplied more 122mm and 130mm heavy guns, light AAA, and the new Strela heat-seeking, shoulder-fired antiaircraft missile. Allied intelligence pinpointed the date of the offensive in February, but heavy US aerial bombardment forced postponement for over one month. Despite sustained air attacks, the invader retained a high degree of initiative when the operation began. South Vietnam is nearly one thousand miles long and very narrow. The invader could attack along the Western border from Laos and Cambodia and spread the assault over a wide front by a series of flanking moves. ARVN forces were compelled to cover the heavily populated coastal regions and commit their reserves to block main thrusts aimed at cutting the country in half. Thus a classical strategic play developed, with the invader enjoying flexibility and the defender being tied to restrained moves.

On 30 March three North Vietnamese divisions thrust toward An Loc, sixty miles northwest of Saigon, and a single division infiltrated through the A Shau valley to fix the ARVN I Division at Hue. Making slower progress, three more divisions moved against Kontum in the Central Highlands. These operations tied up the bulk of Allied air support for nearly a week. In the interval, three additional divisions with heavy eqiupment were deployed across the pulverized DMZ and attacked Quang Tri. As the northernmost province fell, the understrengthened NVA I Division was reactivated in the Mekong Delta in the U Minh Forest area and the reinforced 3 Division captured Binh Dinh Province on the northern coast. The latter two actions were diversionary operations designed to pin down reserves.

After two months, ARVN forces recovered but could not regain the initiative. At the end of six months, they had recaptured Binh Dinh Province and maintained most main coastal communication arteries, but they could not lift the seige of An Loc, clear Kontum Province—although the attack on the provincial capital itself had been repulsed—or recover ground vital to the defense of Hue. Moreover, they had lost theee months and at least three crack paratroop and Marine regiments in a successful attempt to recapture Quang Tri city. Conversely, NVA forces retained the initiative by alternately threatening Hue, capturing the valley and district capital of Que Son thirty miles south of Da Nang, the country's second largest city, and challenging the defenses of Saigon itself.

The US responded to the overt invasion of South Vietnam with a twofold strategy. It substantially increased direct military pressure against North Vietnam by stepped-up air attacks. Over two hundred B-52s were assigned to Vietnam operations and the number of tactical fighter-bombers was increased to over 800. Prior to the renewed aerial offensive, the US had dropped 6.2 million tons of air munitions in Southeast Asis—three times the total tonnage dropped by the US in World War II. The cumulative explosives expended in all SEA to that time equalled 300pounds per person for all North and South Vietnam, Laos, and Cambodia. The total tonnage dropped by the beginning of the cease-fire was 8.2 million. During the nine-month counter air offensive one and a half times more tonnage was dropped than during the entire Korean War.

When the increased bombing did not have the desired effect of halting the invasion, Nixon decided to escalate the pressure by mining Haiphong and six other ports and blockading the North Vietnamese coast against over-the-beaches offloading of supplies—despite the anticipated risks these actions might have on the first US-USSR summit conference in Moscow two weeks later. These sharp increases in US air and naval operations were staged from Thailand and the South China Sea; programed troop withdrawals from Vietnam proceeded on schedule and further reductions were announced in August.

The second aspect of the strategy was to renew efforts to reach a political settlement. Prior to the invasion, Nixon had agreed to the proposal that new elections be conducted in South Vietnam before which President Thieu would resign. Such a concession exceeded the moral bounds and discretion that should be exercised among allies, and was clearly the outer limit of US tolerance. In his 9 May national address announcing the naval blockade, Nixon bypassed the question of a political settlement and discussed only the terms for terminating US involvement. The blockade would be maintained, he stated, until all US prisoners of war were returned and an internationally supervised cease-fire was honored. The mines would then be deactivated and four months later all US troops would be withdrawn from South Vietnam. Because there terms were no longer explicitly tied to mechanical procedures for reaching a political settlement, they gave the impression of being the broadest concessions yet offered Hanoi. But North Vietnam apparently concluded that they could not be extended as a unilateral package unless Washington was prepared to accept charges that it had capitulated. Indeed, Hanoi may have estimated that they were aimed more at the American electorate than its Politburo. To the surprise of many observers, neither the steady increase in US military efforts nor the proffered political terms induced Hanoi to relax its offensive; it retained the initiative and maintained strong pressure against South Vietnam until after the US elections.

What were the immediately perceived consequences of the invastion? A Western evaluation was offered by General Raoul Salan, Commander-in-Chief of the French forces in Indochina in 1954. He predicted that the offensive would ultimately collapse. Giap had made the same mistake Hitler did at Stalingrad: he dispersed the offensive in too many directions. If he had opened the attack on 1 February as planned, or if he had been able to move faster through the Central Highlands and tie down more ARVN reserves, he would have had a better chance of capturing Hue and making it the capital of a new Viet Cong state. Giap apparently calculated that there would be greater local support as "liberation" became more graphically visible. But there was even less public enthusiasm for the Communists than during the 1968 Tet offensive. Giap also estimated that ARVN troops were inferior to North Vietnamese forces, which Salan called the best infantry in the world—better than the Germans at Verdun.[4] But only the 22nd and 3rd Divisions broke under heavy enemy pressure; other units, especially the paratroop and marine regiments, demonstrated determination and proficiency, inflicting far heavier casualties than they sustained. The combination of firm tactical resistance, heavy US strategic pressure, and supply lines over one thousand kilometers long finally brought the offensive to a halt without reaching any major objective.

But the North Vietnamese were neither pessimistic nor discouraged by the results. In mid-July, Colonel Nguyen Dinh Uoc, editor of the leading North Vietnamese military journal, cited the following achievements:

> First, we weakened the puppet army. We killed or put out of
> commission 150,000 enemy troops. Except for the Seventh Disision

all other enemy divisions have been decimated. Second, we contracted the field of action. The enemy has been forced to concentrate troops around Quang Tri and Kontum and other places. They are subject to counterattack. Third, we broke the enemy's defensive line along the Cambodian border. In every battle they were surprised and forced to retreat.[5]

These claims are obviously exaggerated, but they project the confidence that the military operations will have an important influence on the political outcome—that Saigon will have to be more receptive to Hanoi's demands for a settlement.

Political Consequences of the Invasion

A further result of the invasion was the confirmation of China's inability to alter the outcome of the conflict, despite the increased importance of its role in logistic support. The US blockade was far from total. Thousands of tons of cargo were delivered overland from China, reducing Moscow's importance as a sole source supplier, but not measurably increasing Peiping's political influence. The level of Chinese aid did not appear to reach that of 1967-68 period when, for example, 50,000 Chinese helped to keep North Vietnamese communications open. The lower level of cooperation seemed to have been mutually desirable. Peking's coolness stemmed from its objections to an intensification of the war that would prolong the presence of American forces in Taiwan, which Nixon had agreed to reduce as tensions diminished. Further, the invasion expanded Hanoi's dependence on Soviet arms deliveries and the US blockade necessitated Chinese cooperation in transiting these arms—Chinese refusal in 1965-67 to transport Soviet war shipments across its territory had been a major factor in the Sino-Soviet split. But times had changed; for the first time the strained relations between Hanoi and its two Communist allies over its invasion policy were not exploited by either rival. For their own reasons, both Communist giants opposed the offensive, but neither could refuse aid when a fraternal state was sustaining such heavy damage.

While Chinese interests in Southeast Asia to date have been mainly a function of the Sino-Soviet dispute, they are apt to shift northward or to other areas of competition with Moscow after hostilities end in Vietnam. Such a change of priorities would reflect a realistic assessment of the long-term constraints on its policy in the region. China is the only state since 1941 to initiate hostilities against the USSR, emphasizing Soviet vulnerability and Chinese brazenness. As a result of Peking's shift in interest, Hanoi would inevitably lose its leverage against the two giants, but not its importance in Soviet designs. Soviet interests in the area are not as much anti-imperialist as they are anti-Chinese. Since at least 1969, Moscow has been urging the formation of an anti-Chinese mutual defense pact or political coalition hinging on Southeast Asia and containing Peking's influence to its present borders. Hanoi's confidence in its continuing criticalness in Soviet plans must have been a prime factor influencing its decision to invade the South, confidence that was apparently not shaken by the Nixon visit to Moscow and Podgorny's later journey to North Vietnam, when he called for a ceasefire and acceptance of the May 1972 peace package already rejected by Le Duc Tho. At a stopover in Calcutta, Podgorny confirmed that "the USSR will do everything possible to stop the fighting." Moscow's dilemma over cooperating with the invasion was compounded by the desire to expand the degree of conciliation with the US and to advance its image as a peace-promoting state. Following its successful *démarche* into the subcontinent, leadership in a political settlement in Indochina would immensely strengthen Brezhnev's stature at home and abroad and provide a positive matrix for stressing coordinated action against the more militant Chinese.

But Hanoi refused to consider the US proposed cease-fire. Podgorny was snubbed in an obvious show of displeasure that was confirmed in the communiqué issued on 18 June. The wording was one of the most important victories for North Vietnam during the entire southern offensive. Moscow pledged resolute Soviet support for Hanoi until full victory against the imperialist was achieved and promised to provide aid in all three critical levels—military, political, and diplomatic.[6] A shift of this scale suggests that there were new uncertainties now for Moscow as well as for Southeast Asia. Moscow apparently elected not to exacerbate these uncertainties by forcing a confrontation with Hanoi. It probably concluded that there was more to be gained by developing a fall-back position of exploiting Peiping's embarrassment than relieving the American predicament in Asia. Thus, an additional result of the offensive was the further confirmation of Hanoi's latitude regarding Moscow.[a]

---

[a]Probably the most significant consequence of Hanoi's open aggression stemmed from the basic motive for the assault. Hanoi has consistently maintained that Vietnam is indivisible; that there are no foreign troops on the Viet Cong side. It was suppprting civil war insurgents who opposed imperialists and therefore had the right to move its forces freely throughout Vietnam. The drive south was to confirm this notion of sovereignty with an openly demonstrated physical presence. While no key cities or regions fell, the North Vietnamese secured the major objective of gaining US acceptance of the durability of that presence and thereby implied endorsement of its legality. On 9 May President Nixon proposed a standstill cease fire and formally abandoned any hope of demanding NVA withdrawal as the price for a final settlement. Washington was clearly alarmed by Hanoi's ability to deploy virtually its entire army southward despite massive bombing, and by the prospects for effective ARVN resistance. Nixon later justified his reversal on this point by arguing that the contestants should not expect to gain at the bargaining table what had been lost on the battlefield. Saigon complained bitterly that American war-weariness had undermined its claims to independent sovereignty and left it with no option but to continue the military struggle with the invaders and to restore the former shape of South Vietnam. From Saigon's viewpoint American abandonment on the vital principle of sovereignty merely increased the stakes in the military confrontations.

While the US attempted to segregate the issues into those related to the US presence and to a political settlement, the two Vietnamese governments attempted to preserve the integration of the various problems and to reach a total solution. But the various proposals raised by the respective sides (5, 7, 8, and 9 point plans, etc.) all boiled down to two key issues: American military disengagement and the nature of the Saigon government after hostilities ended. The Thieu regime has stoutly resisted suggestions for a coalition government with various ratios of Communist representation. Under strong US pressure, it finally agreed to Thieu's resignation and new national elections in which the Communists could participate as a legal party.

On its side, Hanoi insists that Thieu must be forced out of office and out of political life as a precondition for participating in a responsible government. These demands are based on the awareness that Thieu's demise would be a graphic symbol of Washington's defeat and an acknowledgment of the National Liberation Front's difficulties in removing him if the Americans fail to do so. North Vietnamese representatives have publicly stated that in return for Thieu's sacrifice as the symbol of the status quo Hanoi would accept another government without immediate Communist participation and long-term (ten-year) timetable for solution of the reunification problem. When this offer was rejected, Hanoi sought some formula guaranteeing that neither faction would dominate a future government. The near impossibility of such an exercise indicated an erosion in Hanoi's bargaining stand. Thus the gap between the two positions narrowed slightly, with the political stature of Thieu as the leading political figure in the South and the difficulties in accurately measuring local Communist support remaining the outstanding problems. Hanoi's demand for Thieu demise was his best insurance for continuing longevity. And, when elections are likely to follow the battle lines, is it in both sides' interest to hold and expedite them.

By the fall the NVA offensive had bogged down without making a favorable impact on the US Presidential campaign and ARVN forces were gradually regaining lost territory. New TOW antitank missiles and tactical air bombardment had so decisively defeated NVA armor and artillery that experts began reassessing the future of the tank. Without recommitting US ground forces, the superior fire power of the ARVN had largely reduced the North Vietnamese effort to heavy mortar barrages and battalion level attacks. On 8 October 1972 Hanoi accepted the basic principles of the US proposals of 8 May 1972. But the announcement of serious negotiations discouraged ARVN commanders and troops from vigorously prosecuting the war effort. Hanoi, in turn, misperceived this hesitancy as defeatism and reverted to an intransigent negotiating position.

On 18 December the US launched the heaviest bombing offensive to date against Hanoi. By 31 December the administrative viability of the country had been jeopardized, raising serious questions about the effectiveness of the government itself. When Hanoi agreed to resume serious negotiations, the attacks were suspended. In the meantime Washington had talked "sternly" to Saigon, which was holding out for terms on the sovereignty question that would have taken years to achieve—namely the expulsion of invading forces.

Largely because of US bombing pressure in the North and political compulsion in the South, a cease-fire agreement was signed on 27 January 1973. It included a standstill cease-fire, return of all prisoners, withdrawal of remaining US forces, and provisions for consultations among the rival South Vietnamese about the political future of the country. Only questions relating to the US military disengagement were effectively resolved. Political issues, such as the supervision of national elections and the composition of a national executive body to administer reconciliation, were sidestepped as both forces sought military advantages. The NVA interpreted the cease-fire as a suspension of hostilities with freedom of movement and the ARVN considered it a standstill imposition. Given the two sides' differing political goals, their antagonistic views of sovereignty, and their residual military capabilities, large-scale fighting promptly broke out.

Resumed fighting had two important consequences, with long-term implications. ARVN forces engaged in a wide variety of operations, including extensive air attacks, without US advice or logistic support. "Going it alone" had a galvanizing effect on South Vietnamese morale and confidence. They have reportedly geared the war effort to long-term sustained operations, including large-scale procurement and stockpiling of war materials, in direct violation of Articles 7, 15, and 20 of the Cease-fire Agreement. The second consequence of renewed hostilities was Hanoi's reaction to the ARVN demonstration that it would not collapse without direct US support. The NVA's inability to match the mobility and firepower of the ARVN forced a major decision. To succeed militarily, it would have to abandon fighting the South on its terms and reduce the conflict to a level it could more effectively support. These changed requirements would necessitate a reduction in the intensity of the fighting, though not the geographic distribution, while a systematic logistic build up could be made in the hinterland of occupied South Vietnam. At the time of writing, this consolidation had the appearance of permanency and irrevocability. To protect the southern terminals of the Ho Chi Minh trail and the new links across the demilitarized zone, a major air defense complex was constructed at Kai Sanh, including a jet aircraft-capable airfield. Three new divisions were reportedly brought up and an elaborate roadway system is under construction. To support such an undertaking with a heavily manpower-based transportation system, the North Vietnamese first sought the return of refugees who had fled to ARVN territory and, when this failed, drafted a new indigenous population from the North. This new population brought with it the primitive industrial and limited agricultural capabilities sufficient to provide locally as much support as possible for an army garrisoned abroad. Despite the rugged terrain, occupied South Vietnam is now taking on the appearance of colonialization or annexation, also in open violation of the agreement.

The breakdown of the cease-fire regime and the stalemated political talks between the South Vietnamese was the product of complex political problems that tended to forestall movement until the military contest favored one side or the other. For example, on refugees, Saigon claimed that the several million remaining homeless did not want to return to Communist-controlled territory and Hanoi charged they were forcefully detained. Political activities Saigon saw as subversion and Hanoi as a legitimate political struggle. Saigon saw the Provisional Revolutionary Government as a dangerous ruse that had no capital, few subjects, and little territory but could eventually set up a rival administration on South Vietnamese soil; Hanoi claimed the PRG was legitimate, with its own terms for partnership and legality that were the price for political stability. Saigon saw reunification as an ultimate by-product of its own consolidation process in the South; Hanoi was confident that it would be an inevitable consequence of the revolutionary struggle.

On national elections, Saigon was suspicious lest open Communist activities fan grievances across the entire political spectrum, resulting in protest voting and no genuine measure of support for the Communist platform; Hanoi insisted that since many of its supporters were either in prison or detention all political prisoners must be released and open political activities permitted before an election could register valid public sentiment. In this stalemate, both agreed that elections would merely reflect the existing military configuration and subject Saigon to charges of fraud and expose the insignificant power of PRG. Thus there was little incentive for either side to negotiate seriously and the elections—the first step toward reconciliation—were repeatedly postponed.

With this lack of political good will, international supervision of the cease-fire was seriously hampered. The International Commission of Supervision and Control, consisting of Canada, Hungary, Indonesia, and Poland, was perhaps doomed to ineffectuality from the start. The ICSC was 1160 men strong and divided into twenty-six fixed teams and four mobile teams. Only four of the fixed teams were assigned to the interior and twenty-two were stationed in the large centers where inspection was relatively easy. The smaller mobile teams were severely restricted by the number of units available compared to the size of the task, and by the Communists' denial of access to prohibited areas. Canada informed the commission of its refusal to participate in a body as emasculated as its predecessor, the 1954 ICC, and gave the commission six months to prove its merits. At the end of July 1973, Canada resigned and issued a scathing denunciation of the Communist side for obstructing the commission work, while launching a massive military buildup that clearly violated the agreement. By September Iran had joined the ICSC primarily for prestige purposes; it was far less vigorous in fulfilling its role and the commission was relegated to virtually complete inactivity.

Wins and Losses

Thus after eighteen years of American commitment to Vietnamese self-determination, a political settlement is even more remote than in 1954 and the US has resigned from further involvement. Unlike the 1954 Geneva Accord, the 1973 agreement does not provide for reunification on the basis of a Vietnam-wide referendum. It merely inscribes the hope that the Vietnamese rivals can resolve their differences in the South without prescribing procedures or timetable for this accomplishment. The eventual American resignation left the South Vietnamese society relatively more pluralistic and far less authoritarian than that of North Vietnam. But it was also more corrupt and susceptible to a negative ideology. It lacked charismatic leadership and political maturity. And most debilitating, it was so heavily dependent upon the United States that its compounded frustrations could finally take the form of increasing anti-Americanism. Yet Thieu commanded one of the biggest, best-equipped and trained armies in Asia, giving him confidence that his military options are still credible. Eighteen years of US responsibility for South Vietnamese security had eroded its ally's political maneuverability and forced the contest back to the battlefield, where the outcome is less than certain.

In assessing the great powers' wins and losses or comparative advantages one year after the cease-fire, the USSR seems to have earned substantially more political profit.

1. Moscow failed to protect a member of the Socialist commonwealth from exhaustive destruction, but it provided enough aid to prevent Hanoi's capitulation and successful prosecution of the war.
2. It failed to establish decisive influence over Hanoi but virtually neutralized Chinese authority; the present level of Soviet influence is likely to remain with the protraction of the war.
3. The Soviets failed to provide the "decisive" weapons in either the quantity or quality that would insure the conquest of South Vietnam, forcing Hanoi to rely heavily on the ideological component of the contest. (Drawing from their Canal War experience, they apparently feared US overreaction.) But they agreed to make good whatever losses occurred, allowing Hanoi to keep its military options open. When the NVA forced the US to a military stalemate, it proved the best example yet of the exploitation of proxy forces for the advancement of a great power's political interests.
4. Moscow failed to convert Hanoi's war into a rallying cry for its leadership of world Communist parties and sympathizers, but it guaranteed enough aid for a small power to deny a rival great power its political and military aims in Southeast Asia, inflicting a serious defeat on the US. The NVA

entrenchment on South Vietnamese soil is a Soviet political and ideological victory, and Moscow will claim credit for any further NVA inroads.

5. Moscow was unable to advance directly Hanoi's strategic political interests of establishing friendly or satellite regimes throughout Southeast Asia. But without risking Soviet troops, the US was compelled to withdraw its forces without a compensating NVA retreat and was forced to contract its interests throughout Asia, with serious overtones for the credibility of US obligations in other theaters.

The Soviet-North Vietnamese victory, however, was far from complete.

1. The US retreated under pressure, leaving the enemy in partial possession of the battlefield. But the Vietnamization program has been sufficiently sucessful that the ARVN enjoys unquestioned technological superiority; the will to resist remains the critical integer and continued US presence would have been irrelevant if not counterproductive.

2. Washington's failure to plug Hanoi's breach in its containment barriers was a grave demonstration of the growing obsolescence of military alliances against direct aggression Washington regarded any attempt to rally international condemnation and collective action as utterly useless. But the US was able to thwart Hanoi's forward strategy of regional revolutionary warfare long enough for potential victims to use the growing Hanoi-Peking rift and mounting Soviet involvement to build new political defenses. (It remains an open question whether the Khmer Rouge and Pathet Lao will prove more Chinese than North Vietnamese oriented.) But there is a greater chance now than ever for securing an internationally guaranteed neutrality for all Indochina—despite Hanoi's anticipated obstructionism.

3. The McNamara concept of "limited war" and the ability to fight major wars in Europe and Asia, plus brush fires elsewhere, has proven bankrupt. The US has now formally revised its strategy to a "one and a half war" concept. But this neither negated the necessity at that time for an expanded army nor the persistence of a limited war in Vietnam, with the Soviets heavily committed and deflected from other pursuits.

4. The American massive industrial approach to warfare proved inadequate in meeting anything but the minimum aims, and the American military establishment was unable to provide alternatives of either adequate scale or originality to improve the outcome. But Hanoi's concept of a people's army seems hardly the answer. Paradoxically the NVA estimated it could not score successfully until it committed virtually all of its regular army and élite cadre. At the same time the US dropped its cherished concept of a drafted citizen army that would allow for more intensive training and higher technical skill levels.

5. The US was unable to provide a satisfactory formula for regional stability

that would assure popular aspirations without encompassing Communist subversion. But it was able to prevent a forceful takeover and to exploit the ensuing frustrations of its revals. By reopening the Sino-Soviet dispute with the added dimension of US participation, it successfully minimized the potential gains of its major rivals. This maneuver fixed its adversaries' attention on larger global issues and precluded a surge by either into the vacuum created by America's retreat. Indeed the elevation of Washington's focus to problems of a greater magnitude had an assuaging effect on the despondency resulting from its Asian defeat, however severely it was calculated.

In the final analysis Vietnam is likely to be an American parallel to the Boer War for Britain and Algeria for France. These were manifestations of retrenchment within empires and the contraction of the outer limits of influence abroad, caused by both unrest at home and pressures from overseas. But the analogy is not complete. In Algeria and South Africa, local governments effectively filled the vacuum of declining colonial rule and maintained close ties with the metropolitan power. In Vietnam it is possible to envision continuing civil strife, the rise of anti-American nationalism, or even a radical takeover. Such dire prospects are plausible not merely because of eighteen years of American dominance, but because of the possibility of continued foreign manipulation in Indochina that may prolong American dependence for Saigon. Ironically the most plausible avenue to local stability is via the common ground on this point between the US and China.

As the American society goes through the turmoil of reassessing its involvement in Indochina, several lessons have gained general recognition. While Vietnam became inadvertently America's only colonial war of the twentieth century, the US was not practicing imperialism in the traditional sense. It was exercising, however, an imperial will. It acted repeatedly in its own best interest without regard when necessary for the values, principles, and even lives of South Vietnamese. However noble the motives may have been, policies that are imposed or do not reflect local interests are imperial. The gradual awareness of the self-perpetuating nature of this imperial will that is so antithetical to the principles of self-determination for which the commitments were originally made resulted in the shock over the onerous burden of unilaterally accepted responsibilities for foreign undertakings. It is this seeming abhorence of future unilateral commitments abroad that has projected the image and danger of neoisolationism.

But what is less visible and probably more enduring is the gradual acceptance that undesirable unilateral responsibilities can best be avoided if greater maneuverability against potential rivals can be assured. Latitude for diplomatic initiative and reaction has at last become a valuable end in itself, even when a degree of rapprochement with an archenemy is required. This signals a restoration of diplomacy after being frozen by the Cold War into rigid this or that positions.

The age of adjustment, if fully implemented, will be far more stable than the age of black-and-white commitment, even when bolstered by assured deterrence. Growing awareness of the merits and necessity of adjustment led to intensified questioning of the value of South Vietnam to vital American interests and the consequences of its loss to Hanoi. The majority of Americans seem to have concluded that the new era reduced the importance of Saigon as the embattled outpost of the Free World and that moral and material commitments should be the extent of US involvement. Moreover, even these reduced commitments should no longer be regarded as indefinite or infinite in nature or applicable regardless of the character of the government. This line of questioning marked first an intense societal examination of the war issue and then a gradual indifference and distraction with other issues.

The Chinese Puzzle: Maelstrom or Utopia?

The People's Republic of China has now attained great-power status: it has sufficient strategic deterrence and residual military power that it cannot be compelled to act against its will. This achievement is the most important single development since the nuclear age and the strategic duopoly began. It is more significant than the rise of Japan or the emergence of superpower détente. China finds itself in a singular position: it is the leading underdeveloped nation with sufficient nuclear strength to command respect among the super powers. Moreover, Peking rightly claims that it is practicing the world's most grandiose and most successful experiment in utopian welfare, and argues that it has formulated a model for economic development that is more applicable to Third World countries than any yet devised by either Marxist or Western economists. Thus no other nation has had quite the same leadership opportunity on a global scale, with the potential linkage position between developed and developing nations. (For example, it was India's lack of a credible strategic posture that resulted in its failure to establish effective leadership of the developing nations, and in the revelation that its leadership tool—nonalignment—was an artificial dependency of the Cold War.) But it remains to be seen whether China will develop these leadership options to the fullest. This reservation stems from the continuing priority China places on consolidating its domestic revolution rather than advancing its interests abroad.

Maoism and Chinese Culture

Maoism, history's greatest experiment in utopian development, proposes no less than to change the nature and motivation of man from egocentrism to dedication to the common welfare. China supports progress of the Third World countries but does not purport to export replicas of its revolution. Consistent with the long rivalry with Moscow on the issue of a single source of dogma, China holds that each society must develop its own brand of revolution, incorporating its unique characteristics and problems. Self-reliance is the hallmark of success which will come only with correct party leadership and mass mobilization and their subsequent integration into a seamless collectivized entity. As John Melby has commented, "In a world which has lost faith in its values and ideologies, it may well be that the greatest impact of Maoism will be its demonstrated belief in its destiny, superiority and rightness.[1] In other words, a continuation of traditional elements of introverted Chinese political culture can be expected.

Klaus Mehnert observed after a recent visit to China that Maoism was more entrenched than Leninism was in the USSR. The successful eradication of the "four old things"—tradiaiontal thoughts, culture, habits, and customs—has produced a patriotism and national pride that engendered the present generation with sufficient confidence to discard traditional beliefs and the former compulsion to imitate Soviet models.[2] These basic changes were due largely to fundamental alterations in Chinese social structure. Chinese social development has witnessed a sharp increase in the size of the productive units and a corresponding decrease in the number of units. Most Chinese are now wage earners living and working within the framework of large bureaucratic structures. Personal life has become more regimented, but more secure, predictable, and productive. Income, mobility, and opportunities often depend upon the organization to which one belongs. One of the main purposes of the Cultural Revolution was to reduce these inequalities, to strengthen self-reliance and self-sufficiency of the less fortunate organizations, and to eliminate the budding class consciousness deriving from association with the more affluent or influencial organizations. Greater mass identification with more equal social structures was required to achieve the goal of a society composed of autonomous cells. But inequalities persist, especially among regions, and they are likely to intensify as the pace of industrialization increases. Further changes will be required and will likely remain the dominating concern for Chinese policymakers for the next several years.

China's record in economic development has been one of sharp contrasts, reflecting competition between unsound ideological demands and rational economic planning. The roughly 4 percent aggregate and 2 percent per capita annual growth rate represents fluctuations between rapid expansion during the fifties and stagnation in the sixties. Development strategies were so different that they seemed to project the needs of two separate countries. Policy oscillations, such as the Cultural Revolution, seriously hampered growth; e.g., China's total world trade did not return to the 1966 level of $4.2 billion until 1970 and was off over $500 million in 1968. But progress has been made. In deliberate industrialization China's experience is comparable only to India's record with its massive external support. More significant, it is now on the threshold of an economic takeoff, if the political environment remains stable.

The most serious problem for China-watchers is the assessment of the political durability of present leadership. The Ninth Party Congress in 1969 was convened to terminate the Cultural Revolution, define basic social economic and party policies, and heal the wounds of the various factions. It only ended the Cultural Revolution; factionalism persisted and new guidelines could not be formulated. The official confirmation of Lin Piao's conspiracy and subsequent death revealed the depths of the rivalry and warrants further examination.

As a gesture toward national unity after years of civil strife, the Ninth Party Congress named Defense Minister Lin Piao as Mao's successor. During the crisis

Piao had provided unquestioned support of the armed forces for the Maoist elements and, in an unprecedented gesture, the military received in return one quarter of the seats in the new Central Committee. This new authority at the national political level was partly a reflection of the Army's dominant position in the provinces where it had established a local civil administration loyal to the military rather than to the party hierarchy. Several levels of difference persisted through the Party Congress. Some elements, supported by Lin Piao, advocated perpetuating the revolution and others, backed by Premier Chou En-lai, stressed returning to order and productivity. The issue was more complex than a mere army-party confrontation. Even the army itself was split between the traditionalist officers who insisted on professionalism and modernization and the "ultra-leftists" who demanded ideological purity. Divisions carried over into foreign policy, with the professionals and managerial elements arguing against perpetuating the policy of "fighting on two fronts" by opposing both the United States and the Soviet Union. The leftists insisted on preserving China's self-appointed position as the source of world revolutionary encouragement and active engagement on all fronts of imperialism, reaction, and revisionism.

A second plenary session of the Central Committee was convened in September 1970 to rectify these differences. The deliberations clarified the issues and polarized the delegates more definitively around two leaders, Lin Piao and Chou En-lai. The moderates gained some ground in their argument that top priority should be given to the reconstitution of the party apparatus in the provinces and to the definition of its relationship to the army-controlled revolutionary committees. The Piao faction reportedly tried to block this decision by calling for a National Assembly and attempting to pack the delegations. Lin Piao argued that the destruction of the party apparatus had been necessary and it need not be reconstructed in its earlier image. Until a new model could be formulated, the army was competent to protect the interests of the central authority, as it had throughout the Cultural Revolution. Chou En-lai responded with a call for a return of the legitimizing function to the party so that the revolution could be advanced in other crucial sectors. The National Assembly was not called and the Politburo finally met in December 1970 and ruled against Lin Piao. The Defense Minister, misreading his little Red Book, had estimated that his proposals were more in tune with Mao's thoughts than were those of the Chou En-lai faction. This confidence encouraged him to persist in his defiance of the majority of the Central Committee and the Politburo and to assume the stature of the personification of the continuing Cultural Revolution. But Mao sided with Chou and the deadlock was broken.

In firm control of the Politburo, Chou inaugurated his plan to restructure the provincial party apparatus. To further isolate Lin Piao and insure Army loyalty, he appointed military officers to chair most of the committees created between December 1970 and August 1971. During Edgar Snow's interview of Mao on 18 December, it became apparent that Chou had already "taken power."

Chou moved slowly to reintroduce economic rationality and a more traditional orientation in foreign policy. But Lin Piao still retained control of the news media and maintained a steady flow of anti-Americanism (even while Kissinger was in China) and veiled attacks against Chou En-lai.

A crisis of greater implication than mere personal rivalry was reaching a climax. Massive celebrations for the fiftieth anniversary of the party were canceled and leading figures again slipped out of sight. Unconfirmed reports hold that Lin Piao recognized that he now represented a minority and called for another session in September 1971 of the Central Committee on the guise of making peace. The Central Committee, however, deposed the radical faction and, with a handful of close followers, Lin Piao promptly tried to flee to the USSR. His plans were discovered, however, and his aircraft was shot down inside Mongolia, where the Soviets recovered the wreckage.

The full record of the Lin Piao affair has not been released, but the above reconstruction and the aftermath of his death shed light on the Chinese political process and the outstanding succession issue. The official version is that Lin Piao organized a conspiracy and attempted to assassinate Mao when his demands were not met by the Central Committee. This is the first acknowledged conspiracy in the history of the Chinese Communist party. Earlier cases of Kao Kang, who in 1954 opposed the economic policy, and Defense Minister Peng Teh-huai, who in 1956 objected to the Great Leap Forward, and finally President Liu Shao-chi, accused leader of the antiparty faction during the Cultural Revolution, were never charged with attempting a military uprising. And should the conspiracy charge prove to be an exaggeration by the Chou faction, the fact that it was released abroad rather than at home suggests a sensitivity about the consolidation process that resulted from the purge of the leftists. A bloodbath has not occurred; the Chinese are not Stalinists in this sense. Lin Piao's supporters have been removed from office, yet over half of the 1969 Central Committee are reportedly still at their posts. The purge has passed through the central apparatus and proceeded through the provincial level. The Chinese maintain a humane perspective about the opposition, but it is not tolerated within the official structure. Thus, in this sense the Chinese remain strongly Stalinist. Democratic centralism is still interpreted to mean strict elimination of dissent after decisions have been taken. No attempt has been made to legitimize or guarantee minority views, as the Czechoslovaks tried in 1968. Moreover, the designation of an heir apparent, such as Lin Piao, for the chairmanship is contrary to party statutes and Communist practice. The responsibility rests solely with the Central Committee and is to be exercised upon vacancy.

Thus the extraordinary measures associated with the Lin Piao affair point up the paradoxes in contemporary China. At the grass roots, the Cultural Revolution produced a real and readily apparent spirit of vitality, vigor, and initiative. On the other hand, the same revolution had a divisive and disruptive effect on the leadership that paralyzed policy and generated a conspiracy of unknown magnitude. The endurance of the present dominant faction remains very much in doubt, as does the political succession for the chairmanship. A prolonged political crisis may erupt when both Chou and Mao become incapacitated. After two decades of rule, the Chinese Communists have not been able to legalize or legitimize processes for the normal transition of power. And the vitality of the revolution still remains at the grass roots, rather than at the central authority. Herein lies the most critical contradiction facing China today. The prospects for its resolution and the erection of stable political processes are not promising; indeed, the Lin Piao episode may signal a trend toward modification of the political process.

On the other hand, Lin Piao's conspiracy may represent a reaction against the growing constraints of policy that future leaders must accept or devise such stratagems as cultural revolutions to refurbish central authority. Contrary to the goals of the Cultural Revolution, China is remaining a pluralistic society. Though the striations have changed, it is not a classless, integrated mass society. Emphasis on regional self-interest and self-sufficiency has been counterproductive to the party's efforts to recentralize authority and has nourished traditional Chinese provincial rivalry. Agricultural imperatives and industrial requirements have introduced a new competition for scarce resource allocations. Except for the army, only limited work has been done as yet by Western scholars on the emergence of interest groups in China and their relative influence on policy. But the very rise of nacent interest groups will act as constraints on leaders who could formerly resort to political charisma or ideological zeal to carry through controversial policies. Lin Piao may have been the first victim of the new balance in domestic power and the last to seek rule by revolutionary fervor alone.

Return to Foreign Policy Questions

How do these domestic developments affect Chinese foreign policy aims and how do both relate to US objectives? With the eclipse of the Lin Piao challenge and the steady recovery from the Cultural Revolution, Chou En-lai apparently had enough confidence in the domestic passivity that he could probe new foreign policy opportunities. The change from rabid anti-Soviet and anti-American policies pursued before the Cultural Revolution was noticeable early in 1970. Regarding the classical communist dilemma of whether to stress world subversive revolution or international diplomatic recognition, China now shifted its priority to protecting national interests through responsible actions with legitimate governments. It supported Pakistan in its suppression of the East Bengal uprising and condemned the "Guevarist" rebellion in Ceylon. Sihanouk has been carefully muzzled and aid to the Palestinian guerrilas has wound down. No assistance has been reliably reported going to African insurrectionists; conversely, East African governments have become recipients of sizable grants of Chinese economic aid.

These signs of moderation in revolutionary activities were accompanied by debates in the United States among academics and analysts over whether China was an expansionist or a status quo state. One school argued that Maoism had an international appeal and global aspirations. Another countered that Maoism was usually solicited rather than compulsively exported, and that in the twenty-two instances when the Chinese Communists have used force abroad the aim was defensive or deterrent. In 1970-71 an increasing number of China specialists concluded that Peking's ambitions abroad had become more constrained. The general view held that China's national objectives were those of a legitimizing, rather than expansionist, power. These objectives included:

1. insuring military self-reliance, including strategic deterrence;
2. securing a higher degree of economic autarky (holding out only limited prospects for expanded trade);
3. preserving Chinese cultural and social heritage within the traditional Chinese Basin;
4. sponsoring friendly governments in neighboring states rather than satellites and dependencies;
5. engaging in legitimate influence competition in the modernization processes of the Third World through economic aid programs (China has now become a major donor state, granting $709 million in 1970);
6. curtailing US influence in the Pacific through the progressive withdrawal of the US presence, but not to the point where a vacuum might be created which could be exploited by a potentially hostile power;
7. recovering Taiwan;
8. preventing Japanese rearmament while cultivating cooperation in exploring new Asian relationships;
9. insuring sufficient latitude in the above relationships to maintain leverage against the USSR and prevent Soviet encirclement;
10. orienting all the above aims to the major goal of securing general recognition of China's stature as a great power.

From China's viewpoint the main threat to this ambitious plan was the Soviet challenge. On virtually every international issue, from Germany's Ostpolitik, to disarmament, to Japanese political stature, the two Communist giants were at opposite poles. Only the exigencies of the counteroffensive against North Vietnam produced a limited commonality of interest; but this was short-lived. Thus the main imperatives for Chinese policy prescribed effective counters to Soviet objectives.

The initial dispute with Moscow and the subsequent Cultural Revolution were essential for the desatellization process. Without the catharsis of nationalism and then independence, China would not have had the confidence to confront the Soviets while launching a bold initiative with the US. Sino-Soviet

relations have now been confined exclusively to the national level and are characterized as mutually antagonistic.

Moscow has pursued a policy of steadily intensifying propaganda and
polemical attacks while cautiously advancing limited diplomatic moves. (For
example, in June 1972 a new trade agreement was signed—none were approved
during the Cultural Revolution. In 1970 total trade was only 70 million rubles
($77 million), and in 1971 it reached 139 million rubles. Figures for 1972 were
only slightly higher). On the main grievance, talks about the border disputes
have dragged on since Kosygin's surprise visit to Peiping in September 1969.
The Chinese have demanded a reduction in the threat posed by Soviet forces
along its borders as a precondition for improved relations. And the Soviets insist
on normalization of relations as the prerequisite for reduced tensions and troop
withdrawals. (This is consistent with their demands on European security
matters.) The Soviets are highly sensitive about their exposure along the
Siberian front. They must maintain sufficient forces to counter any level of
attack, as well as to compensate for physical disadvantages. The total front is
over four thousand miles long, and the Far East provinces can only be supplied
by air, circuitous sea routes, and the slow trans-Siberian railway. Impenetrable
forests north of the railway deny the Soviets operational depth. And the railway
itself is vulnerable to Chinese artillery for long stretches and to inclement
weather conditions. Moscow has now deployed some fifty-four divisions in the
border regions against a smaller number of Chinese units. They are superior in
mobility, armor, firepower, air support, and nuclear warheads.

But China has tested tactical nuclear warheads in ranges from 10 to 30
kilotons, and is producing its own F-9 fighter-bomber that could deliver such
weapons at ranges up to five hundred nautical miles. China now has over three
hundred F-9s deployed with forward squadrons and is producing about fifteen
per month. Equally significant, China has abandoned its earlier strategy of deploying primarily militia in border areas and in relying on defense in depth with
regular formations. It is now assigning its first line divisions to border positions,
following a strategy of forward defense. One half of China's 120 divisions
were stationed in the south; some will undoubtedly be reassigned in the northeast
as Vietnam winds down. These build-ups have increased Soviet defense costs
substantially over Chinese expenditures, since Siberia is an extremely high-cost
deployment area and Manchuria is China's lowest-cost area.

This mutual build-up is hardly conducive to the degree of confidence
necessary for troop withdrawals. In March 1972, Brezhnev publicly extended
a compromise package. He called for a treaty renouncing the use of force, which
would allow troop reductions, coupled with settlement of border difficulties,
which would relieve a major source of tension. China preferred to keep its options open and gave a noncommittal reply. Soviet propaganda responded with
renewed calls for an anti-China pact. After three years of talks, Sino-Soviet
differences still appear unbridgeable. A continuing source of Chinese apprehensions

is the Brezhnev Doctrine: the self-proclaimed responsibility, exercised in Czech-oslovakia and reiterated as late as May 1970 in Prague by Brezhnev, to impose the Soviet model for Socialist development wherever deviation warrants. This is an obvious threat to China's Maoist practices, and one motive for the border clashes of 1969. China attempted to demonstrate Soviet vulnerability along the borders and to convince Moscow that, unlike Czechoslovakia, it would resist any level of attack. The Brezhnev doctrine was also one of the main reasons for China's return to the diplomatic offensive in 1970 in Eastern Europe.

Chinese relations with Eastern Europe reached an all-time low in 1967. Trade had fallen 73.5 percent from 1959 to 1967, to a monetary value of only $175.6 million. Moreover, party and state relations had been virtually suspended. In 1969 Chinese interest in Eastern Europe showed a sharp rejuvenation. For example, Chinese foreign language radio broadcasts to Eastern Europe increased from 1967 to mid-1971 by 212 percent. Trade figures showed impressive gains. Rumanian-Chinese trade rose 60 percent between 1969 and 1970 to 803 million lei, not including a 25-million-dollar loan extended Rumania for flood relief. During the same period trade with Hungary rose 14 percent; with Poland 22 percent. These favorable improvements were translated into mutual political benefits. By the end of 1970 full diplomatic relations had been restored between Peking and all East European states, including its former arch antagonist, Yugo-slavia. (Because of Chinese ideological objections, diplomatic relations were not established with the heretical Tito regime until 1955. Finally ambassadors were exchanged as a result of strong Soviet pressure to secure a general rapproche-ment with Belgrade. It was China, however, who resumed the lead of the Social-ist attack in April 1958 against Tito and withdrew its ambassador until May 1970.) In 1971 Yugoslav Foreign Minister, Mirko Tepavac, made the first official visit of a high-ranking Yugoslav to China. His trip was preceded by a visit of Rumania Party chief Ceausescu to China. Ceausescu's ten-day tour was greeted with alarm in Moscow and a mini-crisis erupted in the Balkans.

Moscow and its more conservative East European allies opened a polemical offensive against the alleged formation of an entente between Rumania, Yugo-slavia, and Albania under Chinese sponsorship. Soviet-Albanian animosities were well known. The miniscule improvement in relations between Tirana and Bel-grade and the rather remote Albanian ties with Rumania suggested that the triangulation was more a bureaucratic conjecture than a political reality. Yugo-slav-Rumanian relations had been close but correct, especially since the Czecho-slovak invasion. But the propagation of a crisis, particularly by Hungary, over the marginally improved relations in the southern Balkans indicated Moscow's hypersensitivity to the remarkable Chinese inroads into its own front yard. Polemics against Bucharest for alleged improper Socialist behavior and rumors of renewed Warsaw Pact threats to invade Rumania were intended to dampen the Balkans new opening to the Far East and to demonstrate the outer limits of Moscow's tolerance in Balkan-Chinese flirtations.

This dramatic resurgence of Chinese presence in the Communist world was part of a general diplomatic rejuvenation. During the Cultural Revolution, Chinese ambassadors had been withdrawn from all foreign posts except Cairo. Within several months, twenty-three new appointees were returned to key embassies, and formal diplomatic relations were later opened with some fifty countries. It is important to note that the mission of Chinese embassies after 1970 had substantially changed. Reflecting Chou En-lai's victory over Lin Piao, Chinese embassies were no longer centers for Maoist revolutionary subversion or the focal point for radical forces. They performed the conventional task of representing Peking's interests with the government of the host nation, without undue compromise by contacts with opposition elements. Even espionage, formerly practiced by Chinese diplomats and still an active duty for Soviet representatives, has apparently been suspended—not a single Chinese diplomat has been declared persona non grata since 1970, while over one hundred Soviet representatives were expelled in 1971 from Britain alone. The more legitimate activities of Chinese diplomats represented a more sober view of world problems and China's role and interests in the broader context of interstate relations. For example, Chinese representatives in West Europe have become deeply concerned with such seemingly exclusive European matters as the Common Market, the European Security Conference, and the Mutual Balanced Force Reductions. China is strongly lobbying against the standard Communist line and in favor of accelerated Western integration, and is expressing caution or cynicism on security negotiations and opposition to troop cuts—to do otherwose would encourage or aid the Soviet position. Thus Chinese diplomacy, as well as it can be judged in two years, is noteworthy for the new singularity of its nationalist perspective and nonattachemnt to its former commitment to radical movements, local Communist sentiments, or Soviet demands.

Taiwan Question

China's campaign for diplomatic acceptance culminated in its successful membership bid in the UN. While membership itself was expected by many during the 1971 session of the General Assembly, few predicted that Taiwan would be so promptly expelled. The expulsion of Taiwan advanced Peking's claims both of the singularity of Chinese sovereignty and to the incorporation of Taiwan as a province of the mainland. Correspondingly, it weakened the two-China policy informally adopted by the US. Peking insisted on these terms for its participation and in doing so indicated the strength of its feelings on the issue. When a majority of the nations accepted Peking's terms, Taiwan and its foreign interests were relegated to a back-burner position. But this intensified the issue as a major obstacle in Chinese-American relations because of US commitments to Taiwanese security.

Taiwan has several unique features. Of its 13 million people, only 13 percent are of mainland extraction; 87 percent have little identification with or interest in the mainland. (Formosa was a Japanese possession from 1895 until 1945 and was ruled by the mainland as an occupied territory for four years). The ruling Kuomintang Party comes from the alien minority and has made almost no effort to accept Taiwanese participation in government or political life—only four Taiwanese hold seats in the Parliament. Finally, there has been little integration or intermarriage.

The United States had important moral and material stakes in Taiwan. It has become a model for economic development, a showpiece for Western development programs. Between 1950 and 1965, the US invested $6 billion from public funds in economic assistance that has now been terminated. Only $82 million was spent in military aid in 1971. As a result, the GNP increased twelve times between 1951 and 1971; the annual rate during the last decade was 9.8 percent. In 1972 industrial growth increased 20 percent. Foreign trade is greater than that of the entire mainland and is expected to grow 12.5 percent annually. Real per capita income is growing at 4.5 percent annually—$320 in 1971, three times that of the mainland, it is expected to reach $1000 by 1980. Land reform has been introduced; 80 percent of the people now own their land. Finally, unemployment and inflation are low and rice exports are booming.

Japan is slowly awakening to the opportunities and dangers inherent in the Taiwan issue. Strategically the island is vitally important to Japan. Three hundred million tons of raw materials alone annually pass through the Formosan Straits. Until now the US has given Taiwan stature, status quo, and protection. If these responsibilities should pass to a potentially hostile power, it could pose a serious threat to Japanese economic interests. Moreover, Japan has important investments in Taiwan. Between 1964 and 1970 Japan invested only $80 million in public funds, plus $150 million in government loans in 1965. But private investment has soared. By 1970 Japan was investing 26 percent and the US was down to 62 percent of the total annual funds. And Japan had rung up a trade surplus with Taiwan of $1.6 billion. The comparative economic advantages of the two island states are likely to accelerate trade, with Taiwan supplying agricultural and raw materials in exchange for manufactured goods.

US-Kuomintang relations oscillated between intimacy during the Second World War and mutual disdain after the Civil War. On 5 January 1950 President Truman stated that the US has no predatory designs on Formosa or any other Chinese territory, and that the US would not become involved in a Chinese war for Formosan defense. The US refrained from pledging support for Chiang Kai-shek during the Korean War and rejected his offer to participate fully in the United Nations Command. Not until after the conflict had shifted to Indochina and Washington feared an Asian-wide conspiracy did it accept major responsibility for Taiwanese security. The US responded reluctantly but decisively to the defense of the offshore islands in 1958, confirming its commitments to

Taipei. The continuous presence of US military since then has been regarded as an important contribution to the Pacific deterrent forces.

Washington's New Open Door Policy

From the Chinese viewpoint, Taiwan was the central issue for discussion during the unprecedented Nixon visit to Peking. Change in the US attitude was first apparent in the July and November 1969 pronouncements known as the Nixon Doctrine. At Guam in November the President stated three principles:

1. The US shall keep all its treaty commitments;
2. It shall provide a shield if a nuclear power threatens the freedom of a nation whose survival it considers vital to its security; and
3. In cases involving other types of aggression, it shall furnish military and economic assistance when requested in accordance with its treaty commitments. But it will look to the nation directly threatened to assume primary responsibility of providing the manpower for its defense.

This more eclectic approach to Washington's Asia policy suggested that while previous commitments would remain legally binding, the manner of fulfillment had now changed. The US promptly reassured Taiwan, Thailand, South Korea, and the Philippines of its fidelity to its obligations. But the announced plan to withdraw 500,000 troops from South Vietnam raised speculation among these allies that as US Asian interests were changing so would the nature of our responsibilities change. As reiterated by the President, however, US interests remained relatively constant. The US sought stability and the preservation of the status quo, promotion of local prosperity, and the prevention of hegemony by any nation—the USSR, China, or Japan. What had changed was the policy to implement these goals. The character of deterrence in Asia would now involve only indirect American involvement. This new minimum US accountability and Vietnamization coincided with the development of the potential New Delhi-Moscow axis and increasing Soviet influence in Hanoi. Peking now felt increasingly threatened more by the USSR than the United States.

This was the setting for the transition from confrontation to adjustment in US-Chinese relations. China accepted Washington's overtures for exploratory talks above the level held by their ambassadors in Warsaw without requiring a general improvement in the Asian political climate or a cessation of Vietnamese hostilities as preconditions. The omission of these presumed prerequisites augured well for talks and indicated that Peking had apparently concluded that a change in the balance of power was occurring which imposed a higher priority on fuller participation in the new power constellation than on continued militant anti-imperialism. For its part, the US justified the prospects for rapprochement with several arguments. First, it would offer a positive alternative to the wornout Dulles syndrome of containment and counterideological campaigning. Second, the new power constellation in the Pacific demanded US recognition and unfettered participation to insure stability. Third, a "second chance" strategy would grant Peking the opportunity to demonstrate whether it is truly expansionist, without serious risks to US interests or losses that could not be recovered. Fourth, neither Taiwan nor China expected invasion from the other, and US strategic requirements could be fulfilled from other bases in the Philippines or Guam. Finally, the US alliance with Taiwan has achieved its basic objective: Taiwan was free and economically stable.[3] But by the time of Nixon's visit, the US had not yet adequately thought through the Taiwan issue and was unprepared for the unexpectedly uncompromising Chinese insistence on the matter. Should the US forces remain on the island to insure continued stability, heavier US-Japanese investment, and economic viability after a US Vietnam-pullout? Should the US encourage Taiwanese independence of a two-states-in-one-nation formula? What should be the role of Taiwan in future US Asian policy? Finally, could a "sellout" that would trigger the retreat of other allies toward China be avoided?

During the Nixon visit in February, the Chinese stated firmly that improved relations depended upon US abandonment of its support for Taiwan, renunciation of a two-China option, and formal recognition of the island as a province of the mainland. When Nixon cited Washington's security obligations, Chou replied that China would not use force to liberate Taiwan. (But he refused to include this promise in the Shanghai communiqué.) Nixon then formally agreed to remove US forces from the island when tensions in the region subsided. The US also pledged not to obstruct contact between the two Chinas. The US recognized that there was only one Chinese state, but refused to meet Peking's demands that it included Taiwan. Nixon insisted that this was an issue for the two Chinese governments to resolve.

In Asia the communiqué was widely regarded with alarm. Marshal Green from the State Department was dispatched to the capitals of Asian allies to explain the US interpretation. Kissinger undertook the chore with American newsmen. He explained that the US commitment to Taiwan was dependent upon the island's legal status, which was a Chinese matter. If the Chiang Kai-shek government was determined not to associate with the mainland and to maintain its independence, then the US would honor its alliance responsibilities. This explanation was more soothing for Americans than Asians. The Philippine President announced that because of the new course in US policy, Manila would renegotiate all its treaties with the United States, not just commercial and base rights agreements but its mutual defense pact as well. Within a year all America's Asian allies had made some form of approach to Peking, and Taiwan itself began actively but quietly to foster a two-states-in-one-nation de facto solution. Some Oriental form of de facto accommodation in which mutual claims are quietly dropped may be the most attractive short-term solution from Taipei's viewpoint.

Korea—A Third Divided Asian Nation

It also may be the best solution for the reunification of Korea, the other outstanding Asian divided-nation problem. Like Taiwan, the US has a heavy moral and material commitment to South Korea. Since the Korean War, it has invested nearly $8 billion, averaging about $300 million per year. US private investment has been somewhat below $100 million annually, but since 1970 it has been steadily increasing. And US troops stationed in South Korea contribute about $150 million to the economy per year. Economic growth in South Korea rose by 13 percent in 1968 and 15.5 percent in 1969, causing inflationary pressures and a controlled 10-percent increase for 1970. In general an air of prosperity prevails in South Korea, especially in the cities, where per capita income was estimated to be on an average of 70 percent higher than in rural districts. While these inequalities persist, the per capita income in the South is believed to be several times higher than in North Korea.

Over twenty years of direct US engagement in the defense of South Korea and the continuous stationing of combat forces in the country manifested Washington's continuing obligations to Seoul. The 50-percent reduction in US combat ground forces negotiated by Vice President Agnew after the Guam Declaration contributed to a new climate on the peninsula. Seoul demanded and received major incremental increases in the modernization of its armed forces and the reduction of its expeditionary forces in Vietnam as compensation. But the continued US presence remained the most objectionable obstacle for North Korea to improved relations.

By 1966, Pyongyang adopted a middle-course policy in the Sino-Soviet dispute that gradually earned it leverage against both rivals. During the course of the Cultural Revolution, North Korea established a degree of independence comparable to that enjoyed by Hanoi and exercised this new latitude primarily against the United States. Available evidence indicates that neither Peking nor Moscow was consulted beforehand about the capture of the USS *Pueblo* or the shooting down of the US EC-121. Both neighbors were surprised and unprepared for these incidents; the Soviets actually aided in air-sea rescue operations for the missing aircrew. North Korea's general attitude on these matters was underscored by Premier Kim Il Sung in a press interview: "There was little hope that Soviet or Chinese influence would play any decisive role in improving relations between the United States and North Korea. This was the responsibility of the United States."[4] Clearly he felt Pyongyang would have to rely on its own devices to compel a more conciliatory American attitude. A policy of vigilance and militancy against the South was his preferred instrument.

But Washington's decision to draw down its forces in Korea was made despite Sung's aggressive policy and because of the burdens accumulating from the Vietnam War. This move contributed in the end to an improved climate, but it was probably the shock of the announced Nixon visit to Peking that induced adjustments in both Koreas. Barely six weeks later, both sides appointed

Red Cross representatives to hold talks in Panmunjom about resolving the humanitarian aspects of the division, such as family reunion, etc. One year later, on 30 August 1972, formal negotiations opened in Pyongyang to formalize the humanitarian aspect of the two countries' relations. More important, during May and June 1972 the two sides had held top-level talks and initialed an agreement, released on 4 July, reiterating their mutual desire to advance reunification. There were so many reservations voiced by both sides that the prospects for reunification were remote. The significance of the agreement, however, was that for the first time in over two decades the two Koreas had conducted official talks and agreed to suspend further hostile military actions.

Sung's decision to approach the South was in concert with moves being made by other Asian states, whether allied to China or the US. This general readjustment was due not only to the ambiguous US stand on Taiwan; it was a result more of the general sense of accommodation released by the Nixon visit to China that compounded the insecurity arising from the Guam statement. US policy would now be examined more minutely for signs of perfidy, and at the same time a more conciliatory stand toward China was regarded as only prudent. After all, China is an Asian power by virute of its geography; the US claimed the same rights based only on its policies. In other words, the prospects for Chinese-American conciliation have altered the roles and strategies of all smaller states. No smaller state can now use the same degree of leverage against either rival power. They have quickly sensed the danger of being relegated to a position of growing indifference and the possibility of becoming expendible. One of the noteworthy characteristics of politics in the 1971-72 period was the intensification of diplomacy on several new planes of action: the new four-great-power play, the US, USSR, China, and Japan; the smaller states' overtures to rival great powers; and adjustment among neighboring smaller states, including friendly states such as the ASEAN nations.

Political Implications of the Open Door

Conversely, as the options for the smaller states multiply, the great powers can no longer view their Asian policies in the singular perspective of black-and-white challenge and response formerly associated with the Chinese threat. The United States, for example, must adopt a more variegated approach that can accommodate the variety of national interests in Asia and compensate for the growing lack of homogeneity in security matters formerly induced by the peril of Maoism. (When all factors are weighed, Asia is probably the most heterogeneous region in the world, reinforcing the need for individualized approaches). The sum of these diplomatic activities will not only be a clarification of mutual interests and issues, but may result in a more precise understanding of the relationship between great powers and small powers in an era of continuing great-power influence competition and localized animosities.

The USSR was the main loser from Washington's new Open Door to China. In assessing the accomplishments of the Peking summit, President Nixon stated, "In sum, the visit represented a long first step toward establishing a continuing fruitful dialogue with the People's Republic of China, in a way that will contribute to peace not only in the Pacific but in the entire world. The second and succeeding steps are already being taken with visits to Peking by legislative leaders, periodic ambassadorial meetings in Paris, and other contacts which would have seemed impossible only a year ago."[5] Not only the summit conference but the continuity that persisted created a general shock in Moscow. Sino-American hostilities had been a constant axiom in Soviet calculus of world developments and appropriate strategies. Indeed, the visit shattered the presumed shared interest between Moscow and Washington in cooperating to contain Maoism and Chinese expansion. Moreover, the Soviets regarded as incredulous and naïve the growing Western view that Maoism was not an international threat. (André Malraux, the former French Minister of Culture, expressed the widening belief: "For me, I think Chinese Communism has always been excessively serious inside China, and always been not at all serious outside China.")[6] But by the Peking summit, the US regained the initiative, destroyed this stable power relationship, reopened the Sino-Soviet dispute by allowing China to concentrate its attention on a single front, and diverted world opinion from the expansion of its Vietnam involvement. Moscow also realized that the initiative would not easily be regained and that it would be relegated for some time to a responsive rather than a creative posture. For example, even if Moscow decided to reverse its course completely and to seek full rapprochement with China, it is doubtful if China would reciprocate—Peking now has the best of both worlds and would probably be content to exploit its advantages. The Soviet resentment must have been enhanced by the portion of the Shanghai communiqué that was directed implicitly against it—both sides pledged not to seek hegemony in Asia and implied that they would resist efforts of other states to gain such privileges.

Washington's new role in China's anti-Soviet stretegy was expounded in detail during the July 1972 visits to Peking of US Representatives Hale Boggs and Gerald Ford. Chou En-lai provided general counsel which he admonished the United States to take seriously. The USSR, he claimed, would never live up to any agreement to scale down nuclear weapons, and the US must continue full-scale development of nuclear technology or risk the consequences of the USSR becoming an unrivaled nuclear power. He argued that the US must not reduce its troops in Europe or accept the guise of European security arrangements, since this would either be exploited in the West by Moscow or seized as an opportunity to shift greater pressure against the Far East. With the prospects of increasing all-out Japanese rearmaments and the mounting Indian threat arising from the strengthening of the Moscow-New Delhi axis, China feels tightening pressures of encirclement. Therefore, Chou urged, the US must do everything possible to block Soviet attempts to dominate Southeast Asia. Since the

USSR was now China's main antagonist, Chou requested that US troops remain stationed in Asia for the time being, as the most feasible deterrent against further Soviet expansion.

Whether or not Chou's projection is an accurate revelation of China's new threat estimate is less important than the imagery it suggests. Soliciting aid from leaders of the US House of Representatives to counter the Soviet menace was a reversal that would have boggled the imagination only one year earlier. Instead of a tacit Soviet-American understanding on the desirability of cooperation in containing China (presumed only on the Soviet side and largely by reason of their own anxieties), Chou was conveying the unquestioned impression that China would warmly endorse collusion with the United States to contain the USSR. Projections of this scale illustrate the lack of precision that now permeates the relationships of the three great powers. Policy planners in all three states no longer calculate on the same degree of predictability they formerly enjoyed in plotting interests and strategies. This new ambiguity in Asian affairs, however temporary, is one of the most important consequences of the change in Sino-American relations.

7 Japan: Further American Retrenchment?

In classical balance of power politics, the new triangulation among the three great powers might have been highly unstable. The natural tendency of all three would have been to cultivate the other two, while trying to preserve sufficient distance to remain a balancer by aligning itself with either one or the other. The rise of Japan as the fourth Pacific power has reduced the tendency to seek the balancer role. A new rectangular relationship is emerging, in which the roles of the contending powers remain somewhat unclear.

Japan has not only recovered from war devastation, but in a quarter century has become the world's third strongest industrial state. Moreover, it has virtually established economic hegemony over Southeast Asia. Over one third of Japan's exports go to Southeast Asia. Valued at $19 billion in 1970, they are expected to double by 1975 to $37 billion. Japan is the number one investor in Thailand, number two in Indonesia, and accounts for 60 percent of all new investment in the Philippines. In 1968 Thailand's trade deficit to Japan was $250 million and by 1972 it exceeded the country's total foreign exchange reserves. Japanese private investment overseas is now around $900 million annually. Moreover, Japan now outranks the US as the world's top consumer of raw materials, importing $20 billion worth of goods annually, including 200,000 tons of iron ore and 600,000 tons of crude oil daily. Twenty percent of the world's yearly total of raw materials goes into Japanese products, and this figure is expected to increase by 15 percent annually. Due in part to trade prosperity, the yen was revalued in December 1971 by 17 percent (and later by another 17 percent), yet surpluses continued to mount, reaching $10 billion within a year. To correct this continuing trade imbalance, Tokyo finally reduced tariffs by roughly 20 percent on 2000 of the 2700 imported items, leaving duties of between 8 and 10 percent, or about the same as other industrial nations. These cuts, however, were expected to increase imports by only $340 million annually. In an additional measure, the Export-Import Bank was authorized in late 1972 to make major new investments abroad for production of manufactured goods. Thus, Japan has become the dominant economic power of Asia. But it is also far more dependent upon foreign markets and sources of supply than before the Second World War.

Japan has been content for the past twenty-five years to accept American military protection and the lowest defense budget by far of any industrialized society. Under strong US pressure, it agreed to increase its Fourth Defense Plan, 1972-76, to $16 billion. This figure is $5 billion more than the first three plans combined, but it remains only 0.8 percent of the GNP, while the US spends between 8 and 9 percent. But low defense spending was only one of many factors that allowed the resource-impoverished islands to build an economy that is expected to become number two by 1980. High labor productivity, low wages, paternalism in labor unions, skillful management, innovation and adaptability, and social stability contributed to this economic miracle.

But the scale of the growth lead inevitably to sharp competition with the US, its chief trading partner (in 1971 the US bought $7.5 billion in Japanese goods). The strain in Japanese-American relations developed not only from trade difficulties and economic policies, but over the manner and timing of Washington's opening of the Chinese door. President Nixon had established a warm and personal relationship with Prime Minister Sato. Due in part to this good will, Nixon took an active interest in the return of Okinawa in 1972 to Japan, a step Japan was not prepared for strategically but which bolstered Sato's domestic posture. In return, Sato personally pledged a limit on the export of Japanese cotton textiles to the US. Sato was unable to keep this promise and the close personal friendship suffered. Washington was not unduly concerned about Tokyo's discomfort over its failure to consult Japan about the changes in its China policy. It was also not sympathetic to Japanese criticism when it imposed the 10-percent surcharge and revalued the dollar. Finally, Washington expressed no regret when Sato resigned, on 17 June 1972, and was replaced by his ardent opponent, Kakuei Tanaka.

Tanaka met with Nixon on 2 September, soon after taking office and shortly before visiting China. From the American viewpoint, the most important issue in relations between the two countries was its trade deficit. The Japanese saw the central issue of the summit conference as its future relations with China. The total US trade imbalance for 1972 was expected to reach the record high of $5 billion. (By year's end the total deficit reached $8.3 billion, three times the 1971 record). The US deficit to Japan alone in 1971 was $4.1 billion. Tanaka agreed to short-term trade adjustments that would relieve about $1 billion in the US deficit. In compensation, he asked for US understanding of Japan's decision to consider China's terms for increased trade with the mainland and full diplomatic relations.

This was a difficult decision for Japan. China had imposed stiff preconditions for trade between the two countries and had demanded none from American businesses. China will not deal with any Japanese firm that aids Taiwan or South Korea politically, that makes "substantial" investments in Taiwan or South Korea, that supplies war material to US forces in Southeast Asia, or that engages in joint ventures with American companies. Furthermore, Peking has stipulated three political prerequisites for normalization of relations between the two countries: recognition of the Peking government as the sole authority for China, affirmation that Taiwan is part of China, and abrogation of the peace treaty ending the Sino-Japanese war signed with Taiwan in 1953.

The Japanese believe that the trade potential with the mainland is an important opportunity. China's GNP is about $80 billion, only one third of Japan's. But significantly, China's total trade is only 5 percent as high as Japan's and Tokyo's trade turnover with Peking in 1971 of $900 million represents only 2 to 3 percent of its total trade—but could possibly expand to 5 percent. In some sectors the Chinese market is particularly strong. Sixty percent of Japan's fertilizer production is exported to China. Yet Taiwan's total trade of $3.1 billion in 1970 was nearly that of China, and South Korea's trade was $2.5 billion in the same year. Moreover, Japanese exchanges with these two countries is more valuable than its trade with the mainland. Nonetheless Japanese businessmen for the most part were convinced that a commercial bonanza awaited them on the mainland, if only the restrictions could be removed.

(One of Tanaka's first acts was to reverse a long-standing ban on the use of Export-Import Bank credits for trade with China. And during his September visit to China, he sought a long-standing commitment to supply natural resources in exchange for high technology industrial equipment. In contrast, another segment of Japanese commercial leaders see Siberia as more rewarding and are trying to arrange the $5 billion long-term credit for the construction of an oil pipeline between Tyumen and Nakhodka on the Pacific and for developing the Yuzhno-Yakutsk coal and gas deposits. Competition between these two interests is likely to intensify and may ultimately reduce the euphoria about investment in China).

Tokyo's New Foreign Policy

Both Chinese restraints and Japanese enthusiasm are in part the product of the war: Chinese demands for restitution and Japanese sense of war guilt. The most extreme restraint is the demand to abrogate the peace treaty with Taiwan. The treaty terminated the state of war and pledged Japanese cooperation for Taiwan's defense. The US reportedly asked Japan to reaffirm this commitment to Taiwan's security during the Nixon-Tanaka summit, but the issue was omitted in the communiqué, indicating that Tokyo would like to be released from this obligation. During Tanaka's September 1972 Peking visit, he formally expressed Japanese contrition for the war and announced Japan's readiness to accept Peking's sovereignty over Taiwan, but he could not yet renounce the treaty. Should the Taiwan question be consitutionally settled by the Chinese, the treaty would automatically be abrogated. Tanaka's decision was a heavy blow to Taiwan, which promptly broke relations, and a major victory for Peking. China quickly moved to exacerbate Taipei's growing isolation.[a]

---

[a]The gains for both sides in establishing full diplomatic ties and normalized relations resulting from the Tanaka-Chou summit were impressive. China received an important new credential in its bid for legitimacy and world recognition. Formal endorsement by such a prominent former antagonist was an important certification of the credibility of Peking's new, post-Cultural-Revolution brand of international behavior. In terms of Asian politics

A peace treaty remains an outstanding issue in Soviet-Japanese relations. Japanese of all political stripes are agreed that the preconditions for a peace treaty and complete normalization must be the return of the four groups of Kurile Islands, held by the USSR since the war. Sato believed he scored a major point when he gained Soviet assurance that the Kuriles would be returned when the US relinquished Okinawa. In the wake of Nixon's Peking trip, Soviet Foreign Minister Andrei Gromyko arrived in Tokyo and agreed to open formal negotiations on a peace treaty, without insisting that Japan abandon its territorial claims. In the light of the prospects for Japanese and American accommodation with Peking, the Soviets had lost leverage in Tokyo and have little more than marginal commercial opportunities to offer—the problem in developing Siberia is still labor shortages. (The Soviets have used as enticement the suggestion of convening an Asian Security Conference along the lines of its European counterpart. But the Japanese have insisted upon Chinese and American participation, dampening Soviet interest.) The Soviets are likely to play the Japanese card strongly, especially if Chinese policy should prove more assertive, and Japan may finally receive a peace treaty and at least two of the Kurile Islands.

Such Soviet generosity would not be due to benevolence, but to confusion about the new Pacific power configuration and the appropriate role Japan is likely to play in the future of Asia. Japan's future political role is its biggest problem today. How should Japan achieve political rank commensurate to its economic stature? Can it remain indefinitely an economic giant and a military pigmy? Has it now been relegated the status of an "outsider" by its US patron and other sympathizers? In a world with few friends, are political aspirations even important? Should Japan remain, as de Gaulle preferred, a nation of transistor radio salesmen? If Japan embarks on a political role of global dimensions, how can the accompanying nationalism be controlled? How can other states be assured that the feared cyclical process of "independence," neutrality, Gaullist nationalism, and rearmed super-power chauvinism is not inevitable and can be checked?

---

and diplomatic maneuverability Japanese acceptance was as critical as American for China's attempt to break out of its isolationistic barriers. On Tokyo's side, normalized relations with Peking was a vital step in redressing century-old animosity between the two nations. The retribution China required for World War II grievances was the last major obstacle in Japan's complex task of overcoming its war guilt. Finally reducing tensions with its principal neighbor was a leap forward in Japan's quest for political stature and maturity; Japan's freedom of action was increased by a factor substantially greater than the mere addition of one more player in Tokyo's international calculus.

The magnitude of the changed atmosphere was illustrated by reports that China had sounded out Japan on the prospects of an anti-Soviet entente. During Tanaka's Peking visit, Chou En-lai dropped earlier allegations about Japan's remilitarization. He observed that in light of the augmentation of Soviet armed forces and the reduction of American troops a modest Japanese military build-up would have a stabilizing effect. If Soviet "aggressive designs" resulted in a permanent naval presence in the East China Sea or direct military operations against Japan, Chou reportedly suggested that China might come to Japan's aid, even alongside US forces. If confirmed, Chou's offer would be more symbolic than realistic; a manifestation of China's new quest for diplomatic maneuverability.

In tackling these questions, Japan has several important constraints. To sustain economic growth and yet overcome persistent labor shortages, Tokyo has transferred capital and technological prowess to labor rich countries, and has already created an anti-Yankee type of resentment. Animosity and nationalistic emotions have reached the point that cooperation with other countries in selected instances has been nullified. Further, development opportunities in China and Siberia will probably never be as lucrative as in Southeast Asia, because of China's insistence on self-sufficiency and autarchy, and because of Russian weather conditions and chronic labor shortages. Moreover, unlike West Germany, Japan has no natural geographic area or group of neighboring states in which it can exercise political leadership. It is surrounded by powerful rivals and/or resentful economic dependencies. Its most natural arena for political authority is within the community of Western industrial nations, where Japan is respected. The strategic implications of too close an identity with nations located on the other side of the world impart obvious risks. Yet it is these military factors that figure so precariously in Japanese estimates. Serious rearmament would be resented at home and abroad and would be regarded as detrimental to both domestic and foreign interests. In an era of reduced predictability of power relationships in the Pacific, and without natural allies, Japanese defense policy can be shifted in only two general directions: increased dependence on American protection, or greater self-reliance. Japan has been reluctant so far to commit itself to either alternative. But if public opinion senses that the other Pacific powers are playing Japan off against each other, or that they are making deals at her expense, a shift toward the right and national conservatism might be difficult to control.

The US has officially called on Japan to seek an appropriate role in a "multipolar" world—Kissinger's term, and suggested that it accept a distinction between the different levels of international responsibility and commitment, such as military, economic, and political. Japan is expected to relinquish strategic military aspirations and accept the credibility of American protection, and yet subject itself to commercial practices it regards as detrimental to economic growth.[1] Such simplistic attempts at compartmentalizing authority are resented by the Japanese as chauvinistic and discriminatory. The Japanese cannot be expected to embrace any suggested political role that implies discrimination or subordination. On the contrary, they can be expected to maximize their options and reduce their dependencies, while continuing their own commercial protectionism and exploring in their own way a political role.

Thus, the central point is that Japan must find its international political functions largely by itself. To encourage this process and preclude alarm by those states that must ultimately accept or reject this role, friendly governments should act now to reduce the chances of present relationships deteriorating and eventually causing panic among the Japanese. In other words, the best check against radicalism in Tokyo is the strengthening of friendly ties with states the

Japanese respect and which can give them confidence and security as they
experiment with the democratic processes and the unknown mechanisms for
attaining international political authority. The United States has a particularly
heavy responsibility in this regard: it gave birth to and nurtured democratic
Japan. To ignore its further development before its social and political institutions
fully mature may court resentment, a swing toward anti-Americanism, and the
return to ultranationalism of a society better equipped than ever to generate
international tension.

Japanese-American friendship will not be easily broken, but since July 1971
it has eroded. The Nixon-Tanaka summit reportedly did not restore the degree
of personal familiarity and national intimacy that formerly graced relations between the two countries. Perhaps this growing distance is an inevitable aspect of
the maturation process. But the younger Japanese are becoming skeptical and
even cynical about all these "growth mechanisms" the Americans cite. Indeed,
they may increase their identification with traditional inner Japanese qualities.
Zbigniew Brzezinski has perceptively outlined several recommendations for
Washington to assure continued Japanese friendship.

1. Pay more attention to Japanese developments through increased press coverage and academic study of Japanese affairs;
2. Encourage Japan to assume constructive international responsibilities without
   dominating the Asia region;
3. Encourage Japan's "nuclear neutralism" for the near future, thereby eliminating the complicated decision of acquiring nuclear weapons which Japan
   is reluctant to make; and
4. Reemphasize cooperation in American-Japanese strategic-political planning
   while reducing the visible US military presence.[2]

In other words, convert a former dependent relationship to a full partnership.

New Rectangular Relationships

What future can one foresee for the new rectangular relationship in the
Northwest Pacific? The uncertainties outlined above suggest the difficulties in
attempting accurate predictions on issues and problems that are inadequately
based on precedents and stable interests. But several assumptions can safely be
made at the outset. First, strategic nuclear weapons can no longer be relied upon
as planning factors for the protection of national interests. The Chinese cannot
use their nuclear weapons for purposes other than national survival any more
easily than the super powers.[b]

---

[b]From Japan's viewpoint, the development of its own nuclear capability would not
increase its deterrence or security; indeed, it would produce the opposite results. In the

Second, military prowess will be increasingly measured by the proficiency of general purpose forces. With the Chinese and the Soviets the emphasis will necessarily be on ground forces, and the Japanese and Americans will stress naval and air power. China and the USSR can more readily threaten or invade each others' territory than either or both can the territory of the two naval powers. This disparity in the nature of defense and deterrence will have an intensifying effect on the friendship or the enmity of the two land powers, and will allow the naval power the advantages of distance and restraint. Third, if the prospects for territorial conflict remain low and ideological competition remains relegated to the past, Japan's economic power will become the dominant feature in political interests for all four. Cordial and expansive multilateral economic cooperation among all four remains unlikely, and Japan can be expected to press its commercial advantages and interests on a bilateral basis. In the economic sphere, China will remain the weakest of the four for many years. But its national requirements will remain lower than those of the other four, compensating for its relative backwardness. US-Japanese commercial relations will continue to outweigh the importance of trade with the other partners.

Fourth, if ideology and national will return to importance as the top national asset and international developments evolve so that this asset has value abroad, then China will have distinct advantages over the other three. But the key is whether national zeal can be exported. Ideological fervor will have little impact on the power relationships when it is confined to China, unless it proves disruptive. Fifth, China would become a serious threat to the other three not as a modern, industrialized society or as a unified equalitarian peasant society. The most dangerous course would be if it should collapse in a series of political succession struggles and fall apart as a viable state. It would once again become the focus of foreign manipulation, especially Soviet. The other three would clearly prefer a benign, self-confident, self-satisfied China able to defend its border and operate an efficient economy.

A final assumption is that in this region the Soviet Union will remain the most vulnerable to land attack and inhibited of the four powers. Russia has not been able to reduce the exposure of its Far Eastern provinces since the days of the 1904-1905 Japanese War. Only overwhelming in-being forces, requiring long and costly logistical support, will give Soviet leaders confidence that aggression can be deterred. Because of its vulnerability, the USSR can be expected to act with caution and prudence, yet the size of its in-being forces will remain a source of suspicion and tension. In contrast, effective US deterrence against attack on

---

event of tensions, a small independent nuclear force would invite preemption. Further, Japan has little incentive to provide nuclear protection for smaller states such as South Korea or Taiwan. Thus nuclear deterrence for Japan rests firmly on continued US presence and commitment, plus credible conventional forces. The trick will be for the Japanese government to preserve a climate favorable for a continuing US military presence in spite of growing left-wing pressure for a troop withdrawal. Without this presence the credibility of America's nuclear commitment will deteriorate in the eyes of both sides.

its west coast is more a state of mind than military mobilization. Obviously, of the four Japan is the most exposed to naval assault.[c] China, on the other hand, is threatened mainly on one front and will act in military matters most judiciously against the Soviets.

With these caveats about the nature of the relationships, it may also be suggested that as a new balance develops all four powers will experience an element of release and will pursue more independent policies. All four will feel compelled to establish relations with the other three, yet all four will be subject to the constraints in relations imposed by the others. This is a fluid state of affairs, yet potentially stable. No dramatic realignments are expected in the near term. But wider latitude for initiative will be generated and higher thresholds for tolerance of provocations will be fixed. The basic stability of the new arrangements stems partly from the legacy of previous power relationships. In the past, power either has been institutionalized, "balanced," or governed through coalition politics. The notion of containment through coalitions still gives contemporary leaders the greatest confidence in their ability to control events, or at least to preclude the emergence of unexpected or undesired developments. The quest for coalition will stimulate diplomacy. But the unique features of four different civilizations, political systems, economic structures, and ideological values will inhibit radical changes in existing preferences.

It seems safe to suggest, then, that the future holds only moderate modifications of the status quo.[3] This would include an American military withdrawal from the Asian mainland as adjustments are reached between the two Koreas and two Vietnams. The political viability of Southeast Asian nations, including the Philippines and Indonesia, may be promoted and encouraged through regional cooperative institutions and arrangements, in which both the US and Japan might play an increasing role. China and the USSR are likely to participate in such regional arrangements, but they can be expected to play a less positive and dynamic role. Japan may gradually see its political stature as a function of its participation in these regional organizations rather then in its present preference for bilateral relations. China will probably continue to focus heavily on the Taiwan issue, but will probably settle for some form of association less than full constitutional absorption. A formula may be devised that will allow Taiwan to retain its present economic structure and a degree of political autonomy; both could be advantageous to Peking as a commercial complement and a window to the outside world. The USSR will remain rather less secure and less stable in its relations with other Asian states. It lacks natural contact and affinity with Asian states and suffers from the same resentments of other Europeans. In all likelihood,

---

[c]Japan is not likely to build a Navy commensurate with the size of its mercantile interests. The dimensions of such an undertaking are formidable and would be alarming to all Pacific powers. It is cheaper and safer, though not as reliable, to continue to depend on the US Seventh Fleet to protect Japanese maritime needs; a combination that is likely to foster circumspection.

the Russians will continue to be relatively isolated in the far corner of the Pacific, and yet rather discontent with their restricted ability to make only occasional forays into regional political developments.

8

Appraising Ostpolitik and Political Adjustments in Central Europe

The historic adjustment of national grievances in Central Europe resulting from the successful application of Bonn's Ostpolitik is one of the most significant features of the overall détente process. The negotiations of the normalization treaties with the Soviet Union, Poland, and Czechoslovakia, the *Grundvertrag* with East Germany, and the Four Power Protocol on Berlin confirm that a new era has begun in Germany's relations with Eastern Europe. Collectively these documents codify the rights and principles of states with vital interests in Central Europe. They provide a durable solution to political disputes that were the main sources of the Cold War. In the broader context, Ostpolitik contributed more than any other factor to the political stature of Bonn in both East and West Europe and to the consolidation of the Soviet position east of the Elbe River. This enhanced status of both powers corresponded with their respective national interests and international aspirations: the threat to Soviet legitimacy in Eastern Europe was largely removed and Bonn was relieved to the unwanted legacies of the Second World War. An element of normalcy is now possible in interstate relations for the first time in a region that has experienced constant turmoil and tensions for nearly forty years. By the end of 1974, Bonn expects to have diplomatic relations and strong commercial ties with all East European nations. The scale of this adjustment can be illustrated if it is remembered that West German revanchism was universally denounced for a quarter of a century by the Socialists as the main source of European tensions and the alleged justification for the 1968 invasion of Czechoslovakia. A brief survey of the evolution in West Germany's East European policies will also demonstrate the scope of this change.

During the Weimar Republic, Germany held that the most feasible method of reducing the adverse consequences of the First World War was to seek integration and recognition in the West, affording respectability and security, while regaining hegemony and influence in Eastern Europe, providing renewed sources for its stature as a major European power. These aspirations were regarded as legitimate by most political parties because the Versailles Treaty left Germany with important territorial claims in Eastern Europe. After the Second World War, the consequences of defeat were more drastic. Outstanding territorial claims were compounded by the forceful division of the German nation; 40,000 square miles of former German soil was administered by the USSR and Poland and the historic threat of a Red Prussia had become reality. The highest national priority had to be the restoration of national unity, and Adenauer redoubled Streseman's earlier policy of gaining respectability, integration, and identity of views in the West in order to deal with the Soviets from a stronger position than that afforded by West Germany alone. Close alignment with the US and active participation in NATO were indispensable requirements for the solution of the German problem on Bonn's terms. Adenauer adopted a policy of "maintained tensions": no concessions to the East until agreement was reached on the self-determination of the German people. These demands were fundamentally incompatible with vital Soviet national interests, which prescribed that its strategic borders stretched to the Elbe and that it must retain a decisive influence in the German problem, and in the policies of both German states. A quarter-century-long deadlock developed that split Europe into rival spheres of influence and the world into hostile camps.

Shifts in Germany's Eastern Policy

In general, Western hopes for a new European order were based on achieving a German peace treaty that would produce satisfactory solutions to the residual effects of the war and correspondingly reduce the sources of European tensions. Disarmament and, later, arms-control schemes were envisioned as measures to decrease the risks of potential imperfections in these solutions. The legacy of suspicion about disarmament deals persisted in the West and is still apparent today. For example, Khrushchev proposed in 1963 a nonagression pact similar to the recently concluded Moscow-Bonn treaty, but it was rejected in Germany by both the Christian Democratic Union (CDU) and the Social Democratic Party (SPD) as superfluous and dangerous; without solutions to the political problems, it was reasoned, military détente would weaken the West's most important leverage. Only gradually did the West perceive that a policy of small, confidence-building steps could advance ultimate aims.

A variety of influences generated the new awareness and the shift in orientation. Domestic West German pressures that had made the Grand Coalition imperative released new demands for an activist platform. The changing nature of the policies of Bonn's allies also had a crucial bearing: the 1960s witnessed de Gaulle's flanking movement to the East, Kennedy's search for alternatives to confrontation, Johnson's obsession with the Far East, a wind-down in Western integration, and NATO's acceptance of Soviet strategic equality and the eclipse of asymmetrical deterrence. Signs of polycentrism in Eastern Europe gave rise to speculation that a more individualistic Western approach toward each East European country could foster the growth of their respective national aims, allowing a policy of small steps greater latitude. Rumania's independent-minded policy had been instructive. For one and a half years after establishing diplomatic relations, both Bucharest and Bonn were subjected to concerted polemical attacks and discriminatory policies. But after the 1968 Prague crisis it became apparent to many Eastern leaders that it was both necessary and desirable to deal directly with the West Germans in further stabilizing developments in Central Europe.

In Chancellor Willy Brandt's view, there were four main reasons for the change in Moscow's German policy: the Soviets' growing concern with the Chinese threat; their desire for broadening economic and technological contacts with the more advanced Western industrial states; the need to reach a modus vivendi with the United States; and their realization after bringing Prague to heel of the need to participate in the détente to the same extent as their allies. "What makes the present process of détente so important," Brandt said at the end of 1970, "is the fact that it is going with the Soviet Union and not against it."[1]

While it is difficult to identify direct cause-and-effect relations in the policy changes of the FRG and the socialist countries, one decision can be categorized as an important stimulant of the transformation in East European policy. Bonn's gradual acceptance of the status quo and abandonment of its policy of strength triggered forces in the East that inevitably challenged the traditional stand. In turn, these forces generated responses allowing the FRG to relax further its own terms for accommodation. More than any other single factor, the loosening of the FRG position, especially since 1969, seems to have been the catalyst for the East's receptivity to Bonn's Ostpolitik. Bonn's earlier emphasis on reunification was an anathema to most East Europeans and led to solid support for the GDR's Ulbricht Doctrine, which proscribed normalizing relations with the FRG until mutual recognition was achieved. The breakthrough in FRG policy was the decision to separate Ostpolitik and the diplomacy of adjustment with East Europeans from its Deutschlandpolitik and inter-German relations. Agreement to deal with each state individually about mutual problems allowed East Europeans to break their tandem position behind the GDR and seek an equitable accord.

Formal Accords

In the spring of 1969, Bonn and Moscow opened serious talks on a treaty for the renunciation of force. Sufficient common ground was soon identified that the scope of the treaty was broadened to include virtually all outstanding East European grievances from World War II. The implications of such a comprehensive treaty raised alarm among the Western Allies and the government opposition: Allied approval and ratification were jeopardized. The accord was scaled down to include primarily Soviet-German interests and was signed in August 1970. The treaty took the tone and character of a normalization accord. Moscow in part abandoned the policy aims of its allies. No mention was made of the Munich Agreement, of recognition of the GDR, or of the sanctity of East

European borders in terms acceptable to its allies. This was an abrogation of the Pact's aggregate demands for détente, regularly reiterated since the 1966 Bucharest Declaration. In establishing such a powerful precedent for separatist national contacts with the chief European antagonist, Moscow agreed to grant similar prerogatives to the East Europeans. Furthermore, by accepting something less than what the Czechoslovaks, Poles, and East Germans regarded as non-negotiable terms, their bargaining position on their important grievances was undermined.

It is not surprising, therefore, that each of the major negotiations conducted since then gradually assumed individual characteristics. The case of Poland is instructive. From 1956 to 1958, Poland set terms for establishing normal relations with the FRG similar to those recently accepted, then shifted emphasis to military disengagement in the various Rapacki plans of 1958, 1960, and 1962 and the Gomulka Plan of 1964. After that date, however, Warsaw became virtually locked in position behind the GDR on all aspects of the Pact's policy toward West Germany. When Bonn's policy began to loosen in the mid-1960s, Polish policy aims had become firmly subordinated to those of the GDR, whose main objective was to insure Pact solidarity for the legitimization of its Socialist Unity Party (SED) rule. Poland was unable to assert an independent initiative.

Gomulka's 17 May 1969 speech reflected a willingness to sacrifice this linkage in return for firm guarantees that Bonn would recognize Poland's security interests through the renunciation of all claims to Germany's former eastern territories. Once the talks with the FRG were well under way, however, Polish national prestige became so heavily committed to a successful outcome that the Gomulka government had no choice but to continue negotiating for the best possible terms. It could not afford to overlook such an important opportunity to advance its traditional goals, and, therefore could not return to its former preference for securing East German objectives. Poland rejected the Moscow formula of "unreserved [German] respect" for its borders and continued to hold out for "final, unequivocal recognition." The compromise wording was substantially stronger than the Soviet position, indicating the different values Warsaw and Moscow placed on the same issue. Moreover, Poland not only dropped its former demands for West German recognition of the GDR, but reversed itself by agreeing to establish full diplomatic ties with Bonn. A normalization treaty was signed in November 1970 in which West Germany renounced claims to nearly one quarter of its former territory.

Inter-German Problems

The chief obstacles to the further improvement of Soviet-West German relations has become not the fundamental policies of either state, but those of

East Germany. Up to the final stage of the Four Power Berlin negotiations, East Berlin pursued an assertive foreign policy, unprecendented in its short history, directed against both the FRG and its socialist allies and designed to discourage forward progress of the Ostpolitik. It had become the principal antagonist of the USSR within Pact councils, amplifying its former role as the monitor of Pact policy and relations with West Germany and taking over Rumania's role as the focal point of dissent. The East German government played an even more adroit and determined game than Rumania, however, for the stakes were higher; it was potentially threatened by isolation from its allies, subversion by West German liberalism, and dissent by a restive populace. This was an inevitable by-product of the new challenges from both quarters. As the threat from the West diminished, the GDR's strategic leverage in the Pact was reduced proportionally; it could no longer demand its allies' unequivical support for its interests as compensation for its exposed position.

The gradual revision in East Germany's policy after the replacement of Walter Ulbricht as party leader stemmed apparently from both Soviet pressure and from the conclusion that the trend toward adjustment was irreversible and laden with potential gains for East Berlin. The breach in the common front made by its allies' insistence on higher priority for national interests rather than international commitments allowed East Germany to demand the same prerogatives that could strengthen the its bargaining position against both East and West. After nearly two years of bilateral talks at the state secretary level on transportation problems, the tumultuous West German ratification of the Moscow and Warsaw treaties, and the signing of the Four Power Protocol on Berlin, the two German states announced agreement to open formal negotiations for an accord normalizing their relations. The adjustment in East Berlin's attitude was accompanied by new perceptions in Bonn. During the negotiations, the ratification debate, and the subsequent Supreme Court decision on the constitutionality of the accord, several key issues became focal points of widespread West German public concern: the level of recognition, sovereignty and two states in one nation, nationality, and representation abroad.

As early as January 1970, SPD deputy leader Herbert Wehner, the party's most versatile spokesman, predicted that a situation would arise in which people would no longer argue about the recognition or nonrecognition of the GDR, but would ask whether contractual agreements between East and West Germany could be concluded. Opponents charged that Wehner had accepted recognition in principle, but proponents expanded his argumentation. Legal recognition alone has several drawbacks:

1. Bonn could not make a case for recognizing the GDR under German public law.
2. Recognition under international law connotes that both countries consider each other foreign states.

3. Refusal by one country to recognize another is not identical with considering the other nonexistent.
4. Full recognition of the GDR would entitle East Berlin to consider all refugees living in the FRG as citizens of the GDR and subject to GDR public and criminal laws.
5. Recognition of the GDR would virtually negate Four Power responsibility for all Germany and would undermine West Berlin's legal basis and security.
6. After obtaining diplomatic recognition, the GDR could cut all remaining ties between the two parts of Germany and thereby reinforce the partition rather than perforate it.
7. The partition is a political, not a constitutional, matter and recognition of the GDR would reduce Bonn's leverage against a fully sovereign state to ameliorate the division.
8. There is no evidence that Moscow will accept full independence until legal guarantees can be provided by both German states that the USSR's political influence in German matters will be assured.

The importance of such West German exchanges was shown by the gradual public acceptance that, in Wehner's words, "recognition of the GDR would be too little," or that the formulae of the legal accords were less crucial than the political content behind them. West German recognition would have to be dependent on the GDR's acceptance of substantial additional political conditions for mutual accommodation. Coexistence is also not enough; a degree of intra-German settlement is required. While a formal World War II peace treaty seems no longer probable, the German people must seek an adjustment that relieves their grievances but does not obviate their claims to a final settlement.[2]

Yet on these points deadlock and futility seem insurmountable. Both sides have such opposing views on nationality and sovereignty that adjustment has been impossible. The federal government argued its case before the Supreme Court, asserting that one German nation persisted because of common language, history, and culture. But within this nation two separate states had emerged, with equal rights of nonintervention, mutual respect, and appropriate joint recognition. The East Germans and CDU opposition countered that the test of statehood was the degree of responsibility a government could exercise in the promotion and protection of the inhabitants' interests. When this responsibility was effectively administered and recognized as such by other states, the inhabitants enjoyed the rights of citizenship and nationality. Acknowledgment of these functions of sovereignty was damaging to the government's case; it implied at least de facto acceptance of separate nationalities that was acclaimed inconsistent with the one-nation thesis. The issue was further compounded by the claims of each state to represent all Germans. In a letter of interpretation accompanying the *Grundvertrag* but not embodied in it, the FRG reaffirmed its commitment to the single-nation concept and to the achievement of reunification.

Virtually every major demand raised by the GDR at the Erfurt and Kassel summit meetings has now been accepted in practice. It has been granted bona fide credentials by other states for full particiaption in the community of nations. While Bonn officially endorses the one-nation concept and attempts to devise means for its implementation, other states practicing more conventional notions of international law have afforded the GDR the trappings of full sovereignty.

The bitter accusations that were subsequently exchanged in the Bundestag and the West German press conveyed the widespread dismay in the Federal Republic. While many West Germans believed the elevation of the GDR to equal status was probably inevitable, they were concerned about the speed at which this status was achieved and the price Bonn paid. Bonn entered the negotiations with an imaginative bargaining position and strong leverage against the GDR. The one-nation concept was original and applicable to other divided countries. The treaties with the Soviet Union and Poland and Berlin Protocol were signed before the negotiations, resolving the major sources of tension in Central Europe and denying East Berlin the strength of solidarity. Moreover, the Conference on Security and Cooperation in Europe now assumed a new urgency for the Pact, whereby it could gain international ratification of the *Ostvertraege*. Finally, East German intransigence could be more damaging than ever for its allies' interests. Thus Bonn was in a favorable position to delay until its terms for political adjustment were met.

The reason for the rapid erosion of the FRG position is partially understandable. The concept of two states in one nation is politically attractive and received wide endorsement among West Germans as an equitable compromise. But it was too new to be implemented in haste. There were insufficient precedents or guidelines to improvize the necessary checks and balances required for Bonn's understanding of political adjustment between antagonistic social systems. West German negotiators felt compelled repeatedly to fall back on conventional experience when first technical details and then principles were found incompatible with this unique mode of representation and accommodation. Bonn consistently maintained throughout the negotiations that the end results should contribute to European détente and humanize the partition of Germany. East Germany concurred with the first aspiration, but reserved its interpretation of the second. Soon after the treaty was ratified, East Berlin interjected its individual interpretation of crucial provisions. It reacted vigorously to Western demands at the Conference on Security and Cooperation in Europe for freer exchange of people and ideas by tightening travel restrictions, disrupting inter-German sporting events with political maneuvers, and raising the issue of West Berlin representation abroad by Bonn to such intensity that Brandt's official visit to Prague to sign a normalization treaty renouncing the 1938 Munich Agreement was postponed.

An increasing number of West Germans were bitterly disappointed and disillusioned by what was condemned as the SPD's naive negotiating techniques, the GDR's perfidity, and a "sellout" by Bonn allies. By granting the GDR equal status and international recognition, Bonn had made a concrete contribution to European détente. But in so doing it had failed to secure tangible evidence that the onerous aspects of the division would be removed, e.g. the shootings at the Wall, and had given up much of its former leverage against the GDR. At the time of writing however, the majority of West German commentators seemed cautious and guardedly hopeful that the general détente process will underscore East Germany's anachronistic policies. The threat of international ostracization, so important for a government uncertain of its legitimacy, may produce the political adjustment the Brandt government failed to deliver.

The treaties Bonn has ratified with the Warsaw Pact nations largely relieved the grievances of the East Europeans and forced the solution of the German problem onto the two German states, where it rightfully belonged. The German problem—the proper geographic location of the German people and the social institutions to which they should subscribe and which are acceptable to *all* their neighbors—can only be afforded the necessary universal acclaim if consensus is first reached among the Germans themselves. The *Grundvertrag* omits reunification entirely. It embodies the principles of mutual acceptance and accommodation necessary for defining a modus vivendi, but fails to provide a precise formula. Beyond this stage the prospects for an early solution to broader aspects of the German problem do not look promising.

The Four Power Protocol on Berlin on the other hand, signed in September 1971, represented a significant success for Western diplomacy. Both the Soviets and the Western allies made important concessions in the Berlin accord that made East Germany the principal loser. Its traditional claims that West Berlin existed on its territory were not upheld. Its insistence upon the right to regulate transit traffic as a manifestation of East Berlin's sovereign rights was downgraded. The confirmation of the manifold ties between Bonn and West Berlin voided its former claims that West Berlin was an independent entity. Finally, the Four Powers failed to confirm the constitutional linkage between East Germany and East Berlin, a long-standing GDR demand. Instead, Four Power responsibilities and privileges were reaffirmed in a manner that explicitly restricts East German claims to regulate access between West Berlin and the Federal Republic; the USSR assumed full responsibility for access controls. The Protocol thus delimited GDR claims in the Berlin issue.

The Four Power Protocol also marked an important step in the FRG's quest for political stature. In the past Bonn's obsessive concern with East German reactions to every FRG policy move was a serious constraint on its search for political recognition. The Berlin accord allowed the full fruition of Bonn's Ostpolitik, and relegated its Deutschlandpolitik to a less urgent category. Thus, the gradual defusing of the German policies of the GDR and the FRG allowed both German states for the first time to consider the German problem with less attention and apprehension from their respective allies.

Political Implications for West Germany

What have the West Germans actually gained from Ostpolitik and the *Ostvertraege*? From the Western viewpoint the long-range impact of the treaties appears to be mainly beneficial. Several reasons may be cited.

1. Because their ratification by West Germany was contingent on a favorable Berlin solution, the entire normalization process has been refined to a single frame of reference. The FRG has accepted the existing realities in the West and required that the East follow suit with respect to Berlin. This significantly strengthened the allies' bargaining position in the Berlin talks. The resulting Protocol elaborated the Potsdam Agreement, whereby Moscow was assured continued legal status in West Berlin (and thereby gained leverage against both German states) in return for guaranteed Western access to the city. While Bonn initially argued that the Moscow treaty would neither prejudice nor anticipate a final settlement, acceptance of the Polish and East German demands has conveyed a de facto peace arrangement.[3] Since these and subsequent accords were firmly linked to a Berlin solution, however, the necessity for a final peace conference may be substantially reduced.

2. Bonn's failure to achieve more satisfactory results from its Deutschlandpolitik was in part the consequence of its successful pursuit of Ostpolitik. By separating the two and dealing bilaterally with each government, Bonn reached agreement on all issues, including Berlin, before the hard bargaining began with the GDR. At that juncture it had lost its former leverage among the Pact nations that could have been used to moderate East Berlin's position. East Germany made historic gains by the treaty, but the insecurity of government will make it difficult for these gains to have an immediate impact on public welfare. West Germany's loss of leverage has allowed the initiative on the broad issue of the German problem to pass to East Berlin. But because of the regime's insecurity there is unlikely to be any movement toward solution in terms acceptable to West Germans—this historic cancer in European affairs remains unsolved, though substantially drained of tensions.

3. Bonn learned a lesson from its attempts in 1967-68 to make gains in Eastern Europe at Moscow's expense. In 1969 it started at the top and made an adjustment with Moscow its leading priority. This new orientation was more acceptable to Moscow, and as Bonn gradually relaxed its assertive attitude against the East and expanded the latitude of mutual cooperation, its stature in the West also increased substantially. Integration in the West was the first step and the opening to the East was the second toward establishing Bonn's political authority commensurate with West Germany's economic status as the world's fourth economic power. These coordinated steps allowed Bonn for the first time to extend its policy aims beyond those

of the Weimar Republic, to include security and settlement rather than manipulation and expansion in the East. It is too early to predict the durability of the new normalization policy, but as it is now exercised it represents one of the most important alterations in Germany's traditional Eastern policy in this century.

4. The stretegy of small steps and the piecemeal approach to stability and security have proven more successful than former comprehensive peace plans. The Ostpolitik has been the best example in the history of East-West relations of the merits of confidence-building through microdiplomacy. It is likely to complement the formula of other Western countries and NATO as they seek a military disengagement and political détente.

5. In the wake of the *Ostvertraege* there is a growing feeling among West German analysts that Moscow is attempting to return its European policy to the context of the nineteenth-century Concert of Europe. It has recognized that the FRG is the chief source of European stability and instability, and has elected to drop its former policy of ostracism for one of mutual cooperation. While the distance between the present level of cooperation and condominium of the 1939 variety remains wide, it is essential that the FRG, as the second European power, acts positively to establish and preserve leverage against the USSR. The Moscow treaty provided Bonn with its first substantial initiative and served as an important prerequisite for subsequent moves.

6. The sacrifices embodied in these treaties are more than symbolic gestures that the Germans have accepted at last the consequences of their aggression (welcomed by friends and foes alike). They are an essential step toward rectifying the war guilt and political paranoia that has afflicted so many Germans and their foreign policy. These treaties afford West Germany a measure of international rehabilitation and restored self-respect that is indispensable for a durable solution to the German problem.

7. Critics have charged that the treaties also represented a moral step backward, allowing for the acceptance of injustice and a new climate of cynicism in which the communist system is regarded as being different from, but as good as, a free society. The futility of the twenty-year-long anti-Communist campaign, warrants a new approach, however. The barrenness of the effort has not been due to lack of Western humanity or moral virtues, but to the misuse of arguments against communism, stemming largely from confusion between national communism and Soviet expansionism. Available evidence indicates that peaceful competition between the two political and economic systems can be reasonably expected to lead to more emphasis on human rights than in the era of anticommunism and international tensions.

8. The Ostpolitik has undoubtedly opened new economic opportunities. Otto Wolff von Amerongen, President of the Deutscher Industrie und Handelstag, has predicted that the proportion of Eastern trade in total West German

foreign trade may increase from its present 4.2 percent to 8 or 9 percent. He has also cautioned against immediate optimism because of the restraints experienced by the socialist countries, namely, lack of convertible currencies, strict bilateralism, poor-quality industrial goods, and inadequate marketing techniques for competition in the West. At the same time, he pointed out that there are several largely unexplored areas of cooperation for Western firms, such as buying and selling licenses and technological know-how, marketing Eastern products within Eastern Europe itself and third countries, and financing correlated production in the socialist countries.[4] If such activities prove profitable, traditional restraints may be gradually neutralized and West Germany could become an increasingly important technological power for Eastern Europe.

9. The responses of Bonn's allies to the Ostpolitik are important criteria for its success. Brandt has affirmed many times that the opening to the East is important but not vital to West Germany, while Western integration is a vital interest. Brandt termed the EEC Hague summit meeting of 1-2 December 1969, for example, "the most important event in foreign affairs since I have come to office."[5] Defense Minister Helmut Schmidt has remarked: "Without a firm foundation in NATO there can be no sensible policy of détente in Europe. It would be sheer folly if one attempted to conduct one's policy in the East from any other basis than that of firm Western solidarity."[6] The NATO allies responded positively. Indeed, Nixon asserted the primacy of Ostpolitik for the general détente atmosphere in his 1973 Foreign Policy Report.

10. Thus, Ostpolitik now provides a fuller framework for German policy. Bonn's aims during this decade are likely to remain relatively constant and predictable, and will include preservation of national independence; integration with the West; normalization of relations with Eastern Europe; humanization of Germany's partition, while reserving self-determination as an ultimate right; and cautious testing of its increasing economic and political weight. West German foreign policy has been characterized by the desire to maintain control over its own fate, to obtain and retain a major voice in the solution of the "German Problem," and to do this from a position of strength and a measure of independence. It should be noted that Ostpolitik was essential to reach an adjustment with Eastern Europe and, equally important, to enhance its options in the West. Without a successful Ostpolitik, Bonn would have remained "dwarfed" by the weight of its albatross of "maintained tensions" and its dependence upon external powers, such as France, for the promotion of its interests.

Shifts in the Soviet Position

If this accurately describes West German assessments of the results of

Ostpolitik, how do the Warsaw Pact nations appraise its impact? Several questions are relevant. For example, is the Warsaw Pact now more or less reliable as a political instrument than it was in the wake of the Czechoslovak invasion? Following the explicit negation of Bonn's policies as the "main threat" to East European security and the acceptance of West Germany's political respectability, what new cohesive matrix can be supplied to insure endorsement of ideological discipline in the East? Has a greater degree of coalition politics, à la Rumania, been accepted by the Kremlin, and how should this be measured? Bonn's renunciation of territorial claims and recognition of existing borders has imparted to East Europeans greater mental security than at any time in the past thirty-five years, but does this inject more or less latitude in the formation of national policies? As the bloc countries increase their measure of security, will the Soviets' top priority aim of stability be reduced proportionally? Are there natural levels to the extent of West German influence acceptable in the East? Are they much beyond the present level? With Germany's traditional economic and cultural avenues for influence generally reaching a plateau, what new resources can be drawn upon to strengthen Bonn's desire for political stature? What are the parameters of German reconciliation acceptable to Bonn, East Berlin, Moscow, and the Western allies? Has the relevance of Allied authority and influence been weakened or strengthened by the Ostpolitik? Finally, can German nationalistic sentiments sustain the losses inflicted by the Ostpolitik and frustrations contained in the Deutschlandpolitik for more than several years without degenerating into demands for drastic action—which might entail a more aggressive policy toward the GDR, a Gaullist line toward the West and neutralist stand toward the East, firmer demands in European councils for greater political power, or, conversely, a gradually increasing indifference toward the interests of Bonn's allies?

Such questions indicate that it is problematic indeed to plot the long-range profits and losses for the USSR in its new relationship with the FRG. For more than twenty years Moscow's aims in Eastern Europe have been to consolidate and legitimize its rule (see chapter 15 for more details). An important instrument for this purpose was the specter of West German revanchism, which, raised to doctrinal proportions, became the primary raison d'être for Warsaw Pact solidarity.[7] These tactics were sufficiently successful to enable Moscow to alter its German policy after the construction of the Berlin Wall, and offer in 1964 to open a dialogue with Bonn. Prague, Warsaw, and especially East Berlin reacted so sharply, however, that Moscow accepted their argument that the Warsaw Pact could deal with the FRG only form a position of unity and strength. West German diplomacy in the East to that point had had the effect of aligning the northern tier countries, which feared Bonn's territorial claims, directly behind East Germany's growing assertiveness in challenging both Bonn and Moscow. Rumania viewed this collusion among the northern members of the bloc as a dangerous step toward greater Soviet hegemony and a sound reason for formulating a two-Germanys policy, a precedent adopted by other East European countries only after long and bitter disputes.

At the same time Moscow was becoming increasingly aware that it could not complete its consolidation of Eastern Europe without dealing with the West Germans. The Soviet courtship of de Gaulle had demonstrated the futility of trying to bypass Bonn in settling Central European problems. West Germany's central position in European affairs, its relative technological capabilities, and its contiguous position along Moscow's strategic security frontier made direct contact with Bonn unavoidable. But the USSR could not invite the FRG to participate as a peace partner in Central Europe—the long-standing Guallist desire—without making important concessions to West German interests. The initial concessions, and probably the most durable, were the abrogation of Bonn's threat status and the Pact's commitment to its respectability. While the East European people will continue to fear and hate Germans for many years, the Pact's formal commitment to Bonn's international respectability introduced a fundamental change in East-West relations and Central European diplomacy.

Such alterations of Warsaw Pact aims and methods of policy formulation were fraught with uncertainties about the entire fabric of Eastern solidarity, and raised questions about appropriate parameters for autonomy, coordination, and security. Could the Pact's decision-making apparatus be decentralized in accordance with Rumania's demands for genuine coalition politics without impairing Moscow's interest in preserving regional stability? The use of force against Czechoslovakia and its threatened employment against Rumania established the upper tolerance levels for East European maneuverability. The Brezhnev Doctrine of limited socialist sovereignty has been denounced by ruling and nonruling Communist parties alike, but its implications have been clearly understood and accepted by countries like Rumania. Bucharest's return to Pact councils and deliberations was a signal that it acquiesced, however reluctantly, in the priority Moscow attached to socialist discipline on issues of vital interest to the Kremlin. Rumanian diplomacy since the spring of 1970 has been designed to establish new areas of maneuver and wider freedom of action within the Soviets' level of tolerance. Rumania accepted the importance of conformity and discipline on selected issues, and Moscow could proclaim the Brezhnev Doctrine successful. But the Soviets recognized Bucharest's special status within the Pact and right to establish national priorities within the general parameters of socialist policy.

With Rumanian "conformity," Moscow's Pact policy became clearer. Its chief demand was apparently that its allies remain "little Europeans" and refrain from undue objections to Moscow's great-power policies. As a result, all Pact members accepted legally binding commitments to aid the USSR in the event of Chinese aggression and have assiduously refrained from contesting Moscow's active participation in the defense of Egypt. On its part, the USSR agreed to greater coordination of regional policies and to push more vigorously for a European security conference as called for in Pact meetings since 1966. The failure of the West to accept the Pact's terms for an intra-European gathering and the growing indications of moderation in Bonn's Ostpolitik prompted a change in priorities in December 1969, agreeable to all except the GDR. The Pact decided to place more emphasis on bilateral solutions to national problems while holding the multilateral approach in reserve, to be used as a means of pressuring the West but mainly as the vehicle for maximizing gains made in the bilateral agreements. The preference for bilateral negotiations opened the way for a broader application of the normal processes of diplomacy and the adjustment and compromise required for its successful practice. It also required new methods or instruments for policy coordination. To date, this has been most noticeable in the accelerated pace of individual contacts among leading national figures and the regularization of the semiannual summit gatherings; no institutional modifications have yet come to light.

Thus the forces for rapprochement in Eastern Europe that have required solutions to national grievances gained some temporary ascendancy over those demanding total subordination and solidarity of purpose. Moreover, by accepting the commitment to long-term détente, codified in Ostpolitik, Moscow has opened Eastern Europe to penetration by Western influence, and to confusion about new standards for proper socialist behavior and appropriate relationships between great and small powers. Western influence may become increasingly important in shaping these modalities in intra-Pact relations. It would be unwise, however, to imply that Moscow will remain insensitive to these potentially dangerous forces in its vital sphere of influence, as has been seen already at the European Security Conference (see chapter 15). The Kremlin can be expected to improvise new checks and balances to supplement those of the Brezhnev Doctrine and the bilateral defense treaties; and Soviet armor will remain the basic guarantor of East European respect for vital Soviet interests. Nonetheless, in the next decade Moscow will have to assess and accept to a greater degree than before the individual interests and demands of its allies. More than ever, consensus will have to be negotiated rather than imposed. It remains to be seen whether this process will strengthen or weaken the Warsaw Pact as a political and military instrument.

Impact on US Interests

The implications of Ostpolitik for Washington are several. All the agreements reached deal explicitly with the provisions of the original Potsdam accord that prescribed Allied rights and interests in Germany and Central Europe. While the recent agreements contain clauses stating that the treaties do not abrogate the provisions of other multilateral accords, the accumulative impact of the Ostpolitik vintage documents tends to supersede those of the postwar period. This weakens the claims of both the Americans and the Soviets to jurisdiction over questions of German sovereignty. Theoretically it strengthens the independence of both German states. The contraction of American responsibility may generate a compensating urge within the Federal Republic, leading to greater Western integration. The durability of this tendency remains to be seen, but certainly it should be encouraged by Washington.

A further implication relates to Berlin. The Protocol achieved more than the Germans and Americans expected, without requiring major concessions. Specifically, it fixed for the first time Soviet responsibility for access to West Berlin and therefore for the ultimate welfare of the city. The Soviets viewed this requirement as the most plausible means for securing their top priority aim: institutionalizing Soviet rights, interests, and influence in West German affairs. Soviet access responsibilities are important leverage against both German states that is not likely to be eroded or removed in the near future. Moscow can be expected to exercise these privileges continuously to insure the relevance of its views in trans-Elbian matters. Thus, the treaties guaranteed Western acceptance of the Elbe as the USSR's strategic frontier, but the Protocol assures Moscow influence in future German developments. From this improved position, the USSR can be expected to intensify its diplomacy in Western Europe. Indeed, the West German press repeatedly pointed to the macabre scene during the April-May 1972 ratification crisis in the Bundestag, with three parties navigating the process and negotiating the final compromise: the government, the parliamentary opposition, and the Soviet ambassador. Further, in September 1973 Moscow reopened the issue of Bonn's right to represent West Berlin's interests abroad, claiming the Protocol confined this representation to individuals only, precluding institutions and organizations. It raised sufficient pressure that the normalization of relations between Bonn and Prague was formally delayed.

Sufficient accommodation now has been registered so that political relations in Central Europe, even between the two Germanys, cannot be returned to the level of hostility and distrust witnessed in the 1950s, and as recently as 1968, without a cataclysmic upheaval and surge of tensions. It is safe to speculate that recent events have precluded a direct backsliding to the Stalinist era, when threats and reprisals virtually froze diplomatic activity, without a major change in the entire international system as it has developed. This is a period of change of scale unknown since before the Second World War; a transition without reliable precedents in the memories of contemporary statesmen and diplomats. Only scant evidence is available upon which to base even tentative answers to questions that have plagued analysts for years, and to new queries that have arisen only within months.

Within this settlement, Moscow has now secured its minimum terms for a peace settlement in Central Europe, and the FRG has lowered its conditions for managing the German problem. Accordingly the former vital nature of FRG-US relations to the national interests of both Bonn and Washington has been partially diluted. Questions of grand strategy, nuclear sharing, and conventional armaments no longer dominate US-FRG relations. Emphasis on practical matters has now been confined largely to the relatively mundane problems of troop stationing, offset payments, and commercial matters.

While there was no requirement for the Federal government to consult
with the US during the *Ostvertraege* ratification debates, its worst parliamentary
crisis, German commentators could not help questioning whether this more
than symbolized the decline in US interest in German affairs. Does the United
States retain satisfactory leverage against the USSR in Central Europe to preserve Western interests? Has Washington retained the profound concern over
the German problem that shaped American and Western policy for a quarter
century? Has the United States institutionalized its influence in German affairs
to the satisfaction of Bonn's allies and opponents? Has the Nixon Administration,
with its German-born Secretary of State, returned American perspective from
the aberration of Southeast Asia dominos to its traditional priorities in Europe?

Many West German commentators answer these questions negatively, but
fail to record that the urgency of these seemingly imperative requirements has been
minimized.

9

Western Europe: FRG–EEC–US

One of the harshest shocks in the period of letdown after the euphoria of the Kennedy era was the realization that political unity in Europe was still years away. Throughout the postwar era, the US saw its role in Europe as that of protector and exemplar. World War II was the resurrection of the symptoms and maladies of the World War I experience. Both conflagrations allegedly had demonstrated the ineptitude of European political ethics and dramatized the need for either rejuvenation or complete substitution of values—as in the case of Nazi Germany. The US equated peace and stability with new norms of political behavior; norms that projected state interactions beyond the goals of cooperation to integration and finally unity. The American model for federation was cited as valid evidence that a pluralistic society could be successfully motivated and democratically governed. The inability of Europe to unify created resentment in the US; its desire for a genuine partner was frustrated. The sense of disappointment with other distractions, e.g., Southeast Asia, domestic unrest, etc., diverted US political attention from its former primacy in Europe. American national interests in a disunited Europe began to resemble those of the 1920s, when they centered mainly on ethnic, cultural, and commercial values.

The aberration of US focus on Europe was also due in part to America's unassailable economic hegemony over disunited Europe. Four fifths of the world's foreign trade is conducted among the North Atlantic countries. Yet marketing and organizational problems had created a technological gap that could not be easily closed either by quantitative expansion of the total volume or by conceptual innovations in industry. Joint efforts in space developments, the Concorde supersonic aircraft, and the swing-wing fighter were improvizations designed to exclude the US from European markets and establish competitive sources of supply. Priority for the "fair-share" principle between partners rather than a division of labor and the primacy of national endeavors produced disappointing or financially disastrous results. Moreover, US supremacy in the defense-related and science-based industries had perpetuated America's advantage. Even in sectors where the European potential is strong, such as conventional weapons, there was a conspicuous inability to standardize, or organize merely within the EEC on individual weapons systems. Europe had the technological expertise to reduce the gap substantially; it did not have the political fortitude to suppress the urge for asserting national preferences and privileges.

Continuing European technological dependence on the United States had contributed strongly to US complacancy toward Europe.

Political indifference had produced the danger of losing touch with evolving European realities. For example, the sharp European reaction against senatorial pressure for a unilateral US troop cut was not merely a protest that NATO security would be threatened by such reductions. Many Europeans perceived these motions as a manifestation that they had lost their former preferential position in US foreign policy and a symptom of a growing lack of American identification with European political realities. The United States, they believed, was losing its touch on the European pulse, but they were unable to reach a consensus on alternative plans to offset US dependence. In this seeming vacuum other imperatives gradually changed the orientation of both US and West European interests. Intra-Alliance attention became riveted to growing economic grievances and inter-Alliance focus rested increasingly on security matters— purely political affairs were increasingly avoided in NATO and resolved in the East by Ostpolitik.

French-German Rivalry in the Unification Process

Because of West Germany's dominant economic position and France's overbearing political stature, developments in the EEC over the past decade have been characterized as the process of adjustment of their respective national interests. A poll taken by the EEC in 1963 showed 81 percent of the West Germans favoring European integration (although, to be sure, reunification ranked a higher preference).[1] This suggests that there was substantial consensus within German public opinion as to the utility and the necessity of the Common Market and a certain aura of inviolability surrounding the closely related concept of European integration. But there was a lack of clarity with regard to the final form, nature, and purposes of the EEC. This was especially noticeable once the process of economic integration passed the "negative" stages of tariff reduction and began the effort of creating common "positive" programs, such as central banking and currency structure or unified political institutions. In general, German participation in Western integrative arrangements was deemed necessary largely to obtain support of the Western Allies, above all the US and France, for a policy of strength and moral certitude toward East Germany and the Soviet Union. But by the mid-sixties it had become clear, at least in the original conception, that Western integration as a tool for reunification afforded diminishing chances of success. West Germany's allies were lukewarm and perfunctory in their assurances of support. Moreover, after the Wall, East Germany was well on its way to becoming an economic power in its own right, and the Soviet Union was less willing than ever to see a reunited Germany.

Time brought changes, requiring Germany in effect to choose between favoring a closely integrated or a loose Western community. She was fortunate that the choices were not exclusive nor too closely related, enabling her to maintain close ties with the US, promote further European integration, remain conciliatory and adaptable towards France, take over the position of leadership within the EEC, and keep her options clearly open in both East and West. This balanced policy became apparent when Bonn acquiesced in de Gaulle's two vetoes of British entry into the EEC, agreed to a partial accord in agriculture by accepting a November 1964 French proposal for common cereal prices, reluctantly concurred in France's refusal to endorse further political integration, yet firmly rejected French terms for participating in the *force de frappe.* Under these circumstances there was no possibility of closer political ties with France; France was engaged in an effort to free herself and Europe from American dominance and was attempting to use the EEC to these ends.

By the mid-1960s the strain in French-German relations become increasingly apparent. Ambitious efforts in March 1965 by the EEC commission to create centralized funds and a measure of centralized supranational authority for disposition of these funds provided the occasion for France to block the next step toward union: the provision regarding majority voting due to come into effect in 1966. To emphasize French disapproval it staged a boycott of all major EEC functions as of 1 July 1965. The Germans, while in general approving of majority voting as presented, had their own reservations about its ramifications. In the negotiations and insinuations that followed over an interim settlement, the Germans emerged as the leader of the "progressive" grouping in opposition to the French and a political opponent equal or superior in stature to France within the EEC. The outcome of the Luxembourg negotiations on 16-17 January 1966 was an agreement to disagree, and to keep similar confrontations from arising. In addition, the political powers of the independent-minded Commission were narrowed, tying it more closely to the Council.

With the political decisions held in abeyance for a time, the EEC began once again to pick up the loose threads of economic integration. On 11 May and 24 June 1966, the Council agreed to complete the customs union by 1 July 1968, including the introduction of a common farm policy. At the beginning of 1967, agreements were signed initiating a common, if limited and short-term, economic policy, as well as a "harmonized" system of business taxation (the value-added tax). And in July of that year the fusion of the three executives (of ECSC, EEC, and Euratom) took place as scheduled, an act more of symbolic than of practical importance. Yet Britain was again refused entry, without serious West German objections.

In 1967 the Grand Coalition sought a course of adjustment in the battle over the structure of the Western union and of reconciliation with de Gaulle. It succeeded only when it altered its basic perspective. At that time West German policy was dominated by security needs requiring American presence and the goal of reunification from strength. The French by themselves could not satisfy this latter requirement, even had the Germans been willing to accept their arrogated claims to seniority and to overlook their readiness to bypass Bonn in unilaterally seeking advantages in the East. Thus, the West Germans gradually accepted the view that their interests were better served by an expanded EEC with perhaps lesser political cohesion, but more political potential, than by a smaller unit with more economic authority. Both a heavier balance against France and a partner of sturdier stature for the US were needed.

Thus, Bonn's approach to the EEC since 1968 has been based primarily on general political goals, i.e., enlargement and integration of the community, somewhat at the expanse of national advantages in other areas. Economic gains within the Common Market have gone largely to Italy, the least developed country of the EEC, at the expense of West Germany, the most industralized nation. Moreover, in the agricultural sector from which Bonn has the least to gain relatively by the Common Agricultural Program (CAP), it continues to pay the largest sum into the agricultural fund. Such compormises of national preferences were made on the premise that the "give and take" in coalition politics would advance political economic union. But all EEC members continued to place a higher priority on national advantage than the abstract benefits that might be derived from integration.

As a result, West German policy aims in the EEC from approximately 1968 until the Hague Conference in December of 1969 were primarily aimed at transferring the leadership of the EEC from France to a more progressive and cooperative base. When this goal was at least partially achieved, focus was turned toward developing a structural framework flexible enough to meet the demands of states on the outer ring of EEC and to accommodate broad aspects of European affairs. Thus, the policy approach that evolved was somewhat analogous to the three levels of Ostpolitik negotiations.[2] In the case of the EEC, however, the policy aims deal first with France, second with Europe—the EEC, along with EFTA members and East European Bloc—and third with the Great Powers. The significance of these basic changes for EEC policy was that they registered Bonn's hypersensitivity toward implicit charges from its Western partners about alleged German assertiveness and signalled the gradual abandonment of its former reluctance to accept more active political leadership of Western Europe.

The subordinate position of the Federal Republic to France was gradually modified when Foreign Minister Willy Brandt assumed the devil's advocate role. On 4 May 1968, Brandt advanced what came to be known as the German compromise plan for expanding membership. He urged nations seeking membership in the Common Market to work out an interim agreement on trade with the EEC—such as a 30 percent reduction in industrial tariffs—as the best way of narrowing the gap to accession. Bonn's initiative proved to be important for four interrelated reasons: it placed Brandt (and the Social Democratic Party), rather than Chancellor Kiesinger, in the fore as the promoter of a trial balloon;

it tied the goals of Ost- and Westpolitik to similar SPD philosophies; it represented a divergence from de Gaulle, holding forth a compromise on the entry
issue between France's unequivocal "No" and British demands for a solid
"Yes"; and it signaled a growing awareness of Germany's economic strength
and the outlet it could provide.

Bonn-Paris differences began to crystallize when France imposed curbs on
imports and subsidies for exports in violation of both the last stage of the
programmed EEC tariff reduction and the single-rate external export margin
established by the Kennedy Round of trade negotiations. While the Executive
Commission of the EEC was quick to rebuke the unilateral French action,
Kissinger went so far as to urge a summit meeting on expansion. France responded in September by rejecting the German compromise plan, imposing
what was in effect France's third veto of British entry. It remained the responsibility of Foreign Minister Brandt, in his unique position straddling official
government policy and left-wing political opion, to push the devil's advocate
role one step further, citing the stagnation of the EEC as an open rebuttal to
French leadership.

Events in the spring of 1969, i.e. the resignation of President de Gaulle
(28 April); the monetary adjustments of first France and then Germany in the
fall; and the initial successes of Ostpolitik, further slowed EEC activities. The
first event, in terms of Germany and the EEC, was significant because it weakened the Gaullist voice in the European community by diluting the preeminence
of France. France had been able to pace EEC progress almost from the outset
of the Treaty of Rome; she had maintained a single personality and mentality
which governed her response to the association—thus evoking a seniority among
the member states. Paradoxically, the French themselves now rejected de Gaulle,
but his demise only partially deflated Gaullism. The succeeding Pompidou
government demonstrated a similar singularity of purpose in defining national
preferences, as the subsequent devaluation of the franc indicated.

The massive riots and strikes in May 1968 created major economic dislocations throughout France whose impact was not fully registered for over
one year. On 8 August 1969, the franc was devalued, followed by the revaluation
of the German mark on 24 October. The reasons for the change in parities were
purely economic: underheated and overheated economies. But Bonn seized the
opportunity of converting, at least indirectly, economic strength into political
potency, and thereby partially filling the vacuum in the directional leadership
of the European community. The German revaluation in the wake of French
devaluation marked a break from French leadership in the EEC: the 9 percent
revaluation seriously impaired the economic basis of CAP, a direct blow to
French agricultural interests. Second, it forced the Community as a whole, and
France in particular, to strive for the acceleration of the integrative process,
meaning specifically progress beyond a mere customs union toward a more
comprehensive association revolving on the base of a unified economic and
monetary policy.

The culmination of Bonn's shift in relations with France came at the 1969 Hague Summit Conference. The FRG made the strongest call yet for the promotion of an integrated Europe with expanded membership. Brandt advanced several arguments for British entry:

1. Avoiding the question merely threatened EEC paralysis.
2. Enlargement was in the common interest "when we are trying to bring East and West more closely together."
3. Expansion was necessary for Europe "to hold its own economically with the United States and the Soviet Union."
4. Britain could serve as a balance to West Germany's "economic strength."

In a broader vein, he took the lead in urging the other chief executives to act swiftly in the areas of increased political cooperation; full economic and monetary union; strengthening Euratom; reforming CAP to eliminate surpluses; and expanding development aid to third countries.

The importance of the Hague Conference lies in its substantive achievements. At Bonn's suggestion the conference readopted the basic measures which had been set aside by France in 1965 and not acted upon since. Bonn initially strengthened its position vis-à-vis France within the EEC to consolidate the European community for the sake of integration and the additional political stature earned from its new activities and policy. Bonn was also hypersensitive lest the progress in its Ostpolitik be viewed in the West as "the mad race to Moscow," as Dean Acheson labeled German-Soviet reconciliation. To counter this tendency, it was in Bonn's interest to reaffirm the linkage between its Ostpolitik and Westpolitik by demonstrating a firm commitment to further integration. In this context the FRG deliberately tried to lure the EEC away from the weak fragmentization of Gaullism toward greater multilateralism. At the same time, German policy was aimed at obtaining the support of her European allies, notably France and England, for her Ostpolitik.

Because of the dualism in German policy and the priority attached to Ostpolitik, there were rough limits to the level of integration the FRG could expect. Bonn could not afford to offend *either* the United Kingdom or France in advancing its EEC policy aims without endangering Ostpolitik. Both countries maintained qualified integration stances that tended to cancel each other out and produced only indifferent support for Germany's otherwise complementary Ostpolitik. Bonn was now rather suddenly confronted with circumstances totally removed from the largely dyadic interplay which characterized the previous years of its European diplomacy.

As a result, the period following the Hague Conference began as a phase of rewarming Bonn's rather "cooled" relations with Paris, a move back toward firmer ground. Brandt took this step by appealing to Pompidou in January of 1970 for a renewal of Franco-German cooperation within the scope of Common

Market goals. The success of the German overture was reflected in the 31
January 1970 Brandt-Pompidou meeting and the 7 February approval by EEC
members of a new "package deal" that reignited the integrative process. In the
package France regained her agricultural financing, while the "Europeans"
within the community (headed by Germany) secured limited endorsement of
the European Parliament's control over 3.5 percent of the association's operational budget by 1975. Further, France agreed to end in June 1970 its boycott
of the WEU (begun in January of 1969 over France's allegation that it was a
"backdoor" entry for Britain in EEC), and to the principle that enlargement
should be tied to conditions reflecting the EFTA position—negotiations on
British entry were to begin without further delay. In addition, two committees—
the Werner and Davignon—were empowered to prepare reports for consideration
the following year on further measures of political and economic coordination.

By the fall of 1970, Bonn was finally seeing the partial success of its overtures on the French and EEC planes. Its costs in terms of compromising purist
principles, however, were also beginning to show. By November the Chancellor
recognized that political unity would have to take second place in favor of
further efforts toward integrated economies. This reordering was due to the
urgent need for planning and negotiating an economic and monetary union,
which while in the long run was a necessity for advanced integration, nevertheless tended to obscure more immediate West German political aims. Like the
debates on agricultural policy, the issue of economic and monetary union
turned the impetus of the association's endeavors away from the basic political
implications of enlargement. Bonn feared that in the absence of a real crisis
protracted EEC debate on economic issues, at the expense of key political
matters, could revert the community to the "stagnation" preceding the parity
crisis of 1969.

Expansion and Diffusion

Paradoxically, negotiation over British entry into the EEC in 1970 was
one of the most important political developments in the organization's history,
but it did not significantly accelerate the momentum toward integration. The
achievement of enlargement to nine members was regarded as a triumph of
German persistence over French obstinancy. More than any single factor, it
assured that key policy debates in the future would no longer be conducted
on the bilateral French-German level, but rather on the broadened EEC plane.
Yet this new projection did not immediately ascend to the political realm. The
issues of common laws, institutions, interests, and foreign policies have been
only tangentially cited by some officials, and assiduously avoided by others.
Many European analysts believe that Pompidou's motive in conducting a national
referendum on Britain's entry was specifically to strengthen his hand in dealing

with Germany on the issue of future political integration. But such maneuvers
were rear-guard actions rather than strategies for advancement.

While attention to political integration has not been noticeably intensified,
the importance of political influence obviously has not waned. Again unexpected circumstances developed in Europe which afforded Brandt the opportunity to turn economic strength into a political asset, negotiable both on the
EEC level and in broader Ost- and Westpolitik terms. The occasion was the
mounting dollar crisis. On 10 May Bonn announced the floating of the mark.
While basically motivated for financial reasons, the move also provided the
opportunity to evoke once more political leverage balanced on an economic
fulcrum. As *Die Welt* noted prior to the sliding adjustment:

> There has been speculation that the Bonn government favors a
> floating rate for the Mark as a means of making other European coun-
> tries take similar action so that, in effect, there would be a joint re-
> valuation of EEC currencies in regard to the dollar as suggested by
> Schiller at the Hamburg conference of EEC economic and finance
> ministers, April 27.[3]

As Bundesbank President Klasen's remarks at the time also indicated,[4] Bonn
hoped that the crisis would trigger progress in moving the stalemated EEC
monetary talks. It appears clear, however, that Bonn's decision had an important,
though probably temporary, braking effect on political integration endeavors.

In the fall of 1970 the Werner and Davignon committees made their reports.
The Davignon committee report on political unity resulted in agreement on bi-
annual meetings of the foreign ministers, to be prepared by the "consulting
mechanism" of quadrennial meetings of the political directors of the foreign
ministries. Since the foreign ministers were already meeting within the framework of the EEC, the importance of this step should not be overemphasized in
terms of immediate and practical effect.

The Werner report, reflecting FRG interests, required further deliberation.
It called for a more centralized economic structure, including a central bank
and a common currency. Debate over this report lasted into 1971, with France
cast in the minority role. By 9 February agreement was reached on a substantial
degree of future monetary integration. A common currency was to be introduced by 1980. In the interim, coordination of monetary and fiscal policies
and the narrowing of fluctuation margins of the various currencies were envisioned, as well as the creation of a central bank. A long-term commitment was
made to establish further institutions that would affect national monetary and
fiscal policy, but decisions would not be made on these matters until 1973 at
the earliest. In effect, a general goal and an outline for its attainment was endorsed. The hard decisions would be made along the way.

It was not long before the monetary agreements began to crumble under
the pressures of the growing international currency crisis of 1971. When Germany

floated the Deutschmark—in violation of EEC agreements—and kept it floating despite judgments against the procedure by the appropriate Market institutions, Brandt stated: "As long as we have gone no further in building up the Common Market than where we stand today, recourse to the plea of vital interests is not the privilege of others alone, it belongs to us as well."[5] France objected to this individualistic attitude, a displeasure Brandt was not able or willing to appease at his meeting with Pompidou in early July. The intransigent positions of both states precluded a common front at the scheduled September meeting of the IMF. The Franch-German confrontation was compounded by the sudden US devaluation and the precipitation of a worldwide monetary crisis. Throughout the 1970-71 monetary tensions, a common position was never achieved within the EEC about a joint policy. By the end of 1972 the Community was still trying to regain the harmony which had existed previously in this sphere.

Assumptions About Integration
and German Policy

In light of these continuing crises, several suppositions about how Bonn is most likely to assert its increasing authority can be made. If the SPD remains in office as a coalition partner with the Free Democratic Party, which seems likely as a result of the November 1972 national elections, the FRG is apt to continue a policy of emphasizing the momentum of Western integration, while preserving an image of noninterference in Eastern Europe. It will actively explore the scope and intensity of British interests in European affairs, and try to determine the implications of three additional members for its goals of integration. Foremost among Bonn's priorities will be a prompt determination of whether there is sufficient similarity of interests between the UK and FRG to guarantee that the EEC will not be plunged again into a period of stagnation. Specifically, Bonn will inquire about the extent to which Britain will support its stand against France on fiscal and political integration matters. A noncommital reply or a plea for a period of acclimatization may prompt Bonn to dramatize its former role as the champion of the smaller members in order to maintain integration momentum. The objective of these soundings will be to assure the SPD that integration will proceed as programed for its own sake and to provide the necessary stature and leverage to achieve the ultimate goal of Ostpolitik. If the SPD cannot make acceptable progress toward this objective in reasonable time, the entire philosophy behind Ostpolitik and its explicit sacrifices could be exposed as bankrupt. An indignant electorate could swing to the right and increase endorsement of the CDU.

Several assumptions can be offered regarding changes in Bonn's foreign policy if the CDU is returned to power. Both major West German parties agree on fundamental foreign policy issues. Their differences are on timing, implementation, and the extent of national self-reliance. The CDU will continue to

view the Market as an economic necessity for the FRG, but also privately as a
potential political albatross of small states clamouring for authority and prestige
beyond their legitimate stature. Bonn accepted these liabilities at a time when
its own legitimacy and acceptance were critical for national self-assurance—days
that are past. A key reason for Bonn's former dwarfish political stature was its
obsession with, and impotency in, dealing with East Germany. Bonn must now
be careful not to allow its obsession with Western integration to become an
equally constraining influence. Thus, the CDU places less emphasis on the correlation between Western integration and East European dividends. While firmly
dedicated to integration, the CDU views other options as more readily available
levers. Moscow's continuing vulnerability in Eastern Europe has not been fully
exploited. Any amelioration of Europe's partition can only be made by the
Soviets, not the French, British, or Americans. Therefore, the CDU would
accept a relaxation in the pace of integration and a formulation of far looser
commitments, while focusing greater attention on gains in Eastern Europe.

The CDU argues that what is needed is a new formula for relations with
Moscow. It proposes to use the Federal Republic's growing economic, technological, and political strength as bargaining counters with the Soviets in
devising a more comprehensive settlement for Central Europe. This schema
would not negate Bonn's fundamental Western orientation or its allegiance to
the Atlantic Alliance. Only through these commitments can it preserve its
security requirements and preclude Soviet intimidation. But the proposal is
an unabashed recognition that only the Federal Republic and the Soviet Union
can assure a durable settlement in Central Europe. Such a settlement will require
a mutual acceptance of both powers' respective national interests in this region.
The Soviets must understand the need to humanize the partition, and West
Germany must finally acknowledge that Moscow's strategic frontier lies along
the Elbe. Soviet progress on this issue would permit a redirection in the military
character of its strategic frontier. In the past it was argued that the partition
could not be perforated until the GDR liberalized its regime and raised the
general standard of living. This estimate is still true, but less applicable if gradual
progress made in both spheres is coupled with the CDU's acceptance of Soviet
strategic interests and abandonment of hopes for common institutions in both
Germanies. The fundamental issues at stake are Moscow's insistence on guaranteeing the durability of its interests in German affairs—a "right" France has insisted on for over one thousand years—and Bonn's insistence on the right to
exercise self-determination in formulating German destiny. A quarter-century
of futile efforts has demonstrated the necessity of ceasing to view these vital
issues as contradictory or mutually exclusive. The CDU acknowledges that the
SPD accelerated the adjustment process in Central Europe and preserved Bonn's
options of German and European settlements. But the CDU insists that the
SPD's preference for Western integration and the expected agreement on the

European plane is less realistic than a reorientation and adoption of a policy
to solve the German problem between Germans and Soviets.

In drawing nonpartisan conclusions about the FRG-EEC relationship,
German policy preferences as well as diplomacy regarding the EEC are still in
the embryonic stage. Suffering from a "military-phobia" as a result of the Second
World War, the Bonn government has begun to test its voice within the European
community by relatively unprovocative measures. To date, it has discovered that
a policy "European" in form and pragmatic in substance has made it possible to
assert, via linkage, its national interests. With the successful negotiation of
British entry in 1971, German interests in the EEC have increased by a factor
greater than the number of countries admitted. The scale of the integrated
economies will place Bonn in the tacit leadership of the second largest economic
power and the first trading power in the world. The population and industrial
capacity of this power will be substantially larger than that of the USSR, its next
largest rival. Its combined GNP is three fourths that of the US, and it controls over
four times the currency reserves of the US. The awesome prospects of the misuse
of this power has caused soul-searching throughout Europe. The Germans realize
this, and have begun to press for action in the noneconomic sphere as a counterbalance. Foreign Minister Scheel stated this quite clearly on 29 July 1971, at the
end of negotiations with Britain: "What is gained in European cooperation must
not be lost in the Atlantic partnership."[6] More specifically, Scheel began to urge
a permanent secretariat for the biennial meetings of the Atlantic foreign ministers,
grounding his position not with appeals to past treaties or European ideals, common threats or future hopes, but quite simply on his view of what it would take
to maintain US presence in and partnership with Europe.

West Germany's foreign policy goals now require both a substantial US
presence and a strong European community. Whenever forced to choose, they
have usually opted for the US position—not out of esteem or perfect congruence
of interest, however light the American hegemony might be, but out of necessity,
given their goals of sovereignty, security, and reunification. Yet Bonn has recognized that both props of their foreign policy are in some respects unsteady and
unreliable. The US has shown itself weary of its world role, desirous of détente
with the Soviet Union, impatient over the slowness of European integration and
apprehensive over its present results. The West European countries have
demonstrated circumspection about making further sacrifices for the sake of
integration, manifested a resurgence or a reappearance of nationalism (or at the
very least an extremely pronounced parochial attitude), and at times exhibited
signs of schizophrenia in their relations with the US. With the entrance of Great
Britain into Europe and the continuing obstinacy of France, the EEC will remain
for the foreseeable future a loosely structured economic community with little
prospects of further political integration, even under the threat of a trade war
with the US.

American-Common Market Difficulties

How do these developments and questions affect American interests in
Western Europe? With only 5 percent of its GNP coming from foreign trade,
does the US have sufficient incentive to promote international fiscal reform or
foster a genuine economic partnership with the EEC? Does the US predilection
for viewing its European interests in strategic terms inhibit its ability to perceive
the relevance of a more integrated Atlantic political association? Can smaller
states be expected to place credence in a system of coalition politics that is
based heavily on special or preferential relations with Washington? How can
US interests in Europe that have been taken for granted for the past two decades
be reassessed without creating undue shock? Lastly, to what extent is a US
military presence on the continent necessary to defend American interests,
harness German ambitions, and insure progress toward fuller integration?

The politization of economics has now become the overriding Alliance
issue in urgency, possibly rivaling strategic and security matters in long-term
importance. The crisis is focused on three main areas: trade and fiscal policy,
reformation of institutions and principles, and burden-sharing within the
Alliance. In the first category, the United States has lost its relative economic
authority in the world and contributed to severe dislocations and uncertainties.
A few figures illustrate the change. In the last ten years Japanese exports to
the US increased 543 percent and imports from Europe by 295 percent. During
the same period, US exports to Japan increased by only 134 percent and to
Europe by 133 percent, leaving the US with overall trade imbalances. Despite
steady annual growth increases, the US percentage of the world GNP dropped
dramatically from 50 percent in 1950 to 30 percent by 1970. EEC percentage
rose from 11 to 20 percent and Japan from 1.5 to 8 percent. In 1950 the GNP
of the European members of OECD amounted to 55 percent of that of the US;
by 1970 it rose to 80 percent. In automobile production the US dropped during
this period from a contribution of 76 percent of the world's supply to 30 percent. In steel production its percentage of the world's total fell from 46 to 20
percent. And most startling, the US holdings of the world international reserves
tumbled from 50 percent to 8.8 percent in July 1972—before the 1973 sustained
drive against the dollar.

There were several apparent reasons for this steady decline—the allocation
of Marshall Plan funds, the drain of the protracted Vietnam War, the rise of other
economic powers, lagging interest in developing countries, favorable circumstances
for a rise in investments abroad (totaling $86 billion by 1971 at book value),
and the failure of commercial leadership that could have provided new guidelines and principles during the current transitional stage in economic relations
and possibly could have curbed the present rise of reciprocal protectionism.
These causes of the American economic decline are not all sources of alarm.
The Western industrial nations have been trying since 1944 to establish an

equitable international economic balance based on efficiency, comparative advantage, stability, and growth. The adjustment in the cited production figures indicates for the most part the success, not failure, of these efforts. But they also reveal that the US was unable to absorb the strains of the war within an economy infected by chronic inflation and unemployment. Yet the US preserved its lead in the science-based and technological industries which remained important stimulants to trade and investments abroad. Direct US investments in Europe, the chief recipient of advanced industrial components, increased from $6.7 billion in 1960 to $27.6 billion in 1971 at book value. Net income from total foreign investments has reached $7.3 billion annually, and incomes from royalties and license fees rose ten times, from $200 million in 1950 to $2.1 billion by 1971. Moreover, until 1972, the US had produced the lowest inflationary rate of any major industrial nation and had sustained a reasonable economic growth rate. It was the increasing competitiveness of other industrial nations on selected commodities and the general US agriculture crisis of 1973 that exacerbated the international monetary instability and commercial protectionism.

US transactions in agricultural products in 1973 created severe strains in Atlantic relations and were indicative of the growing commercial tensions. In January, Washington signed the largest feed-grain deal ever with the USSR, which generated local price increases, government subsidies for shipping lines, transportation dislocations, and inflationary pressures. At the same time large shipments of wheat were sent to South Asia and Africa and major deliveries of soybeans were made to China and France. Grain prices soared and soybeans soon tripled in price, resulting in export embargoes and the imposition of price ceilings. Livestock raisers, housewives, and foreign traders were the hardest hit, but the US had for the first time since World War II succeeded in reducing its grain surpluses and in cutting its subsidies and massive storage costs. EEC finance ministers met in emergency session to examine the consequences of the agricultural embargos. France reacted sharply, demanding EEC support for the extensive development of alternative sources of feed-grain supplies that would remain less vulnerable to "discrimination." Its partners sympathized but argued that US actions were part of a worldwide shortage, and failed to adopt measures that would have resulted in reciprocal protectionism.

The US harvested record crops in 1973, but it was not enough to force foodstuff prices back to 1972 levels or to sustain its expanded markets abroad. Federal agricultural spending was reduced substantially, but growing domestic pressure forced diversion of increasing stocks to home markets at the expense of foreign deliveries. While the US attempts to secure its new position as a permanent grain supplier for the Soviet Union for political reasons, traditional markets are likely to suffer and be forced to seek alternative sources. Agriculture remains the most nationalistically oriented component of economic policy, with peculiarities and incongruities that defy standardized policies among trading partners. Each nation seeks the broadest self-sufficiency possible in foodstuffs, leading frequently to national preferences that override international obligations and possibly to trade retaliation. The US agriculture dilemma is a case in point. To reduce burdensome surpluses, it capitalized on exports that forced prices up, creating serious international inflationary pressures that sustained the continued attacks on the dollar and disrupted traditional markets without adequate warning or compensation, inviting retaliation.

The 1973 agriculture crisis was merely one facet in the deteriorating trade situation among industrialized nations. Tariffs on industrial goods were reduced during the Kennedy Round of negotiations to between 6 to 12 percent. But hidden charges persisted and nontariff barriers often imposed even higher penalties. The principles of nondiscriminatory free trade and most-favored-nation treatment were being openly circumvented. The EEC, with its inherent regional discriminatory premise, was the prime mover in the direction of the erection of barriers. In September 1973 more than sixty nations met in Tokyo to review the principles of the original GATT conference and to recommend new means of introducing discipline and order into the commercial world. The further reduction of tariffs, the elimination of nontariff restrictions, agriculture problems, and monetary questions were discussed, culminating in the euphoric claims that usually emerge from such gatherings. The United States and Japan led the majority opposition group against the EEC and discriminatory policies. These two states suffer the most from EEC preferential practices, but were unable to arouse sufficient interest among other delegations to compel a modification in EEC tariff structures. If anything the growing pressure is likely to increase EEC resistance, especially that of France. In the near future, foreign pressure growing from EEC's rejection of GATT trading ethics will confront it with hard choices about its future development. Will it remain simply a customs union predicated upon discriminatory practices against the outside world, or will it be able to forge sufficient cohesion to form the necessary political authority to move in new directions and drop its regional preferences?

Fiscal Problems and Alliance Solidarity

The EEC's confidence to take such a bold step will depend upon the resolution of the current monetary crisis and the prospects for a stable international fiscal atmosphere. The most unexpected feature of the 1973 monetary crisis was that, unlike previous attacks on the dollar, which reflected criticism of US domestic policies, the entire international monetary exchange system was now the subject of doubt. The American economy was regarded as generally sound, but there was no confidence that the dollar could remain a stable reserve currency, resulting in massive selling of dollar holdings and the forced underevaluation of the dollar (in June it reached $1 to 2.20 marks). Another new additive was the role of multinational corporations and part US-owned subsidiaries.

US corporations have generally followed the principle of borrowing money locally for local operations. This practice allows them to borrow where money is cheap, invest where it is most profitable, and use an international division of labor in a responsive manner. While they are backed by the assets of the parent body, they often trade commodities and transfer funds from one subsidiary to another. Reserve holdings for trade and investment across national borders, therefore, must be in a currency with the least possible fluctuations. (Seldom can multinational corporations afford pure speculation in parity changes.) As former German Finance Minister Schiller stated, corporations are often more rational about money matters than governments. Without a reliable system for convertibility, the corporations could not afford to hold reserves for current and future operations in currencies that are subject to devaluation. With activities abroad that are estimated to range as high as $200 billion annually in fully and part-owned US assets, these corporations will continue to convert dollar accounts to harder currencies at whatever level desired to support prescribed activities, until such time as a more rigid par value convertability system is instituted by national governments.

On 15 August 1971, the US announced the inconvertibility of the dollar into gold, and in December the Smithsonian agreement established parity realignments. But the accord was soon obsolete. Continuing attacks on the dollar forced most trading countries essentially to float their currencies against the dollar though not against gold. During speculation runs, other nations were compelled to buy dollars to check inflationary tendencies, then sell them to the United States, where they were, in turn, lent to corporations at high interest rates. Increasing US prime lending rates was the main brake in the entire cycle. If it was anticipated that a devaluation of the dollar would exceed the interest rates on amounts needed, the corporations were forced to sell in time to preclude losses in excess of the rates being paid, and hopefully in time to earn enough to pay for the next loan. The other industrial nations were displeased. They were absorbing the inflationary pressures and costs for these multibillion-dollar transactions, while the United States offered no relief abroad for its own currency. In one sense, the US was pleased with the 42 percent devaluation of the dollar in relation to the mark in three and one-half years (from 4.05 DM in September 1969 to 2.20 in June 1973). Theoretically this made prices for US products abroad that much more attractive, stimulating sales and production. In practice, however, sales were far less than anticipated, and capital outflow due to currency fluctuations significantly reduced the total impact.

The EEC members concluded from these events that the US was in sufficient domestic difficulty that it was unprepared to support its own currency, leaving the responsibility and the penalty of the corresponding rise in price for their own commodities abroad to its trading partners. By the September Tokyo conference, the threat of a parity race among the industrial nations was looming on the horizon. The United States and Japan argued that currency values should be a function of trade and that the liberalization or elimination of discriminatory practices was the most equitable means for stabilizing the monetary system. The West Europeans countered that some form of preference will always remain a national prerogative, even if for only emergency situations, such as the world food crisis, and that the mechanics and system for value accumulation and transfer is the heart of the money problem. The EEC members generally held:

1. The dollar must be replaced by an international unit of account for purposes of transfer and liquidity;
2. The US must cover its basic deficits with its own reserve assets;
3. For this and other functions, greater use should be made of the International Monetary Fund and its Special Drawing Rights, whose role should be expanded; and
4. Smaller and more frequent changes in par value should become routine and central to the process of adjusting values in changing competitive conditions.

New Atlantic Charter?

The incongruity of these approaches to mutual problems indicates that no facile solutions are possible, and that any movement in either direction by any trading partner rests partly on political decisions. So fundamental are the differences that far-reaching political judgments are now required if harmony and compatability are to be restored to the commerical world. The Kissinger/ Nixon call for a new Atlantic Charter is an attempt to shift the focus of the Western nations from their economic differences to a redefinition of their political affinities. The process of redefinition and the reassessment of common institutions and principles will, it is to be hoped, include economic problems and project trading difficulties in the proper perspective.

Secretary Kissinger alluded to the political facets of the task of achieving a new equilibrium in trade and monetary relations in his April 1973 call for Atlantic revitalization.

> We see these negotiations as an historic opportunity for positive achievement. They must engage the top political leaders for they require above all a commitment of political will. If they are left solely to the experts the inevitable competitiveness of economic interests will dominate the debate. The influence of pressure groups and special interests will become pervasive. There will be no overriding sense of direction. There will be no framework for the generous solutions or mutual concessions essential to preserve a vital Atlantic partnership.[6]

He stressed that a blueprint for a new Atlantic Charter should build on the past, without creating constraints against change that would permit dealing with the problems resulting from the earlier success and that would encourage Japanese participation. "Our challenge is whether a unity forged by a common perception of danger can draw new purpose from shared positive aspirations." Specifically, the blueprint must include the new dimensions of economic competitiveness, continued shared common defense without the former umbrella of assured deterrence, and the changing nature of diplomacy among traditional nation-states. In economic matters, he complained that regional integration was being constructed at the expense of the United States and other nations, particularly in agriculture, which was fueling protectionist tendencies that could adversely affect relations in other areas. Reassessment of our respective interests on all outstanding problems was in order.

In identifying the major Alliance questions from Washington's viewpoint, Kissinger left it to the Europeans to hammer out a common response. By September 1973 NATO's Eurogroup of Foreign Ministers had agreed to a common agenda and accepted the US proposal for a summit conference that fall. But the Europeans remained lukewarm to openly skeptical about the conference and its outcome. France vigorously opposed the idea, preferring bilateral contacts where they would not be cast in the minority opposition on virtually all agenda items. (Since the SPD came to power, it consistently sought the institutionalization of routine NATO summit conferences, as are held by the Warsaw Pact. France has vetoed the motion each time it has been raised. The US initiative launched to end finally French obstructionism on this point was made only after affirmative responses came from other allies.) Other NATO members feared that Washington was now apprehensive about the child it had tried to foster for so many years in EEC, and regarded it as a competitor whose further integration and unity must be deflected.[7] They were most consistently concerned about the apparent US attempt to capitalize on Europe's security dependency in order to gain concessions in monetary and trade matters. During 1973 Washington repeatedly tried to tie trade and tariffs to troop cuts and burden-sharing. Europeans criticized the "packaged three T's" as a callously veiled maneuver to gain leverage in burden-sharing in exchange for preferential treatment in trade, seeking only favorable terms for US products, not the advancement of principle of nondiscrimination. EEC fears were not unfounded. As the US made slow but noticeable progress at SALT II and MBFR talks, the danger arose that the momentum for troop cuts would outpace European leverage against the US on this issue, thus NATO's strong preference for separation of problem areas.

It is doubtful that a crisis of confidence exists in the Atlantic Community, but certainly a condition of chronic malaise has seized all members in varying degrees. The lack of urgency may be even worse than an emergency. As Kissinger pointed out, "If we permit the Atlantic partnership to atrophy, or to erode through neglect, carelessness, or mistrust, we risk what has been achieved, and we shall miss our historic opportunity for even greater achievement." The proposed 1973 NATO Summit Meeting, the first since 1957, can only launch the process of reevaluation—it is unfair and unwise to expect that it can resolve such outstanding differences in such a short span.

While the process of redefining the principles of partnership will be a time-consuming and possibly an interminable problem, the issue of burden-sharing and a more equitable formula for defense responsibilities remains uppermost in American appraisal of its European commitments. Again Kissinger clarified US priorities on this point:

> The President has asked me to state that America remains committed to doing its fair share in Atlantic defense. He is adamantly opposed to unilateral withdrawals of American forces from Europe. But we owe to our peoples a rational defense posture, at the safest minimum size and cost, with burdens equitably shared. This is what the President believes must result from the dialogue with our allies in 1973.[8]

Burden-Sharing and US-FRG
Special Relationship

Following the termination of the occupation status of Western military forces, means for continued financial support were needed from the new Republic to offset the costs of maintaining strong NATO forces on FRG soil. This was accomplished in the early and mid-1960s by West German purchases of American military equipment. In the late 1960s German procurement of military hardware from the US dropped as the equipping of the Bundeswehr was completed and European production took up a greater portion of the requirement. From fiscal year 1968, new agreements have included nonmilitary transactions, i.e., FRG purchases of US securities and pledges not to convert dollar reserves to gold. The inclusion of fiscal expediencies has been regarded as unsatisfactory by both sides.

The size of the financial burden of supporting the US military element in NATO is substantial. In 1969 the total of US expenditures related to NATO reached $12 billion. In 1969 direct outlays to support the half-million US military-associated personnel in Europe reached a new high of $1.6 billion. This figure included $950 million spent in Germany alone. In fiscal year 1970, US defense expenditures affecting the balance of payments problem totalled $1.731 million. This accounted for almost one third of the national balance of payments deficit in 1970. In 1971 the estimated costs involved, not surprisingly, continued to climb. The US Defense Department placed the overall annual expenditures for maintenance of US troops in Europe at $2.9 billion. Of this amount, $1.9 billion went for personnel costs, which the US felt should be fully offset. The remaining $1 billion would be considered the US fair share and written off. The FRG established a Committee of State Secretaries chaired by the State Secretary of the Federal Chancellory to seek solutions acceptable to FRG interests in the alliance and in maintaining frank and friendly relations with the US. Defense Ministry itself reacted by seeking contributions by other NATO members. In 1970 Schmidt stated that increased FRG offset payments would not be an acceptable solution, because such funds would have to come from the FRG defense budget and would adversely affect NATO interests. The December 1971 meeting of the Defense Ministers of the Eurogroup (ten European NATO members) announced a planned increase in the European share of NATO's 1972 defense budget of over $1 billion. This was a significant addition to the European contribution to NATO, which already stands at 90 percent of ground forces, 72 percent Air Forces, and 80 percent naval forces in the European area.

This move increased the European share of the burden for defense of Western Europe but it did not cut the US costs. The US-FRG offset agreement expired in June 1971, when negotiations terminated inconclusively. In October 1971 Schmidt offered Secretary Laird a substantial contribution of funds to help improve living conditions for American troops in Germany. This offer was the key innovation in the offset accord signed on 10 December 1971. Of the total $2.03 billion for a two-year period, $184 million was earmarked for the troop billets program. This direct FRG budgeting involvement is an unprecedented procedure, breaking past offset practices, and was a compromise with the US request that the FRG assume all housekeeping costs—regarded by Bonn as onerous reflections of the occupation period. Still, the heart of the agreement centered on Bonn's decision to purchase 175 Phantom F-4 jet aircraft at a cost exceeding $1 billion. The $2-billion figure represents 80 percent of the balance of payments outflow caused by military commitments, and should strengthen Nixon's position in countering charges that the US can no longer afford large overseas military commitments.

Directly related to the offset problem is the question of the amount of treasure the West Germans should be expected to contribute to their own military establishment. The US spends 8 percent of its GNP on defense, compared to an average of 4 percent by European NATO members. And the US tends to fulfill military planning goals both quantitatively and qualitatively, while the continental allies do not. Further, the FRG defense budget is likely to plateau at about 20 billion marks, with annual increases reflecting only inflation and larger national budgets. This leveling-off tendency in defense spending is due to SPD preferences for improvement in other sectors of government and growing voter apathy about military programs. Indeed, even a clear CDU majority probably would not be able to improve drastically the FRG's defense budget.

Given these domestic restraints, Bonn is likely to continue viewing its immediate security requirements as a function of US support. If the Cold War climate diminishes and movement toward Mutual Balanced Force Reductions becomes a reality, reliance on US deterrence will be proportionally curtailed. But Germans are likely to continue to emphasize the necessity of "buying" the present level of US presence by reducing the gap between US and European burden-sharing, possibly through increasing direct budget support and more multilateral cooperation. As an interim measure, it is feasible to expect that a more reasonable balance in burden-sharing can be achieved.

In formulating recommendations for policies that will govern American-European relations for the next decade, a warning must be sounded. The specter of a premature withdrawal of American forces from the continent is an overbearing handicap. For a generation Western Europe has enjoyed a high degree of security because of its confidence in American commitments. The Europeans are most unlikely to fill gaps created by a substantial US withdrawal. US troop redeployments in 1966 and 1967 to the States triggered similar reductions in force strengths among Europeans, a pattern that will likely be followed in future cuts. Moreover, any major reductions that were not Alliance-wide would proportionally increase the weight of the Bundeswehr, a universally agreed undesirable goal. The Europeans are apt to conclude from a unilateral US cut that a significant shift in the relative weights of East and West has occurred, and to question their former confidence in American credibility. The resulting strain in relations between Americans and Europeans will undoubtedly provide the Soviets greater freedom of maneuver than they exercised during eras of increased NATO solidarity or than their physical strength warrants. Even more critical, confronted with this seeming shift in the political center of gravity toward the East, Europeans are likely to lose confidence in themselves. This would follow from the rationale that the US withdrawal stemmed primarily from domestic problems and not from a clear concept of NATO priorities, a farsighted Alliance perspective, or the military requirements of its partners. Furthermore, if no structural or strategic alternatives emerged in the Alliance or no compensating change in Warsaw Pact strength accompanied US actions, it would be interpreted widely as a retreat in which the Europeans have been abandoned. Despite the American ability to return troops to the continent under fire, the fact that they withdrew for lesser considerations would plant permanent reservations in European minds about the reliability of a US decision to return under fire. These reservations would be underscored by the knowledge that the withdrawal would eliminate the intermediate stages in NATO's deterrent and require the introduction of theater nuclear weapons much sooner than either the Americans or the Europeans are psychologically prepared to accept. Moreover, Europeans fear that fundamental changes in US nuclear policies are unlikely to be adopted after a troop cut has been initiated. For similar reasons, the Europeans are becoming increasingly nervous about the impact of the SALT deliberations on the Alliance. It is not so much a fear of a US-USSR deal at their expense or the erection of a tacit condominium applied to selected issues, as a fear that the US may develop such a stake in its bilateral relations with Moscow that it would risk less than formerly to support its Allies' interests.

Conversely, as the Europeans begin to lose confidence in American leadership, a tendency may emerge where both sides of the Atlantic would reduce the political and psychological investment in the other. Western Europe would likely become more parochial and disposed to accommodate the Soviet Union— a European power by virtue of geography, not policy. "Finlandization" after all has not been so distasteful for the Finns or armed neutrality unpalatable to the Austrians. It is quite conceivable that Europe would become bitterly nationalistic and protectionist toward the US, allowing dormant Gaullist tendencies present in most European countries to dominate future policies. Such a development could confront the US with nationalistic, dynamic movements in both Europe and Japan and render the evolution of a coherent international system based on mutual cooperation between Japan, North America, and Europe virtually impossible. In view of the continuing Soviet challenge, an unquestioned American tactical nuclear guarantee and the continued presence of strong in-being theater forces is critical for security in these vital regions, until alternative strategies and supporting policies have been adopted. The proper order of priorities recognizes that security is the cornerstone for détente and that only after détente has progressed to the point of insuring normal relations can security requirements be relaxed—not vice versa. Kissinger stressed in his April address that a linkage should be maintained between redressing the Alliance's economic and political grievances and the simultaneous revision of strategic doctrines that will allow NATO to cope with the military challenges of the 1970s with greater confidence.

**Part II
Security Requirements
in the Age of Parity**

Introduction

An assessment of US national security requirements in the 1970s necessitates an appraisal of the comparative military strengths of the great powers and their respective alliances in the various areas of potential confrontation or hostility: strategic nuclear capabilities at the intercontinental level, general purpose forces at the theater plane, and naval forces in the maritime area. The exercise of analyzing relative military postures ranges in difficulty from the complex to, often, the futile. In modern defense policy there are no simplistic arms progressions whereby the acquisition of a new weapon can be either duplicated or offset by increased procurement of existing arms. From the outset of the Cold War, arms rivalry assumed an asymmetrical character. Each side necessarily tried to compensate for the opponent's advantages not by meeting his assets on a one-for-one basis, but by emphasizing its own advantages. As the great-power competition expanded, the asymmetries in their military capabilities increased. Therefore mere quantification of force structures was a false indication of total military capabilities. The differences in postures, quality of weapons, and the missions for which they were intended were compounding factors in these estimates. The intensity of the conflict and the closed nature of Soviet society led Western strategists too frequently to measure Soviet military prowess by Western strategy concepts. It was often assumed that the two sides had identical missions and therefore should have similar force requirements. American supremacy in strategic nuclear weapons and command of the high seas equated into a concept of deterrence based on assured destruction: the ability to retaliate at the strategic level after absorbing any intensity of attack and inflict unacceptable damage on the Soviet Union. Assured destruction was regarded as so absolute that deterrence at the strategic sphere was expected to work at the theater levels as well. Indeed, the US began shifting its priorities for the general purpose forces to the role of counterinsurgency, an area where the Communist threat was regarded as most lethal and where we were inadequately prepared.

The Soviet perception of the weakness in the singularity of the assured destruction strategy led to a major effort during the 1960s to overcome the numerical inferiority of the Soviet strategic forces. As rough parity was achieved at the intercontinental level, Moscow was able with only modest investments of resources to emphasize the different missions designated for its theater and naval forces. The erosions of assured destruction allowed the Soviets to claim parity for their smaller forces in other spheres by assigning them missions commensurate with their capabilities. Thus a significant change has occurred in the nature of the military confrontation and role of military forces in political negotiations.

In light of this shift, has there been a corresponding modification in the threat perceived by either side, as is so often claimed in the public media? For prudent Western observers, the military threat from the Soviet alliance still persists. There has been no alteration in concepts of operation, training levels, and force structures. Indeed there has been a steady modernization of Pact forces, introducing advanced systems comparable to those in NATO. In some areas the Pact has distinct advantages, especially in the implementation of an integrated doctrine for the use of tactical conventional and nuclear weapons. Thus, the Pact's military capabilities are not declining and the potential threat remains unchanged—what *is* changing is Western response to it.[1] NATO can no longer view the Soviet challenge in the same perspective as it could under the comfortable shelter of assured destruction, and new countermeasures are required.

In exploring the security needs of the Western Alliance in the age of parity several general questions will be posed as the framework for inquiry. As parity is gradually attained at all levels of engagement, can the West place as much confidence as it did under the Johnson Administration in the deterrent quality of military uncertainties? What are the standards for measuring parity—which should be applied universally and which selectively? Is parity to be equated with a military status quo, stalemate, or stand-off, and to what extent does it contribute to the present negotiations for the consolidation of an age of cooperation? If parity represents a status quo, is it a prerequisite for mutual arms reductions? Is parity merely a slowing of the arms competition that is less influential on reductions than nonmilitary factors? Is parity and its political consequences conducive to the improvement of military efficiency through changes in doctrine and weapons quality? Can it foster fundamental shifts on both sides necessary to convert force structures from offensive, provocative postures to defensive, reactive forces? Was the collapse of assured destruction and erection of strategy parity a consequence merely of numerical aggregation of military capabilities, or the recogniton that such power could only be used to acquire vital interests from an opponent, an aim to which neither side aspired? Can the renunciation of such aims be transposed to lesser levels of violence? After repeated calls by the Nixon Administration for West Europeans to become more aware of their capabilities and responsibilities, what role should American forces play in Europe? What should be the function of credibility in US commitments in a post-MBFR Europe? Should all parties anticipate and prepare for a Europeanized Europe? What should be the unified Western aims at the CSCE and MBFR? At what level of force reductions will structural changes occur, and can such destabilizing and uncertain developments be offset on the political plane? What kinds and sizes of forces are desirable to insure a continuing US engagement in Europe and what force structures are necessary to give Europeans confidence that they can compensate for Moscow's political preponderance by their own political latitude and fortitude? What kind of a NATO strategy will encourage the political growth of Western Europe without impairing great-power interests elsewhere or endangering the general international system as it is now known? With one third of present Western defense budgets allocated for the maintenance of manpower and material reserves, would it be prudent to reassess the nature of war, and to pursue a defense policy that would channel potential conflicts into areas where the West has more advantages and opponent has greater disadvantages, rather than vice versa?

The following chapters will explore the impact of parity at the various levels of possible hostilities and discuss policy options for the improvement in Western military efficiency along the lines raised by these questions.

10 Strategic Parity: The Impact of the Loss of Assured Destruction on NATO Nuclear Policy

The 1962 crises in the Himalayas and Cuba demonstrated convincingly to the Soviets the superior strategic mobility of American conventional forces. The US Navy effectively quarantined Cuban waters and the Air Force airlifted air-defense and communications equipment and crews to the Indian Army fighting the Chinese. The Soviets were physically incapable at that time of matching such a performance or of mounting a credible overseas strategy. When they became involved in the Congo, for example, the Soviets were forced to draw back because they lacked the logistics support and potential military presence to bolster their protégés. The decision must have been made in 1963 to correct these deficiencies; soon after, evidence began to appear that Moscow was developing a stronger naval posture, and later that it was prepared to make the necessary sacrifices to challenge the US intercontinental strike capability.

It is not clear whether the Soviets were able at that time to calculate with precision the full implications of their challenge at the strategic nuclear level. From mid-1950 to 1960, Soviet defense policy followed a strategy of minimum force posture, with superior strength in only sufficient categories of weapons systems, such as submarines and tanks, to compensate for the inferiority in others and render the composite structure a credible deterrent. The achievement of a favorable imbalance in general-purpose forces in Central Europe and a less favorable balance in blue water naval forces was a successful projection of this strategy. Advantages at theater levels later became direct by-products of the policy change regarding intercontinental forces. At the strategic level the Soviets decided to abandon the constraints of minimal force postures and to seek full parity or superiority. The achievement of parity at the intercontinental level increased the weight of theater forces by a factor much larger than the reduction of the constraints imposed by minimal force policy warranted. Medium-range weapons systems, such as bombers and missile-equipped submarines, could be transferred to theater missions, increasing total inventories without requiring additional investments. More important, parity at the intercontinental level introduced constraints on the United States unprecedented in the nuclear age. For the first time, the US had to modify its policy of assured destruction and confine its vast strategic reserves to only the defense of vital national interests. There were few tactical situations which either warranted or could be influenced by a strategic nuclear exchange. Because of the geographic and political configurations of its alliances, the decoupling of strategic and theater levels of conflict

131

compelled the US to invest substantially greater resources to achieve the same
degree of security at both levels. It should be emphasized that by achieving
parity in strategic weapons, the Soviets were able to insure a high degree of
parity in the various theaters of potential tactical engagement without having
to follow the exhaustive action-reaction syndrome of matching the opponent
gun for gun and ship for ship. Thus the Soviet attainment of strategic parity
is the key factor in the defense policies of both adversaries and will remain the
focus of security calculations for the remaining 1970s. (This chapter will
deal only with the military aspects of parity; chapter 12 will consider the
political and diplomatic features.)

Salt I

On 26 May 1972, three documents were signed in Moscow by President
Nixon and Party Secretary General Brezhnev: a formal treaty limiting anti-
ballistic missile systems (ABM), an interim agreement on the limitation for up to
five years of offensive strategic systems, and a protocol outlining the constraints
on submarine-launched missiles (SLBM).[1] The ABM treaty permits construction
of two sites armed with one hundred launchers to defend an existing ICBM
complex and the national capital. Each launcher is limited to a single missile
with a single warhead. The size of radars is not restricted around the capitals,
but the numbers are limited. The numbers are unlimited for radars at the
ICBM sites, but their sizes are restricted. The Soviets have sixty-four Galosh
missiles at their Moscow site and have not yet begun construction on an
ICBM defensive site. The US is completing its Safeguard ABM site at Grand
Forks, North Dakota, and has abandoned all other sites, retaining only the
option for a second site at Washington.

These quantitative restrictions do not apply to qualitative improvements.
Both sides retain the option to modernize both missiles and radars, within the
size parameters specified. According to the President's 1973 Foreign Policy
Report, the Soviets are continuing development and active testing for an
improved ABM that may replace the Galosh and later be installed in the second
site. The US will gain operational ABM experience when the Safeguard system
becomes fully deployed, while continuing development of the Hardsite system,
with its larger number of smaller sized radars. Thus the efficiency of the ABM
systems on both sides can be expected to improve over time. The treaty can be
reviewed at five-year intervals but is of unlimited duration, giving an aura of
permanency to the present restraints of strategic defensive weapons systems.
The upper limits on quantitative deployments and functional symmetry have
been codified, although neither may choose to expand to those levels. Both
sides view ABM deployments as a direct correlation to developments in the
area of offensive missiles.

The quantitative restrictions on offensive missiles include a rather mysterious formula. No specific figures are mentioned, implying high confidence in intelligence estimates; or, as the President attests, minor errors in numbers have little consequence when calculated at the magnitude of strategic delivery systems. The total number of submarine-launched ballistic missiles (SLBM) launchers is based on the number operational or under construction as of 26 May 1972, and ICBM launchers will not exceed the number operational or under construction as of 1 July 1972. No additional "heavy" ICBMs of the SS-9 type are to be deployed and the size of silos is confined to that of those operational or under construction (the one hundred silos under construction at the time turned out to be larger than SS-9 silos, indicating that the Soviets are holding open their options on the "heavy" missiles). Within these limits modernization and replacement of submarines, launchers and missiles is freely permitted. Pre-1964 ICBM launchers and "older" submarines may be traded for an equal number of new SLBM launchers. Within this modernization process, however, there are upper limits. The US may have no more than 710 SLBM launchers and no more than 44 modern submarines (the US presently has 656 SLBMs in 41 submarines, and could trade 54 Titan-2 ICBMs for SLBM launchers in three new Trident submarines). The USSR is authorized up to 950 launchers in not more than 62 modern submarines, and a total of up to 1618 ICBMs (only 1530 are presently operational; the remainder are apparently being held for follow-on missiles). The USSR can have 740 SLBMs in 56 nuclear submarines operational or under construction, plus an additional 210 launchers in new submarines as replacements for an equal number of SS-7 and SS-8 ICBMs, provided the number of boats does not exceed 62 and SLBMs remains under 950. The US can replace its Minuteman 1-2 and Polaris force with Minuteman-3 and Poseidon MIRV systems and continue development of the Trident submarine with 24 6000-mile-range missile launchers. The Soviets have equal freedom to modernize and are presently developing three new ICBMs: a new, very large missile which could have a greater capability than the SS-9, with its 25-megaton warhead; a smaller ICBM, possibly intended as a follow-on to the SS-11; and a solid propellant ICBM, probably designed to replace the SS-13 or possibly to provide a mobile capacity. These new missiles may well carry highly accurate MIRVs. The USSR has also begun deployment of a new submarine capable of submerged launch of a 4000-mile-range missile.[2]

Both the present and potential number of launchers favors the USSR. In early 1973 the USSR had an estimated 2090 launchers, of which 740 were SLBMs. If its 66 launchers on its diesel-powered submarines were retained, the maximum number of 2424 launchers could be reached. The US has a total of 1710 launchers, of which 656 are SLBMs. This former figure can not be exceeded, and the shift to SLBMs can only rise to 710. The reason for this discrepancy, according to the President, was that the range limitations of both missiles and submarines required that the USSR have three boats for every two US vessels to achieve the same amount of on-station time. (But as longer-range missiles and nuclear submarines came into operational service, this ratio would be corrected to 1 to 1). Second, some quantitative factor had to be included as compensation for the qualitative superiority of US warheads. (But as Soviet MIRVs become operational, the vulnerability of US land-based systems will be increased, jeopardizing the current strategic stability).

The importance of the Soviet numerical superiority is that it now has much wider latitude in shaping its future force structure. It can opt for a maximum SLBM force with 950 launchers and greater survivability and flexibility. Or it can gradually modernize its existing SLBM force with 740m launchers, introducing longer-range missiles and a new generation of quieter submarines and reserving the diesel-powered submarines for theater targets, while converting its ICBM force to a more economical, reliable force of advanced missiles. The latter option would assure superiority in numbers of both SLBMs and ICBMs and require minimal resources. The former would assure greater flexibility, but it would cost substantially more to construct and operate such a fleet of submarines.

While numerical advantages provide greater flexibility in selecting policy options, important qualifications persist about the relative strength of both strategic forces. The interim agreement does not include bomber aircraft, a category in which the US has a distinct advantage. The US presently has 450 B-52 bombers and 76 FB-111 medium-range bombers (for greatest efficiency, the latter aircraft must operate from forward bases). The Soviets have only 140 slower, older, and shorter-ranged bombers. US B-52s alone have an impressive advantage in payloads over their Soviet counterparts: 30.5 million pounds (33.4 million with the FB-111s), compared to 4.8 million pounds, or 2000 warheads compared to only 420 Soviet warheads. When the US Short-Range Attack Missile (SRAM) becomes fully operational in 1976, the total number of deliverable warheads carried by B-52s will rise to over 3500, while the Soviets are not expected to make any substantial gains in this area.[3] The Americans are developing a follow-on B-1 long-range bomber, but the Soviet Backfin reportedly has only a medium-range capability. Moreover, the survivability of the B-52 force has been increased by decreasing the time required for takeoff and by developing new basing concepts. This will reduce the threat from the growing force of Soviet ballistic-missile submarines.[4] The Americans have placed considerable faith in this bomber force and are likely to continue to do so. It is increasingly survivable and is manned, allowing for choices in flight. But it is relatively vulnerable to hostile defenses. Nonetheless, the bomber is an important component of a second- or third-strike force that will be difficult to supplement completely by missiles. The Soviets, however, are not likely to pursue this option and will be content with redundancies in numbers of ICBMs as compensation for reduced versatility.

The second qualification lies in the number of deliverable warheads. By 1972 the US had deployed its Multiple Independently Targeted Re-Entry Vehicles (MIRV) in 200 Minutemen-3 ICBMs with three warheads each and in 10-14 warheads in 160 Poseidon SLBMs. When the Multiple Re-Entry Vehicle (MRV)-equipped Polaris SLBMs with a triangulation-burst capability and the strategic bomber force are taken into consideration, the United States can strike theoretically 5580 aiming points; and the Soviet Union can strike only 2510. Should the US convert its Titan-2 ICBMs to Poseidon SLBMs and complete the MIRVing of the scheduled 550 Minutemen-3s, it will be able by the expiration of the interim agreement to strike 7800 targets, and some 3500 targets with warheads on strategic bombers. By the end of 1973, the USSR had only begun the deployment of its first MRV system on SS-11 missiles, and had flight-tested its first MIRV. By the expiry of the agreement, the Soviets would not be able to threaten more than 3800 targets with all systems, since its MIRVs would not yet be deployed. Moreover, the short range of the USSR's present SLBMs precludes more than 40 percent of its submarine force being on-station at any given time, while the US maintains 60 percent of its capability on-station. (The Soviets would have the initiative and could conceivably have more boats deployed in a "maximum effort," but the exact number would be contingent upon warning and mobilization rates; in other words, the subject of conjecture). Given the existing ratio of on-station boats and the upper limits for SLBMs under the interim agreement, the US could have some 425 launchers in firing positions by 1975, and the USSR only 380. The 1973 US force can fire 3150 warheads at about 2710 targets; the current Soviet submarine force has only 1750 warheads available. By the agreement's end, the US Navy could have a maximum of 5650 warheads deliverable on 5450 targets, while the Soviet Navy without MIRVs could have only 1850 warheads aimed at the same number of targets.[5] Thus, the Soviet Union is clearly ahead in the number of launchers and has greater leeway in selecting future options, while the United States has marked advantages in force mix and number of deliverable warheads.

The discrepancy between these two postures was a product of missile size and throw-weight and the level of warhead technology. The 309 SS-9 carry a 25-megaton (MT) warhead, the 210 SS-7 and SS-8 carry a 5-MT payload, and the 970 SS-11 a 1-2-MT capability. The 54 Titan-2 carry a 5-10-MT warhead and the Minutemen force only 1 MT. Therefore, the total throw-weight of the Soviet ICBM force is 400 percent greater than that of the US ICBMs. Indeed, the US has been reducing total yields as it has increased the number of deliverable warheads. It is estimated that the total US ICBM and SLBM force has a maximum theoretical capability of 2400 MTs, and the Soviet counterpart force about 11,400 MT, or five times greater.

But these figures are partially misleading. Destructive nuclear power is a product of both yield and accuracy in delivery. There are diminishing returns in high yields; beyond certain levels, increased yields add little to the total blast and are essentially wasted energy. As delivery errors are reduced and accuracy approaches "near-zero errors," the destructive power increases by factors of 100 to 1000 over yield.[6] The United States opted for increased accuracy, permitting greater efficiency and precision in the destruction of most targets. The Soviet Union, on the other hand, persisted in the development of heavy missiles, giving it a greater overall megatonnage and wide options regarding its future disposition, as well as hedges against technological backwardness. The USSR is believed to be at least five years behind the US in both its MIRV and MRV programs. But there is no reason why it should remain permanently handicapped. The danger in the size of the Soviet megatonnage is its potential for refinement. When the Soviets reach the present US level of a second-generation MIRV capability, they may be able to multiply their 500-percent advantage in throw-weight by a factor substantially larger in deliverable warheads, while the US will be unable either to increase total warheads or multiply their accuracy.

The explicit provisions authorizing modernization along any line either government chooses is the principle reason why the agreements on offensive weapons systems are regarded as interim in nature. There are no obvious balances or permanent counters for any system, and each side has reserved the right to exploit any technological advantage it presently enjoys. Neither side presently has the capability of disarming the opponent by a preemptive first strike against his strategic forces. While the US delivery capability is largely pegged to presently forecasted maximum levels, the Soviet levels remain more open-ended. Should the Soviets seek and achieve the present level of US warhead technology, their delivery capability would be sufficiently increased that a first strike would be plausible. The Soviets could attack in-place strategic nuclear forces without fear of reprisal. They would retain an overwhelmingly invulnerable retaliatory capability that would render the US second strike option useless—there would be no point in attacking a few Soviet cities when Moscow's reprisal would spell national destruction. Both sides are apparently seeking some format in SALT II that would codify the present imperfect balances with their respective advantages for modernization that could be exploited should the accords later fail, without undue expenditures of resources at the present level. Such a formula would place a high degree of confidence in intentions to compensate for underestimated capabilities and presumed disadvantages.

Weaknesses in the SALT I Limitations

There are several holes in the present accord that must be considered in any future agreement. First, the US sought unsuccessfully in SALT I to gain a limit on all ICBMs, including the 60 SS-13 mobile missiles, and the follow-on missile the Soviets are testing. No "zero-limit" would be plausible without adequate verification; procedures that are difficult to envision for mobile systems. The attempted inclusion of a system that defied absolute verification indicated that the US was prepared to introduce new criteria for agreement. Both intention and capability were regarded as valid standards for accord. The Soviets probably refused a "zero-limit" because there was no commensurate

quid pro quo the Americans could offer, and because they placed less faith
in intentions than capability.

A second category for consideration in SALT II is American strategic
bombers. The present force of 450 B-52s and 76 FB-111s will be retained in
service only if no agreement is reached necessitating their retention, and if the
development of the B-1 is blocked by Congress. It is presently anticipated that
the B-52 force will be reduced to 250 aircraft by the end of the 1970s. Because
of their proven value in conventional bombing in Southeast Asia and their
potential as a third strike force, the US will probably place a high priority on
retaining a sizable manned strategic bomber force, making it an awkward
possible bargaining counter for Soviet mobile ICBMs.

Another category of weapons that must be treated is air-to-surface
missiles (ASM). The Soviets first developed ASMs and deployed them with their
medium-range TU-16 bomber force. These aircraft are now estimated to have
been reassigned to theater missions and their ASM capability is not relevant
to SALT. The United States, on the other hand, has developed ASM capability
for strategic use. At present one B-52 carries three or four-gravity bombs and
two Hound Dog nuclear ASMs. By the end of 1975, the deployment of SRAM
system will be completed, allowing each B-52 to carry up to twenty SRAMs
and the FB-111 six SRAMS each.If only SRAMs are included, the expected
bomber force in 1975 will be able to carry over 1500 independently targeted
ASMs. The low-level penetration capability and maneuverability of US bomber
aircraft are versatile delivery platforms for the SRAM that can be fired from
low levels at fixed targets over the horizon or at targets of opportunity from
higher altitudes. There is no comparable system in the Soviet inventory.

Against this bomber threat the USSR has deployed over 3000 interceptor
aircraft and 10,000 SAMs, including the most advanced aircraft on either side,
the Foxbat and Flaggon B. The US has only 500 interceptor aircraft, which
are rapidly being phased out, and 800 SAMs of only marginal utility. If SALT II
follows the pattern of earlier proceedings, a high priority may be placed on
curtailing defensive systems along with their corresponding offensive system.
It will be difficult for air-defense systems to be included, however, especially
from the Soviet side. They have exclusively defensive characteristics and dual
utility against both strategic and tactical aircraft. Finally, strategic bombers
are not critical to the posture of either side.

Antisubmarine warfare (ASW), however, is an area of defensive systems
that is becoming increasingly important to both sides. Since each side is
likely to shift an increasing proportion of its strategic offensive capability to
SLBMs, defenses against submarines should receive greater attention. Each navy has
oriented the bulk of its ASW capabilities to date to protecting surface vessels.
To distinguish between boats assigned to surface shipping protection and
submaring hunter-killer mission is probably impossible. Detection and destruction techniques are unlikely to be considered, since the US is reportedly about
five years ahead of the Soviets in both areas. Further, the capabilities of NATO

allies are highly advanced and would remain outside the context of a bilateral accord. Therefore, the Soviets might be expected to seek a merely numerical advantage in a limitation on nuclear hunter-killer submarines. Numerical limitations at this point would not be a serious restriction for either side, since the offensive system has a wide margin in effectiveness over the defensive in submarine warfare.[7]

These separate weapons categories are important individually to the overall balance, but are still peripheral to the central issue of the numbers, yields, and accuracy of deliverable warheads. Total launchers and throw-weight have been partially fixed by the 1972 accords. The United States entered SALT II pledged to reduce the adverse implications of the numerical disadvantages it had surrendered in SALT I, and thereby to place SALT II on a more durable basis. Within the context of SALT I, this could only be achieved by the destruction of existing launchers or a ban or limitation of the proliferation of warheads. Many Western observers believe that the Soviets will steadfastly refuse to destroy in-place missiles and will be more likely to discuss limitations on proliferation, but only after they have achieved an operational capability and a numerical advantage over the United States.

Relevance of Theater Nuclear Systems

On the Soviet side, the most likely single trade-off for a limitation on Soviet MIRVs is the Forward-Based Systems (FBS). The relative numbers and capabilities of German-based US F-4s and MIRVed SS-9s are militarily incomparable, as the US repeatedly points out. The FBSs, however, have important psychological implications for the East-West balance that focus more sharply on internal NATO susceptibilities than any issue since the achievement of strategic parity and the decoupling of US strategic forces from European commitments.

During SALT I, Moscow sought to include all NATO FBSs on the agenda. The US reportedly replied that a reduction of European-based nuclear systems with a potential range to strike the USSR would have to be accompanied by a reduction of medium-range bombers, missiles, and submarines targeted against Western Europe. A deadlock developed over terminology and the appropriateness of equating intercontinental systems with theater forces. The US apparently agreed to reconsider the issue at round one of SALT II, but reportedly firmly rejected the Soviet argument that all FBSs were strategic systems. It appears safe to assume that the US side would not have accepted this proposal so readily without indications of Soviet agreement to participate in MBFR talks and to discuss the MIRV issue at SALT II.

At the 1973 Copenhagen Minister Meeting, the United States reportedly implied to the NATO members that the US strategic forces have been effectively decoupled from NATO security requirements. For planning purposes, it was no longer appropriate to include strategic retaliation in European deterrence. These forces can now only be employed for defense of the continental United States. Consequently, Europeans have shifted the burden of US credibility in its NATO commitments to US FBSs. American forward nuclear forces have become the chief remaining demonstration of US determination to deter the Soviet nuclear threat against Europe. Under these circumstances, the psychological and political importance of the US FBSs have been heightened, without improving their military effectiveness.

Under the broadest definition, FBS would include the F-4, F-111, Pershing missiles, carrier aircraft, and SACEUR-assigned Polaris submarines. In ascending order of effectiveness, the Pershing has a range limitation of 740 km and cannot strike Soviet soil unless deployed to the Bayerische Wald, where it would be highly vulnerable, or into Warsaw Pact territory. It is extremely unlikely that the Pershing would ever impact on Soviet soil. The F-4 has severe range limitations when launched from Germany on a low penetration and recovery flight profile; only a fringe of Soviet territory can be struck even with in-flight refueling. The F-111 also has only a marginal capability because its operational bases are located in England. Greek and Turkish F-104s are more suitably deployed, as would be US carrier aircraft if they could be launched from the Aegean Sea. But the survivability of carriers in the Eastern Mediterranean is highly questionable. Further, the two carriers assigned to the Sixth Fleet relinquished the nuclear strike role years ago and crew proficiency is now probably negligible, even if the weapons are aboard for a secondary capability.

The only real threat to the USSR from a US FBS is the five or six Polaris submarines assigned to SACEUR. These boats operate in European waters and their MRV missiles can strike the Soviet interior with a high degree of accuracy. But while the submarines are by far the most effective system, they are less viable to the European public than USAF aircraft. Many Europeans insist that without a major US component to the SACEUR Strike Plan in the form of manned aircraft, Washington would feel compelled by numbers alone to withhold its SACEUR submarines in the event of attack to bolster its second-strike capability. The US could justify such a withholding on the grounds that its second-strike capability would be the only genuine deterrent left—the Europeans would probably concur. Thus, the reduction of US strike aircraft would be more disturbing for European sensitivities than the complete withdrawal of the unseen submarines.

Yet when the numbers of US strike aircraft available are calculated, the marginality of their strategic performance is further underscored. There are presently 475 F-4s and 76 F-111s assigned in Europe for all combat missions—air defense, ground attack, interdiction, and nuclear strike. Approximately 340 of these aircraft are committed to the SACEUR Strike Plan under optimum conditions.[8] To generate this force level, however, presupposes maximum alert, zero maintenance outages, and 100-percent crew availability. An 80 to 90 percent aircraft availability with several days' warning would be more realistic. Moreover, if the conflict intensified at the conventional level, a decision would probably be made to commit an increasing portion of this force to the conventional ground support role, reducing the number of aircraft remaining for the Strike Plan. Finally, the NATO allies have no first-line aircraft held as reserves or replacements; all reinforcements must come from the US, which includes only about 450 first-line tactical combat aircraft. Except for a limited number of F-111s and aging F-105s, most of the F-4s and A-7s in reserve are not configured for and the crews not trained for nuclear warfare. Because of time needed for nuclear reconfiguration and expected high attrition rates among conventional forces, US replacement aircraft by necessity will be assigned to conventional missions.[9]

This is a meager force for conducting nuclear warfare in Europe. Further, the declining number of NATO strike aircraft available to SACEUR do not total a satisfactory force structure and merely heighten the symbolic value of USAFE strike aircraft. (The FRG has recently converted two F-104 strike wings to F-4 conventional wings, and eventually all six F-104 wings will be assigned nonnuclear F-4. See below.) Because of this new symbolic value, USAFE strike aircraft have become a psychological reassurance for West Europeans and an important negotiating priority for the Soviets.

Advocates of unilateral US troop reductions have testified that tactical aircraft can be redeployed to Europe in a "matter of hours."[10] This is true under given conditions. First, optimum alert conditions must be achieved. This has not yet been accomplished in any Soviet-initiated crisis (see chapter 11). Second, forward bases, command and control centers, and nuclear storage facilities must remain intact and serviceable. A growing school of thought among American analysts now contradicts earlier thinking that the Soviets would be deterred from general war, especially along the Central Front, but might attempt smaller-scale ventures. The new school argues that with the increasing awareness of strategic decoupling and the growing importance of in-place theater forces for the defense of European interests, the Soviets may be tempted to achieve expanded aims with a massive assault along the Central Front. Or they may seek lesser objectives by mere threats of a large-scale attack. This thinking suggests that to achieve either set of goals the Soviets are likely to employ force in a traditional continental manner—the use of whatever military power is necessary to secure political aims in the shortest possible time, including even the employment of nuclear weapons against nuclear facilities. Should such a scenario take place, the Soviets would rapidly overrun many of the forward bases and neutralize vital nuclear facilities. Forces deployed from the US would have to fight from rearward bases, probably in the UK, reducing their effectiveness.

Finally, the decision to deploy US strike forces to Europe is a political one and must be made in time to strengthen the deterrence or, if that fails, to bolster European defenses. But the decision is complicated by the awareness that the deployment of strike aircraft may be perceived by the opponent as an escalaroty rather than precautionary action, which might trigger preemptive Soviet strikes against nuclear facilities that could render these aircraft largely useless. Moreover, despite direct assertions to the contrary via the hot line, a danger exists that Moscow would view any explanations from Washington as pleas and indications of weakness that would reinforce its determination.

Of these three uncertainties, the gravity of the decision to return strike aircraft to Europe is the strongest justification for leaving them in place and reducing conventional ground forces first if necessary. This viewpoint is reinforced conversely by the presumed Soviet reasoning in pressing for a solution of the FBS question—namely, by securing a withdrawal of even a portion of the US strike aircraft, the SACEUR Strike Plan would be more psychologically discredited than militarily dismembered. But the effect could be the same. The Europeans could lose further confidence in US credibility and Washington could feel compelled under certain circumstances to withhold its Polaris submarines for second-strike purposes.

An element of agreement was reached apparently during SALT I about the relationship of the FBS issue to the larger context of strategic arms limitations. Both sides seem to have agreed that if US territory was granted immunity from nuclear attack by a great power, then the USSR should be granted the same degree of sanctuary. The implication was that the great powers could exercise mutual restraints regarding nuclear warfare better on a bilateral basis than on a multilateral one, even though there was no question of either one transferring nuclear weapons to their respective allies before the outbreak of hostilities. Full implementation of such an understanding would deny NATO partners warheads for any systems that could strike the USSR. The difficulties in assessing the impact such a denial would have on the Alliance and in gaining a corresponding reduction in the Soviet threat to Western Europe were the most likely reasons for delaying further deliberation on the matter during SALT I.

But the US made an important unilateral concession as evidence of its good faith on this ussue to which the USSR attached such importance, agreeing informally to suspend nuclearization of all follow-on systems for obsolete NATO systems that had a "strategic" range. The F-4s presently being purchased by the FRG are all nonnuclear. Other allies presently seeking replacements for the F-104 are being offered only conventional aircraft. While no formal ban on modernizing NATO tactical aircraft has been reached, all parties realize the enormous costs and time required to reconfigure a conventional model for a nuclear role. If this policy persists, the nonnuclear NATO countries will be denied their present "strategic" responsibilities under the Strike Plan roughly by 1975, the expected end of SALT II. The NATO partners were reportedly informally told at the Copenhagen Meeting that a unilateral nuclear "freeze" had been imposed on all NATO systems in the FBS category.

Far more important than their sacrificed responsibility under the Strike Plan is the erosion of these countries' ability to use these systems for nuclear interdiction missions on non-Soviet territory—their primary mission today. For example, the FRG will lose the service of six wings of strike aircraft and be reduced to only one hundred nonreplaceable Pershing missiles. Moreover, the nuclear interdiction role will become almost exclusively the responsibility of the United States, an uncomfortable dependency for many Europeans.

The relevant questions now facing the West Europeans are:

1. Since the nuclear "freeze" on European FBSs will eventually eliminate the commitment of the nonnuclear NATO's responsibility to the SACEUR Strike Plan, will their influence in theater nuclear policy be proportionally reduced?
2. If their territory is likely to be the first violated or the target of nuclear weapons, what level of authority should they rightfully exercise over Alliance nuclear strategy?
3. Are the new generation of US battlefield nuclear weapons efficient enough to assure tactical success, or must the battlefield be interdicted with nuclear weapons to provide that confidence?
4. Does the necessarily increased reliance on US FBSs inherent in the "freeze" improve the prospects for a successful tactical outcome by lowering the level of violence, or does it spell disaster by reducing the deterrence to the opponent's conventional preponderance?
5. Without the negotiating burden of the Allies' FBS, will the US be more prone to trade off its own FBSs for limits on Soviet warhead proliferation— an issue that has only marginal application to European security?
6. What assurance do the Europeans have that the US will attach the same priority they do to symmetrical reduction of NATO FBSs and Soviet medium-range delivery vehicles?
7. Does not elimination of the FBSs or even their redeployment rearward reduce the Strike Plan and NATO nuclear policy to virutal insignificance?

Thus the political and psychological implications of the FBSs is far graver for the Western Alliance than their military effectiveness. It is uncertain whether the Soviets divined from the outset the magnitude of the FBS dilemma for the West, but they are likely to press the advantages that are now discernible. Indeed, they can be expected to try to focus SALT II heavily on this issue, possibly at the expense of MIRVs.

The military implications of SALT I and II are likely to have far-reaching ramifications on the purely technical aspects of arms control, strategic force postures of smaller nuclear powers, and long-range US strategic objectives. But persistent uncertainties will influence the negotiations; after years of experience, the scientific and technical properties and side effects of certain high-performance weapons systems fundamental to NATO deterrence still remain the subjects of extensive speculation. The duration and lethality of ionization clouds, Electro-

Magnetic Pulse effects, penetrability, warhead insulation, and reliability of radars and communications in a nuclear environment are all subject to laboratory calculations and conjecture. For example, the general apprehension for several years about the Soviet submarine ballistic missile threat was the so-called "pin-down effect." Soviet warheads need not be detonated on ICBM sites at the outset of hostilities, but at synchronized intervals at high altitudes along the known climb-out trajectories of all US ICBMs. The X-rays released in the ionization cloud could penetrate the missile and disarm the electronic circuitry in the warhead, rendering it useless. Because of the present limited Nuclear Test Ban Treaty, the US cannot conduct experiments on ionization effects, and there is no agreed position among American scientists about the potency of this threat or the effectiveness of prescribed countermeasures. Pessimists claim that the US ICBM forces will be unable to launch through the cloud and will remain "pinned down" in their silos until the heavy Soviet ICBM impact.[11]

Scientific uncertainties aside, the position of third parties, the smaller nuclear powers, is likely to remain just beneath the surface of SALT II deliberations. The Soviets have expressed repeatedly their apprehension about the growing Chinese nuclear capability. During SALT I the Soviet side pressed the United States to accept an anti-Chinese nuclear pact—a pledge for joint retaliation in the event of a Chinese attack against either party.[12] Leonid Brezhnev sought to broaden the joint curb to include all nuclear powers during his summit conference in the United States in June 1973.[13] The United States declined to participate in a anti-Chinese understanding, but agreed to a broader commitment for consultations regarding nuclear provocations from any nuclear power. This concession was due in part to Washington's own inability to assure its allies' respect for or acceptance of SALT-type restraints on their independent nuclear forces.

The French Nuclear Contribution

The French *force de dissuasion,* always a difficult foster child for the United States, is likely to become an even more problematic factor for the great powers and the NATO members if SALT negotiations cannot satisfy the Europeans' anxieties about the FBS issue. The motivation behind France's independent nuclear power was based on de Gaulle's belief that the risks of thermonuclear war were so great that no state would be willing to take them unless its interests were directly imperiled. Thus the possession of a small deterrent by a threatened state was worth more than a large strike force of a purportedly protective ally. The merits of collective security, therefore, were marginal. In the event collective security failed, as the Gaullists predicted, the security of each member would depend upon the errors and weaknesses of its adversaries. The only two states not affected by this formula were the US and the USSR. They had established sanctuaries unassailable by lesser powers, a new criteria for national security. It was natural, then, for states in the "subordinate" position to seek the elevated, more secure status of a sanctuary.[14]

> Behind this explicit argument is another which is, quite certainly, General de Gaulle's deeper reasoning: That a state ceases to exist as a state to the extent that it is deprived of the means of self-defense. That this purely national defense might be insufficient without the help of allies is possible, but this insufficiency is no reason for abandoning it. In other words, to de Gaulle's way of thinking a *défense nationale* is as much an end as a means. Even if it afforded less protection than America's atomic might, he would go on demanding it, since it is the symbol and consecration of France's political self-affirmation.[15]

In the words of one American analyst,

> The logical out-growth of the American strategy, which seeks to reduce the automaticity of nuclear response to aggression and cushion the successive shocks that could lead to a nuclear exchange, has been to create pressure from those European allies who disagree with that strategy for greater control over the nuclear weapons. And the US reluctance to yield a degree of control satisfactory to the allies may have reinforced previous tendencies to maintain or create national nuclear forces.[16]

Thus, in the ensuing diplomatic jockeying that dominated Alliance politics for over a decade, the US was striving for strategic options and de Gaulle was seeking political ones.[17]

Throughout the past decade, France placed top priority on the creation of an operational nuclear capability that was to provide this political stature. This force presently has a first-line strength of 36 Mirage IVA 1200-mile-range mach 2.5 aircraft capable of low-level penetration with 70-kiloton atomic bombs (three to four times the yield of the Hiroshima weapon). The range of these aircraft can be extended to 2500 miles at optimum altitude by 12 US C-135F tankers for aerial refueling. This force can be dispersed to about ten unsheltered bases in southern France and is directed from a hardened command post at Taverny. Construction is completed for two intermediate-range (1875 miles) missile complexes, each housing nine missiles in silos hardened to 300 psi. They are located in Haute-Provence north of Marseilles and will be capable of delivering 150-KT warheads into Western USSR. A third site of nine missiles has also been started. The *force de dissuasion* is also programed to receive five Fleet Ballistic Missile Submarines (FBMS) by 1975; two are presently operational and carry 16 Polaris A-1 type SLBMs. The French nuclear program has already cost over

$12.7 billion (the Mirage IV force with ordnance costing nearly $2 billion), and is expected to total well over $16 billion by the time it reaches the target of 100 megatons in 1975.

France's nuclear force is the victim of several inherent weaknesses. Its first-generation deterrent, the Mirage IV, is subject to many variables. Air speeds are seriously reduced and fuel consumption is roughly tripled at low levels. If denied refueling over the FRG or East European airspace because of the superiority of hostile air defenses, the Mirage can not reach key targets. Even if it refuels over the Adriatic and penetrates neutral Austrian or Yugoslav defenses, it can not hit Kiev, and refueling over the Baltic it cannot penetrate beyond Leningrad. Second, the Mirage force is vulnerable to a preemptive strike. A maximum twelve-ship force could remain on aerial alert for an extended period, but the remainder would survive only through random dispersal (not to predetermined auxilliary bases). This would be a complicated maneuver and would seriously compound the command and control problem, and yet would be subject to enemy satellite surveillance after only a short period. Third, even if the Mirage force was successfully dispersed to twenty additional bases, it could still be struck by only 5 percent of the USSR's first-generation SS-4s and SS-5s with one-megaton warheads, or by MRV-equipped second-generation intermediate-range missiles, representing less than 1 percent of the total Soviet 2000-plus MRBM-ICBM force. Fourth, the addition of eighteen to twenty-seven more targets when the French MRBMs become fully operational will not seriously complicate Soviet plans. For maintenance and servicing economies, the total force is confined to an area less than 200 square miles, an optimum siting for MIRV coverage or MRV triangulation. Thus the tremendous costs to produce France's second-generation nuclear capability can probably be neutralized with a 0.9 probability of kill by an expenditure of 0.1 to 0.5 percent of the USSR's total missile inventory.[18]

Fifth, if five Fleet Ballistic Missile Submarines are constructed by 1975, France will be approaching an invulnerable capability. But at best only two boats will be on-station at once; during periods of prolonged tensions, a third might possibly be at sea. The accidental loss of one on-station boat would be even more crippling than the crash of six Mirages in Spain in 1967. (It is not comforting in this regard to note that the French Navy has the worst submarine safety record of any modern navy). And by 1975, Soviet sonar tracking capabilities should improve to the point that departures of FMBSs from their two bases can be readily monitored by hostile U-boats. Moreover, even if the maximum number of FBMSs were on-station during hostilities, they could not be used as the strategy of the *force de dissuasion* envisioned, i.e., in single salvo launches to induce conflict termination. When one missile is launched; the position of the remaining fifteen becomes known.[19]

Sixth, the 100-megaton target is in itself not enough to insure self-sufficiency. In development of penetration aids, MIRV warheads and missile defenses, France is likely to remain at least one decade behind its adversary. France's vital communications for its nuclear force are likely to remain vulnerable and its heavy dependence upon US and NATO for tactical and strategic warning will likely persist indefinitely. Finally, none of these inherent weaknesses take into account the probable attrition rates Soviet air and missile defenses are likely to inflict.

Thus, the mere acquisition of nuclear power has not afforded assured deterrence. Nuclear weapons are not the "equalizers" formerly envisioned between small states and the great powers. Even in the nuclear age, the relationship between defense and offense remains relatively constant, i.e., the range and weight of arms determine the radius of defenses and the size of fortified areas. Without adequate defenses or a credible first-strike capability, the Franch nuclear effort remains just that—an effort of dubious military consequences. Its initial conception did not incorporate an important axiom of military strategy: a credible war doctrine cannot be devised independent from that of the potential enemy or countermeasures improvised that do not take his strategy into account. As McNamara warned years ago, the threat of an incredible action, such as launching an inconsequential independent nuclear strike, is not an effective deterrent. Indeed, the very existence of a marginal force invites national suicide, not self-affirmation.

As a result, de Gaulle failed to achieve both the minimum and maximum aims of his nuclear force. France's possession of nuclear power has not guaranteed access to privileged knowledge held by the super powers. It has been excluded from NATO's Nuclear Planning Group, the focal point of Alliance nuclear policy formation originally envisioned in de Gaulle's proposed nuclear triumvirate. West Germany now plays a more influential role in determining strategy and nuclear policy for the Western world than France. Through consignment to the periphery of Alliance strategy formation, France has also not been able to enhance its international stature during crises in the 1960s that did not directly affect its vital interests—from Cuba to Prague to the Suez. Even when the *force de dissuasion* reaches maturity in 1975, the United States will be more likely to deter to German than to French interests in any crisis in Central Europe. Thus, France's nuclear stature has increased neither its authority among its allies nor its deterrence against its adversaries.

The reason for the ineffectuality of the French force was its conceptual obsolescense, demonstrated even before it was fully deployed. Originally it was envisioned that the French force would be dispersed and relatively invulnerable, so that a major nuclear adversary could destroy it only by expending so much of its own capabilities that he could no longer deter the smaller power's major ally. On the other hand, by preempting it was supposed to reduce the adversary's forces sufficiently to make it vulnerable to attack to the rival great power. The inability of the French force to perform either mission indicates how little it can contribute independently to the overall security of the United States or the Alliance. Its only strategic leverage against the U.S. is the possibility

of irresponsible actions. Gaullist writers insist that political independence is a
function of strategic independence.[20] The inconsequence of the French force
employed unilaterally and its dependence upon foreign support systems even
for marginal effectiveness reveal the obsolescense of the concept and its irrelevance to the future course of European developments. Many Europeans now
conclude that the French nuclear capability is politically useful, but to a marginal extent, only in its relations with the FRG—a tiny step only toward its
original objective.

Prospects for a European Nuclear Force

The futility of such a small independent nuclear force has raised repeated
speculation about the feasibility of creating a joint Anglo-French basis for a
European Nuclear Force (EUNUFOR). The British could make a decisive con-
tribution to the viability of a EUNUFOR. It presently has 4 FBMS with 16
Polaris A-3 (MRV warheads) and its own Ballistic Missile Early Warning System.
For tactical operations, the UK has one carrier with two strike squadrons; eight
Vulcan medium bomber squadrons that could still be used in strike roles; three
Buccaneer strike squadrons; and possibly four F-4M strike squadrons. This is
several times the number of strike aircraft and total payload available to France.
Moreover, the British retain use of US nuclear artillery, Lance and Honest John
SSM warheads, which the French now have been denied and cannot fully replace
by the introduction of their 75-mile-range Pluton SSM.
      Thus, the British have substantial assets in both strategic and tactical
nuclear forces. Its Polaris SLBMs have over twice the range, one third more
throw-weight, and three times more warheads than the French counterpart,
the MSBS M-1. The Buccaneer is equal to the Mirage IV-A in both range and
payload. The F-4M has double the maximum weapons load of the Mirage.
Finally, the British force has greater survivability. The future of the present
force will depend partly on a decision whether to accept the obsolescense of its
Polaris SLBM and abandon its submarine role, or to purchase the Poseidon SLBM
with its MIRV warheads.
      Numerous proposals have been raised about an appropriate framework and
division of labor for a EUNUFOR. The erection of a joint political authority
with two military planning staffs for naval and air systems under primarily
British and French respective responsibility is the most plausible suggestion.
Such a joint authority could formulate political guidelines for joint release of
nuclear weapons and targeting criteria for weapons assignment. The contribution
nonnuclear powers could make to this force would be financial aid and manu-
factured components for supporting systems. On political and military planning
aspects they could participate at a level commensurate to their knowledgability
about weapons characteristics and the nuclear powers' decision to allocate a
delivery capability to nonnuclear forces.

Problematic but not insurmountable impediments emerged as the Europeans undertook serious assessment of a EUNUFOR. The French object to participation in a formal arrangement. The size of the present force is too small to wield equal political weight with the British. Such an association would inevitably undermine the philosophical arguments about sovereignty upon which an independent national nuclear capability is based. On their side, the British see no need to consider seriously any proposal that might jeopardize their continuing special relationship with the United States until the advantages are clearly worthwhile. The FRG has refused to date to become the financier of a EUNUFOR without a "seat on the Board of Directors." The Germans expect the same degree of confidentiality from the European nuclear powers it enjoys with the United States. They insist upon a full exchange of views on weapons characteristics and targeting philosophies. The accepted manifestation of mutual trust in security matters is the allocation of nuclear delivery capabilities by a nuclear to a nonnuclear power. The French have categorically refused to allow German participation in any way in the *force de dissuasion.* Bonn has asked on several occasions for the weapons spectrum of the Pluton, a tactical SSM that can only be detonated on German territory until the French Army advances to the Polish frontier. France's repeated refusal to divulge such information has led to the cynical observation that French nuclear policy is designed as much against German as Soviet interests.

Under these circumstances, the prospects for a EUNUFOR are dim indeed. The most that can be expected is a slight improvement in coordination of target allocations and weapons assignment, with each government retaining undiminished authority over its national nuclear forces. But without greater assurance of joint, coordinated action, this is an insufficient boost for European confidence.

With this option barren, the NATO partners have little choice but to continue reliance on the United States, despite the seeming decline in priorities the US attaches to European security. Many Europeans are now convinced that the FBS issue and the impending damage to NATO's nuclear punch is likely to create an alliance crisis of major proportions. Factors that could ameliorate European anxieties will be difficult to produce. Possibly two areas hold some promise: development of a more efficient tactical nuclear capability and doctrine that could provide high confidence in the credibility of European defenses; and development of systematically programed long-range strategic objectives that can provide NATO the assurance that individual security interests are mutually compatible, and the certitude that ends are no longer the product of a haphazard pursuit of random means. The first factor, the development of a tactical nuclear doctrine, has traditionally been the more controversial of the two and a key source of Alliance malaise. The necessity for allied consensus has reinforced US indifference and may gradually shift American priority to the second factor. The US has traditionally shown a proclivity for formulating

defense policy at the strategic level and in a post-SALT II era may be
compelled to intensify its attention on this plane. (For a detailed discussion
of tactical nuclear questions see Chapter 13.)

Strategic Planning Objectives

The difficulties in formulating systematic long-range strategic objectives
were identified in part by President Nixon when he foresaw the need for a reassessment of national security policy and requested appraisals of several per-
tinent questions: What doctrine is appropriate for US strategic forces in an era
when the threat of massive retaliation alone is no longer credible in all circumstances and decisive nuclear superiority is probably unattainable? What should
the relationship be between the programs required for maintaining our strength
and proposals for limiting strategic arms through negotiations? How can we
simultaneously satisfy pressing domestic needs, meet our responsibilities abroad,
and maintain the credibility of our forces in a period when nonnuclear challenges
are an important dimension of the security problem? And how can we, in coordination with our allies, strengthen our mutual defense in a manner that
retains their confidence in our reliability but permits them to play a more
prominent role?[21]

The linkage between credibility of force structures and commitments and
strategic objectives was demonstrated when the Soviet capability to construct
250 ICBMs annually forced the United States to acknowledge its loss of nuclear supremacy and to define a set of strategic aims within the limits of its
existing resources. The resulting formula for a posture of "sufficiency" was,
however, a hybrid of former concepts. Sufficiency consisted of four criteria:

1. Assured destruction: The United States would at all times have the capability
    to respond with high confidence to a Soviet surprise attack of the United
    States homeland and to destroy a substantial part of Soviet society.
2. Crisis stability: Strategic forces of the United States would be designed not
    to create instability during a crisis whereby one or both sides would be
    tempted to launch a preemptive nuclear attack.
3. Relative advantage: The United States would seek to avoid a situation in
    which the Soviet Union might be able to gain a substantial advantage in
    terms of relative destruction in a nuclear war.
4. Damage denial: The United States would develop a capability for denying
    other powers, including China, the ability to inflict damage on the United
    States with their strategic nuclear forces.[22]

(Supporters of the Jackson Amendment to the ratification of the 1972 ABM
Treaty voiced reservations about strategic security, claiming that criteria 3 and
4 had been sacrificed during SALT I. The amendment put the administration

and the Soviets on notice that a strong body of American sentiment held that national security required restored credibility in all standards of sufficiency.)

Whether or not the posture of sufficiency has retained its plausibility will remain open to debate. More to the point, it lacks the perspective and flexibility to serve as an outline for long-term goals—its utility has been in providing guidance for interim objectives. A. W. Marshall has devised a more elaborate schema that goes beyond the conditions of sufficiency. The principal aim of his approach is to control and guide the character of ongoing strategic arms competition in a manner that will preserve stability, remain consistent with arms control negotiations, improve US military efficiency, enhance US competitiveness, and complicate Soviet problems of maintaining competitive positions.[23] Since both competitors have relatively fixed resources over any given short period of time and numerous complications in internal decision-making processes, strategic objectives should be intentionally designed to slow and diffuse the opponent's ability to react to technological opportunities and to reduce the efficiency with which resources are used. In devising such a strategy several questions must be asked at the outset. What are the areas of technology and military operations where the United States has an advantage or disadvantage? Where are Soviet advantages and disadvantages? What problems confront the Soviets, and how can the US move the competition into areas where it has advantages and the Soviets have difficulties? The Soviets have achieved rough parity in strategic weapon systems, and they have also achieved a high degree of parity in the amount of resources allocated to military missions. Over time the US cannot allow the Soviets to use their resources more efficiently than the US does.

Several examples are sufficient to demonstrate the importance of efficiency in arms competition. Strategic parity released medium-range vehicles for missions at the theater level where they can be more efficiently employed. It is estimated that the 500 Tu-16 Badger and 200 Tu-22 Blinder medium-range bombers assigned to the Long Range Air Force have been now tasked with dual missions: 75 percent are assigned targets in NATO and 25 percent allocated to the Far East, as primary missions, with secondary missions as tertiary strike forces against the United States. They could follow the 140 long-range bombers and submarines in their preplanned countervalue second strike with a deliberate follow-on third strike against surviving targets. Likewise, virtually all the 210 diesel-powered submarines have probably now been assigned primary responsibilities in theater waters. These additions substantially increase the nuclear delivery capability of the Soviet forces without the expenditure of new investments. Further, the psychological ramifications for NATO are expected to be more destabilizing than the mere increase in launchers, indicating an additional dimension of the efficiency on this move.

A second illustration of effective moves in arms competition was the US development of Polaris submarines. The Soviets had only two options in countering this new omnidirectional threat: develop a nuclear hunter-killer submarine capability, or construct an antiballistic missile system. Because of the state of their technology at the time, the Soviets felt compelled to invest heavily in both options simultaneously and after ten years still do not have an effective defense against SLBMs.

To pursue the long-term aim of becoming an effective competitor—which Marshall holds the US is not—several measures should be incorporated into Pentagon force planning procedures. More accurate tools of analysis must be devised, possibly with planning gaming techniques, that will illuminate the action-reaction or nonreaction syndrome in arms competition.[24] Greater insight into the Soviet decision-making process and the nature of contending domestic interests is imperative. Model-building techniques should be developed to incorporate alternative Soviet force posture trends. And Bayesian methods for decision-making under uncertainty which permit improved risk balancing should be practiced.[25]

Probably the greatest single area of uncertainty in the arms competition now is general-purpose forces. The impact of the Soviet achievement of rough parity in strategic weapons has been a drastic change in the nature of theater war. The decoupling of strategic forces from tactical commitments has increased the responsibility of local in-place combat forces for the defense of theater interests. This shift of emphasis raises fundamental questions about the relative competitiveness and efficiency of opposing theater forces—a major problem for long-range strategic planners.

11 Parity in Theater Level Forces

In his 3 May 1973 Foreign Policy Report to Congress President Nixon asserted that rough parity existed between NATO and Warsaw Pact forces. Relative force strengths, equipment capabilities, and training levels have been the subject of endless debates among Western officials and analysts. These discrepancies stem both from honest differences about standards of measures and from politically motivated preferences.

Some authorities assume a given level of mobilization and a probable ratio between regular, reservist, and recruit troops. In tallying only in-place first-line units, different formulae are used for the appropriate "division slice," or logistic personnel required to support a combat unit, and the proportion regarded as nonessential in wartime. Accordingly, NATO authorities vary widely in their estimates of Pact troop strengths. For example, Alain Enthoven, former Assistant Secretary of Defense, has testified before Congress that NATO has 30 percent more men under arms than the Pact (5,470,100 vs. 4,200,000), and that NATO has more manpower presently available in the Central Region than the Pact (677,000 to 619,000). "Even at the rifle platoon level, NATO has as many men immediately available as the Pact."[1] On the pessimistic side, former British Defense Minister Dennis Healey has announced that "NATO is outnumbered by the Pact on the Central Front by more than two to one in infantry formations and nearly three to one in armored formations; after mobilization of first-line reserves, this disparity increases. Pact superiority in aircraft is nearly two to one." Mr. Healey admits,

> A Russian division has only about half the strength in manpower of a NATO division, NATO forces have a superiority of 50 percent in antitank weapons, NATO has a higher proportion of multi-purpose aircraft than the Pact and NATO aircraft are superior in factors such as range, payload, loiter time and crew training. No one would deny the need to take qualitative factors into account, but we are still a long way from deciding which factors are relevant and what values should be attached to them. What is clear is that the Warsaw Pact has advantages in two particular respects so great as to render doubtful any prospect that NATO might have of putting up a successful conventional defense for more than a few days. These advantages are in numbers of tanks and surprise. Strength in armor is likely to be decisive in any

operations in the Central Front, especially in the open country
of North Germany. . . . This advantage is compounded by the
advantage gained by the Soviet Union from the fact that she
would be the aggressor.[2]

Such diametrically opposing views illustrate the inconsistencies prevalent at
the highest levels about standards for estimating the threat to national security.
After two decades of exhaustive deliberations, no consensus on criteria has
been established.

Comparative studies of relative force strengths are not only confronted with
the problem of criteria for measurement, but more important they must resolve
the relative advantages arising from the existing asymmetries in force structures,
dispositions, and missions. The organization, equipment, and deployment of the
various forces have been designed to capitalize on national assets and the
opponents' perceived weaknesses. In reality other influences, such as national
weapons production capabilities and limitations, foreign procurements for
economic or political reasons, public image of the army forces, and foreign
policy constraints on national defense policy, may be even more important in
determining force structures.

In the period of assured US strategic superiority, calculations of asymmetrical disparities could be made in imprecise terms. To offset imbalances in
specific categories or the possibility of underestimation, deterrence at the
theater level was linked directly to the US strategic response capability, with
in-place tactical nuclear warheads as a secondary reassurance. The Soviet
achievement of strategic parity has decoupled intercontinental responses from
tactical or theater requirements. In-place combat forces now have a much greater
relevance in the defense of theater interests. This increased importance of line
units has coincided with the movement toward Mutual Balanced Force
Reduction. Both factors have contributed to a reexamination of comparative
strengths and disparities. Formerly such exercises were initiated to determine
deficiencies that must be corrected or offset to insure deterrence. The renewed
efforts attempt to ascertain the degree of parity that exists and the areas where
reductions can be made without impairing security.

Assorted Asymmetries

The most obvious asymmetry lies in the geographic configuration of the
alliances. The Pact is a classical continental coalition based primarily on ground
forces to defend an intact concentric front from the Arctic to the Black Sea. It
enjoys relatively secure internal lines of communications and has no overseas
territories, outposts, or commitments that are vulnerable to attack or for which
it will risk war. Finally, it has the necessary self-sufficiency in natural resources
and war materiale to wage a war of attrition.

The Atlantic Alliance, on the other hand, is a maritime coalition that must rely heavily on naval forces to sustain its land forces. Its fifteen members are scattered around the North Atlantic and Mediterranean basins. They enjoy multiple contiguous frontiers only in the relatively small and confined area of the Central Front. As maritime nations, most NATO states are heavily dependent upon sea transportation for the components for industrial production and, to a lesser extent, for foodstuffs. The least dependent on mercantile interests is the United States, then Canada, France, and West Germany. Despite the expansion of the Common Market and the aggregation of a GNP 80 percent that of the United States, the Central Front countries, West Germany, Benelux, and possibly France, cannot fight a war of attrition. They lack geographic depth: their lines of communication are subject to interdiction and their industries are vulnerable to air attack. Only when the vast resources of "Fortress America" can be brought to bear on a continental conflict can a war of attrition be feasibly waged by NATO. This requires sufficient control of the high seas for mobilization and deployment of reserves and resources with minimum inter- ference. This is a formidable task, especially since any member of the Alliance, from Turkey to Norway, may be subject to any level of attack, requiring Ameri- can reinforcement. Clearly the West has substantial geographic liabilities that must be compensated for in other facets of defense.

Population resources and total men under arms are often cited as amelio- rating factors for such discrepancies. Total ground forces presently under arms for NATO (including France) are 3,091,000; for the Pact, 2,806,000.[3] These figures include Soviet forces in the Far East and American units in the Pacific and continental United States (CONUS). They also include the 34,000-man Canadian Army, deployed over 4000 miles at home and 3000 miles from any possible engagement. NATO totals also include the 328,000-man French Army, which may not be committed, and the 306,000-man Italian ground forces that can only aid the Central Front with difficulty—indeed, the bulk of the Italian forces cannot engage the enemy until *after* the Central Front has collapsed. The 18,000-man Norwegian Army is concentrated in the more populated southern portion, leaving the middle and northern sectors vulnerable to even battalion-level attacks—only one brigade holds the northern sector against four Soviet divisions. Finally, the Portuguese Army of 179,000 is partially confined to Africa and the remainder is irrelevant to any conceivable NATO engagements. These disparities are underscored when the numbers of in-place combat and direct support troops during peacetime are calculated. Excluding French and Portuguese forces and reserves in Britain, the United States, and Canada, there are 580,000 land forces assigned to Northern and Central Europe and 1,000,000 Pact forces, of which 650,000 are Soviet troops, including such units in the Western USSR Military Districts that would likely be committed. In Southern NATO, figures include Italian, Greek, Turkish land forces and assigned British and American units, and total 530,000 ground forces. Warsaw Pact forces in Hungary, Rumania, and Bulgaria and such Soviet units in Hungary and southern

Russia that might be committed total 350,000, of which 90,000 would probably be Soviet.[4]

But peacetime figures are only partially relevant to anticipated strengths at given levels of hostilities. Again, estimates of mobilization and reinforcement capabilities and rates vary widely. In total armed forces there has been a substantial change in manpower levels for both the US and USSR over the past two decades. In 1952 the US had 3.5 million men under arms and the USSR had 4.6 million. In 1960 the US reduced its forces to 2.514 million and the USSR to 3.623 million. Subsequent increases for the US peaked in 1968 at 3.547 million and then fell to 2.2 million in 1973. Soviet forces fell to 3.15 million in 1965, then climbed steadily to 3.375 in 1972. US forces are thus about one million men below those of the USSR, a differential Moscow has consistently maintained.

Despite such wide discrepancies in in-place forces, one point seems irrefutable: the relative overall advantage of each side is likely to be a function of the degree of mobilization it can achieve before hostilities and that can be sustained during the conflict. The pace of mobilization is dependent upon the length of political warning time, logistic capabilities, and the level of initial hostilities. Enthoven makes the startling revelation that NATO has a greater reinforcement capability that the Pact. "No less important," he concludes, "NATO can maintain this rough equality during a build-up of forces on both sides. While the Pact has certain advantages in reinforcing the Central Region during a mobilization, these are not large enough to attain a decisive force ratio.[5]

Such rationale can be faulted on several points. The number of logistic and administrative personnel required to support Pact combat elements is substantially lower than the number required in NATO armed forces, especially American. Since Soviet equipment is more rugged and less sophisticated, more of the total troop strength can be assigned to combat rather than support functions. (The reason for the higher proportion of support to combat personnel in American armed forces is that these units are manned to provide optimum heavy maintenance abroad rather than in domestic depots, as do the continental forces. These discrepancies are being slowly redressed under the "heavy brigade" concept, whereby two service companies are replaced by weapons companies in each brigade.) The different levels of maintenance inherent in deployed units reflect divergent views of the mission of ground forces, as well as the pace of mobilization that can be expected.

Enthoven's last assumption that NATO has a larger physical reinforcement capability is apparently based upon the assumption that both would perceive a danger nearly simultaneously, that the coalitions would promptly reach consensus about the opponent's hostile intentions and would authorize mobilization at a maximum rate, i.e. a level allowing unimpeded deliveries from continental United States. NATO reactions during the Czechoslovak crisis indicate the difficulties in defining the adversaries' intensions and authorizing appropriate countermeasures. A more realistic scenario than Enthoven's might be that Moscow would seek reasonable assurance that important segments of the NATO Council could be neutralized by a crisis. Then, by clandestinely initiating partial mobilization plans at a leisurely pace, an advantage could be gained. When the West finally responded, the Pact could quickly move to full mobilization, transporting as many as 100,000 men with equipment per week into the Forward Area. The success of such an operation would depend upon the degree of secrecy and deception achieved during the initial phase, avoiding a World War I type of race for mobilization. Indeed, it is conceivable that the Pact could even secure such a preponderance that it might attempt to blackmail subregions of NATO with only conventional arms.

The plausibility of such a scenario was demonstrated during the 1968 operations against Czechoslovakia. From this evidence, it must be concluded that the Pact is far ahead of NATO in organization and training of reserves and mobilization experience. The Pact relies heavily on reservists to flesh out existing understrength second-line divisions and to form third echelon units. Their mobilization is frequently exercised, and indeed ten full divisions reportedly participated in the Czechoslovakia operations.[6] Moreover, rear services are also periodically exercised, providing experience that allowed the Pact to sustain 100,000 men in the field for three months in 1968 and then to launch an "offensive" without major logistic dislocations. (The units involved in initial deployments on 7–8 May probably had only short notice, since the decision to use military pressure was probably not made until after Dubcek's return from Moscow on 5 May.)

Rather than rapid mobilization from a well-prepared reserve posture, NATO has emphasized immediate readiness and nuclear retaliation. (There are few reserve units in Western Europe and the only comprehensive program is in the United States, over 3000 miles from the battlefield.) The reason for European reluctance to embark upon a large-scale program for ready mobilization has been their abiding faith in NATO's ability to provide adequate political warning so that the laborious process of converting to a wartime economy could be achieved. NATO governments' confidence that they can accept the risks of a complete Soviet surprise attack is based in part on the minimal fear voiced in Western Europe about a premeditated Soviet attack. What frightens many is the possibility that new eruptions in Eastern Europs, à la Hungary, East Germany, and Czechoslovakia, and the Soviet reprisals, might expand across the Iron Curtain. In no instance, however, have the NATO partners concurred on an accurate prediction of Soviet intentions regarding even limited use of force, neither in Budapest, Berlin, nor Prague. The invasion of Czechoslovakia has now raised grave doubts about the wisdom of permitting NATO strategy to remain dependent upon a period of warning. "Political warnings" might be ambiguous at best. Mobilization and plans for an invasion of West Germany could be hidden under the cloak of Warsaw Pact maneuvers, and the availability of reliable intelligence does not guarantee accurate evaluation of its meaning.[7] Indeed, no political guidelines have been formulated that would allow NATO planners to determine when simple alert might be a provocation and when it would be a precaution. This is a dilemma primarily for the Western side; a NATO surprise attack is simply inconceivable.

Discrepancies in Defense Spending

Comparisons of defense expenditures to national economies also reveal marked discrepancies. While there has been a steady growth in GNP in both alliances (the USSR remains at one half that of the US GNP), there has also been a general decline in the per cent of GNP allocated for defense in NATO countries and rise among Pact states. The US defense budget rose from $78.7 billion in 1971 to $83.4 billion in 1972. But as a percentage of GNP, defense fell from 9.3 in 1968 to 7.3 in 1971. During the same period, the USSR percentage remained the same. Other Pact countries rose one or two percentage points, to a high of 5.9 for East Germany and 5.8 for Czechoslovakia. In NATO countries percentages fell by two to three points, e.g., Canada from 2.7 to 1.8; France, 4.8 to 3.1; FRG, 3.6 to 2.8; Greece, 4.9 to 3.3; and Turkey, 4.5 to 3.3. These percentages for 1971 were substantially lower than those of most Middle East states, e.g., Egypt, 21.7; Iran, 8.5; Iraq, 6.5; Israel, 23.9; Jordan, 11.3; Saudi Arabia, 8.9; Sudan, 7.4; and Syria, 9.8. When defense expenditures per capita are compared, national variations are even sharper. Figures for Bulgaria, Hungary, and Rumania are less than half those for Czechoslovakia and East Germany. They are roughly equivalent to those for Greece and Portugal, but two of three times higher than for Turkey. They are also about the same for those of representative nonaligned nations.[8]

Several generalizations can be drawn from these and related figures. The military resources and expenditures in terms of real assets or economic capabilities are sharply divided in both alliances along lines of national preferences. Length of service, size of armed forces, and the percentage of men of military age in service also seem to reflect nonmilitary imperatives, to the point that no standard criteria exist on either side. Military manpower levels of the southern Pact members are the same or lower than most nonaligned nations, and defense expenditures for all East European states is four to six times less than those of Egypt or Israel; yet all these states started at approximately equal training and equipment levels in the mid-1950s.

From these observations it appears that national peculiarities, historical, geostrategic, and economic imperatives, have precluded establishment of alliance-wide consensuses on the nature of the threat or the importance of global security commitments. In other words, the temperatures of the Cold war have fluctuated rather sharply among the respective allies, forcing both great powers to assume reluctantly correspondingly greater defense burdens. Both have complained for years to their respective allies about the imbalance in burden-sharing.[9]

Weapons Characteristics

Equipment levels are particularly difficult to estimate. For accuracy they must be comprehensive, including effectiveness, reliability, serviceability, handling characteristics, interoperability, susceptibility to countermeasures, and life expectancy. These characteristics determine a weapon's military efficiency. Because of the complexity of modern weapons systems, only technicians can make the required estimates. But the composite of a single service's estimate is often the product of personal persuasiveness, previous military experience, and professed political insight into enemy intentions. At the all-service level, individual weapons estimates can be diluted by the challenge of competing systems, imperatives of resource management, and domestic and international political factors. Paradoxically, this weapons-estimating syndrome applies to a surprising degree to both friendly and opposing weapons. Estimates of opponents' weapons are clouded by normal shrouds of secrecy. Estimates of friendly weapons may be qualified by the inability to perform tests in combat conditions, e.g., the ABM system. In the West, friendly estimates are also complicated by the lack of standardization; there are several thousand different motor vehicles alone in NATO inventories. Thus, weapons capabilities are probably the most difficult single factor in the comparative force strengths to calculate with confidence.

Yet broad observations can still be safely made. Several illustrations without the technical specifications will demonstrate the general contours of weapons estimating. In Northern and Central Europe, there are 16,000 Pact main battle tanks in peacetime, compared to only 6000 NATO tanks. Pact forces are rapidly transitioning to the T-62. The Soviets have traded cruising range for gun caliber. The number and caliber equate into a maximum mobile shock force. NATO's armored deficiency stems from its primarily defensive mission and recent improvements in individual antitank weapons. Shoulder-fired antitank missiles can now defeat any movable armor. The remaining difficulties are training, munition replenishment, and mobility. When mounted on Cobra helicopters, TOW missiles were highly effective against tanks in South Vietnam and in field exercises, scoring as high as 30 to 1 kill ratios. Important advantages have apparently shifted from the offensive to the defense on the battlefield.

In the air war, the US designed the F-4 Phantom as the optimum tactical aircraft. It has extended loiter time for the reconnaissance role, unrivaled range and payload in the fighter-bomber class, both conventional and nuclear potentiality, and an interceptor option. The Soviet Union has neglected the fighter-bomber mission. It has developed limited medium bomber and nuclear missile forces for deep penetration strikes. This composite does not have the versatility to match NATO's long-range fighter-bombers. (Soviet medium bomber force of TU-16 and TU-22 would most logically be used for conventional attacks only through the opening days of hostilities and then withheld and dispersed as a secondary or tertiary nuclear follow-on force.) In air superiority aircraft, however, the Soviets are ahead in some categories of interception.

The MIG-25 Foxbat and SU-11 Flaggon B have superior speeds, altitude, and avionics to the F-4E. Israeli F-4s were unable to engage Soviet MIG-25s over the Sinai because of altitude limitations, and the Foxbat has a "look-down, shoot-down" radar and missile fire control capability that is not operational in the West. The Foxbat is a long-range interceptor designed to counter the B-52 and B-1 threat. Both the Flaggon B and the Phantom are tactical interceptors designed primarily to counter bombers and fighter-bombers, and are not air-superiority aircraft in the true sense. When the F-15 becomes operational, it will have comparable specifications. But because of Soviet tactical deployments, high-performance interceptors are confined to the USSR beyond the range of European-based F-15s. These incongruities in performance capabilities are a product of the long lead time required to design, test, modify, and produce advanced weapons systems. Changes in prescribed threats accelerate the obsolescence of single mission systems, forcing producers to either perfect threat estimates or develop more versatile but less efficient systems.

Command Experience and Military Proficiency

Asymmetrics also exist in training levels and methods of leadership. American forces have received extensive combat experience in Southeast Asia. They have been able to test and modify equipment and procedures under the pressure of active hostilities. This experience generated new command and control techniques, revolutionary bombing tactics, and drastic changes in concepts of logistic support. Most important, it provided a seasoning ground for the individual American serviceman. The Seventh Army in Europe includes a large percentage of veteran soldiers and NCOs, and is heavily engaged in digesting and applying the lessons of Vietnam (including the drug and race problems).

It is more difficult to estimate the training levels of peacetime armed forces. No Soviet unit has experienced combat since 1956. For nearly thirty years training has been conducted largely in the artificial environment of simulated hostilities. For example, Soviet ground forces reportedly conduct more extensive training in chemical and nuclear warfare than do NATO units. But Pact aircrews fly fewer hours. Because of less expensive unit costs, the Soviets have retained their preference for single mission systems and have been able to build sufficient numbers that systems simplicity can be compensated for by redundancies. Simplicity also facilitates training proficiency. Thus Soviet aircrews, for example, are reportedly ahead of the West in low-level and aerial-controlled interception, and have an unquestioned lead in tactical air mobility.

The Czechoslovak invasion was the best test to date of the Pact's proficiency in deployment, command and control, and logistic support for large-scale forces. While difficulties apparently developed that warranted relieving several Rear Services commanders, the entire operation demonstrated a high degree of military professionalism and efficiency, especially at the troop level, where actual combat requirements are most exacting. In general Pact forces appear to be well trained for the limited missions they are tasked to perform, but lack the versatility in experience and mission flexibility now attributed to NATO forces.

Alliance cohesion and allied reliability also pose uncertainties for both sides. The Warsaw Pact is organizationally less integrated and cohesive as a military instrument than NATO. It has neither a unified command nor integrated force structures, as NATO does. All armed forces remain under national command authorities in peacetime. During hostilities they will either be assigned to national fronts or, more likely, detailed to a Soviet command on an ad hoc basis. Thus, no command structure like NATO's Allied Forces Northern Europe or 4th Allied Tactical Air Forces exists in the pact.

The functioning of the Pact's command and force structure was witnessed during the Czechoslovak invasion. The Czechoslovak campaign was virtually a Soviet operation. Units of four other Pact countries participated but were assigned to inaccessible areas just over the borders (except for small symbolic contingents flown into and later confined to Prague international airport). All maneuver battalions and tactical aviation units were Soviet. The USSR provided field communications, air transport, and logistic support. The overall operation was commanded by Soviet General I. G. Pavlovsky, CINC of the Soviet Ground Forces, logistics were directed from Minsk by General S. S. Maryakhin, Soviet Deputy Minister of Defense for Rear Services, and air transportation was under Marshal of Aviation, N. S. Skripko, CINC of Aviation Transport Command. Inspections of Pact units deployed from May through August were conducted by Soviet Defense Minister Marshal Grechko, his political commissar, General Epishev, and the key Soviet commanders, Marshal Koshevoi, CINC Group of Soviet Forces Germany, and General Bisyarin, CINC of the Carpathian Military District. The CINC of the Warsaw Pact Forces, Marshal Yakubovsky, and his Chief of Staff, General Shtemenko, accompanied these inspections, but there is no evidence that they held any command responsibilities during any phase of the operations. Indeed, their presence was probably a reflection of their positions in the Soviet High Command rather than in the Pact hierarchy. Clearly the heart of the operation was largely Soviet, with units from other Pact members participating mainly for psychological reasons. It is not clear whether the inconspicuous allied contribution was due to East European hesitancy in becoming politically overcommitted or to Soviet reservations about the Pact's utility as a vehicle for military intervention.

The Czechoslovak operation also suggests that the political cohesion of both alliances will determine in large part their military utility. There has been a high degree of proliferating national interests in both coalitions that has made consensus difficult on main alliance problems. There are noticeable differences between northern and southern members on both sides that might not be papered out by merely a limited confrontation on one of the flanks. Indeed, the gravest crises in the past decade have not been interbloc, but within each respective alliance: France's challenge to American nuclear monopoly and withdrawal from NATO's military organization and Rumania's "cold war" with East Germany and successful struggle for Soviet recognition of its claim to a special status within the Pact. It is safe to assume that if tensions should escalate seriously the members of both blocs would close ranks. Uncertainties remain for members of alliances, however, about whether during détente their individual national security interests warrant the sacrifices required by collective efforts. France, Iceland, Greece, Turkey, and Portugal have demonstrated a determination to pursue independently specific national problems that affect the security interests of their allies. The enforcement of the Brezhnev Doctrine gives the USSR an advantage in insuring the political reliability of its alliance that the Western coalition will never be able to emulate.

Theater Nuclear Weapons

In the final analysis, miscalculations and risks inherent in these asymmetries have been covered by the existence of nuclear weapons in both alliances' arsenals. These are the ultimate equalizers for any decisive advantage an opponent might gain. But even in tactical nuclear weapons serious disparities persist. Less is generally known about the Soviets' theater nuclear capabilities than about NATO's. In the late 1950s and early 1960s delivery vehicles for tactical nuclear weapons were introduced into operational units of the Soviet armed forces. While many of these systems remain in service, there has been a consistent trend toward modernization. The liquid-fueled SS-4s or SS-5s of the Medium Range Ballistic Missile (MRBM) force are slowly being replaced by the one-megaton-warhead-equipped SS-11. There are an estimated 600 older launchers still deployed, most against Europe, and 100 solid-fueled, highly reliable SS-11s. In air delivery vehicles, the number of TU-16 Badger medium bombers targeted against NATO has been increased as the intercontinental mission has been taken over by the Navy and the Strategic Rocket Forces. Moreover, this aircraft is being replaced by the supersonic TU-22 Blinder; the transition is now more than one third complete. The Yak-28 Brewer has been in general service since the mid-1960s, replacing the 1950-vintage Beagle, and has a limited nuclear capability. The SU-7 Fitter and MIG 21J Fishbed both have a limited nuclear capability, but are being augmented by the Mach 2.3 Flogger with greater potential nuclear capability, both in terms of lift and penetration assurance.

The Blinder and the follow-on bomber, Backfire, the most impressive systems, would be used for interdiction and deep-penetration strikes. The attack aircraft suffer from limited range, small payloads, and relatively simple avionics. All aircraft, however, have a low-altitude penetration capability. And the limited range of the attack aircraft can be offset by the use of sod fields just behind friendly lines. Further, overall limitations are compensated for by numbers of available aircraft, allowing for a substantial attrition rate in mission accomplishment.

Ground delivery systems consist of SCUD-B 150-mile-range missiles (estimated at 18 launchers per division slice), FROG-6 or -7 15-50-mile-range rockets (3 launchers per division), and some 8-inch modified howitzers. The number of delivery vehicles for battlefield warheads is substantially smaller than the Western counterpart, but the discrepancy is less severe for interdiction and deep-penetration targets.[10] Indeed, even the number of theater nuclear warheads is believed to be only one quarter to one half the number of US warheads presently in Europe (1800 to 3500 Soviet warheads for Central Europe, as opposed to 7000 US warheads in NATO countries, not including several hundred air-delivered British tactical warheads and a lesser number of French.) But the individual yields are estimated to be much larger than the NATO equivalents.[11]

There may, however, have been an undetected upgrading and modernization of Soviet tactical warheads over the past six to eight years. (Soviet weapons characteristics can never be confirmed—only a few Soviet underground tests were recorded abroad between August 1963 and January 1971 in the under-20-kiloton range, as opposed to 120 US shots. But Soviet detonations in the sub-kiloton range would probably not have been detected; therefore, this is indicative of only our detection capability, not an accurate reflection of warhead upgrading.) The Soviets must be credited with the technological capability to modernize their stockpile.

It is generally believed that a unique feature of the Soviet theater nuclear posture is that all warheads are probably stored within the USSR and maintained by elite KGB units. Transient storage areas have been constructed in East Germany, Poland, Hungary, and presumably now in Czechoslovakia. A typical exercise scenario prescribes that specially configured aircraft transport both warheads and custodial troops from the USSR to the transient sites where they are transferred to recipient units, usually by helicopter. KGB troops remain with the recipient units throughout the nuclear phase of exercises and would presumably do likewise in hostilities. It must be assumed that these movements would likely come under Western surveillance and initial departures from the USSR would be regarded as a major escalaroty step, inviting precautions in kind or preemption. These cumbersome security procedures are the price the USSR feels compelled to pay for the questionable reliability of its allies.[12] (In a scenario of low-profile and long-term mobilization, these movements to the Forward Area could be accomplished by train, but the warheads would still be stored in transient sites. In contrast, all US storage sites in Europe are within easy helicopter flight distance from recipient units and the transfer of warheads would be more difficult to detect.)

While there has been no perceived change in tactical warheads, there has also been no known change in Soviet tactical nuclear doctrine. Virtually all Pact exercises have been conducted in a simulated nuclear environment (the exception was Exercise Dnepr in 1967, conducted for the first time exclusively by Soviet troops on USSR territory and at a time of intense debates mainly with Rumania about the utility of existing military doctrine and future policies).[13] All other major Pact exercises have had one feature in common. From the perspective of Western planners, it is less important that tactical nuclear warheads are introduced into the exercise than that they are used massively. There is no evidence in Soviet military writings or war games that tactical warheads are viewed as they are in the West—of deterrent rather than operational value, to be used in a selective, piecemeal fashion as demonstrations of intent, not integers in the tactical balance. The Soviets envision nuclear warheads as an extension of artillery efficiency to be expended at whatever level of intensity required to neutralize enemy forces and dominate the battlefield. The consistency with which the Soviets have held to the doctrine of maximum warfare, as opposed to the US-endorsed notion of minimal force, may have inhibited the need to concentrate on very low-yield clean warheads.

Thus, until further evidence is available, Western planners should calculate that the USSR possesses an adequate number of tactical nuclear warheads, predominantly in the "low-intermediate" range yield (20-200 KTs), that can be delivered on short notice to well-trained Soviet and Pact forces in the Forward Area, and that it has the fortitude to use these weapons at any time during hostilities when it appears advantageous. Moreover, when tactical weapons are coupled with the 600+ MRBM force, the USSR must be credited with a high degree of nuclear parity at the theater level.

Because of the American preference for minimal war, the US sought a wider flexibility in the potential use of tactical nuclear weapons, ranging from land mines to air defense weapons and short- and medium-range surface-to-surface missiles to 8-inch artillery. This greater versatility in delivery vehicles required a larger number of warheads. Most of the warheads were designed in the 1950s and have been in the inventories from ten to fifteen years. Their design characteristics reflect the state of the art at that time. They are relatively large-yield, "dirty" weapons that have little military utility except in a strategy of massive retailiation. Accordingly they have been consigned a largely psychological role (for further discussion see chapter 13).

Albert Wohlstetter argues that no strategic arms race has occurred in which the alleged action-reaction sequence compelled ever-increasing escalations or progressions. Decisions regarding strategic weapons reflected a wider assortment of factors than merely the estimated threat, e.g., resource management, budgetary constraints, domestic political considerations, that sometimes resulted in nonaction or overreaction.[14] The disparities in warhead yields, operational doctrines, and training levels between the NATO and Pact forces partially reinforces this argument. Because of widespread fears that Sputnik had created a missile gap neutralizing US retaliatory capability, Washington agreed to expand its existing bilateral nuclear agreements with its partners into a broader theater-

wide capability with greater participation and responsibilities in nuclear war.
The presence of such a massive retaliatory capability compelled Moscow to
develop a deterrence in kind. Its MRBM force was augmented with a limited
variety of battlefield weapons that could be dispersed to its allies. A parallel
theater nuclear capability was perceived as mutually desirable. But here the
parallelism breaks down. Each side placed a higher priority on mission accomplishment than on weapons imitation. Each side had a different mission for
its theater forces and each designed its weapons first to meet specific mission
requirements and then to counter the opponent's systems. More than any other
component, the discrepancies in tactical nuclear forces emphasize the asymmetries in the missions of the two opposing armed forces.

Asymmetrical Missions for Theater Forces

NATO has never enjoyed a singular notion about the kind of war for which
it must be prepared. The American conception calls for a mobile conventional
defense with an in-place, in-depth logistical support capability that will provide
for prolonged resistance—up to ninety days. At that time, the economic mobilization from peacetime to wartime requirements is to be completed and American "industrial warfare" capability will be brought fully into play. Americans
in general have maintained an unabiding faith in the superiority of industrial
warfare over more conventional forms. Industrial warfare allows superior
economic resources, managerial capabilities, and technological assets to be
organized in such ways that whatever force necessary can be expended with
minimum costs in manpower. More conventional doctrines also stress economy
of manpower, but recognize that since men still walk to victory control of the
battlefield is indispensible to the march forward. Other "stand-off" or remote-
controlled means of damaging an enemy's war-waging capabilities are important, but are no substitute for incapacitating him on the battlefield.

Paradoxically, the continentals partially abandoned these honored concepts
and the NATO partners switched positions. The Europeans feared the Pact's
overwhelming conventional capabilities and minimized NATO's operational
depth, mobilization rates, and political determination. Accordingly, force
structures, logistic stores, and reserves are designed for a forward conventional
defense in sufficient strength to preclude incursions and to determine the
attacker's intentions. They are not large enough to assure protracted resistance.
The Europeans also fear the massive destruction that would result from the
extensive use of tactical nuclear weapons that could occur in a stalemate of
conventional forces. Thus, they have intentionally confined their conventional
strength at a level low enough to insure an early US strategic retaliation, allowing
technology to minimize the expenditure of manpower.

Since the United States hopes to preserve as many options as possible before crossing the nuclear threshold, it has felt compelled to strengthen the staying power of its conventional forces and then demand an adjustment in burden-sharing. Greater conventional staying power has resulted in widening the logistic train and exacerbating known problems, e.g., there is no standardization of logistics across national lines and interests, only minimal interoperability exists between similar national weapons systems, and US logistics lines run north-south rather than east-west, with only limited in-depth, prepositioned reserve stocks. No attempt has been made to devise new mission requirements that would minimize dependency on logistical support.

Logistical dependency is a graphic demonstration of the mission differences between the Soviet and American forces in Europe. The Soviet doctrine of maximum force stresses shock and mass. In operational capabilities the Soviets have been able to add increasing mobility to the shock of their forces at the expense of staying power. This formula is the product of the limited mission prescribed for their forces in Europe. The Soviet forces in Europe are not structured or equipped for a conventional war of attrition. On the contrary, a successful European war can only be a blitzkrieg, in which the main centers of allied resistance are promptly identified and neutralized and the principal political and industrial prizes preserved intact. These objectives must be achieved before the US is able to recover and mobilize its vast reserves. A protracted war would risk destruction of the fruits of the campaign in the West and possible damage to the Russian heartland itself. Thus, the mission of the Pact forces in Central Europe is the destruction of Allied forces in West Germany, paralysis of the country by occupying key centers, and the capitulation of the Bonn government within two to three weeks. The conquest of West Germany is the only prize worth the risk of general war. A prompt and decisive campaign would present the US with a *fait accompli*, compel the surrender of Belgium, the Netherlands, and Denmark, and force Finlandization on France, Norway, and the neutral nations.

The Soviet doctrine of maximum force leads to a second observation. Because of excessive congestion and lack of operational depth for NATO forces along the Central Front, the possibility of the Soviets' initiating hostilities with a preemptive nuclear strike against the West's theater nuclear capabilities cannot be ruled out. For example, all US combat aircraft in Germany are assigned to only six airbases. Together with nuclear weapons storage sites and command and control facilities, they are the most feasible targets for the vulnerable and outmoded Soviet SS-4s or -5s, leaving the air-delivered weapons for deploying NATO ground units. The use of whatever force necessary to incapacitate an adversary and to achieve the assigned objectives is only logical to Soviet military writers.[15] The early first use of nuclear weapons would fit this formula for military success; the Soviets would have the advantage of first use against armies and statesmen who are not prepared for nuclear assault and who insist that conventional attack is still the most probable and credible mode for hostilities. Indeed, one could argue that the greater emphasis placed on conventional arms by one side, the greater the likelihood of an opponent seizing the opportunity for early first use of nuclear weapons in a counterforce mode. At any rate, why should the Soviets opt for a form of attack that provides less prospects for victory and allows the enemy the advantage of early first use? In the past two decades, the answer has been that the fear of US strategic reprisals has deterred Moscow from an attack against NATO.

Thus different missions have dictated dissimilar force structures, concepts of operation, and training. US forces in Europe still retain an expeditionary profile that has had a sharp imprint on overall American defense policy. The Soviets, on the other hand, have prescribed a mission requiring strong initial forces with only limited capability for sustained operations.[16]

In estimating comparative military strength and degrees of parity, it is inadequate merely to tally force structures, calculate weapons capability, and ascertain training proficiencies. These standard criteria must be judged within the context of the overall strategic balance and in relation to tactical nuclear weapons. Most important, all these indices of force must be correlated to the mission for which they were designed. It is dangerously misleading to assess an opponent's capabilities from the perspective of one's own mission requirements. Too often this is the case, resulting in confident assertion that since the Soviets do not have the same staying power claimed for NATO forces the West retains a favorable balance. But if it is asserted that the mission of Pact forces in Central Europe has been established independent of other great-power global imperatives, and the estimates are conducted in an individual and separated environment, equating capabilities to missions, the conclusion cannot be avoided that Pact forces are as well equipped, organized, and trained for their specific mission as NATO units. Indeed, if such military tangibles as strategic paralysis, tactical surprise, and alliance cohesion can be achieved, Pact forces are better prepared to accomplish their mission objectives than their Western counterparts. In the final analysis it must be concluded that under those conditions in which military operations are most likely to be conducted in Central Europe, the place where vital interests are most apparent for both sides, the parity balance has already slid in the Soviets' favor. NATO can no longer argue about the importance of preserving its lead; it is imperative that mission and force structures be so drastically changed that the imbalance may be corrected before an incentive emerges for the Pact to resort to force or threaten the use of force to achieve political objectives in Western Europe.

12 The Arrival of Naval Parity

Historically Russia has been regarded as a continental power. Centered on the Eurasian heartland, it was adjacent to no strategic oceans whose control was vital to its national security. When it ventured onto the high seas in strength in the eighteenth and nineteenth centuries, it had felt compelled to use naval power as a manifestation of its global stature, confirmation of its attainment of world power status. Its rivals in this category were either maritime nations or possessed territories and interests abroad that required protective fleets. British interests in the Mediterranean, the Middle East and Persia, South Asia, and the Far East served as the prime constraints against Russian expansionism. The repeated confrontations between these two nations in the one hundred years after Napolean from Europe throughout Asia led the Russians to conclude that England was their chief adversary, and that only these two states, with national interests on a global scale, were truly world powers. A quirk of history forced the two onto the same side during World War I; a quirk resulting from the cyclical nature of Russian foreign policy, whereby it was focused on the West, South and East in turn and would shift when compelled because of adversary resistance, or when lucrative opportunities and threats emerged in other sectors. After its 1905 defeat by Japan in the Far East, Russia was free to return its undivided attention to Europe and the emerging Balkan crisis. Its humiliation by the Japanese and the threat to its security posed by the Balkan unrest compelled Russia to seek alliance with the maritime nations against rival continental powers.

After both World Wars the threat to the Russian heartland was again posed by maritime nations—states that could inflict unacceptable destruction while remaining secure behind oceanic barriers. Russia reacted as it did in the nineteenth century and constructed a blue water navy to counter this threat and, more important, to demonstrate its arrival at global stature. By 1973, the USSR had virtually the same number of major combatants as, and far more submarines than, the US (231 to 243 surface warships). The meteoric rise of the Soviet Navy to global stature and its relative strength compared to Western fleets is one of the most puzzling questions for détente analysts. Overall, less is known about Soviet naval proficiency than that of other services, despite the increasing exposure to Western observation of Soviet warships. Weapons training is confined to restricted areas, and the Soviets have not engaged in hostile activities

169

for over a quarter century. The resulting enigma has contributed to uncertainty about the strength of Soviet global deployments and their value and relationship to theater requirements.

Is the world's second largest navy its second most powerful navy? Does it have characteristics that enhance its posture in restricted waters, such as the Mediterranean, as opposed to high seas? What are the foreseeable trends in naval policies, ship construction, and concepts of operation? Is great-power maritime warfare now possible or a form of limited war between the two states plausible? Does the West's increasing dependency on foreign trade—in oil alone—increase its relative vulnerability proportionally and afford incentives for Soviet coercion? Are the Soviets trying to win a naval challenge without combat, or are their naval capabilities even to be taken seriously? If intended primarily for political purposes, how is this power to be used and what countermeasures are appropriate? Is the Soviet Navy still intended primarily as a delivery vehicle for strategic nuclear weapons and, otherwise, for the defense of home waters? Has the USSR achieved, as it claims, a sufficiently balanced navy that it can undertake the entire spectrum of naval tasks throughout the world? Finally, is the USSR preparing to challenge the US for control of the high seas or to establish mastery over limited seaspace vital to Western interests?

These are the questions that are being asked in the present debate in naval literature (both East and West) about Soviet capabilities and intentions, and whether parity has been reached and the implications this would have for the West. For détente analysts, the prospects of maritime tensions are almost as enigmatic as the threat of strategic nuclear exchanges, and the appeal of peaceful oceans may be even more seductive for world opinion than the codification of nuclear sanctuaries.

Soviet Naval Policy

Michael McGwire has accurately observed that the consistency of Soviet naval policy (as opposed to operational concepts) has been striking. Some forty years ago the Soviet Union grasped the fact that maritime strategy is not some universal science, but particular to the country concerned. The Soviet Union finds herself opposed to the traditional maritime powers, but the strategy that she must adopt to counter this threat to her security need bear no relation to the "classical" use of sea power.[1] In the past, Russia's naval requirements have been dictated by her 23,000-mile coastline and the fact that four separate seas required four self-sustained fleets for their protection. Thus, while nominally a land power, for the past two hundred years Russia has maintained the third or fourth largest navy in the world. Yet she was never regarded as a leading maritime power, because in part of her assiduous avoidance of confrontations with first-rate navies. (When it engaged the smaller, less experienced Japanese fleet in 1905, it was disastrously defeated). Indeed, Russia's only naval victories were against the inferior Turkish and Arab fleets, and the most decisive, as in 1827 off Thrace, were in combined operations with French and British fleets. This backwardness in naval proficiency was due mainly to training and administrative and logistic practices, because in other aspects of naval operations Russia became a leader. In maritime innovations, for example, it was the first to use high-explosive shells, torpedoes, mines, and various aircraft.

After initial setbacks in the wake of the Revolution, the Soviet Navy once again received a high proportion of national resources under the First Five-Year Plan. A Twenty-Year Naval Program (1928-47) directed an 80 percent increase in shipbuilding, including 9 battleships, 30 cruisers, 200 destroyers, and about 400 submarines; the largest inventory of submarines in the world. The construction program received relatively low priority until after Soviet involvement in the Spanish Civil War demonstrated the superior interdiction capabilities of other naval powers. Moscow then unsuccessfully sought to purchase battleship blueprints from the US, and launched a crash construction program for capital ships, including aircraft carriers—six hulls were captured by the Germans in Leningrad.

After World War II, the USSR was again confronted by the traditional maritime powers who had demonstrated their capability to transport continental-size armies over the high seas and sustain them for extended periods. Moreover, these powers also had developed strategic nuclear weapons that introduced a new dimension into potential overseas operations. To offset its lack of a high-seas capability and its nuclear inferiority, the USSR adapted an increasing portion of its submarine fleet to strategic missions. By 1949-50, the feasibility of submarine-launched ballistic missiles was confirmed, and a nuclear warhead was developed by 1955. Finally, the first series-produced nuclear submarines were delivered in 1958 (N-class SSN and H-class SSBN). On the other hand, the USSR commissioned in 1946 yet another Twenty-Year Naval Program to build a fleet of 40 cruisers, 200 destroyers, and 1200 submarines (only 180 for strategic delivery). The initial thrust of this program was mainly defensive, for the protection of the homeland against sea-borne invasion.

By 1953-54, however, the economy was recovering satisfactorily, the regime's domestic position had been consolidated, and hydrogen weapons technology had been mastered. A defense review during this period downgraded the threat of foreign landings and concluded that hostile maritime capabilities should be neutralized in a nuclear war as far from friendly shores as possible. Consequently, the optimum area for engaging Western aircraft carrier forces and maritime convoys was on the high seas, before their aircraft were within range of land targets and their convoys could be supported by land-based aircraft. This new rationale was the justification for converting an ever-increasing proportion of total naval assets to a high-seas capability.

Moscow's Novel Innovation in Missiles

The decision to return to the high seas prompted an inevitable and pro-tracted debate about preferred weapons systems. Should the USSR follow the historic notion of attempting to match a rival gun for gun and ship for ship, and thereby construct the number of carriers and heavy cruisers equal to those of the West? Or should new innovations be sought that would minimize the size, numbers, and costs of individual units required? Moscow decided against both guns and tactical aircraft in favor of a novel gamble on surface-launched long-range cruise missiles and antiaircraft missiles. This innovation, as daring as its development of the torpedo, revolutionized naval concepts. Surface-to-surface missiles could be carried on nearly any size vessel, even coastal cutters. Accordingly, the existing cruiser program was promptly curtailed and thirteen curiser construction ways, including four allocated for aircraft carriers, were converted to other needs. Destroyers and frigates under construction and pro-gramed were fitted with missiles rather than heavy guns, and within three years the naval budget was cut in half.[2] By 1962 a new family of nuclear missile-equipped vehicles had become operational: the long-range J-class submarine, the Kynda-class frigate, and the TU-16 Badger C medium-range bomber, armed with Kipper air-to-surface missiles.

In the early 1960s, the main threat had shifted from carriers and amphib-ious landings to the Polaris submarine, requiring neutralization of the submarine on the high seas or an ABM system to intercept launched missiles. But against both carriers and Polaris vessels, Soviet concept of operations at that time re-quired that its units survive only long enough to discharge its missiles or tor-pedoes. The USSR did not have the resources to insure the survivability of its forces in a hostile environment. This glaring deficiency has now been overcome as a more balanced naval force was gradually instituted.

The wisdom of the Soviets' decision to opt for missiles rather than aircraft is still being debated in the West, though less convincingly than at the time of US naval supremacy. Based largely on Allied experience in the Pacific, not the Atlantic, and the use of carriers during the Korean, Suez, and Vietnam wars, naval air proponents argue that tactical missiles do not have the throw-weight or the sustained rate of fire to project naval force onto the land dimension, nor do they have the versatility or reliability for use as countership weapons. This rationale has carried weight because of the circumstances cited above, where naval power was heavily land oriented. Since World War II Western control of the high seas has been virtually complete; there has been no surface fleet chal-lenge. In this situation, a relatively small number of carriers, with their superb force-generation rate, mobility, and versatility, was the appropriate weapon system for projecting US naval authority throughout the world. As an example of carriers' force-generation capability, during the first bombing offensive of North Vietnam, US carriers were at sea 75 to 80 percent of the time. In 1965 carriers conducted 30,993 combat sorties over NVN and 25,895 sorties over SVN in eleven months. During the monsoon season of March through June 1966, 10,349 sorties were conducted over NVN and 12,065 over SVN.[3] Equally impressive is the carriers' versatility. By changing the aircraft mix aboard, the carrier can be assigned a variety of tasks, from nuclear strikes to antisubmarine warfare.

Future Carrier Missions

But the carrier now faces an uncertain future, because of the changing nature of naval warfare and the new threats posed by the Soviet Navy. US foreign policy during the 1970s is likely to follow the Nixon Doctrine regardless of who is in the White House. As a result, there will probably be fewer international crises in which the US will intervene with military forces. The most likely occasions will be by invitation and with other like-minded nations in tertiary Third World states where internal stability is threatened by external influences. The number of instances when determined resistance and opposed marine landings that would require the use of carriers will probably be small to nonexistent.

True, carriers still retain the mission of adding NATO forces on the Central Front during general war. But carriers could be available in strength only in a protracted conflict. Many analysts now maintain that war in Europe would most likely be short and swift, providing insufficient time for carriers to react. At any rate, there is little justification for retaining fifteen carriers, as presently configured, in the hope of their being able to influence a European war. (It should be noted that because of range limitations and constraints imposed by other missions on readiness requirements, the US Navy relinquished to the Air Force F-4s in the late 1960s the nuclear strike role of its carrier aircraft).

Aware of the declining utility of the carrier, the US Navy devised the concept of the Sea Control Ship, introducing multiple roles for each carrier and an equitable allocation of aircraft between attack, intercept, ASW, and support missions. The difficulty with the new concept is that an equitable but static aircraft mix proportionally dilutes the effectiveness of any single mission and does not provide the flexibility the multirole concept seeks. Proponents argue that it is difficult to anticipate the optimum aircraft mix for any contingency. Opponents point out that the fixation on the "necessity" to provide fleet air protection, for example, is a myth that has penalized carrier efficiency. Fleet protection is only relevant in a hostile air environment such as the Eastern Mediterranean until 1972. There is no need for US naval forces to steam within range of Soviet coastal defenses, and Soviet carriers are not likely to challenge Western carriers for at least a decade. Thus, on the high seas, there is no danger from high-performance aircraft. The main air threat in those waters where the

US Navy is most likely to be committed is the cruise missile and ASM missile launched from long-range bombers. Early-warning aircraft are designed specifically to detect low-level aircraft and missiles in time for interception by shipborne defenses. (Further the probability of even an A-14 downing a cruise or ASM missile in flight is extremely low; quick-reacting SAMs and guns are the preferred defense).

The air-cover syndrome is only one example of "tunnel vision" that has constrained naval conceptual development. Because of numbers alone, the main naval threat remains the Soviet submarine. The chief limitation of the cruise missile is the necessity for target location data. In actual combat conditions this is likely to negate its over-the-horizon range and force the submarine into closer quarters with its target and its defenses. The main threat to the submarine is the helicopter, until the Soviets acquire a Submerge Launched Anti-Aircraft Missile (SLAM) presently in production in the UK. If fleet or convoy protection is to be one of the carriers' future missions, it must be equipped against the main threat.

Thus, the Sea Control Concept requires modification. To assign such carriers to the Pacific where there is no tactical aircraft threat is inappropriate. Helicopter carriers and Phalanx-equipped destroyers would be better suited for this duty. This reasoning leads away from the conversion of each attack carrier to multirole missions with the accompanying curtailment of effectiveness in each role. Carrier specialization or rapid convertibility from one role to the other is the only sound future for the carrier. The latter concept calls for aircraft transfers at sea as one mission is accomplished or a new threat develops. This is presently done on an aircraft-by-aircraft basis. The transfer of a squadron of different aircraft types, however, requires the rapid convertibility of that squadron's entire maintenance support. To achieve convertibility without endangering the task force would be complicated and expensive. Duplicate spare parts for each mission would have to be prepackaged and stored aboard accompanying replenishment vessels.

An alternative, less expsnsive concept is the assignment of a particular mission to each carrier. Only three would be retained in the classical conventional role to which all are now basically oriented. Seven should be assigned fleet protection or screening duty (Greenland-Iceland Gap), configured similar to the ASW Essex-class with a slightly larger fighter component. The remaining five, including the two nuclear carriers, should be assigned exclusively to the nuclear strike role. The carrier remains ideally suited for the role of a third strategic nuclear strike force; i.e. after the initial exchange and the follow-on strikes by Polaris submarines, carriers could be the only survivable nuclear force available to exploit any advantages that may be discernible from earlier strikes. If sailed into the South Atlantic or around South America for security purposes during periods of high alert, these carrier task forces would likely be the most viable fighting units left during the reconstitution phase of a nuclear war that could still threaten the Russian heartland. The survivability of a force this size is a distrinct advantage the Soviets cannot equal, and would justify retention of a large carrier inventory and the elitism of the naval air arm.

Missile Versus Aircraft

The new Soviet threat is the other reason for the changing role of the carrier. The US preference for aircraft over missiles has had serious repercussions now that the Soviet surface fleet poses a challenge. The US has no comparable missile capability and has no option but to retain for the time being its tactical air power for deployment as antiship weapons, regardless of the suitability of advanced aircraft for this mission. The present high-performance jet fighter-bombers were designed in the early 1960s for the delivery of nuclear weapons, and target accuracy was less important than assured aircraft penetrability. Thus accuracy in weapons delivery was sacrificed for speed and range at low altitudes. The 1965-68 Vietnam bombing campaign is incontestable evidence of the difficulty of using high-performance aircraft for precision bombing of defended targets. Average bombing errors were five to ten times greater than the width of Soviet SSM-equipped warships. Thus the use of antequated World War I dive-bombing tactics by present-generation aircraft conventionally armed to inflict hull damage against relatively small, highly maneuverable, heavily defended Soviet warships is an unequal contest. Excessive aircraft attrition rates, with minimal losses of Soviet warships, would have to be expected. (What is excessive? The US lost 143 aircraft during the Battle of Midway Island, but was able to inflict irreparable damage on Japanese carrier forces. It is doubtful if a similar proportion of expended aircraft could inflict commensurate damage on the Soviet fleet.)

The advent of "smart bombs" or stand-off guided weapons is the first revolutionary change in conventional tactical bombing techniques since the development of the aircraft. The pilot no longer has to physically align the aircraft with the expected bomb trajectory. Stand-off weapons are guided to the target by various homing devices, significantly improving accuracy. The performance of these weapons during the second bombing offensive against Hanoi demonstrated that they have sufficient accuracy to be employed effectively against warships. But serious limitations persist in all the homing devices that restrict their optimum employment.

Antiradiation missiles can be deceived by ECM, changing frequencies or shutting down the equipment. In later models target coordinates can be fed into an inertial guidance system, but this mode is ineffective against a mobile target. Further, because of the missiles' limited range, it can only be released within the ship's air defense envelope, exposing the aircraft to attack. Finally, the warhead is only 250 pounds and will detonate in the electronic gear aloft rather than penetrate the superstructure. (Today's warships can be incapacitated more easily by destroying their electronic capability than by sinking them. But the difficulty with attacking antennae rather than hulls is that to assess whether the bomb damage is irreparable requires the exposure and possible expenditure of another aircraft).

Laser guidance systems are tamperproof: they cannot be deflected or jammed. They are ideally suited for hull damaging caliber ordnance. But it is not a self-contained package; the pilot must continually illuminate the target until impact, exposing the aircraft to hostile actions. TV guidance systems can be released from 30 n.m. range and the pilot can take limited evasive action. But, like optical systems, TV is restricted by weather. It cannot penetrate haze, cloud, or darkness, and therefore would have limited utility in North Atlantic operations. Thus, until an all-weather, medium-range, large-caliber missile can be developed, naval air will have to continue relying heavily on classical dive-bombing techniques with "iron" bombs.

It was with an understandable sense of desperation that the US Navy belatedly began developing a cruise missile to counter the Soviet surface threat. The US had pioneered the development of cruise missiles with its Regulus I and II and Triton missiles, but they were abandoned in the early 1960s and valuable development expertise was lost. When the US returned to the cruise missile field with the development of Harpoon, all of its major NATO partners had already deployed SSMs of their own development and manufacture. The Harpoon has a 50-mile range, 1000-pound payload, terminal radar guidance, a surface-skimming capability, and can be launched by aircraft and ship. It was flight-tested in 1973; full production is scheduled for 1975; installation is expected on vessels commissioned after that date. Thus, by the end of the decade, the US will have a limited cruise-missile capability, but with characteristics that may already be dated by Soviet standards.

Regarding other systems, US reliance on aircraft precluded the prospects of close-in fighting and allowed abandonment of further gun development. Since World War II no improvement in guns was made until the development of the new 5-inch, Mk 45 5″/55. But it fires only twenty rounds per minute, less than half the capability of the modern guns of several NATO navies. In contrast, the Soviets now have the fastest-firing, longest-ranged, and most maneuverable guns afloat in the world. (In the interest of maneuverability and acceleration, the Soviets pioneered in 1962 development of gas turbine propulsion).

On the other hand, the US has made spectacular improvements in torpedo technology, both in homing devices and submerged launching for aerial torpedoes, SUBROC. Emphasizing its interest in endurance, the US has developed a nuclear capability for a significant portion of its surface fleet, giving it extended on-station time which rivals must compensate for by a larger total number of ships. In shipborne air defenses, the US is reportedly leading the world. The Standard-T SAM, Sea Sparrow Point Defense, Tartar D fire control system, and follow-on Aegis guidance system, plus the antimissile Phalanx gun which fires 6000 rounds per second, and sophisticated ECM equipment provide a formidable defensive capability.

Soviet Warships and Weapons Capabilities

The credibility of shipborne air defenses is central to the arguments about aircraft versus missile and the offensive or defensive character of the Soviet Navy. During the 1950s the Soviet Navy relied heavily upon submarine-launched cruise missiles and air-delivered ASMs. Over 11,000 missiles in these two categories reportedly have been produced and 5000 are currently deployed among 300 TU-16 and 60 TU-22 medium-range naval bomber aircraft, 51 long-range submarines, 21 major warships, and over 100 coastal aircraft. When the USSR decided to advance its defensive perimeter forward by installing these cruise missiles on surface vessels, Allied air supremacy made ship survivability crucial to the accomplishment of the naval mission. Until the early 1960s SSM warships were designed primarily for general war, adopting a "shoot-and-scoot" defense. Only some vessels had a SAM capability, a naval adaptation of the high altitude SAM-2 with limited effectiveness on the high seas. Heavy reliance had to be placed on radar-controlled AAA. In 1962 the Soviets introduced the Kynda-class frigate, carrying two quadruple SSN-3 launchers with a 450-n.m. range and a full load of 16 missiles, plus twin SAN-3 low-level surface-to-air missile launchers and two twin 76-mm. AAA guns. This ship indicated Moscow's determination to construct survivable warships and a blue water fleet.

The Kynda frigates were followed by the Kresta I-class cruisers carrying two twin SSN-3 launchers, a helicopter for limited-range target location data for its missiles and ASW operations, two twin SAN-3 launchers, plus 57-mm. gun mounts and impressive air surveillance and electronic warfare equipment. In June 1970 the 7500-ton Kresta II was reported, armed with eight SSN-3 launchers, two twin SAN-3 launchers, ASW torpedoes, two helicopters, and 3-D radar.

In 1968 the Soviet Navy turned a corner with the introduction of the Moskva ASW helicopter carrier. At 18,000 tons, it was the Soviet's largest warship and carried a complement of 20 Ka-25 helicopters and ASW rockets for sustained area defense, plus two twin SAN-3 launchers. This was the first serious Soviet effort at aerial antisubmarine warfare, but they remain at least five years behind the West in ASW operations.

in 1971 the USSR introduced a "pocket battleship" the 3800-ton Krivak-class destroyer armed with a quad launcher for a SSN-9, surface-skimming missile, two retractable SAN-4 launchers, two twin fully automatic 76-mm AAA mounts, eight torpedo tubes, two 12-barrel ASW rocket launchers, and minelaying facilities aft. The ship is also equipped with semihardened sensors and gas turbines that generate a top speed of over 35 knots. Relatively small in size, the three ships in this class are the most versatile, self-defensive, and lethal warships in the Soviet inventory. There is no comparable warship in the West.

Moscow's latest entry is two 30,000-ton Essex-class aircraft carriers under construction at the Nikolayev Nosenka shipyard on the Black Sea. The Soviets have traditionally favored armament over endurance and size. Because of size limitations, the carriers will probably have to carry only the Freehand VSTOL (vertical takeoff) aircraft for air defense and attack missions and helicopters for ASW operations. VSTOL aircraft are less effective than conventional fixed-wing aircraft, but under favorable conditions the Soviets will be able to control a limited air space for a limited period.

Does the development of a Soviet carrier force vindicate those who have argued in the past that without carrier-borne air cover the Soviet fleet was sufficiently vulnerable that it would not venture onto the high seas during hostilities? The Soviets' ability to operate on the high seas has been recently demonstrated in two ways other than new weapons systems: naval exercises and out-of-area deployments. On 14 April 1970, Moscow announced the beginning of the largest and longest naval exercise in USSR history. Over 200 ships and 500 aircraft were involved (103 in the North Atlantic and Barents Sea, 15 in the Philippine and Japanese seas, 18 in the Indian Ocean, and 45 in the Mediterranean). In the Norwegian Sea alone there were ten SSM warships and 30 submarines; bomber and reconnaissance aircraft conducted over 400 sorties. Entitled "Okean," the exercise included all aspects of naval operations: amphibious landings, simulated ballistic missile launchings, coordinated maneuvers by vessels from all three western based fleets, gunnery training, and even screening exercises by missile-equipped cutters in the Norwegian Sea. The main purpose of Okean, however, was to test simultaneous communications on a global basis.[4]

But the key operational aspect of the exercise involved a simulated engagement of the Western navies in the North Atlantic. This was the first such exercise of its kind, and while weaknesses were noted, it was generally regarded in the West as an impressive demonstration of the USSR's new capabilities on the high seas. Indeed, the Norwegian Defense Minister, Gunnar Hellesen, later lamented that the Soviet Union now had sufficient naval strength in the North Atlantic to be able to attack from an exercise posture, with Baltic and Northern Fleet warships already at sea, anywhere along the entire Norwegian coast.[5]

Soviet Navy's Political Mission

After Okean was terminated, the Soviets used the opportunity to demonstrate the second aspect of their new capability, the psychological and political impact gained by out-of-area deployments. Many of the participating vessels proceeded to more distant waters for rounds of port calls. One group went to the Cape Verde Islands and then to ports in West Africa, where the USSR has maintained routine combat patrols ever since. Another flotilla called at Mauritrius, where in July 1970 the Soviets has leased limited docking facilities. Another contingent visited ports around the Indian Ocean littoral, and finally six warships, including an Echo-II-class cruise missile-equipped nuclear submarine, entered the Caribbean, steaming at one point to within fifty miles of the Mississippi coast. (As the latter force approached southeastern United States and Cuba, its cruise was coordinated with the flight of two Soviet Bear-D long-range reconnaissance aircraft, exercising target location and communication between aircraft and submarines).

These visits underscored a growing trend in Soviet out-of-area deployments, indicating Moscow's increasing appetite for constrained gunboat diplomacy and new concepts of operation for its high-seas fleet. The coordination of long-range aircraft reconnaisance with submarine activities in the North Atlantic has become routine. The aircraft penetrate the Icelandic air defenses at low level and then search for important shipping in the North Atlantic. Accurate target data are then passed to prepositioned submarines armed with 150- or 400-n.m.-range cruise missiles. The aircraft can either recover at Cuba or return to home bases flying appropriate low-level profiles. This coordinated effort will pose a serious threat to Western wartime resupply efforts, especially since the reconnaissance aircraft operate beyond the range of land-based air defenses and can avoid shipborne systems.

The Soviets have now established a relatively permanent presence in the Cape Verde Islands Basin. Soviet warships in these waters are probably directed to complicate defensive operations of the newly established NATO IBERLANT Command, composed of Portuguese and American air and naval forces guarding the approaches to the Mediterranean, to attack Allied convoys entering the Gibralter Straits, and to counter US Polaris submarines operating from Rota, Spain. In these waters, maritime activities and target data could be passed by nuclear submarines to cruise missile-equipped warships off the African coastline before diving in the relative protection of the unusually deep trough off the Iberian-Moroccan continental shelf.

A more immediate mission in African waters has been political: the defense of Soviet state interests. Several incidents are noteworthy. In February-March 1969, three combatants were deployed off Accra to pressure for the release of two Soviet fishing vessels held by Ghana. Second, since November 1970 the USSR has maintained usually three warships continuously at Conakry, Guinea, as a deterrent against further Portuguese-sponsored attacks and as visible support for Toure. Finally, the USSR dispatched a Kashin-class destroyer to Freetown, Sierra Leone, in May 1971 to deter a rumored *coup d'état* against self-proclaimed President Siaka Stevens. All three moves achieved Moscow's aims.[6]

Soviet naval activities in the Caribbean and Cuban ports have been a source of continuing American alarm. Four times in 1970, major contingents of Soviet warships entered these waters, and auxilliary vessels have established a permanent presence. The US Coast Guard reported to a Senate subcommittee that it could not adequately detect naval movements even in the Florida Straits, and that some Soviet vessels had remained unobserved for as long as four days.[7] The establishment of a nuclear submarine base in Cuba would significantly reduce transit times from the USSR and increase proportionately the amount of on-station time for these boats in geographic areas where the US is the most vulnerable.[8] The seriousness of this potential threat contributed to the US-USSR crisis of confidence in September and October 1970 (which was compounded by harassment on Berlin access routes and violations of the Egyptian-Israeli cease-fire). Only after negotiations between Foreign Minister Gromyko and President Nixon was the issue resolved. On 17 November, the State Department announced that an understanding had been reached with the Soviet Union whereby Cuban ports and facilities would not be used for nuclear submarine bases or other strategic offensive weapons systems. This understanding, however, cannot preclude the normal servicing of Soviet vessels in Cuban ports. In no way does the understanding impair routine cruising by Soviet warships in the Caribbean or inhibit development of long-range SSN missiles. Thus, while the US used this "mini-crisis" to register the seriousness it attached to the Soviet build-up in these waters, it could do little to effectively deter the new threat.

The establishment of a permanent Soviet presence in the Indian Ocean is also potentially critical for Western interests. In March 1968 a Soviet cruiser, missile-equipped destroyer, and ASW escort opened this phase of Soviet naval expansion with the longest series of port calls in Soviet naval history, visiting ports in India, Pakistan, Ceylon, Aden, Somalia, and the Persian Gulf. In 1970 29 Soviet naval vessels cruised the Indian Ocean and in 1971 18 entered these waters, including several nuclear or conventional submarines and 10 combatants and several supporting auxilliaries. By 1972, these units have paid over fifty official visits to ports of sixteen littoral countries. The Soviets have secured commercial harbor facilities in Singapore and in Aden, and a 144,000-dollar oil-tank farm has been constructed at Mauritius. They have provided harbor improvement assistance for South Yemen, Yemen, Somalia, Upper Egypt, Malagasy, Iraq, and the Indian Naval Headquarters at Vishakhapatnam. So far, however, they have not been granted any naval bases. Fleet anchorages have been established in Seychelles Islands and at Socotra off Arabia.

Soviet commercial interests in the Indian Ocean have expanded rapidly. The Soviet fishing fleet is the largest in these waters, yielding a two-million-ton annual catch, or one third of the USSR's total catch, larger than that of the combined local fleets. In November 1971 the USSR started passenger ship service in South Asian waters, with charter service between Singapore and

Australia. The USSR probably has as many as one hundred other merchant vessels on any single day in the Indian Ocean, many transporting Arab oil. Indeed, in 1971 more than five hundred Soviet merchantmen called at Singapore. Soviet trade turnover with Indian Ocean countries increased from 275 million rubles in 1959 to 766 million in 1967 and 1060 million in 1970, or a 12-13 percent increase per annum. These figures represent only 5 percent of all Soviet foreign trade, but show a slightly higher annual increase than the 10-percent growth in overall Soviet trade. In balance, only 20 percent of Soviet foreign commerce is seaborne. Very little trade between European Russia and the Soviet Far East is carred by sea (200,000 tons in 1967—before the Canal was closed—versus 24 million tons by rail). Nonetheless, with these trade and fishing interests in the Indian Ocean, the USSR has become one of the important regional maritime powers, and is now confronted with classical naval requirements of protecting commercial interests. Unlike Japan, who has greater commercial interests in these waters but has refrained from taking military measures for their protection, the USSR has followed the more traditional approach of initiating naval operations commensurate with its commercial activities. Conversely, these mercantile activities provide valuable services for Soviet naval operations. But Soviet merchantmen are also hostages for Soviet good behavior and compound Moscow's problems of providing adequate protection. The USSR is not likely to interfere with Western shipping without accepting the risk of interference with its own merchant fleet.[9]

The closing of the Suez Canal has seriously hampered the Soviet naval build-up in the Indian Ocean. Virtually all naval support has had to come from Pacific fleet. Soviet Pacific Coast ports are severely restricted by fog in spring and fall and ice in winter, and are over 6000 miles from the south coast of Arabia. From the more favorable Black Sea ports to Arabia is nearly 11,500 miles if Africa must be circumnavigated, but only 3200 miles if the Canal is reopened. (From the US East Coast to the same destination is 11,000 around Africa and 6600 miles through the Canal).[10] Thus, if the Canal is reopened, the USSR will be the closest naval power to the Indian Ocean, with important economic and political incentives to enhance its authority in this region, but with sufficient problems stemming from this new posture that it may intensify its efforts to reach a mutual great-power circumscription of strategic naval forces in these waters.

Soviet Naval Threat

Thus, the Soviets have demonstrated a convincing capability to operate impressive forces on the high seas during peacetime that must be regarded as a serious threat to Western maritime interests during hostilities. The Soviet Naval High Command has designed a shipborne air-defense capability in which it has high confidence. Ship survivability has been based on self-sufficiency, a trend now adopted in US naval policy. The effectiveness of its air defenses has allowed the USSR to advance its SSM-equipped warships onto the high seas without carrier cover.

In a lengthy series of articles in the authoritative Soviet journal *Morskoi Sbornik* (Naval Almanac), the Commander-in-Chief of the Soviet Navy, Admiral Sergei Gorshkov, indicated why Moscow was interested in a carrier capability. After years of preaching the superiority of missiles over aircraft in both the offensive and defensive modes, Gorshkov stressed the importance of a balanced fleet disposition that would permit employment in both primary and secondary theaters of interest and for both military and political objectives. He repeatedly emphasized the strategic importance of the Navy and the need for a global power to have the capability to perform a wide variety of naval tasks. Gorshkov implied that the carrier was a means of exploiting the Soviets' arrival on the high seas, not a means of achieving access to the world's oceans. The Soviets now have greater flexibility in selecting options for the use of naval power. The least likely option will be to use carriers to challenge the West for control of the high seas. There is no need for another Midway Island contest between rival carrier forces for mastery of the seas. As John Erickson has stated,

> It is late in the day for the Soviet naval command to place its faith in the mobile power of the aircraft carrier when the improved ship-to-ship missile offers growing tactical advantages, and, even more, when such missiles do not have to be launched from surface ships. In what seems to be the present stand-off between carrier and missile weapons systems, the Soviet command does not appear to have relinquished even a particle of its faith in the missile.[11]

But does mere appearance on the high seas imply the achievement of naval parity with the powers that have heretofore controlled the oceans, as Gorshkov suggests? This is the cardinal question. The Soviets would like general acceptance on the point and the US refuses to grant such recognition. Therefore, the relative naval strengths under given circumstances are subject to conjecture.

In attempting such an assessment, it is important to appreciate the Soviets' understanding of their naval mission. The Soviet Navy is no longer charged merely with the defense of home waters and support for the army, as it was in the wake of the two world wars and periods of national reconstruction. Officially the Soviet Navy now has two missions: a deterrent role in peacetime and combat role in wartime. In peacetime it has been assigned: to defend the territory of the Soviet Union against any preemptive imperialistic attack; to counter the threat posed by the nuclear missiles of the submarines and carriers of the Western navies; and to launch missiles against targets in Western countries which are far removed from the sea, as well as against naval targets. In time of hostilities, the tasks of the Soviet Navy are to insure the fulfillment of the three peacetime missions; to cooperate with the Soviet land forces, especially in mounting seaborne landing operations; to harass the enemy's sea communications; to destroy the enemy's surface ships, submarines, and aircraft; and to help in the defense of the coastal air defenses.[12]

These priorities have several notable features. Defense of the homeland remains the highest consideration for the Navy, as it does with any other maritime nation. Second, the emphasis placed on participation in and coordination with the broad air-defense system reflects earlier Soviet apprehensions about vulnerability to low-level penetrating aircraft over its seaward approaches. It can now be assumed that SAN-destroyers and escorts will be stationed in screening positions, adjacent to land-based air defenses, to counter low-level penetrations over its own sea lanes. A unique feature of the USSR as a maritime power is that in wartime it will rely mainly on its existing continental resources, and therefore does not have the heavy escort requirements that burden NATO. Accordingly, its primary offensive goals are not to secure control of the high seas, or even to deny the enemy portions of his own vital sea lanes—the chief aim is to destroy his warships, making his sea lanes and airways progressively more vulnerable to interdiction. The USSR's peacetime mission is, of course, deterrent, but the wartime mission has now been augmented by an offensive role reminiscent of the force allocations between other smaller and larger navies, e.g. the German navy during both world wars. (In both instances, the mere presence of German light battleship task forces in friendly ports succeeded in tying the vastly superior British Home Fleet to the North and Norwegian Seas, denying these resources for the protection of vital North Atlantic and Mediterranean sea lanes.) *The Soviet offensive threat, then, is designed to force the Western navies to commit far greater resources for the protection of vital sea lanes than posed by the actual Soviet danger, and thereby reduce the overall potential challenge to the homeland, while affording greater Soviet latitude on the high seas. Therefore, the Soviets need not seek a numerical parity with the West. Merely a credible offensive threat consisting of reliable weapons, survivable warships, and maritime proficiency will create sufficient military parity.* In a relatively short time, then, the Soviet Navy has been expanded from a primarily defensive to a powerful offensive naval force that has been assigned a wide variety of military and political tasks.

How is the new flexibility and versatility afforded Moscow by its ship construction policy and its achievement of long-range sea and airlift capability most likely to be used in accomplishing these missions? Policy guidelines for planning a commensurate force structure apparently stressed the aim of forcing the West to commit far more of its offensive resources for protection of vital maritime interests than the USSR would be required to threaten them. From this point of departure, it is appropriate to examine the possible types of conflict the USSR has envisioned in its naval policy and the comparative suitability of the USSR and US naval units to each situation.

Possible Naval Contingencies

Several military contingencies can be itemized for conveninece of analysis:

1. *General War Involving Both Great-Power Alliances.* In the past both Soviet and Western military writers have usually considered that any great-power conflict would inevitably become nuclear in a short period. The Soviets' classical scenario for bloc military war games involves either massive retaliation or rapid escalation; e.g., NATO attacks the Pact conventionally, the Pact counterattacks conventionally, NATO responds with tactical nuclear weapons, and the Pact retaliates in kind. In general war these are four sets of circumstances that bear on the outcome of this scenario: tactical and strategic warning and no-warning situations. (a) It is conceivable that a defender can be attacked without any prior warning of impending hostilities. In other words, any combinations of strategic and tactical forces can be struck by a preemptive attack without warning, as apparently occurred at Pearl Harbor. (b) A defender may have confirmed indications that an adversary is mobilizing with hostile intentions. The extent of his preparation and tactical deployments may not be known, but it is evident that his national resources are being readied. In this situation the attacker may achieve complete tactical surprise and the defender would have had strategic but not tactical warning, as occurred in the 1968 invasion of Czechoslovakia. (c) A defender may gain both strategic and tactical warning of an impending attack, or may have been fully alerted upon receipt of strategic warning so that no tactical surprise was gained. This would be a case of adequate strategic and tactical warning, as seen in the 1943 Battle of Kursk. (d) Upon receipt of strategic warning, a state may attempt to preempt the opponent's attack, such as conceived in the strategic concept of launch-on-warning. In each of these warning situations, the conflict may be either conventional or nuclear and may involve any combination of allies or friendly states.

2. *Limited Wars Involving Great Powers.* American policy-makers have sought to reduce the possibility of a nuclear holocaust by advocating a strategy of flexible response. But US leaders remained preoccupied with the notion that maximum readiness for general war would necessarily deter the Soviet Navy from initiating *fait accompli* actions. As practiced in Southeast Asia, flexible response became a strategy of minimal force. The US became increasingly aware of the dangers at the lower spectrum of violence. On the other hand, the Soviets have never formally adopted a strategy of flexible response and are equipped and trained for a maximal use of force to achieve any given objective. But as their weapons systems become more sophisticated and their political interests more refined, and as the risks of a strategic nuclear exchange magnify, the Soviets have demonstrated a keener interest in the prospects for containing a conflict with the West or the US to a less-than-

total engagement. Both great powers may now envision limited conflict as the most probable means of applying military pressure against its adversary. It is, then, conceivable to foresee a limited great-power conflict, either conventional or nuclear, either tactical or strategic, either with warning or without warning.

3. *Conflicts Between Local Contestants.* This is the most likely mode of great-power involvement in military operations in the near future. In view of the full spectrum of local conflict in the twentieth century and the prospects of local disputes in the 1970s, the opportunities for great-power intervention are enormous indeed, and are likely not to decrease but to proliferate. Both great powers now have the physical capability to intervene in selected local conflicts, and the Soviets' appetite for intervention may be cautiously increasing while the US is becoming progressively disinterested in foreign involvements, especially in unilateral operations. Thus it is conceivable that either or both great powers could become involved in a local conflict, unilaterally or in conjunction with a variety of allies or friendly states. Such an involvement would almost certainly remain conventional.

4. *Great Power Peacetime Rivalry with Only the Threat of Limited Naval Action.* The threat of limited naval action has been used at least once in every one of the past fifty years, except 1944. It has been used by twenty-four states against fifty-two separate countries, some without even a coastline. In the 1960s, there were at least two and usually more instances per year. It is important to note that the threat of naval action is a highly refined instrument of policy, applicable to only a small minority of disputes. It has not been employed in European water, for example, for the past thirty years, yet the Soviets effectively deter Israel from further attacks against Egyptian ports by permanently stationing warships in October 1967 in Port Said and Alexandria.[13] The optimum use of the threat of naval action requires a balanced naval force that can provide maximum mobility and flexibility. The ability of either great power to employ naval threats will remain a function of the refinement of their fleet composition, rather than raw numbers of firepower indices, and the dexterity with which it is applied. Nonetheless, it is likely to become an increasingly useful tool, especially for the Soviets.

Achievement of Naval Parity

Has parity been achieved in any of these contingencies? There is no such thing as military equality or absolute parity. The influence of one nation on the policies of other states depends largely upon their calculation of the power that can be applied against them and their estimate of how it will be used. Strategic parity in a given region, then, is a function of the degree of symmetrical deterrence and the calculus of risks and uncertainties inherent in any policy or action that may alter the status quo to the detriment of an adversary.

While strategic parity is a relative factor, it can be measured by several criteria. To what extent can a great power protect its respective interests in any given crisis, unilaterally if necessary? To what extent can either power exploit the weaknesses of the other? To what extent is either prepared or capable to protect the interests of clients or allies? By these standards, both great powers suffer important constraints, yet enjoy limited maneuverability.

In terms of military force, the Soviets have achieved powerful deterrence against the US in waters important to Western interests, e.g. the Eastern Mediterranean, the Norwegian Sea, the Japanese Sea, the Yellow Sea and the North Atlantic. If the Soviets achieved complete tactical surprise and launched a pre-emptive nuclear strike against only American capital ships and key bases in these regions, it could inflict severe damage, and it would be a long time before sufficient replacements could be deployed to restore the balance. On the other hand, if both sides had adequate warning of an impending nuclear engagement to initiate appropriate defensive precautions, the Soviets would probably sustain such losses that surviving units would no longer constitute a viable fighting force, while the US would likely forfeit its key warships and numerous aircraft. In a protracted bilateral conventional engagement, the US would have sufficient advantages from the outset that in-being Soviet forces and reinforcements could be effectively neutralized with minimal US losses. If NATO were involved in a conventional conflict with the Soviets and their allies, it would likely conclude in the West's favor as "superb live-fire exercise." The number of forces alone ensures that the West can sustain significant attrition rates and still protect its interests. Thus the degree of military parity exists in proportion to the level of conflict: at the lower end of the spectrum, the West retains sufficient advantages to impose asymmetrical deterrence when important interests are threatened, but has diminishing advantages as the scale progresses toward a no-warning nuclear war. On the other hand, the US has been forced to recognize the USSR's similar status, since under low-risk circumstances, Moscow can also intervene militarily by invitation, in combination with local forces or unilaterally, with sufficient force and staying power to present the US with a *fait accompli* when its important interests are threatened. In other words, the Kremlin now has the strength to alter the status quo in its favor when propitious conditions occur; it is unlikely to seek such advantages when favorable prospects do not exist.

Moscow's advantage at both ends of the conflict spectrum must afford it general recognition as a major naval power. Sufficient military deterrence has been achieved that Moscow must now be regarded as a political equal with the most powerful local state or coalition in many regions throughout the world. In these waters, the Soviets' minimum conditions for regional stability can no longer be ignored by other interested powers. While still inferior to the US or Western navies in terms of balance, Moscow has altered its maritime ambitions

to fit its capabilities: to compel the larger power to operate or fight more on
its terms than ever before and to commit substantially greater forces that it
itself deploys. Moscow has succeeded largely in its aims through incorporating
a wide variety of conceptual and technological improvisations. With this new
posture, Moscow apparently has now concluded that in selected contingencies
it could inflict sufficient damage against Western or US forces and interests to
deter its opponents from risky undertakings, affording it an adequate degree of
military parity to significantly expand its political maneuverability. The final
test of parity is not Soviet desires, but the reactions of recipients or those affected by any change in the status quo. The final test of parity cannot be made
until the Soviets challenge important American interests. But there are sufficient
areas where the Soviets could prudently expand their maritime interests without
endangering those of the United States that the expected test could be delayed
for some time.

In assessing how this new untested but presumed degree of great-power
parity is most likely to be applied by the Soviets, several assumptions can be
made. In the foreseeable future, the military contingencies listed above involving
a direct confrontation with the US Navy will be avoided as counterproductive.
Moscow will prefer US acquiescense to changes in the status quo rather than
the risks inherent in a naval clash. Rather, two alternative approaches to the
same end are likely to be employed.

First, an attempt to erode or compromise US influence through indirect
means can be expected. Moscow is likely to demonstrate its new prowess through
the various modes of gunboat diplomacy to influence local contestants.
They are likely to argue that the judicious use of naval power is more rewarding
than open clashes. By first deterring the US and then constraining its freedom
of action, its influence may wane. Only when the imperialists' power to intervene militarily has been contained, Moscow may argue, can the legitimate aspirations of local powers be achieved. Courses of action that ignore this schedule
are likely to arouse resistance rather than induce acceptance. This prescription
underscores the indispensability of the Soviet naval power in resolving national
grievances of selected regional powers.

A second alternative use of Soviet naval power is to foster great-power
cooperation. The USSR has already indicated that there are issues and regions
where great-power collaboration would be mutually beneficial. Moscow negotiated and signed the May 1972 accord on reducing incidents ar sea. The provisions are not stringent and the issue is rather artificial, stemming from
provocations by Soviet warships steering collision courses resulting in near-
misses with US destroyers in the Pacific. The agreement is relevant only when
there is an intent by either party to provoke the other.

Of greater potential interest is Moscow's apparent concern with naval stand-
off in the Indian Ocean. One year after establishing a naval presence, Moscow

indicated to the US its interest in a mutually agreed naval stalemate in the Indian Ocean. According to Under Secretary of State U. Alexis Johnson before the US Senate Foreign Relations Committee on 1 February 1972, the US had approached the USSR at an earlier date about arranging a mutual limit on naval armament in the Indian Ocean—the Soviets would presumably like to discourage Polaris submarines and the US would be interested in prohibiting Soviet carriers. Such asymmetrical trade-offs are risky but the suggestions raised by both sides indicate that each is considering the feasibility of some form of maritime order in acknowledged "seas of influence," armament limitations in waters of marginal interest, and no restraints in regions of potential competition.

Central to these initial great-power sallies into a maritime dialogue is that the US agreement to talk, as at SALT, is de facto acceptance of a high degree of Soviet naval parity—there is no need to bargain when one side holds the important cards. On its side, the USSR can be expected to exploit even proposals for great-power talks as a means of consolidating and gaining recognition of its stature as a global naval power.

A final factor lends credibility to the interests of both powers in seeking some form of naval limitation. Both powers are now reducing the numbers of their general-purpose warships. Between 1968 and 1974 the US reduced its total active fleet ships from 932 to 523. The US has one of the largest coastlines, and has a far less defensible geographic position than the USSR. Indeed the Soviet position with three fleets flanking Europe, however confined, in wartime, may be more influential in local affairs than US fleets based on the other side of the ocean. In both Europe and Asia, Soviet fleets are stationed in better locations to promote Moscow's peacetime intentions than are US fleets at Norfolk and San Diego. Thus the reduction of inventories will affect both but could hurt the US proportionally more—possibly even compromising its advantages in numbers accrued from nuclear propulsion. There seems to be sufficient incentive to seek limited understandings on issues of no immediate threat— even at the risk of sanctifying Soviet naval parity.

The above reasoning suggests that the most immediate dividends from the Soviet arrival at naval parity will be political. The motive behind expanding its defensive posture by acquiring a blue water fleet seems to parallel its nineteenth-century desire: to use naval power as a demonstration of Russia's ability to overcome geostrategic restraints and as certification of its global rank. The political applications of military power are tortuous indeed to fathom. The 1972 expulsion of the Soviet Advisory Mission from Egypt suggests that Moscow has confronted many of the pitfalls encountered earlier by Western powers. Before the Soviets employ their naval parity more advantageously, the US would be wise to adopt a policy of decoupling the political-military linkage whenever possible by isolating and quarantining Soviet naval presence in the most constrained area possible—an imaginative political undertaking that would at the same time relieve Western naval defense problems.

13

Toward a NATO Tactical Doctrine for the 1970s

The phenomenon of strategic parity has reduced the former degree of linkage between strategic and tactical warfare. It is now difficult to relate the outcome of a great-power strategic nuclear exchange to conceivable tactical situations. Thus, a new emphasis is being placed on the relevance of theater forces for the defense of local interests. Discussions in earlier chapters have suggested that Europe remains the chief source of contending vital interests for both great powers, and that new tactical doctrines and postures must be devised primarily for a European confrontation. Earlier observations also indicated that there is sufficient parity and such massive general-purpose forces that conventional war in Europe would be far more destructive than it was in Southeast Asia. Finally, as naval parity becomes more widely recognized, the utility of naval power, especially in Europe where force really counts, is likely to be curtailed. Thus, changes that have occurred in the rival military alliances over the past five years now make it imperative to develop more efficient force structures and doctrines for their employment, primarily for the general-purpose forces in Western Europe.

The most plausible option available under conditions of intensified regional security requirements is not, as has been traditionally argued, to enhance firepower and weapons' destructive potential, but to refine firepower and insure its more discriminate employment. To outline the advantages of discriminate over indiscriminate weapons is not entirely satisfactory. In order to project more adequately the necessity, feasibility, and desirability of developing proposed new weaponry an appropriate doctrine, concepts of operations and supporting troop levels should be briefly sketched. As a contrast, or framework for comparison, a summary of the current NATO tactical nuclear doctrine is warranted.

As early as 1960, Henry Kissinger identified the need for development of a doctrine for the employment of tactical nuclear weapons. "The lack of a concept and capability for tactical nuclear war—conceived as control of the battlefield—is one of the greatest gaps in the present military posture of the United States as well as NATO."[1] This failure to devise a comprehensive doctrine for tactical nuclear warfare or to develop forces clearly designed for it remains a crucial obstacle in the present plans for a Western response to a continental assault. A former NATO official observed nearly ten years after

Kissinger's comments that NATO no doubt has a variety of ways to use nuclear weapons in the initial stages of a conflict, if absolutely necessary, but a plan and capability for tactical nuclear war "conceived as control of the battlefield," or as part of the total deterrent posture—definitely not.[2]

Thirteen years after his initial observation, Henry Kissinger again lamented the failure of the Alliance to develop a tactical nuclear doctrine. "A great deal remains to be accomplished to give reality to the goal of flexible response: There are deficiencies in important areas of our conventional defense. There are still unresolved issues in our doctrine, for example, on the crucial question of the role of tactical nuclear weapons."[3]

The role of tactical nuclear weapons in NATO defenses has been the subject of endless controversy. The US has deployed over 7000 warheads in Europe. The average yield per warhead is approximately equal that of the bomb detonated at Hiroshima. The aggregate energy of these warheads if released is well in excess of 400,000,000 tons of TNT.[4] This is roughly one half of the total megatons of the US ICBM force, formerly regarded as an excessive overkill capacity even for the USSR. When decoupled from the strategic exchange, the idea of the release of such devastation by the Western side alone within the confines of Europe conveys the irrationality of the weapons. General awareness of this destructive potential has been an important constraint on policy and an inhibition on discussions of nuclear matters.[5] These restraints have been magnified, moreover, by the unchallenged assumption that both sides would naturally seek complete victory and military advantages that would require endless escalations and catastrophic consequences.[6] The incredibility of the massive use of the present weapons and the political and psychological constraints against discussing alternative applications have virtually paralyzed discussions of nuclear policy within the Alliance.

The present tactical stockpile was conceived and designed in the 1950s and the ideas for its employment are of the same vintage. Secretary of Defense Robert McNamara stressed in his 1962 Ann Arbor, Michigan speech that US deterrent calculations depended exclusively on strategic reprisals and ignored the impact of tactical warheads in Europe. The deployment of a tactical stockpile to Europe was regarded as the necessary price to assuage NATO fears and French taunts about the credibility of US fidelity. But the majority of the 7000 warheads were and still are programed for release *after* the strategic exchange, making their impact on either the local or global conflict negligible.[7] Individual strikes could be requested, as could strikes against highly circumscribed selected targets. In 1969 NATO's Nuclear Planning Group outlined the concept of nuclear first use in the Provisional Political Guidelines for the Use of Defensive Tactical Nuclear Weapons, which suggested, the initial release be confined to demonstrative purposes. No provisions have been made for additional increments of nuclear weapons in the event the demonstration fails, and the next option theoretically is the last one of the opposite end of the scale, massive retaliation. Opponents of the present concept argue that unless tactical nuclear weapons are calibrated into a more systematic, incremental targeting strategy and the weapons supplied and crews trained to support the strategy, the demonstrative first use makes little military sense. It must be expected that the Soviets would have anticipated this risk in their calculations for successful aggression and would not be deterred, if their objectives remained below the limits that might trigger massive retaliation. But Washington has consistently opposed NATO attempts to further specify the increments in its flexible response as unwarranted constraints of its exclusive nuclear release authority. Moreover, Washington's prolonged indifference toward tactical nuclear warfare and its seeming obsession with conventional armaments have further undermined Allied confidence in nuclear options and reinforced the Alliance's unwitting and reluctant continued reliance on massive retaliation at the theater level. On their part, the Europeans abhor the prospects of a massive exchange confined to the theater level and would prefer a doctrine that envisions early first use and large incremental steps of nuclear weapons leading to an early strategic exchange. Despite differences in the size and timing of nuclear options, all NATO members perceive the Western strategic choices as unwavering linear escalations anchored to the final massive retaliation. Ironically, this ghastly dependence is precisely what Kennedy tried to overcome by formulating the flexible-response strategy.[8] And the Alliance continues to be saddled not only with a stockpile of politically incredible weapons, but also with an incredible doctrine for their employment. No concerted effort has yet been made to replace the doctrine of escalation with a doctrine of genuine force integration.

The solution lies not in attempting to resurrect and perfect a doctrine for flexible response, with all the uncertainties and agonizing dilemmas witnessed in only its conventional application in Vietnam. What is needed is a doctrine for the rational use of whatever force is necessary to achieve prescribed goals—a doctrine that will not merely delineate when to use nuclear weapons by defining scenario-like guidelines, but one that will outline the best application of military power for efficient achievement of objectives.

Assumptions Relevant to Doctrinal Innovations

At the outset, several recommended premises pertaining to the state of the Alliance and general military policy should be outlined for a new overall strategy that may assist in formulating appropriate concepts of force employment and models for force structures.[9]

1. In the age of diplomatic maneuver, the Alliance should stress psychological determination in formulating policies to achieve what is militarily necessary

to prevent war, while encouraging what is politically feasible to strengthen détente.

2. Policy should aim at the dual goals of providing assured security for NATO without creating insecurity for the opponent—protection without threat.

3. Deterrence is only credible as the opponent's estimation of the effectiveness of our local defenses—emphasis should be placed on active defense and the combination of vagueness and credibility of escalatory intentions to produce uncertainty.

4. To preclude *fait accompli* operations, any form of aggression must be countered automatically and reinforced by a willingness and capability to respond at any level of attack, not the opposite—"a more flexible, flexible response."[10]

5. Conflict in Europe must remain under that level regarded as tolerable by Europeans; e.g., there is little point in retaliating after absorbing a massive first strike, if the opponent still has an assured, preponderant second-strike capability directed against Europe.

6. To insure that a potential conflict remains at the lower levels of violence and to deny the USSR sanctuary rights if deterrence fails, Europe must develop its own assured second-strike capability, preferably a more integrated British-French effort.

7. Force structures for the next decade must reflect a decline in national investment in military spending and a gradual American disengagement, resulting in a curtailment of NATO's conventional capabilities.

8. From a position of unprovoked attack, there should be no moral compunctions against destroying an aggressor by whatever means are available; the use of tactical nuclear weapons in itself should not be regarded as repugnant, but it is vital to insure their discriminate, controlled employment. No one can rationally justify the indiscriminate use of nuclear weapons; yet, after Vietnam, neither can anyone advocate unlimited expenditure of conventional ordnance. Within these parameters, a sound strategy can be formulated, relying on existing or proposed defense budgets, weapons technologies, and force strengths. In other words, new concepts can be devised to insure more effective utilization of existing theater resources.

Maximum Defense Strategy— Conceptual Integration

The proposed new strategy might be labeled a Maximum Defense (MD) strategy, and should be designed to provide a compatible doctrine for the employment of both conventional and nuclear theater resources, independently or in unison, with minimum reliance on non-European assets and reinforcements, and structured to maximize defensive postures without impairing security. Unity of conventional and nuclear doctrines has been constrained in the past by the self-imposed US firebreak concept, which must be downgraded. The integration of nuclear and conventional fire should be regarded as complementary to the underlying premise of the proposed strategy; namely, that concepts of operation and force structures should be designed to maximize a defensive posture, increasing budgetary economies while enhancing the onus and cost of aggression without impairing general security. The rules of engagement should stress that the purpose of a maximum defense posture is to reduce the opponent's perceived national interests jeopardized in a given crisis against his risks and possible losses—bona fide deterrence. The basic difference between the proposed strategy and earlier ones is that deterrence is related primarily to defensive operations rather than offensive retaliation. But to achieve this transition without endangering security, a heavy reliance must be placed on nuclear weaponry and force reposturing.

The first principle, then, governing force employment in a Maximum Defense strategy should be that concepts be devised, plans formulated, and troops trained for simultaneous, integrated nuclear and conventional warfare. This conceptual unity would peg the level of violence to the intensity of threat or attack and to specific types of combat. It need not automatically prescribe the use of nuclear weapons for all contingencies, but for serious aggression, it would force the aggressor to accept the onus for starting a nuclear offensive and remove barriers to escalation, thereby strengthening the deterrence of theater resources.

Theater Tactical and Strategic Weapons

To facilitate the decision to employ nuclear weapons in a conflict, a distinction should be made between tactical and strategic theater nuclear weapons. The existing arsenal can be categorized as weapons optimally employed to support maneuver battalions and those for damaging war-waging capabilities, through interdiction or facilities destruction. A separation can also be made between first-use theater warheads and second-strike, invulnerable systems. Finally, a distinction can be made between weapons employed against countervalue and counterforce targets. Battle-winning, first-use, counterforce weapons should be targeted against enemy maneuver battalions, logistic facilities, command posts, and communications that directly support his ability to attack the defender's positions and are within a geographic line seventy-five kilometers behind the Forward Edge of the Battle Area (FEBA). Military targets beyond that point would be subject to escalatory strikes and would serve as an interim step to the release of SACEUR's strategic, second-strike theater force, capable of ranges between 400 and 2300 miles and yields that could be countervalue.

This force consists of long-range fighter-bombers, British and French bombers, IRBMs and ballistic submarines, and US Poseidon submarines.

The segregation of theater nuclear resources into more readily controllable incremental categories, with clearly defined and published thresholds for each, would enhance the defensive profile of the MD strategy by forcing the aggressor to assess more carefully the advantages of concentration and unity over dispersal and survivability. Designation of strategic weapons systems and missions would signal the likely withholding of these weapons against medium level attacks, but would also imply that no barriers existed to their employment should escalation be required. Moreover, the employment initially of only battle-winning weapons would indicate that absolute victory or capitualtion were not the tactical objectives, allowing the enemy an alternative to expanding the conflict. Finally, the distinction between tactical and strategic theater weapons would facilitate a more comprehensive understanding among all Allies about the optimal use of specific weapons and strengthen control over their disciplined employment. Thus the second principle for an MD strategy is that a tactical doctrine for integrated warfare whould provide categorization of targets and warheads appropriate for firm control, maximum military effectiveness, and prompt release.

Nuclear Release Authorization

The third principle follows from the second: the necessity to insure the early first use of battlefield nuclear weapons. The use of nuclear weapons should be a deliberate decision, made with the full knowledge of the probable consequences and impact on national objectives, rather than a hasty choice, made under duress and with inadequate, possibly faulty, information. The use of nuclear weapons is now programed as a cataclysmic spasm, signaling the exhaustion of all other options and the imminent collapse of other forms of resistance. The use of nuclear weapons in such circumstances would be irrelevant to the local conflict and the values and aims for which earlier sacrifices and losses were made.

Criteria for deliberate early first use must be devised in a manner that will contribute either to deterrence or to containment of the conflict. Specific indices for presidential release authorization could be constructed for the most likely foreseeable contingencies, thereby reducing agonizing appraisals and excessive delays. The intent behind the indices would be to facilitate early first use in order to buy time, by forcing the attacker to disperse, and allow the West to accelerate its mobilization, clarify its intelligence, and consider additional counteractions. Furthermore, a decisive intial response to block the aggressor as near the political border as possible, where there would be little loss of face or forces, would offer him suitable alternatives to escalation—before becoming too deeply committed, he could desist. First use of nuclear weapons, then, should be as early as possible, before the military situation deteriorates and the aggressor calculates that he can wait out the impending collapse without escalating the conflict.

Ideally, release of selected types of defensive nuclear weapons could be preplanned for release under "anticipated authorization," whereby purely defensive ADMs, ASW warheads, plus several demonstrative air strikes against predetermined penetration routes in friendly territory would be designed for release within minutes after a significant incursion had been confirmed. The use of a small number of very low-yield, accurate weapons on friendly soil would buy valuable time, allow the attacker to withdraw, and reduce the impact of unforeseen contingencies, such as tactical surprise. "Anticipated authorization" would not infringe upon the President's exclusive prerogatives, but such ultra first-use procedures would require thorough planning and precise training.

Disciplined Command Procedures

A fourth guideline for the MD strategy relates to the command and control procedures for the broader scope of nuclear warfare—deliberate and discretionary release. After the attacker's intentions had been probed by conventional forces and "anticipated authorization" procedures and determined to be sufficiently hostile, additional force increments would be required. If several thresholds have already been established for the employment of various types of theater warheads, their early introduction into the conflict can be discrete rather than spasmodic and publicized as precautionarey rather than provocatory. The incorporation of satellite communications has reduced the time lag between requests at corps level and release by national command authorities. For the first time in the nuclear age, the state-of-art in command and control facilities is approaching the requirements imposed by the speed and mobility of tactical nuclear situations, though field facilities lag behind these improvements. But this should not be viewed as an excuse to maintain presidential control over each weapon authorization. The perpetuation of the existing nuclear procedures will ossify the present tendencies of field commanders to intentionally overestimate situations and make requests for anticipated developments rather than actual ones. Existing concepts and excessive delays also increase pressures for blanket requests and unintentional saturation bombardment.

Thus, the MD strategy should provide for presidential release of all warheads designated for a specified increment of nuclear force which would include weapons types, yields, target parameters, and constraints in offensive employment. The field commanders should be allowed freedom to assigned warheads to each target from his total existing assets. In the past, nuclear warfare was regarded as too serious to be left to the military. But if it is integrated into a total tactical doctrine and not employed as a death knell, the field commander will probably show more restraint than his political counterpart. He is likely to be more aware than higher authorities that nuclear assets represent the ultimate weapons in his sector of responsibility and should be used accordingly. This formula allows military professionals to exploit whatever asymmetries may exist between NATO and the Pact in force structures, equipment, and training and not force them to act as if these discrepancies did not exist. Thus precise political control should be exercised over the release of each increment of integrated nuclear and conventional force, and military commanders would be entrusted with devising the optimal use of each increment.

Maximum-Minimum Force Employment

The next principle for an MD strategy relates to targeting policies. The objective of military coercion should be to deny the aggressor his war aims and to indicate the unfavorable calculus between his perceived national interests and potential risks in any given situation. The opponent's will to resist, the aim of the former philosophy of "offensive" deterrence, must be abandoned. If the opponent is confronted with the onus of launching a nuclear war, it must be concluded that he is sufficiently determined to persevere. Rather than attempting to induce reasonableness by purely psychological means, stark punitive measures should dictate Western reactions. The preference for psychological persuasiveness has introduced such circumspection that minimal force and gradualism have replaced coercion in the applications to date of flexible response, without always achieving the desired results. Efforts to convince an adversary by demonstration are no substitute for those that incapacitate him.

The formula for specifying each force increment should be determined as the level of damage to the opponent's battle-winning potential, then if necessary, his war-waging capability that *cannot be absorbed.* Force levels should be measured as the maximum required to achieve desired results, but which will not result in irresponsible overkill. Optimum weapons and delivery systems should be employed to intensify the impact of each increment. Minimal force allowances may provide the opponent adequate time to calculate the upper limit of one's commitments and his ability to absorb future responses. Under these conditions, the adversary may resort to protracted conflict or over-escalation, negating the effect of the initial increment and requiring even larger allocations.

The main constraint in optimizing punitive responses in theater conflicts is that they must be confined to tactical forces and capabilities, leaving intercontinental strategic resources intact until ultimate values are jeopardized. Attacks against any facilities that support the opponent's capability to retaliate strategically are likely to trigger a preemptive strike. A fine distinction, then,

should be made between inflicting sufficient coercion to induce a cease fire
or stalemate while keeping the level of violence as low as possible. Yet adequate
resources should be available for employment of the follow-on force options
when the first stage is initiated. A credible threat of escalation is a vital component of incremental use of force. The introduction of the next calibrated step
in a relatively short period precludes the recovery of the opponent's battle-
winning potential and implies that the defender has established a deadline for
either cessation or the application of the next increment. As a hedge against
overreaction by the adversary, however, inducements to desist should be
proffered in a similar magnitude to the sanctions imposed. This calibration of
maximum forces will likely make any rung in the upward transition to the
next less, rather than more, probable—an approach US preferences have heretofore rendered difficult to apply. This broader understanding of increment force
more accurately reflects the parameters of doctrinal integration than does the
concept of minimal force and sterile escalatory moves.

Improved Conventional Weaponry

The sixth governing factor for the new strategy pertains to weapons modernization for conventional arms. The devastating firepower of nuclear weapons is
now being supplemented by a revolution in conventional firepower that is
swinging the balance formerly held by offensive arms in favor of defensive
weapons. In the last five years major breakthroughs have occurred in personal
antitank and antiaircraft short-range missiles that have registered marked
improvements over earlier crew-served weapons. The new man-portable, shoulder-
fired missiles will provide virtually every large patrol with antitank and antiaircraft defenses. Tanks and aircraft, the main offensive instruments, will still
have greater mobility and more sustained firepower over the individual patrol,
but the capability of single infantrymen to defeat any movable armor or the
fastest low-altitude aircraft, or the use of missile-equipped helicopters to counter
the mobility of mechanized units, means that defensive redundancies, or
defense in depth, can now be planned on a scale and economy never before
envisioned. Every enemy foray must now expect to encounter devastating
fire anywhere within hostile territory, making penetration and survivability
more a function of larger numbers than of maneuverability, firepower, speed,
or surprise. Yet concentrated forces will become vulnerable to nuclear fire and
immediate devastation. Revolutions on this scale are of the same magnitude as
the progression from bolt-action rifles to machine guns, and restore the primacy
to defense after fifty years' subordination to tanks.[11] But revolutions on such
a scale are now only technologically feasible; like earlier quantum changes, it
may take years and possibly a war before tactics and training reach the level
necessary to capitalize fully on major technological innovations. Short of

complete utilization, other measures, e.g. early first use of tactical weapons, will be required.

Equally important for defense has been the emergence of new concepts of air power and air mobility. NATO countries have by far the largest aggregate of tactical airlift aircraft in the world, and they are integrated into the close ground-support operations of lifting supplies to forward tactical units, even under siege conditions. This marked improvement in battlefield airlift capability is vital to sustain the main component of the new air-mobile concept—the air-mobile division. Air-mobile brigades with light fire support can now be lifted and sustained for extended periods 75 to 100 kilometers behind the FEBA on the Central Front with its own internal transport. Each brigade can move independent of roads and logistics bases within the FEBA "fire support zone," or 75 kilometers from friendly mobile defenses, engaging enemy reserves, interdicting logistics, and identifying major targets for nuclear fire. These unique features of the air mobile units would be a valuable contribution to the peculiar characteristics of the MD strategy with its emphasis on defensive posture. While a nonprovocative profile is desirable, sufficient offensive power must be available in mobile warfare to assume the initiative and to prevent consolidation. As a lightly armed unit, the air mobile division is not normally regarded as a truly offensive force. But the mobility and coordinated nuclear fire support would make these units ideally suited for the counterattack role and an optimum component in the offensive/defensive force mix for an MD strategy. An important reservation, however, must be added. For full implement- ation of this concept, air superiority must be assured or night-flight operations risked. On balance, aerial deliveries can be made beyond the FEBA at night and low altitude, but aircrews will encounter the inaccuracies of night work and ground fire that is more difficult to counter at night.

Probably the most important aspect of the revolution in conventional defensive weapons is that the NATO countries are far ahead of the Warsaw Pact in developing these new weapons systems and concepts. The Pact is still equipped and trained for a World War II type massive offensive, supported in the main by relatively large-yield nuclear warheads delivered primarily by missiles and high-performance aircraft. Every effort should be made to accelerate the pace of the revolution in conventional defenses and thereby under- score the discrepancies between the Pact's preponderantly offensive force postures and the West's defensive profile.

Improved Nuclear Weaponry

A seventh principle envisages a similar revolution in the modernization of nuclear weaponry. The equivalent of at least fifteen megatons of high explosives were expended by the United States in North and South Vietnam. No total

costs for the air campaign that delivered most of this ordnance are presently
available, but they must be the highest figures of all other similar operations
if all procurement, training, losses, armament, and support facilities are included.
Yet no other country of comparable size has sustained such extensive collateral
damage from modern warfare. Such extensive destruction to other targets not
specifically designated for attack was due to excessive bombing errors—high-
performance aircraft were designed to deliver medium-yield nuclear weapons,
not relatively small conventional bombs. In view of such discrepancies between
results achieved and undesired damage inflicted, it is appropriate to inquire
whether more positive results could have been accomplished at smaller costs and
with less unwanted damage through the use of improved tactical nuclear weapons.
The emphasis of the MD strategy on a battle-winning doctrine stresses the importance of accurately acquiring and destroying military targets with minimal
collateral damage. The best means of reducing collateral damage without
impairing the ability to neutralize military targets is to increase delivery accuracy
and reduce weapons yields. Near-zero impact errors are now possible through the
use of new weapons such as the Walleye and Condor missiles and laser-guided
bombs. It is also now possible to reduce individual yields by factors of 100 or
1000 over those in the existing arsenals, and to virtually eliminate onerous
contamination.

Improvements of this magnitude are contributions neither to nuclear
blackmail nor offensive retaliation, but to the positive use of defensive power to
repel aggression, and must be exploited. Moreover, economies of force on this
scale would allow a multiplication of available warheads by several hundred.
Mental phobias, not technological and engineering know-how or production
costs, remain the basic restraints against improving existing stockpiles of
obsolescent weapons. Indeed, economic imperatives of savings in production,
maintenance costs, and manpower are strong arguments supporting conversion
to new generations of nuclear weapons.

(Budgetary considerations are one of Washington's reasons for not modernizing its nuclear arsenal more quickly. This reluctance may be overcome by extending the costs to NATO burden-sharing programs. Since the improved weapons
would be used almost exclusively for continental defenses, European contributions to their production should be expected. Actual production would remain
American responsibility, but formulation of weapons requirements and financial
obligations could be largely the responsibility of nonnuclear states. Funding
could be managed either through expanding the existing infrastructure system or
by an independent financial consortium. Development and production of delivery
vehicles and supporting equipment could be consigned to defense industries of
nonnuclear states, ameliorating both the burdens and the economic rewards for
all members.)

Several specific suggestions can be offered as indications of the types of
weapons improvements currently possible. Fusing devices can be installed in

battlefield and aircraft delivery systems similar to those in modern air defense weapons that would allow battery commanders and pilots to dial a desired yield into the warhead before firing. Thus increments of the same maximum critical mass, e.g., 0.5, 2.0 or 5.0 Kts, can be controlled to specific burst overpressures. In another example, the construction in the Pact of aircraft shelters has increased by four or five times the number of nuclear weapons required to destroy a hardened airbase. The number of tactical aircraft required to inflict 80 percent damage against a single well-defended, hardened airbase deep in hostile territory is likely to be high. A nuclear cluster munition, similar to the conventional cluster bomb (CBU series) used so effectively in Southeast Asia, could be designed to dispense five or six nuclear bomblets. Development of such a munition would restore the former one aircraft to one target ratio and allow important economies in the present limited aircraft resources. (Production costs for such a weapon would undoubtedly be drastically lower than the delivery aircraft, an example of how greater weapons efficiency can impart significant savings when cost effectiveness is equated with assured destruction.) Finally, one of the restraints against employing ADMs has been the difficulty of achieving the prescribed implantation and the danger of pro-ducing a relatively high proportion of collateral damage compared to durable structural destruction. But the use of existing shaped charges with a very-low-yield nuclear warhead could insure adequate penetration of hardened surfaces and increase cratering and secondary structural damage many times. Multiplica-tion of munition effectiveness and conservation of physical assets on such scales can now be readily available.

The purpose in developing ultra- and very-low-yield weapons and increasing substantially the total numbers available would be to afford NATO an optimum defense-to-offense ratio by capitalizing on the crushing advantage of nuclear firepower over mobility and warhead availability over speed. Reinforced platoons could compel the aggressor to amass forces several times larger to mount a conventional assault. Yet such concentrations would provide tactical warning and present lucrative targets for nuclear fire, while denying the attacker targets appropriate for his relatively scarce and probably larger weapons. Thus, for relatively moderate costs compared to NATO's total budgetary outlays, the strongest tactical defensive posture since the days of US assymetrical deterrence is feasible. Indeed, the adverse impact of great power strategic parity and Pact advantages in Europe can be neutralized.

Clean Weapons—Neutron Ordnance

Western security needs do not now demand a more powerful bomb or great-er delivery speed to insure military effectiveness. In tactical warfare, efficiency is seldom equated with maximum destruction. If for no other reason, economy of resources defines efficiency as the discriminate use of force. When the nuclear dimension is added, weapons should be not only efficient but politically credible.

The first criterion for a new family of tactical weapons is that they must meet the classical standard for military effectiveness: maintainability, low costs, handling ease, survivability, reliability, flexibility, and accuracy in delivery. Flexibility and accuracy, however, are not sufficient to insure discriminate use of nuclear fire. The second criterion is that warhead design must be modified both to compensate for human error under combat and to minimize adverse effects. Distinctions need no longer be made between sources of energy (conventional or nuclear), but between the impact that energy has on a military target and its immediate environment. The new weapons must maximize discrimination between immediate military and residual civilian objectives.

A third criterion relates to the political credibility of the system, and therefore to its military utility. The erection of the most efficient military *defenses* possible is a government's national responsibility; its actions become a threat to international peace and stability when they acquire a distinguishable offensive capability. There appears to be little logic in the argument against improving defenses, even when it requires radical innovations. And in view of contemporary political reality, the final specification for the new system should be the incorporation of highly defensive and self-limiting or nonescalatory characteristics.

The present stockpile of tactical warheads consists in large part essentially of weapons with strategic-level yields. The energy source for these weapons is primarily the fissioning of relatively large masses of uranium and plutonium which release enormous blasts and vast amounts of longlived radioactivity. Their lack of precision and indiscriminate effects impart a similar magnitude of destruction as most warheads delivered by strategic vehicles; warhead reductions cut size, weight, costs, and adverse effects. But even in lower yield ranges, destructive and contamination penalties outweight the political risks or even total national costs to achieve desired goals. The present weapons do not meet any of the specifications outlined above.

There are two technologies that can produce the desired weapons effects. The first is to miniaturize fission warheads to the range of very low yields, or tons equivalents rather than kilotons. This process reduces the heat and blast effects and proportionally increases the prompt radiation effects (the neutrons and gamma rays that last only a fraction of a second). Human beings are more susceptible to radiation than to the blast effects of nuclear fire. Therefore, the antipersonnel effect is partially increased as the yield is reduced. In other words, it is possible to attack enemy troops in towns without inflicting significant structural damage. To produce comparable casualties by blast would require increases in energy intensity of possibly one hundredfold, with the resultant collateral damage and residual radiation witnessed at Hiroshima. The new miniaturized artillery shells being considered by NATO forces have these preferable characteristics, which permits for the first time realistic discrimination in nuclear fire.

A second option deals with fusion rather than fission. In the early 1950s it became possible to force the fusion of light elements such as hydrogen and lithium rather than the fission of heavy uranium and plutonium. Fusion reactions create even more discriminate detonations by reducing blast and increasing prompt radiation, while releasing *no* residual or longlived radioactive products. For example, a fusion reaction releases about 80 percent of its energy in high energy neutrons—antipersonnel radiation. By contrast, in a similar sized fission reaction only about 5 percent of the energy is released as prompt radiation. Thus a kiloton fusion bomb may have the prompt radiation effectiveness of a fission warhead fifteen times larger, or a Hiroshima-size yield. Moreover, the blast and heat effects in the fusion device would be only a fraction of a kiloton, since its energy would have been dissipated as prompt radiation, and it would release no residual contamination.[12]

As early as 1963 the US acknowledged that it was conducting research on fusion weapons. A major obstacle in perfecting the warhead has been the triggering device—the problem is how to induce the fusion reaction without using a fission or atomic detonator. It is now widely believed among experts that a solution is imminent.

How would an enhanced-radiation, clean, neutron warhead affect tactical operations?

1. A neutron bomb can be delivered in such a manner that the physical, ecological, and social structure of the civilian population need not sustain serious damage or dislocation, except when the enemy intermingles with civilians.

2. Since urban structures do not normally provide sufficient mass to attenuate high-energy neutrons, hostile troops will be less likely to use cities as primary centers of resistance, but would enter urban areas mainly to mingle with the population and thereby preclude attack; the net effect, however, will likely be to return tactical hostilities to the battlefield and a truly counterforce struggle.

3. The intensive antipersonnel aspects of enhanced radiation weapons will magnify the need for protective cover, suggesting that a higher premium will be placed on fixed military defensive positions rather than urban centers which could alter the entire scope of tactical warfare.

4. The decline in physical destruction will reduce the amount of rubble and debris that often impedes movement, adding greater unit maneuverability when friendly exploitation is appropriate.

5. But enemy exploitation and maneuver can be retarded by "salting" or introducing an additional element into the fusion process which becomes

an irradiated longlived contaminate.[13] The range of prompt radiation and its anti-personnel effects can be varied also by altering the height of the burst.

6. The normal kill-to-wound ratio of 1 to 3 will be reversed, with three times more deaths than wounded; and fewer wounded will be maimed or crippled and can be fully recuperated, since the blood supply is both the main source of contamination and resuscitation.

7. Hard targets requiring destruction can be efficiently struck by either extremely accurate delivery or by using warheads with varying levels of fission components and corresponding increases in blast effect.

8. Neutron ordnance is more versatile than fission weapons, and can be made even more flexible by the incorporation of existing operator devices that select desired yields and effects.

9. Most important, fusion weaponry contains inherent firebreaks—it is nonescalatory. Beyond a certain relatively low yield, the warhead loses its unique features and military efficiency. The use of neutron warheads, therefore, should be regarded as less provocative or subject to escalation than any fission weapon presently available.

In the event that the perfection of fusion weapons proves illusory, full advantage should be made immediately of integrating the new discriminate miniaturized artillery shells into a plausible tactical doctrine. This new capability is the most important contribution yet made to the sane conduct of military operations in Europe, but its utility is likely to be largely ignored or dissipated until an MD-type strategy is developed.

Force Structures

A further factor that should be considered in an MD strategy relates to force structures and dispositions. If tactical nuclear weapons are used as integral components of an MD strategy and not as a substitute for lack of conventional staying power, what size total force would be needed and how should it be organized, trained, and deployed? Several criteria for minimum strengths can be established. The absolute minimum level of in-being forces armed with modernized nuclear warheads must be a sufficiency to protect all available nuclear resources, delivery vehicles, logistic support systems, and command and control facilities in order to insure the credibility of the theater nuclear defenses.

A second criterion is that sufficient conventional forces must be in-place to support all nuclear options in the event of a no-warning offensive. In-place general-purpose forces for the conduct of massive conventional campaigns are unnecessary, but enough conventional power must be available to exploit the use of nuclear weapons or their presence becomes irrational and their employment incredible. Force strengths needed for decisive exploitation of nuclear options and assurance of favorable termination of hostilities depend upon the anticipated intensity of violence. Even if Warsaw Pact forces are maintained at the present level throughout the next decade, a gradual reduction in Western troop strengths will be possible as modernization improves mobility, firepower, command and control, and logistics. By 1975, a 30-percent troop cut and by 1980 a 50-percent decrease would not be unrealistic, providing that savings in real terms are converted to modernization programs and that doctrinal changes are incorporated to optimize weapons improvements. (Weapons modernization, force reductions, and doctrinal changes must be closely synchronized: a disastrous situation would result if a new strategy was devised independently of the forces and equipments required to support it, or vice versa, as Senator Mansfield advocates).

In the intermediate stage, a 30-percent reduction of the present 28 2/3 divisions on the Central Front, the remaining forces should be structured and equipped for both maximum mobility and staying power. The core of the mobile contingents could be three US air cavalry divisions plus one West German, one British, and one French paratroop or air-portable division. These six divisions, stationed in Europe, would form the basis for a theater strategic reserve for both the Central Front and the Flanks. On the Central Front, they would require the staying power of approximately fifteen independent nuclear artillery brigades, the present air-defense units, and the same Pershing missile forces that form part of the theater strategic forces. The Central Front would also require a conventional in-place forces of six mechanized divisions, emphasizing antitank and self-propelled artillery rather than armor, to insure the credibility of the nuclear deterrence and to support nuclear operations. In-being tactical air forces would not be reduced during this stage because of the requirement to fulfill both conventional and nuclear missions simultaneously, a dual capability for which there are presently insufficient available aircraft. Moreover, to increase the numbers on hand, conventional reconnaissance missions would be facilitated by the use of aerial drones and theater read-out terminals for satellite sensors, while immediate tactical requirements could be met with aircraft armed with pilot yield-dialing devices for multiple nuclear weapons. Finally, the present number of Fleet Ballistic Submarines assigned to SACEUR should be increased by one third and equipped with MIRV warheads as the most plausible means of countering the Soviet MRBM force.

Countering the Soviet MRBM Force

One of the most complex requirements for an MD strategy is how the formidable Soviet MRBM forces can be countered or neutralized. In partial response, nuclear facilities and support functions must be dispersed. Since the

Soviets know as much as the West about tactical nuclear technology, the present security measures for the stockpiles are excessive. These measures should be downgraded to those of regular munitions (local thievery will still be directed against high explosives, not nuclear warheads), allowing for dispersal to utilizing units and important budgetary savings. Delivery systems must also be scattered (for aircraft dispersal, see below). Alert procedures for SSMs should be accelerated so that in simple alert, say, units are fueled and moved out of garrison and held en route until full alert, when they would proceed to randomly selected launch sites. Finally, QRA functions can be dispensed with, thus gaining important savings in manpower and funds. Under the above nuclear release procedures for integrated early use of tactical nuclear weapons, the present policy of confining a portion of air and SSM units to alert compounds is unnecessary and costly. Such concentrations are too small to deter effectively, but large enough to invite attack.

Second, as suggested above, the planned number of eight European Fleet Ballistic Submarines should be increased by one third (either constructed in Europe or purchased from the US and fitted with British warheads). This increase in second-strike capability would allow a more credible deterrent to be on-station at all times and possibly one hundred launchers afloat during Reinforced Alert or 176 missiles for a maximum effort. The FBMs force should not be targeted against the Soviet MRBM force, which would increase the incentive for Soviet preemption. Rather, they should be directed against the Soviet tactical nuclear capabilities, such as storage sites in the USSR and the Forward Area. The USSR would probably not move tactical warheads forward during a mobilization phase, because of general security precautions and fear of detection, escalation, or preemption by the West. Further, the relatively smaller number of Soviet nuclear-support facilities increases their vulnerability. Thus, even after a Soviet first strike, storage facilities and known recipient units would still be vulnerable to incapacitating retaliation from an invulnerable NATO second-strike force.

A targeting policy emphasizing the susceptibility of Soviet tactical nuclear forces to incapacitation would reduce Moscow's incentive to launch disarming attacks against similar NATO nuclear facilities. But even if the deterrent failed, a high confidence in Western retaliation against like Soviet resources would impose a rough ceiling on the level of violence, since the massive use of tactical warheads would be denied both sides. Nuclear warfare would not be totally canceled out, however, since NATO could be resupplied from stockpiles in the US and the Soviets could transfer warheads from the Chinese front. But in a situation requiring rapid resupply of tactical warheads the West is believed to have important advantages: a relatively larger total number of warheads available in the continental United States than in the USSR, and the probable Soviet reluctance to deplete its resources in the Far East. Even the possibility of a modest US edge in resupply, however, would weaken Soviet confidence that in-theater nuclear assets could be neutralized and its preponderant conventional power assured the defeat of Western forces. Such a scenario reveals the extent that a strengthened Western MRBM posture could play in both the deterrence and the war-winning capability of an MD strategy.

Military Reserves and Mobilization

Consolidation and reequipping on this scale could seriously impair European security interests, unless they were accompanied by additional improvements of similar proportions. Local militia should be organized for optimum implementation of a forward defensive strategy. The marked improvements in mobility and the devastation of the attacker's nuclear fire have drastically reduced the value of static fortifications. Training of long-term militiamen with the relatively simple, high-firepower individual missile weapons should produce a high degree of proficiency and reliable resistance against medium-level incursions.

Another precondition for a one-third force reduction should be the institution of a comprehensive, standardized, NATO-wide reserve training program that would organize the vast manpower resources of Western Europe for rapid mobilization. Paradoxically, NATO has based all former strategies on the assumption that no major offensives would occur without adequate political and strategic warning of the imminence of hostilities, but has maintained large ready forces and deemphasized reserve capabilities. The only large-scale organized reserves readily available to NATO are presently in the United States. In comparison with the Pact's formidable manpower mobilization capability, the sparse European contribution to NATO staying power must be corrected before major reductions of in-place forces can be seriously considered.[14]

In terms of readily available deployed forces at any stage of mobilization or level of conflict, NATO should strive for a battalion to brigade or 1 to 2–3 *disadvantage.* Escalation to the next degree of mobilization or violence option would be warranted under several conditions: the threat of a large-scale loss of tactical nuclear weapons, jeopardizing both defensive operations and the ability to exploit greater increments of force; high attrition rates among ground forces, threatening the collapse of a given sector; and excessive aircraft losses, endangering the success of ground operations. The decision to escalate should coincide roughly with the commitment of corps level ready reserves and the attrition of roughly one-third of the available tactical aircraft.

The actual numbers involved would remain a function of the intensity of the conflict, the amount of strategic warning provided and the degree of matériel and manpower mobilization achieved and sustained to that point. Mobilization is the indispensible element in a sustained war effort under an MD strategy. It depends upon the organization, depth, and availability of war matériel and manpower commensurate with any contingency. (At present, stockpiles of war matériel on the continent are adequate for only several weeks' combat and the possibility of retooling European defense industries to meet large-scale demands on a crash basis is almost nonexistent. Thus, the vast bulk of both manpower reinforcements and matériel supplies, conventional and nuclear, must now come from the United States.)[15] In these awkward circumstances, NATO's rate of mobilization is disproportionately dependent upon the degree of strategic warning of enemy intentions available to political leaders.

Warning and Reaction

An additional premise for an MD strategy, then, relates strategic warning to mobilization and force availability. Providing strategic warning of impending actions by a closed society, such as the Soviet Union, is a particularly hazardous game for relatively more open Western nations. Nonetheless, NATO has consistently predicated all its potentially hostile actions on the predictability of the Pact's political intentions. But the West, especially the US, has not yet accurately forecasted Soviet moves. The adoption of the Acheson Plan and the deployment of large US conventional forces to the continent was totally irrelevant to the subsequent Soviet decision to erect the Berlin Wall. Soviet duplicity during the Cuban missile crisis was finally revealed by military intelligence, not political forecasting. The introduction of a policy of "gradualism" in the Vietnam War was based on the fear that US "overreaction" would force the two Communist giants into collaboration, but even the intensified bombing of the North did not heal the split—indeed, it increased tensions within the Communist camp. Finally, the political pundits successfully divined that the Pact would not invade the West during the Prague crisis, but they failed to predict the invasion, its timing and scope. Virtually all analysts, including notably Czechoslovak, Rumanian and Yugoslav officials, were confident that Moscow would not intervene.[16] This is clearly an unsatisfactory record of predictability that will give the Soviet Union important advantages of secrecy and surprise.

Since accurate political forecasting is likely to remain a fundamental premise for Western responses and also is likely to be continually hazardous, especially when the opponent has the initiative or a wide variety of options, can improvements be made? Few recommendations can be offered for strengthening either the model or techniques presently used in forecasting Soviet political intentions (see chapter 10). But several suggestions can be made that could reduce the adverse impact of future inaccuracies and errors, and minimize the uncertainties involved in Soviet behavior:

1. Establish NATO-agreed criteria for precautionary and provocative actions in crisis situations, allowing the Alliance to initiate measures for its

self-protection without hesitation; measures that will not also exacerbate tensions.

2. Institute realistic civil defense and evacuation procedures, especially in the forward defense zone.

3. Expand East-West détente measures, such as mutual reductions of existing restrictions against military attachés, and establish a tactical "hotline" between Soviet and American tactical air force headquarters to avert shoot-downs of aircraft that inadvertently penetrate the opponent's air space.

4. Install passive surveillance along common borders, i.e., the installation of remotely operated, unmanned, electronic sensor surveillance devices to a depth of twenty-five miles on the friendly side of the border.

5. Systematize Alliance consultative machinery to include mutual assessments of Pact intentions and East European reliability, and the exchange of friendly plans for bilateral contacts that might invoke adverse Pact reactions.

6. Institutionalize intelligence interface within the Alliance framework and bilaterally in an effort to bolster European confidence in NATO's ability to reduce tactical surprise. This could be fostered at the NATO level by the US granting access to processed satellite intelligence, without divulging collection capabilities, and by introducing the exchange of more sensitive data on a bilateral basis.[17]

The most important single factor in improving NATO's warning-mobilization capability, however, is the formulation of agreed criteria for initiating each stage of response. Once agreed upon, the publication of representative indices for mobilization would notify the opponent that hesitation and reluctance among the allies had been overcome and that incremental mobilization should be regarded as a prudent precaution rather than a blatant provocation. Establishing and announcing the fine distinction between the two interpretations should strengthen deterrence by reducing the possibility of miscalculation. Yet publishing mobilization criteria would not divulge to the opponent the state of mobilization at any given juncture or the number of units deployed at any given time, since decisions escalating mobilization would not be revealed. Thus the advantage of tactical surprise could be contained within the framework of a well-planned preparatory posture that would minimize the impact of erroneous warning information and miscalculations.

Concept of Operations

The last premise for the Maximum Defense strategy governs the concepts of operation for the gradually reduced NATO forces. Highly proficient militia would be assigned a mobile border warfare mission and expected to block minor incursions and provide sufficient time for engineers to implace ADMs and other obstructions against major penetrations. Air mobile troops with greater staying power would be airlifted into presurveyed forward positions. Regular maneuver battalions would provide defense in depth and gradually relieve the air mobile units in the forward defense role, allowing them to resume their strategic reserve mission. Reservists' units would be assigned local security missions and the more proficient battalions would be deployed as corps reserves and support for nuclear artillery batteries.

If the aggressor achieved complete strategic and tactical surprise, tactical aircraft would be the principle defense force, using conventional ordnance until enemy intentions were discerned, the scale of the attack determined, and main thrusts were identified. If the scale warranted, armed nuclear strikes could then be directed against developing spearheads and dispersing maneuver battalions. As ground formations established contact with the aggressor and the FEBA began to stabilize, aircraft would be reassigned to the conventional missions of air defense and close ground support, relinquishing the primary nuclear task to ground forces, but retaining an on-call secondary responsibility for armed strikes. Extensive use of nuclear strike in the initial phase, however, imparts the risk of retaliation against friendly air bases by hostile SCUD or MRBM missiles. A hard choice may develop in a no-warning situation between the expediency of committing aircraft in a nuclear role to halt an attack and the desire to maintain a minimum level of violence, by precluding massive retaliation.

In the more likely scenario, when there would be strategic warning but tactical surprise, ground forces would be in some phase of alert, probably fueled and armed ready for movement forward. In this case the first use of nuclear munitions would probably be the ADMs and Lance and Honest John rockets assigned to forward patrols. Friendly forces would be deployed in a dispersed posture down to company level, and nuclear responsibility would rest primarily with the ground forces, leaving tactical air forces free to conduct conventional missions of air defense and close support.

In either scenario, the credibility of NATO's defensive posture would be increased if the tactical air forces were deployed along functional lines. Air-delivered nuclear weapons represent the bulk of SACEUR's strategic retaliatory capability. As part of the distinction between battlefield and strategic weapons, coupled with the desire to demonstrate the withhold of strategic forces whenever possible, those units assigned to support strategic reprisal plans should be redeployed as far *rearward* as possible during peacetime, and certainly in high phases of alert. In the Central Front, this would mean the transfer of aircraft or their missions to remote dispersal bases in Belgium and Britain. This transfer would improve aircraft prelaunch survivability in a no-warning attack and stress the precautionary nature of NATO's posture. Mission accomplishment for deep-penetrating nuclear strikes would not be seriously impaired if those crews were qualified in aerial refueling or if those missions were planned on a "gas-and-go" concept, where aircraft would be refueled at preplanned forward dispersal bases either inbound to or outbound from the target. Aircraft assigned a nuclear strike role during the initial attack would employ the same concept until ground forces assumed responsibility for nuclear fire support. Then these aircraft too would be dispersed rearward in the hopes of securing sanctuary rights for nuclear bases.

Sanctuary rights for rearward nuclear air bases may be illusory. But effective dispersal and hardening would substantially increase the number of missiles and medium bombers the Pact would have to expend on a first strike, raising the dimension of the undertaking to the massive retaliatory level at the outset, without the certainty of effectively neutralizing dispersed aircraft *and* the other strategic retaliatory vehicles. Furthermore, as an incentive for sanctuaries, NATO would refrain from attacking the Pact's theater strategic resources at the outset.

Rearward deployments of US strike aircraft is a probable solution to the Forward Based Systems issue at the MBFR talks. To date the suggestion of rearward deployments of nuclear components has met with sharp resistance by military commanders. But redeployments of tactical air units along functional lines and the elaboration of concepts of operation that incorporate greater integration and utility of strike aircraft would improve, not impair, theater nuclear defenses.

As evidence, rearward dispersal would have the advantage of allowing deployment of all reinforcement aircraft directly into bases in the forward area, where they could be assigned conventional missions—crews in follow-on forces are usually not trained and their aircraft may not be configured for nuclear operations. Thus, rearward dispersal could both streamline subsequent air operations in the battle zone and signal NATO's self-protection measures regarding its prime theater strategic capability.

These inherent advantages in the proposed new strategy/doctrine/force structure/concepts of operations when employed under conditions of some strategic warning and moderate mobilization should result in marked asymmetries favoring NATO. The pact will be faced with hard choices between opting for its traditional preference of mass and shock and the option of matching NATO's refined nuclear fire with its own nuclear bombardment. With the former choice, the Pact could expect extremely high losses, and with the latter, it would probably expend its divisional compliment of nuclear missiles and possibly resort to air-delivered weapons without achieving its goals. The MD strategy's programed battlefield superiority will force the attacker to consider cessation or escalation, either by expanding the geographic dimension or the intensity of the conflict. The onus of aggression will be compounded by the consequences of escalation.

Conclusions and Prognosis

The Alliance now needs a strategy for the next decade that will reduce the historic differences between America and Europe on security matters, while enhancing respective national interests in the collective effort. Influence over Alliance policy will continue to be roughly proportional to contributions for the total enterprise. The new strategy should emphasize European allocations in manpower, material, and concepts, and should be directed toward providing an improved defense against the most likely type of continental conflict— limited, localized aggression. A less provocative defensive posture than exists would not sacrifice self-protection but it would foster political détente and accelerate the Europeanization of continental defenses. Moreover, greater reliance on an indigenous defense capability for Europe would restore the original perspective of the Alliance. Initially the US was to provide only enough strategic resources to prevent European interests from being endangered by intercontinental conflicts and sufficient tactical forces to insure the compatibility of political commitments within the Alliance—leaving the burden of local defense requirements, in both resources and concepts, to the Europeans. Finally, when the full impact of parity and the consequences of declining American domination of Alliance policy becomes generally accepted on both sides of the Atlantic, the stage may be prepared for promoting a European nuclear defense force; a more integrated Anglo-French force with sufficient institutional flexibility to remain integrated with American strategic resources and battlefield warheads, yet with enough autonomy to remain under national control.

If a new, European-oriented strategy is not acceptable to the various ministeries of defense, major renovations in existing NATO policies and concepts can be made by SACEUR without clearance from the national representatives. SACEUR could measurably improve NATO's defensive potential by developing a doctrine and plans for tactical nuclear warfare, retargeting tactical aircraft, redeploying existing forces, expanding the present program for maximizing force survivability, pressing for modern nuclear weapons, streamlining the infrastructure system with the aim of consolidating logistics, and furthering standardization. Such actions are clearly within SACEUR's purview and, if initiated, would heighten the self-protection image of the Alliance and prepare a more receptive atmosphere for adoption of broad measures requiring ministerial approval.

Thus, the national interests of both Europeans and Americans prescribe that immediate attention be directed to the formulation, without the duress of threatened troop withdrawals, of a comprehensive strategy compatible with both progress toward a coherent, mutually beneficial international system and the gradual reduction of national resources allocated for military purposes. The national priorities within NATO, then, must be increasingly focused on positive measures that will promote Western concepts of international progress without endangering collective security needs. In the age of intercontinental parity and US paralysis at the strategic level, the initiative in solving regional security problems may shift to the Europeans. If not, it is likely to be assumed by the Soviets.

**Part III
The Political-Military
Relationship in the
Détente Process**

Introduction

The Soviet achievement of strategic parity with the United States is the most important single development in the nuclear age, and one of the fundamental turning points in military history. It basically changed the nature of the great-power confrontation at the strategic level and destroyed the former "axiomatic" precepts of assured destruction. By decoupling US strategic capabilities from its Alliance commitments, Moscow was able to multiply the effect of its own medium-range nuclear weapons and to force the US to significantly augment its own theater nuclear posture. Thus, parity at the intercontinental level has had a direct impact on the military dispositions at all other levels of potential great-power conflict.

The word *parity* is sometimes wrongly used to imply equivalence or symmetry in military capabilities. As was pointed out in Part II, in the present international system great-power military relations must be calculated on all possible levels of potential conflict and for all possible contingencies. Strategy is not the study of the formulation of national values, aims, or behavior. Strategic theory deals only with the organization and execution of the means of achieving whatever aims have been prescribed by political authorities. There is no military science as such; there are few universal truths about strategy. There are incongruities in the sources of power and ideological motivations behind state behavior. These incongruities result in dissimilar national objectives and military capabilities. To compensate for known asymmetries in aims and capabilities, most nations attempt to establish the broadest latitude possible in dealing with known challenges and future contingencies. An effective strategy must be flexible in the achievement of consistently held values and principles.

In many ways, bipolarity of the Cold War was an aberration. First it froze political objectives into stereotyped formats and then calibrated military capabilities on predictable progressions. As a means of escape from this syndrome, the concept of flexible response was not a unique innovation; it was the logical extrapolation of the immobility imposed by the Cold War. Even at a time of assured destruction, effective deterrence at all levels had not been achieved. Flexible response theoretically provided latitude and options in countering the continuing threat. Misperceptions about the opponent's aims and intentions and anxiety about the danger of nuclear war led to further distortions. When applied in Southeast Asia so much constraint was exercised under the concept of minimal use of force that American power was dissipated through the practice of "gradualism," which contributed to the final defeat. The incongruities

215

between the US and its Asian adversaries are well known and preponderant
power at the strategic level could not be employed to compensate for asymmetries in the local hostilities.

At a time when multipolarity has injected greater fluidity into both strategy and diplomacy, military parity between the great powers also has been
achieved. In a potentially less stable international system, has great-power
parity increased mutual deterrence and improved the balance of the system?
The measurement of parity or comparative military strength deals only with
capabilities, roles, and missions. Deterrence is the correlation of military power
with intentions. It is an attempt to ascertain an adversary's aims and then to
build a military posture that will dissuade him from aggression by presenting
him with risks he is unwilling to incur. During the period of American preponderant power, Soviet security depended in part on US benevolence and a
posture of minimal forces. Moscow regarded this as an excessive dependency
and adopted a policy of pursuing parity. Theoretically, parity should make
mutual deterrence more secure.

If parity has been achieved, has strategy become the static effort of attempting to preserve the status quo? Indeed, is military power even usable, if
its chief utility has become merely the guarantor of the present balance of
comparative advantages? Is disarmament at last now feasible; can it be achieved
by merely mutually curtailing research and developments efforts for follow-on
systems and allowing obsolescence to attrite naturally great-power arsenal?
What is the function of military power in the post-SALT and post-MFR world?

First, the United States must continue to present a credible deterrence
against the threat or use of force against it and its allies. The US will also have
to retain sufficient forces to prevent an adversary from obtaining by military
aggression exclusive dominance of areas vital to its national interests, i.e., a
"counterintervention" capability.[1] Until a better knowledge is attained of the
relationship between military force and political influence, national security
will continue to require modern armaments. Since defense budgets, like other
governmental expenditures, will remain under constant duress to provide maximum benefits for minimum costs, there will continue to be pressure to modernize and upgrade weapons' efficiency. Arms competition will remain a permanent
feature of the détente process, though it need not be as uncontrolled as before.
Because of the growing complexity of modern weapons systems and the difficulties in testing them under the combat conditions they were designed for,
the problem of assessing comparative strengths is likely to become even more
hazardous. In reality the relative power or degree of parity is seldom as facile
as analysts claim, and even when balances are universally acknowledged they
are always subject to intentional disruption by either side. Thus, the principal
ingredient in deterrence remains political: the adversary's intentions. At a time
when the military balance still remains somewhat imprecise and the aims and
durability of the present Soviet leadership are so uncertain, it is imperative to

maintain a strong military posture to insure that Western interests will not be neglected while the parameters of détente are under negotiation.

Finally, the most binding reason for maintaining a maximum defense posture is that parity is the underpinning of the entire détente process. Only when mutual or equal security was gradually acknowledged by both great powers was it conceivable that adjustment on political differences could be made. In 1971 Marshall D. Shulman called for a balance of conventional forces as well as strategic systems as the antecedent to a sane world.[2] Rough parity has now been achieved and the détente process has been accelerated, but an unexpected imbalance would likely generate political tensions that would endanger the delicate mechanism.

The change in Cold War political relations has not been merely the decline in the numbers and kinds of issues that are likely to deteriorate into threats of war. It has been more profound, including also the extent and nature of cooperation that has become possible between two highly competitive social systems. The chapters in Part III are an attempt to assess the interdependency of military and political policies in the era of peaceful coexistence, and to examine their influence on the détente process.

14 Progress Toward Military Détente

Détente is a highly ambiguous term—few authors or statesmen are agreed about its meaning, implications, or limitations. It will be discussed in the following pages in either a political or military context before attempting to define its characteristics. This chapter will survey the efforts of the great powers to reach a common ground on selected issues; matters on which there was either little controversy or strong international pressure, or an intense mutual desire to avoid further tensions. The issues range from the 1959 Antartica Treaty to the military use of the seabed. The respective positions of both powers and other interested states will be examined and the compromises reached will be assessed to determine the nature and degree of flexibility of both powers. The extent and character of this give-and-take may provide insight into the nature of change in great-power relations, their respective perceptions and evolving values and interests.

The thirteen-year span of these negotiations included the tenures of four US presidents and two Kremlin factions. More important, they took place simultaneously with divisive developments in great-power relations, e.g., the Vietnam War, the space race, the Arab-Israeli dispute, the Cuban missile crisis, and the strategic arms race. During this period cautious changes began to occur in the perceived threat and the vital interests of each power. Inherent in these changes was the common desire to calibrate and categorize issues for influence competition and adjustment, thus compartmentalizing the Cold War into a more manageable framework.

Early Efforts: Antarctica

The great powers sought military détente in the 1950s through various schemes for general disarmament in the form of complex packages submitted as draft treaties (the USSR in 1959 and the US two years later). The comprehensive general disarmament plans, however, proved too complex to negotiate; issues such as accuracy in estimating adversaries' capabilities, contents of military budgets, and political intentions could not be resolved with sufficient assurance for either side to accept the risks of sudden unilateral or cautious joint actions. The US regarded verification procedures for any accord as vital to national

security; the USSR viewed them as a potential threat. These difficulties did
not diminish the desire to find some form of accommodation in the arms race,
and gradually it became apparent that progress could be made on selected,
technical, highly refinable issues.

Such a selected issue was the peaceful use of the vast continent of Antarctica. In 1959 President Eisenhower extended an invitation to the other eleven
nations which had participated in the International Geographical Year (1958)
to join the US in seeking to assure the continued peaceful use of the frozen
continent. The resultant conference, which included the US, USSR, Argentina,
Australia, Belgium, Chile, France, Japan, New Zealand, Norway, the Union of
South Africa, and the United Kingdom, submitted the Antarctic Treaty for
signature on 1 December 1959. After ratification by the twelve nations the
treaty entered into force on 23 June 1961.[1]

The most significant aspects of the treaty are: its stipulation that Antarctica be used only for peaceful purposes (Article I); the eschewing of any new
territorial claims or enlargement of existing claims in Antarctica by signatory
states (Article IV); prohibition of nuclear explosions and disposal of radioactive
waste in the continent (Article V); and the right of signatory nations to have
their own observers inspect all foreign installations in Antarctica, unrestricted,
at any time, including departing and arriving ships and aircraft (Article VII).
In a press release of 13 October 1970 President Nixon reasserted US objectives
in Antarctica: to maintain the terms of the treaty and ensure that the continent
remains peaceful and does not become an area or object of international discord;
to foster cooperative scientific research for worldwide and regional problems;
to protect the Antarctic environment and ensure wise use of its resources.[2]

The significance of this treaty may appear somewhat diminished by the
fact that the great powers were in essential agreement on the issues from the
outset, and did not have to make any compromises regarding their vital interests.
They appear to have been motivated more by a desire to make a contribution
to the interests of science, and perhaps showing a commitment to the principle
of détente, than by a feeling of urgency that they were confronted with a problem area which was in need of soul-searching appraisals. Although there may
have been some real advantage to the nuclear development programs in using
Antarctica for weapons tests, the limited Nuclear Test Ban Treaty was still
several years away, and it probably did not seem worth the potential jeopardy
to scientific progress to dispute the issue.

But 1959 was the height of the Cold War. The second Berlin crisis and
alleged missile gap drove tensions upward. The fact that the great powers were
able to reach such rapid and comprehensive agreement at that time on any issue
was remarkable. The liberal inspection provisions, although by no means duplicated in any subsequent agreements of this scope, have served as a model for
future verification procedures and precedents for the Nuclear Test Ban proposals.

Hot Line Agreement

Another selected issue on which the great powers were able to reach agreement was the "hot line" between Washington and Moscow. This teletype communications link was largely a result of the frightening experiences of the 1962 Cuban missile crisis. During the crisis the two world leaders found themselves resorting to national news broadcasts to communicate with each other—the only really rapid method available to them. Normal cable transmissions between the two capitals required a period of hours.

In spite of initial fears that such a direct communication system would be dangerously subject to sabotage and/or wire-tapping, the hot line went into effect in September 1963. It consisted of two separate systems: a duplex wire telegraph circuit which goes from Washington to London by undersea cable, thence by wire to Copenhagen, Stockhold, Helsinki, and Moscow; and the emergency back-up, a duplex radio telegraph circuit, which utilizes a relay station in Tangier, Morocco. Messages are sent in coded form, providing a certain amount of security, and the system is tested at least every hour. To date there have been no reported failures during the tests.[3] The hot line was activated twelve times during the 1967 Arab-Israeli War.

Speed limitations of the system (only about sixty words per minute) and its obvious susceptibility to sabotage led to the signing of an agreement between Secretary Rogers and Andrei Gromyko on 30 September 1971, calling for a meeting between the US and USSR early in 1972 to work out arrangements for a new system, which utilizes communications satellites. The new system consists of two separate duplex circuits, one employing the Soviets' Molniya-2 satellite, and the other Intelsat. Four ground stations handle the transmission and reception.

Prior to the agreement there was some opposition to the use of the Molniya by the Soviet military, who did not want to water down the satellites' military uses or risk giving the US any insight into their operation. The US was opposed to the use of the Defense Satellite Communications System, two stations of which were scheduled for launch into synchronous orbit in November 1971, for the same reason. The requirements for assured crisis communications, however, overrode these differences (the Soviets already had six Molniyas in orbit, including those used for military purposes and public telecommunications).[4]

In evaluating the significance of the original hot-line agreement, a "step in the right direction" represented the upper boundary of importance. It signaled no change in the nature of the adversary relationship; indeed, the very intensity of the hostility level following the events in the fall of 1962 made the rapid-communications system necessary. Whereas the Antarctic Treaty was motivated by a desire to further the cause of science through negotiation of a nonvital issue, the hot line was a response to reservations about accidental infringements of vital interests. The rapidity with which the obstacles and cavils to this venture were overcome, however, must be viewed with caution. At that time the Soviets also reached the decision to strive for strategic parity, and may have regarded the hot line as a limited assurance against US overreaction before parity was attained.

Limited Nuclear Test Ban

Great-power détente underwent the first major transition in 1963 with the negotiation of the Limited Nuclear Test Ban Treaty. The negotiations were notable for several reasons: the great powers were now dealing directly with their ability to improve existing and develop new weapons systems; the ultimate agreement was finally made in spite of substantive disagreements between the great powers at the outset (although these disagreements were largely bypassed rather than resolved); and the smaller states took an active part in the proceedings.

On 12 February 1963 the United Nations' Eighteen Nation Disarmament Committee (headed by the US and USSR, boycotted by France) convened with the specific purpose of considering a ban on nuclear-weapon testing. A series of letters between Kennedy and Khrushchev, as well as three-power talks between the US, USSR, and Great Britain, had delineated quite clearly the areas of agreement and on the need for: the use of nationally manned and controlled seismic stations for the detection and identification of seismic events; the installation of automatic (unmanned) seismic stations in the territories of the nuclear powers, and in adjacent countries, as a check on the proper functioning of nationally manned stations; and the need for some annual quota of on-site inspections "to determine the nature of suspicious events."

Disagreement centered on both qualitative and quantitative issues. The Soviets called for two to three annual on-site inspections, while the US was in favor of eight to ten (this was reduced during the negotiations to seven). The USSR wanted three unmanned seismic stations, the US seven. In order to determine the necessary quota of both inspections and seismic stations, the US advocated the technical examination of such details as the composition of in-spection teams, the criteria of eligibility of events for inspection, the area to be covered by each inspection, how events would be chosen for inspection, and the location of the automatic stations and equipment. The USSR insisted on *first* establishing quotas by some mutual agreement, without going into the details of *how* they were to be determined. They asserted that the quotas themselves were the main question, and that going into too much detail would unnecessarily protract the negotiations. During the spring and summer several compromise proposals were submitted by the smaller states, calling for three or four truly effective inspections yearly. The UN Secretariat, at the request of India, compiled a synopsis of all the suggestions offered by the nonaligned countries for consideration by the nuclear powers in arriving at a compromise. But the problem was that they were aiming at a *comprehensive* test ban, and apparently neither great power was ready to halt nuclear testing completely.

The Limited Nuclear Test Ban Treaty was finally worked out between the US, USSR, and Great Britain, and signed by their foreign ministers in Moscow on 5 August 1963. Nuclear tests were banned only in the atmosphere, outer space, and under water, and there were no control provisions. Following the initialing of the treaty, all participants in the Conference of the Eighteen Nation Committee expressed satisfaction with the results of the Moscow talks—satisfaction that has been diluted over the years by the inability to attain a comprehensive ban. While over one hundred nations have now ratified the treaty, France and China remain notable exceptions. Both great powers have remained faithful to its provisions, despite the impact this denial has had on the development of both strategic defensive systems and certain types of offensive weapons.[5]

Probable great-power motivations behind the Limited Test Ban Treaty included protection of the environment from excessive nuclear fallout; restriction of future nuclear developments of the smaller states; and protection of their own options for nuclear-weapons development (i.e., underground testing). It can be argued that the US was more genuinely interested in a truly comprehensive ban, since their initial position advocated effective controls. But there was no reason to believe that the Soviets would accept the control proposals which would have codified their strategic inferiority. The US refusal to accept the principle of unilaterally imposed restraints, due to distrust of the Soviets, indicates that they were just as jealously protective of their rights to future weapons refinement as the negotiators from Moscow. This was a period of misperceived threats and restraints. The US insisted that in light of its strategic preponderance, its restraint in applying this force should be regarded as a demonstration of good faith. On the other side, the USSR argued that with only a limited deterrent capability its offer of limited verification procedures should be regarded as a restraint. Such mutual protestations of constraint, however, did not outweigh the mutual perception of threat.

The Limited Test Ban was not a compromise on the issue as such. The crucial aspect was merely dropped, rather than resolved to anyone's satisfaction. It was significant that the negotiable features were separated from the nonnegotiable and a limited agreement reached, establishing a procedural precedent for negotiations in the area of chemical/biological weapons.

Agreement on Outer Space

The success of the Limited Nuclear Test Ban Treaty of 1963 proved to be the last major progress toward détente for almost four years; the change in

Kremlin leadership had ushered in a new, more cautious era. The Outer Space Treaty of 1966 broke the inactivity. It was sucessfully negotiated mainly because the concessions made during the negotiations by the great powers were relatively minor and the issues were of little interest to other states. Further, there were common advantages in restricting great-power rivalry from outer space.

In June 1966 both the US and USSR submitted draft treaties to the UN Committee on the Peaceful Uses of Outer Space. Although there were several details which remained to be reconciled between the drafts, they were in basic agreement on substantive issues. The motivation was primarily a desire to keep the arms race from expanding into outer space, for both security and economic reasons. The similarities with the Antarctic Treaty of the previous decade are apparent: it was another virgin frontier in which both countries shared extensive scientific interest, but which nonetheless had the unfortunate potential of degenerating into a nuclear proving ground if restraints were not exercised from the outset.

One of the areas where there was a difference of opinion was the issue of exchange of information. The US, in its draft, called for free exchange of information on scientific progress between all parties to the treaty. The Soviets were not prepared for such open provisions. A compromise was reached in Article II when the US revised the wording to require the parties to merely "take note of the desirability of the fullest exchange of information," and submit reports and information to each other "to the extent feasible and practicable."[6]

The US also acquiesced on the issue of access to foreign facilities in outer space (such as moon laboratories). In the original draft it called for virtually unlimited freedom of access between nations' facilities, along the lines of the Antarctic Treaty. But the Soviets insisted that any visits to their installations be arranged and agreed to beforehand, with a definite time specified. The overt reason for this was to provide for necessary safety precautions and avoid hindering any work that might be going on. The Soviets saw the US proposal as something akin to on-site inspections, and therefore reacted negatively. The US subsequently agreed to a provision for "appropriate consultations."

The wording of the article dealing with the use of military equipment on celestial bodies was the subject of a third US concession, albeit a small one. The USSR thought such equipment should be "forbidden," while the US called on signatories to "refrain" from introducing military equipment on heavenly bodies. In Article IV of the final draft it was "forbidden." This exchange typified a characteristic of great-power negotiations not uncommon in other areas: the USSR advocated blanket prohibitions, while the US, skeptical of the implications of such broad bans, sought to keep its options open.

A final important provision incorporated into the final draft was the result of a British suggestion. It provided, in Article IV, that responsibility for compliance with the treaty would be shared between signatory states and international organizations which might conduct operations in space in the future. The final treaty was approved by the General Assembly on 10 December 1966. Several smaller countries expressed disappointment over the fact that only "celestial bodies" had been specifically designated in Article IV to be free from nuclear weapons, and not the totality of space (implying that the rest of space could be used for nonpeaceful purposes). But it was presumed that all activities in space, as specified in Article III, must still be in accordance with the UN Charter; thus reducing the possibility of their fears being realized through any legal loopholes.

The military aspects of the treaty, then, were the prohibition of military installations on celestial bodies, and of nuclear weapons and other weapons of destruction from earth orbit. There was no provision for inspection, because it was regarded as technically feasible for national intelligence facilities to conduct their respective surveillance of adversary compliance.

Nuclear Non-Proliferation Treaty

Another characteristic of great-power negotiations that became apparent on selected issues was the tendency to join forces when faced with determined small-power opposition. The Nuclear Non-Proliferation Treaty, signed in July 1968, became a classical example. The idea of nonproliferation was an outgrowth of the campaign against nuclear testing that had become a key international debate in the early 1950s. By the early 1960s the Irish, Swedish, and Indian delegations to various world disarmament bodies had presented a series of proposals that dissected the issue of proliferation from general disarmament and, to a lesser extent, from nuclear testing. Several factors influenced the great powers to refrain from active, genuine involvement in these deliberations: the persisting general hostility of the Cold War, which was dissipating slowly and only through peripheral matters; Soviet distrust of Western attempts to create multilateral nuclear forces to appease alleged West German security needs; and the proposals by smaller states requiring great-power guarantees for the nonnuclear powers in lieu of developing their own nuclear weapons, and positive great-power steps toward disarmament. But as the Cold War continued its gradual erosion, NATO's Nuclear Planning Group replaced the more threatening MLF concept and some key nonnuclear states began to take a more pliable stand. Thus the great powers were encouraged to take a more active role in exploring and refining the issues at stake.

Bilateral US-Soviet discussions on nonproliferation preceeded the eighteenth-National Disarmament Conference (ENDC) in February 1967. The opening statements gave a glimpse of some of the complexities involved in the negotiations. Prime Minister Wilson urged a link between nonproliferation and a ban on underground testing; William C. Foster read President Johnson's message designed to reassure nonnuclear powers that an NPT would not hinder the development of the peaceful uses of atomic energy; and Aleksei Roshchin stressed the importance of West Germany's cooperation in the proceedings.

One of the main areas of conflict was the subject of inspection. The USSR called for International Atomic Energy Agency (IAEA) inspections of the non-nuclear nations of EURATOM (Germany, Italy, Belgium, Netherlands, and Luxembourg), which was regarded by EURATOM as tantamount to industrial espionage by Communist states (who are IAEA members). The European nations maintained that EURATOM inspection procedures were even more stringent than IAEA's, but this was rejected by the Soviets as self-policing and too lenient. The US generally agreed with the Russian viewpoint, but could not antagonize its allies. It offered a compromise, providing for a three-year transition period after the treaty entered into force, during which IAEA inspectors would gradually be introduced into the safeguards process in EURA-TOM. This proposal was changed in April to accommodate the unyielding European position; rather than phasing in gradually during the three-year period, IAEA inspectors would be *prohibited* from the process during this time. The new proposal was in turn rejected by the USSR. As a result the first draft avoided the issue entirely for the time being by leaving the article dealing with controls blank. Leaders of the opposition in EURATOM were Germany and Italy, who insisted that they be allowed to withdraw from any eventual agreement if IAEA inspectors took over. Other major areas of disagreement between the nuclear "haves" and "have-nots" were the lack of guarantees, prohibition of peaceful explosions, and Germany's objection that there would be no chance of a "European option," that is, a united Europe becoming a nuclear power at some future date.

The first draft treaty was submitted jointly by the US and USSR on 24 August 1967. Basic provisions were:

1. The nuclear powers were not allowed to transfer nuclear weapons or other explosive nuclear devices to nonnuclear countries, or to give them control over or aid in the manufacture of these devices;
2. The nonnuclear nations agreed not to manufacture or receive nuclear weapons or other explosive nuclear devices;
3. The treaty would not affect the right of all nations to develop nuclear energy for peaceful purposes;
4. Any party to the treaty could in the future propose amendments to it, which would require the approval of a majority of member states, including *all* nuclear nations and the IAEA board of governors;
5. Five years after going into force a review conference would be held in Geneva by member states to determine the future of the treaty;
6. The treaty would enter into force when all nuclear signers and an

unspecified number of the nonnuclear signers had ratified the treaty; and
7. The treaty would be of unlimited duration, but any member could withdraw from it if it felt that further membership was contrary to its national
   interests.

This first draft met with a reception varying from lukewarm to hostile.[7]
India, Nigeria, and Italy, among others, faulted the draft for discrimination
against nonnuclear states, general inadequacies of guarantees, and failure to be
more comprehensive regarding issues such as an underground test ban. The US
and Britain, in an attempt to dispel fears of discrimination, offered to open their
own territories to the safeguards specified in the treaty, whatever they might
be, "subject to exclusions for national security reasons only." The fact that the
Soviets did not reciprocate rendered this attempt at conciliation largely ineffective.

Two more drafts were tabled on 18 January and 14 March 1968. The 18
January draft included many of the nonnuclear nations' demands: a separate
article (V) now dealt with the availability of the benefits of nuclear explosions
and research to the nonnuclear states for peaceful purposes, ensuring them
that they would be available through both international procedures and bilaterally; negotiations in good faith on disarmament were required of signatories in Article VI; and on the matter of controls, Article III left it to the
nonnuclear states to conclude separate agreements with the IAEA on inspection
procedures, specifying that the use of existing safeguards, i.e., EURATOM, was
desirable.[8] Changes in the 14 March draft were minor, being mostly increases
of emphasis on such things as the desire to halt the arms race, rather than substantive alterations. The nonnuclear nations' dissatisfaction remained over the
lack of sufficient security guarantees, although their desire for peaceful nuclear
sharing had been accepted. A joint resolution on 7 March by the US, USSR,
and Great Britain, promising immediate assistance to the nonnuclear states
should they come under nuclear attack, did not actually go any farther than
existing UN charter obligations, and failed to reassure such holdouts as India
and Germany, who wanted guarantees against threats and nuclear blackmail
as well.

The third draft was finally approved by the General Assembly on 10 June
and opened for signature simultaneously in Washington, London, and Moscow
on 1 July. Germany refused to sign at the time, citing a "whole series of world
political problems" which had to be solved first.[9] France denounced the treaty
but said she would abide by its provisions in the future. France's contention
that the question of complete disarmament was much more important than
nonproliferation (which attempted merely to "castrate the impotent"), was a
cavil shared by most of the treaty's detractors. The language of Article VI
provided for no way to force the great powers to pursue their "negotiations
in good faith" to halt the arms race. As a result many signatories stipulated

that their ratification would depend on what progress, if any, was being made in regard to disarmament.

Although the treaty went into effect in March 1970, with 95 signatures and 47 ratifications, the placing of the smaller nations' survival in the hands of the great powers under the aegis of the Security Council has continued to maintain the frictions present from the outset. The nonnuclear nations remain hypersensitive to the implicit provision of the treaty equating nuclear protection as directly proportional to the level of great power cooperation in a given situation—a formula that has not been tested and may not impart the desired deterrence because of the existing adversary relationship. Although the "most discriminatory" treaty ever negotiated, it remains a milestone in great power cooperation that has clearly become a vital precedent for subsequent joint undertakings.

Uwe Nerlich has argued convincingly that the protracted negotiations over the NPT were due partly to misperceptions and other influences on both great powers. The USSR concluded that Bonn's reluctance to sign the treaty because of industrial espionage was an excuse to keep its military options open. This led to a time-consuming exercise of "containing the inactive." The United States gradually increased its stakes in successful outcome because of seeming domestic interests. At a time of mounting civil unrest and growing uncertainties, President Johnson calculated that a major accord with the USSR on security matters would distract his opposition.[10] Both great powers finally agreed to postpone further discord, without abandoning their positions on verification. Individual ratification became contingent upon inspection procedures worked out with IAEA. As a result, the FRG signed the treaty in 1969 but did not initiate the ratification process until 1973, when it became the subject of national political infighting on related issues, e.g. MBFR, CSCE, and NATO strategy. The ratification debates reflecting personalities' contests over broader political issues that was again misread by the Soviets and may have been a contributing factor to their resurrection of the Berlin issue at that time.

Bans on Chemical and Biological Weapons

On the issue of chemical/biological weapons, agreement between the US and USSR has been less than complete. On 10 July 1969 the United Kingdom introduced a resolution in the expanded ENDC called the Conference of the Committee on Disarmament (CCD), proposing a ban on production, possession, and use of biological methods of warfare.[11] This proposal separated biological from chemical methods of warfare for several reasons, such as differing modes of delivery and levels of effectiveness, logistical support requirements, and vast differences in lethality and unpredictability of long-term effects. The enormity of the effect of biological weapons and their unpredictability were regarded as sufficient to make their use irrational, and therefore largely beyond the requirements of stringent verification procedures.

The US responded shortly after with President Nixon's announcement on 25 November 1969 of unilateral suspension of production and stockpiling of biological weapons.[12] This was followed by a similar statement on 14 February, unilaterally banning toxins as well. On both occasions the President endorsed the UK proposal governing biological weapons and reaffirmed the US renunciation of the first use of lethal or incapacitating chemicals. The draft finally approved by CCD and sent to the General Assembly on 30 September 1971 (sponsored by the US and USSR) contained the basic provisions of foreswearing the stockpiling of bacteriological weapons, while avoiding the issue of chemical agents. The verification procedures were relatively simple. Suspicions of violations were to be reported for investigation to the Security Council through the Secretary General.

On April 10, 1972 the signing ceremonies were held simultaneously in Washington, London, and Moscow. Significant absentees from the more than forty signatory nations were France, which felt that control provisions were insufficient, and the People's Republic of China. President Podgorny took the occasion to express the hope of the Soviet government that similar prohibitions on chemical weapons would soon be forthcoming.

In line with Article IX of the treaty, which calls for continued "negotiations in good faith" on chemical arms control, the Soviets submitted a proposed convention to the CCD on 28 March 1972, providing for essentially identical prohibitions on chemical weapons as the above-mentioned treaty makes on biological ones. Chances for an early agreement, however, hinge on difficulties of verification. Verification is more complex with chemical agents' than with any other instrument of mass destruction, since virtually all of the agents used for military purposes are produced for commercial reasons as intermediary ingredients in the manufacture of dyes, paints, plastics, insecticides, pharmaceuticals, and other chemical compounds. The gross production of the worldwide chemical industry was estimated in 1968 to exceed $150 billion, and annual global production of phosgene, responsible for 80 percent of the World War I deaths, exceeds 100,000 tons. Annual production of hydrogen cyanide, required for the synthesis of many commercial organic compounds as well as toxic gases, is in excess of one million tons.[13] The interrelationship between toxic compounds and commercial activities is so complex that the chief Soviet delegate commented before the CCD that verification in the form of control posts and on-site inspections would be simply impossible to exercise from a practical point of view; controllers would have to be assigned to practically every laboratory in the world. Yet the Soviet armed forces are known to possess vast stores of nerve gas in particular, and to devote far greater time to training in chemical warfare than Western armies, rendering the Soviet provisions for self-inspection and good faith clearly unacceptable to the US.[14] Thus, without on-site inspection rights, prohibitions against chemical agents appear remote.

Both the chemical/biological issue and the Non-Proliferation Treaty register
a growing awareness on the part of the great powers that possession of ultramodern methods of destruction, although dangerous enough when enjoyed by
them exclusively, is a far greater risk to humanity if allowed to spread to the
rest of the world. Although this attitude is often labeled as discriminatory, it
also represents an increased sense of responsibility. It is unquestionably in the
interest of world peace to take action to prevent a smaller state from precipitating a worldwide holocaust by the small-scale use of weapons of mass destruction
against one of the great powers or its allies. Prevention of such an occurence
was one of the motives lying behind the reluctant but persistent movement of
the US and USSR toward arms-limitation accords.

But there is also the ever-present and thinly drawn line delineating vital
interests, beyond which the great powers refuse to go. The USSR has always
refused to accept meaningful on-site inspections on her territory, and the US
has usually declined to rely on trust and self-inspection, except where the
irrationality of the weapon's use rendered inspection unnecessary. Thus there
was some evidence up to this date to the charge that the closest coincidence
of great-power interest centered on issues requiring verification on other states'
territory, not their own. But more important, all the agreements to that time
had contributed to a growing understanding of the technical aspects of inspection and relative risks and benefits related to verification of a growing category
of negotiable problems.

Seabed Exploitation: Weapons Ban
and Commercial Development

In the history of détente politics there has been no issue more complicated
or fraught with conflicting interests between the great and small powers than
the twin issues of nuclear-weapon placement on and exploitation of the seabed.
The question of the peaceful uses of the oceans and seabeds was originally
raised in 1967 in the UN General Assembly. During its 1968 session, the CCD
discussed the military aspects of the problem. The great powers were at odds
initially over the limits of territorial waters and the issue of completely demili-
tarizing the ocean floor; the US and USSR advocated three- and twelve-mile
limits respectively. The US regarded the Soviets' proposal to ban installation
of any "object of a military nature" from the area beyond national jurisdiction
as impractical, due to the joint military-civilian nature of communication and
navigation equipment. But a compromise was reached, the US agreeing to the
twelve-mile limit and the Soviets accepting limits on only weapons of mass
destruction proposed by the US. The smaller states, however, complained that
the great powers were promoting de facto legislation for the high seas, without
adequately guaranteeing verification procedures. Accordingly, US and USSR

agreed to cosponsor a draft treaty, hoping that the appearance of closed ranks would dispell the reservations of the opposing states.

But reactions of the majority of the conference members, including most maritime powers, were so adverse that the great powers agreed to revise the draft. In the second draft submitted to the UN General Assembly for endorsement on 30 October 1969, the nuclear powers' right to veto amendments to the treaty was deleted and a five-year review clause was incorporated; the majority rule and the review clause had been incorporated in the original American draft but had been dropped upon Soviet insistence. Other minor concessions were made, but the central issues were sidestepped and the smaller states again rejected the joint great-power effort.

At stake were four basic problems:

1. The "security gap" imposed by the differing interpretations of territorial limits (the treaty wording provided that each state could continue to apply its own definition; about thirty states claim three-mile limits, another fifteen between four and ten, about forty claim twelve miles, and twelve insist upon jurisdiction as far out as two hundred miles);
2. difficulties in adequate verification (the opponents insisted upon physical access to marine installations, while the proponents argued that this was unnecessary, costly and dangerous);
3. the matter of assistance in verification (most riparian states do not have the technical capability to undertake independent inspections of their continental shelves, and the nuclear powers did not want to get involved, because of their advanced oceanographic capabilities, in the role of umpires in local tensions); and
4. the rights of nonnuclear coastal states (this lack of independent verification procedures and dependence upon the great powers' technical facilities produced a dichotomy in which the smaller states viewed their interests as the subject of either great-power collusion or competition; accordingly, they sought some form of universal inspection with the participation of the respective states).

The two great powers submitted a third draft treaty to the CCD on 23 April 1970, incorporating many of the recommendations made by the opponents of the earlier drafts. More than half of the substantive aspects of the draft's text dealt with verfication procedures. Although this revision represented significant concessions by the US and USSR to the smaller states—in fact, the text of Articles I and II dealing with definitions of the area of concern was essentially that presented by Argentina in a working paper—agreement was still one more revision away. During the summer of 1970 a number of changes were suggested by smaller countries. Not wishing to have their fourth revised joint draft treaty suffer the same fate as their previous efforts, the US and

USSR representatives "consulted extensively" with all members of the committee in inserting the latest proposals into their next revision, which was submitted to the Committee on 1 September and approved by the General Assembly on 7 December 1970.[15]

Important changes were incorporated into this final draft. The most significant simple concession was the right of small states to invoke great-power technical cooperation to inspect alleged violations. This was the clearest manifestation of the combined leverage of the smaller states against the great powers in codifying international cooperation. The universal pressure of the other maritime powers of the CCD maneuvered the great powers to where their technological prowess could be demanded in regional crises. The potential embarrassment to great-power interests will be an important constraint in future relations with client states. No other treaty has established such potentially severe limitations on great-power actions. In the final analysis, it was the siding of both great powers' allies with the opposition that was instrumental in compelling this unique concession.

The issue of peaceful uses of the seabeds had been developing along parallel lines since approximately 1968, when a 1967 UN ad hoc committee was elevated to the status of a special committee designated the Seabed Committee. While the CCD addressed itself to prohibition of nuclear weapons on the seabed, the Seabed Committee concerned itself with the equitable distribution of the ocean's resources. Although there have been no important differences of opinion between the great powers in the committee's negotiations, and hence no painful compromises in the interests of détente, an examination of the proceedings to date reaffirms the important role smaller states can play in negotiations regarding issues of strong concern to the great powers. The US position on the matter of seabed exploitation was made public in a press release by President Nixon on 23 May 1970, in which he called upon all nations to renounce national claims over natural resources of the ocean floor beyond the point where the water reaches a depth of two hundred meters. The area beyond this point he referred to as the "common heritage of mankind," and proposed the setting up of an international regime to oversee its exploitation.[16]

Nixon's proposal, in addition to being a further attempt at securing international agreement on an issue of common interest, is aimed at assuring the broadest possible use of the ocean's resources, and in working out a way by which the developing nations and noncoastal states can share in their benefits. The plan calls for a "common pooling" arrangement for mineral royalties to be used for international community purposes, including economic assistance to the developing countries. In addition the President called for rules governing the prevention of interference between nations, protection of the oceans from pollution, maintenance of the integrity of investment for exploitation, and the peaceful and compulsory settlement of all disputes.

In order to accomplish those goals, Nixon proposed the establishment of two different sets of machinery. For the area within the two hundred-meter depth line, as far as the boundary of the traditional continental shelf, the appropriate coastal nations would exercise control as trustees. For all areas beyond, some unspecified type of international machinery would be designated. In the trustees' areas the coastal nations would exercise broad authority, within the context and spirit of the international treaty defining their trusteeships. They would, for example, be charged with authorizing and regulating exploitation by all nations in their respective trusteeship zones, enforcing the general rules established by the treaty, granting leases, and preventing and punishing violations.

The Seabed Committee, which considered the proposed plan in the summer of 1970, was unable to reach agreement. The Soviets challenged the proposal at this stage, calling for total demilitarization of the seabeds, and objecting to the ideas of international authority over the oceans and sharing revenue with the developing nations. Progress was made, however, on 17 December 1970, when the General Assembly adopted by an overwhelming vote US-sponsored Resolution 2749 (XXV), which was a declaration of principles governing the seabed and ocean floor, and Resolution 2750 (XXV), also US sponsored, regarding reservation of the seabed for peaceful purposes. These resolutions cover such general principles as the need for an international regime to control the ocean area beyond national jurisdiction, the need for equitable distribution of the ocean's resources among all nations, especially developing ones, the rights of coastal states, and the nature of the ocean's resources. In part C of 2750 (XXV) the Assembly stipulated that a conference on the Law of the Sea was to be convened in 1974, with the Seabed Committee to hold preliminary meetings in order to undertake the extensive preparations necessary to make possible a successful conference.[17]

One of the main areas of conflict was the scope and nature of the international regime to be created, especially regarding licensing. Was the regime to govern all uses of the sea, or only exploration/exploitation? Should it have strong or limited control? Britain advocated a limited regime with liberal licensing for individual exploitation, and the establishment of national quotas (to set aside and save for the future certain areas of the ocean for smaller states which do not have the capability to take advantage of seabed exploitation at the present). Chile, Mexico, Panama, and many other Latin American countries were opposed to licensing. The US was for a strong regime with the broadest possible jurisdiction, and the establishment of the twelve-mile limit.

Another area of conflict was the definition of the "area." Some nations preferred to define the limits of national jurisdiction in terms of nautical miles from shore, varying from three to two hundred. Others chose the isobath definition, and here recommendations varied between two hundred and twenty-five hundred meters. Some nations would not accept the trusteeship idea.

Essentially the conflict was between those advocating the maximum international area concept, and the defenders of broad rights of the coastal states. The Soviet Union submitted a draft treaty which simply left blank the areas of definition, licensing, and distribution of benefits until such time as the issue of national jurisdiction was settled.

The exploitation issue arouses strong feelings. The US, as the initiator and chief protagonist of the concept of an international regime for the seabed, has actively participated in the preliminary proceedings. The USSR has not. It is significant, however, that its initial criticisms of President Nixon's basic principles were laid aside when it became clear how important the matter was to other maritime nations. The USSR's limited side-taking on the emotion-charged issues, such as area definition, suggests that it is reserving its stand until a more definitive stage is reached. Such prudence, not now unusual in Soviet diplomacy, is a contrast from its more provocative nature in the 1950s. The controversies over exploitation are more complex than those over early weapons bans and the crystallization of issues is bound to take longer. But as this process develops, the USSR is likely to conclude that on many issues it will have a greater commonality of views with the US and the Western maritime nations than with the smaller coastal states. But the virtual isolation of the US and USSR that occurred in the weapons-ban negotiations is not likely to be repeated.

Levels of Cooperation

How can the contrast be measured between the almost euphoric results of the earlier progressions in military détente and the harsh realities of the SALT discussions? (See below.) Certainly there was a cumulative positive effect gained from the initial efforts in arms control. Indeed, they must have been in part responsible for cooperative measures in other fields, e.g. expanded trade agreements, accords on scientific and technical matters, creation of the international "think tank," space cooperation, the protocol on naval and maritime principles, and enriched cultural exchanges. And the combined pressure of these broadening contacts are likely to point the way to further cooperation.

But several observations can be made relevant to the issues the great powers have selected as negotiable and the character of the negotiations that may indicate the direction and limits of further contacts. Initially the great powers chose issues that did not impair national security (Antarctic Treaty), or provided a mutually advantageous utility function (Hot Line), or provided marginal political benefits without serious risks (Limited Nuclear Test Ban, Weapons Ban in Outer Space). The next sequence of accords focused attention on the threat of proliferation or use of weapons of mass destruction (Limited Nuclear Test Ban, Nuclear Non-Proliferation Treaty, Ban on Bacteriological Weapons, and

Ban of Weapons of Mass Destruction from the Seabed). In the first series, the great powers acted virtually in concert with the smaller nations; in the second, the smaller nations became increasingly aware of their national interests involved in each issue, and concerned about the degree of great-power collusion for the sake of détente. By virtue of their technological privileges, the great powers tended to view these issues as falling primarily in their exclusive domain. The resistance of the smaller states was unexpected and forced a closing of ranks between the two that was not anticipated, but projected a brighter image of cooperation than actually existed. The seeming isolation of the two powers and the defection of their allies to the opposition (especially on Seabed questions) gave the impression that the great powers had a stronger commonality of interest between themselves than with their traditional friends. But this ad hoc realignment pertained only to individual issues with a single common denominator— they had only a marginal impact on immediate great-power security requirements.

The question of the consequences of violations (especially in the NPT and the Seabed Ban) reinforced this perception of great-power "togetherness." Since only these two states could effectively enforce compliance, the smaller states concluded that there must be a strong motive to establish joint policy that would dissuade possible violators. Clearly the prospects of taking joint action to compel compliance would be a difficult choice for both powers, and would strengthen earlier efforts toward dissuasion. The increased responsibilities to preserve the discriminatory qualities of the treaties they sponsored, imposed in some cases upon reluctant smaller states, proportionally enhanced the prospects for combined great power actions. Or did they? It is just as likely that the two powers would not go beyond the level and extent of consultations already conducted during the negotiations for the NPT. Neither the maximal nor the minimal response can be anticipated, and neither can be precluded. The opportunity for either is available, but the reaction obviously will depend upon the prevailing circumstances.

The image of collusion was only slightly dispelled over the issue of verification, which was a more accurate indicator of great-power interests than in enforcement or nuclear guarantees. Verification procedures were the most consistent obstacle to great-power agreement on the more controversial issues. Accords were only reached when national verification procedures were mutually considered as adequate. No breakthrough was made on mutual inspection rights between the two; indeed, surveillance was imposed on smaller states but rejected by the nuclear powers. Great-power insistence (primarily the Soviet Union) on preserving national discretion over monitoring international agreements was probably the most significant development in these initial détente moves. It delineated precisely the upper limit of any arms limitation arrangement. Mutual acceptance of this prohibition allowed the two to open SALT. But the importance of the underlying principle, the protection of national security interests, was one factor that was misread by the US during SALT I and has become the brake on SALT II.

The sharpest realities after a decade of confidence-building measures toward a military détente are that there are fewer and fewer marginal issues upon which to temper great-power intentions and determination. Both sides must now face more squarely the hard choices of reducing their standing military forces and destroying selected weapons systems, or accept the status quo in military détente. Until now disarmament advocates placed great faith in an allegedly self-perpetuating mechanism inherent in the confidence-building process. If advanced to a sufficient, but unidentified stage, the great powers would presumably recognize that enough common ground existed between them that the era of cooperation would be consolidated. The difficulty is that there is no agreement on the definition of that stage and both sides are now compelled by default to face the prospects of reducing or limiting capabilities at various levels in SALT I and II, CSCE, and MBFR.

15

Multilateral Negotiations on Political Détente: The Conference on Security and Cooperation in Europe

Few analysts predicted or even suspected that the security interests of both East and West would be under active negotiation on three separate but closely interrelated planes in 1973. By then all parties had concurred on the wisdom of fractioning out the substantive aspects of security matters for individual consideration at the Conference on Security and Cooperation in Europe (CSCE), the Mutual Force Reduction talks (MFR), and the second round of the Strategic Arms Limitation Talks (SALT II). The three levels of negotiation were regarded as interdependent, with the CSCE gradually assuming a political character rather than the security function designated by its title. As the West slowly acknowledged the logic of the Pact countries, it became increasingly clear that progress would have to be made first on the political sphere, before military disengagement could be initiated. Thus, the rough framework for political accommodation became the indispensable prerequisite for reductions in the military confrontation, and this responsibility was arrogated to the CSCE. The alignment of these priorities was one of the most difficult single factors in the détente process because it focused directly on the central features of the former stalemate of the Cold War.

For years the West had consistently maintained that progress toward military disengagement of military détente was the precondition for movement toward political reconciliation. Just as consistently, the East maintained that the relaxation of political tensions was indispensable for a reduction of the military confrontation. The West felt that it had consistently dealt with the Pact nations with restraint and in good faith, but could no longer rely either on political promises or proclamations of Soviet intentions—military capability and dispositions were more reliable indicators of possible political options. But the Pact states held that regional tensions were a result of NATO's refusal to accept the consequences of World War II and the present realities in Eastern Europe; these political attitudes had to be modified before the threat to Pact security could subside. Thus, the dilemma of where adjustment should first be made—at the military or political level—produced the deadlock in East-West relations throughout the Cold War era.[1]

Soviet Interests in European Stability

Moscow's political and military interests in Europe are well known, and can be itemized briefly:

1. Insure the security of Eastern Europe and gain recognition of the Elbe River as the USSR's strategic frontier;
2. Gain recognition of the legitimacy of the friendly governments in its security zone in Eastern Europe;
3. Establish and maintain influence over all potentially destabilizing factors in both halves of Europe;
4. Guarantee indefinitely its present role in the politics of both Germanys as insurance of its continuing authority in the solution of the German problem— potentially the most serious destabilizing factor in Europe;
5. Project the image in Western Europe of responsibility and respectability; and
6. Gradually decouple the Atlantic Alliance and reduce US influence in Europe as its reputation for correct interstate behavior is enhanced.[2]

The most remarkable aspect of these aims is not their content, but the consistency with which the Kremlin has pursued them over the past quarter century and the alacrity of tactical adjustment that preserved this overall continuity. The Soviets skillfully attached minimum and maximum priorities to their objectives that facilitated their attainment. The minimum Soviet aim remains the security and legitimization of its hegemony in Eastern Europe. After nearly twenty-five years, Socialist rule in Eastern Europe has not run the full course of gaining genuine public acceptance and endorsement. This is not owing to failure, but to success. The new ruling élites have succeeded in uprooting traditional agrarian social structures and imposing industrialization from above. But the process is incomplete, and these societies remain in a highly transitional stage in which instability and unrest are endemic. The autocratic political character and the frustrations stemming from unfulfilled egalitarian ideological expectations add more uncertainties to those of societies in similar stages of development.[3] Thus the internal dynamics of these societies, as they progress from mobilization to modernization goals, as they shift from utopian aspirations to development targets, will likely continue to generate social unrest and political instability detrimental to Soviet vital interests. Further, as has been demonstrated several times in recent years, the close interdependence of Pact countries nurtures mutual infection by the virus of social protest, compounding Moscow's security problems.

American political and military interests in Europe have been largely reactive, the by-product of the overall dimensions of the Cold War. While it is difficult to designate responsibility for the origins of the post-World War II tensions, Marshall Shulman has observed,

I believe we must give central place in the assignment of prime causes of the Cold War to the combination of the Soviet effort to improve its national power position in the disordered condition of the postwar world and the ideological perceptions and expectations of the Communist leadership. In speaking of the influence of ideology on Soviet behavior, it seems useful to identify the particular functions it has performed. Chief among these functions has been the ideological influence on Communist perceptions of non-Communist systems as inherently and intractably hostile, with the consequent conviction that conflict at some level was inevitable. The companion of this perception has been the fundamental expectation of Soviet ideology regarding the future course of history: that non-Communist societies were fated to collapse and be succeeded by societies molded on the Soviet pattern. It has been this component of the Soviet outlook that has made Soviet dynamism more complex and less susceptible to territorial stabilization than if it simply reflected the bursting energy of a nation-state entering upon a virile stage of development.[4]

The basic incompatibility of these contending East-West views fostered in NATO, and in the United States particularly, distorted estimates of the danger posed to the international system and national security by the Communist challenge. The misperceptions and overestimations by the West had the cyclical effect of producing distortions in the Soviet perspective of Western behavior and in their own calculations.

The Pact countries have a long documentary record of expressed concern about European security matters, but each was a response to specific Western policies, rather than a proposal raised on its own merits. Molotov's 1954 call for a European security conference was aimed at blocking West German rearmament. The 1957 Rapacki Plan, and its refinement one year later into a proposal for nuclear free zone in Central Europe, was intended to dissuade the US from distributing tactical nuclear weapons to its NATO allies. The 1963 Gomulka Plan for a nonagression treaty between the two military blocs was aimed at curtailing German participation in the proposed Multilateral Nuclear Force (MLF). Poland's renewed call in 1964 for a European security conference was a second expression of anxiety about the MLF.

NATO rejected these bids because of their suspected propaganda quality, the continuing Cold War and the Pact's unwillingness to meet Western demands for reconciliation, and a general underestimation of the degree of latitude Poland, for example, could exercise in pursuing its own national security interests. Fortunately, a wide assortment of dissimilar political and military influences converged to crystallize the positions of both sides and then to add impetus to force relations off dead center. The separate initiatives of Kennedy, de Gaulle, and Erhard failed to achieve the end of improving relations with Pact countries and created differing responses, but contributed to the increased

insecurity of the East Europeans. The growing Cold War between Rumania,
the GDR, and the USSR on economic matters introduced for the first time
a polarization of the Pact that created new uncertainties for the Soviet leadership. The Sino-Soviet dispute and China's challenge to Soviet authority reached
its height by the end of 1965, and posed grave dangers for the Kremlin's prestige throughout the Communist world. Finally, Rumania's self-appointed role
as the mediator in this dispute and as guardian of smaller Communist parties
raised the possibility that Bucharest would use additional issues as multipliers
in its bid for an autonomous status within the Pact; multipliers that could
accelerate the polarization process within the Alliance.

Evolution of the Pact's Position
on European Security

As a result of these and similar factors the new Soviet leaders felt compelled
to develop a new initiative that would restore Soviet authority in its most vital
quarter—the European theater. During the first eighteen months in office, the
Brezhnev-Kosygin leadership merely attempted to content with the momentum
and omnidirection of Khrushchev's "harebrained" policies. When the most
serious problem, the Chinese challenge, gradually subsided, the new leaders
felt it was imperative to improve Moscow's position on its other flank, in Eastern
Europe. The renewed Soviet attention emerged in the attempt to coalesce Pact
interest in European security. The fact that this was the first major policy
initiative by the Brezhnev leadership created general alarm in Rumania. Gromyko's
Easter 1966 announcement in Rome of a renewed bid for a European security
conference was followed on 8 May by Ceausescu with a resounding reaffirmation
of Rumanian independence. Brezhnev himself went to Bucharest two days later
to ascertain the extent of Rumania's complaint. Ceausescu apparently argued
that the Kremlin could not introduce such far-reaching proposals in East-West
relations without consultations with its allies most affected. It was agreed that
all Pact members should meet at the policy level for a general review of their
common Western policies.

Two meetings unprecedented in length were convened in Moscow in June
at the defense-minister and foreign-minister levels. For its own reasons the new
Soviet leadership had concluded that a "united front" with its allies was now
important, and sought to convince them that the timing was appropriate for
a new Pact initiative in security matters. The defense ministers were entertained
at Semipalansk with demonstrations of ICBM firings and wide-ranging discussions
of the implications of the Soviet decision to achieve strategic parity with the
United States. The Soviets were probably uncertain about the full effect that
parity would have on East-West relations. But apparently they tried to convince
their allies that within two years the Pact would be in the strongest military

posture ever and the United States would no longer be able to bargain on security matters from a position of strength. In order to take full advantage of this favorable new position, the Soviets probably argued, the Pact must begin immediately conditioning Western opinion.

The very scale of Moscow's expectations was disconcerting for Rumania. The majority of the Pact members argued that the new balance of power would allow them to compel NATO's acceptance of détente on the Pact's traditional terms, i.e., a resolution of political differences. Bucharest was unconvinced, holding that the Soviets would not be able to achieve parity undetected and that the suspicion of the Kremlin's aims would convince the United States of the importance of preserving its technological lead and of the necessity of launching the next progression in the strategic arms competition. For Rumania, the Soviet bid for parity posed the danger of accelerating East-West rivalry unless some move was made at the political level to dampen Western anxieties. Rumania sought a middle-of-the-road position: an attempt should be made to meet NATO demands by a call for the abolition of military blocs, the withdrawal of all foreign forces stationed abroad, and the opening of negotiations on mutually acceptable security arrangements between the two halves of Europe. At the same time, the Pact could insist upon Western endorsement of the political status quo in Eastern Europe. Only by moving simultaneously on both the military and political planes could the disastrous arms escalation be contained and the political advantages of parity be fully exploited.

The East Germans particularly reacted so vigorously to this argumentation that the Rumanians walked out of the Foreign Ministers' meeting and negotiated a compromise solution bilaterally with the Soviets. (This maneuver established the precedent repeatedly used by Ceausescu and Dubcek, that a Pact nation could reserve the right to deal bilaterally with its allies when it was unlikely that its interests would receive adequate attention at the multilateral level.) A broad compromise was expressed in the July 1966 Bucharest Declaration of the Pact's Political Consultative Committee (PCC). A new formulation for the Pact's Western policy was announced. A consensus was expressed about the chief threats to European stability and security: West Germany revanchism, NATO militarism, and American imperialism. Under this umbrella of unanimity, each Pact member inserted for the first time its respective political aspirations or grievances regarding the West: legal recognition for the DDR, acceptance of the Oder-Neisse border for Poland, etc. Rumania was able to secure incorporation of its call for military disengagement. The Declaration concluded with a renewed bid for a European security conference. The Declaration was a modest gesture toward Rumania's insistence upon simultaneous movement on both military and political planes.

Ceausescu apparently was not satisfied by either the compromise or its implementation. Without some political tranquilizer, the Soviet bid for strategic parity must have been regarded as dangerously destabilizing. Accordingly, only six months after endorsing the PCC Declaration, Bucharest undermined Moscow's new initiative by adopting a two-Germanys policy. Granting Bonn full diplomatic recognition was a major political concession toward the FRG's aspiration of gaining wider respectability in Eastern Europe, and created the sharpest crisis in intra-Pact relations since 1956. The GDR responded by demanding Pact compliance with the Ulbricht Doctrine, which prohibited recognition of Bonn until the FRG recongized the GDR, and by strengthening its security position by concluding a series of bilateral mutual defense treaties, which insured the military commitment of its immediate Socialist neighbors in the event of a future Rumanian boycott of joint Pact security policies.

Shifts in the Western Position

The resulting two years of infighting among Pact members on the appropriate approach toward European security political issues was superseded only by the development of the Czechoslovak crisis. The Pact invasion of Czechoslovak was directed at both Prague's "liberalism" and Bonn's "revanchism." The invasion and the subsequent military threats against Rumania were unambiguous signals to the FRG that it could not follow the same policy it had with Bucharest throughout the rest of Eastern Europe. If there were to be changes in Eastern Europe, they would only be made with Soviet endorsement. No destabilizing influences would be tolerated in Moscow's security zone, even if the ultimate result would be greater regional security. Foreign Minister Brandt acknowledged this error during his October 1968 meeting with Gromyko, and agreed to deal first with the Soviet Union rather than individual Pact members in implementing Ostpolitik. This reversal of priorities in the Ostpolitik was the first major step since 1966 in moving Europe toward a security conference.

The second significant move in this direction was the FRG decision to separate its Deutschlandpolitik from the Ostpolitik, i.e., to deal with inter-German problems on a separate plane from the resolution of political differences with other East European states. After the East German rebuff to the Deutschlandpolitik at Erfurt in 1969, Bonn decided to shelve further consideration of the German problem until after it had reached agreement with the East Europeans. This decision confirmed the reversal in Bonn's preferences in relations with the Pact. Formerly it has insisted that the solution of the German problem was a precondition for the settlement of outstanding problems with all Pact members. By reordering its priorities for a settlement with all Pact countries, Bonn encouraged the East Europeans to reduce their allegiance to the Ulbricht doctrine and to seek their own individual solutions to the "German threat" to their security. This break in the tandem position of the East Europeans behind the GDR was confirmed at the December 1969 Warsaw Meeting of the PCC, when it was agreed to shift emphasis temporarily from the earlier plan for a multilateral approach to European security to negotiations with the FRG on individual national grievances. This mutually acceptable change in diplomatic techniques facilitated the conclusion of the normalization treaties with the USSR, Poland, and East Germany.

Sufficient progress was made in West German-Soviet contacts in the six months after the Brandt-Gromyko understanding that the Budapest PCC Communiqué of March 1969 dropped for the first time the traditional charge that German revanchism was the main threat to European security. This omission implied Pact acceptance of Rumania's logic that there were "good Germans and bad Germans," and the best way to reduce the influence of the bad Germans was to strengthen the confidence and stature of the goods ones by recognizing them and affording them respectability. The Budapest Communiqué also responded favorably to NATO's reply to the growing East European chorus calling for a European security conference. The Reykjavik signal, as NATO later referred to its initial 1968 response, acknowledged the appropriateness of European security as a subject for deliberation for the two alliances, but insisted that any formal consideration of the issue would have to be accompanied by specific moves toward military disengagement. The Budapest Communiqué implied that the Pact did not reject this linkage, but viewed the military aspects of European détente as an integral portion of the broader process of political adjustment that would be appropriate for an all-European conference. Shortly after the Budapest meeting, the USSR made a formal gesture toward the Western preferences by opening negotiations with the FRG of a treaty on the renunciation of the threat or use of force. After SALT I was opened in November 1969 and the US seemed convinced that the USSR was prepared to negotiate seriously on military matters, the terms of reference of the negotiations with Bonn were broadened to include the political components of a treaty of normalization of relations.

But NATO was reluctant to abandon its insistence on tangible evidence of military disengagement based only on the uncertain outcome of SALT I, and tied participation in a European security conference to the successful conclusion of the Ostpolitik treaties and the Berlin accord. At that juncture, both sides still considered the issue of military détente as appropriate for consideration by a security conference. Because of the complexity of the SALT deliberations and the continuing reluctance of the Soviet side to present concrete proposals for military disengagement, however, it became apparent that the incorporation of this issue in a security conference would probably doom it to a premature death or a protracted paralysis. It was mutually agreed to conduct separate negotiations of political and military aspects of détente in Europe. NATO persisted, however, in demanding a firm linkage between the two: Western participation in a security conference must be tied to Pact participation in force-reduction talks. When Moscow finally agreed in September 1972 to an acceptable timing for the opening of the force-reduction talks, the West agreed

to hold the initial session of Preparatory Consultation for the CSCE in Helsinki
in November.

Preliminary Positions

The main task before the preparatory body was to adopt an acceptable
agenda. The Pact countries had proposed the following items: the ensuring
of European security and renunciation of the use of or threat of force; the
expansion of commercial, economic, scientific, technical, and cultural relations;
and the establishment of an organ for questions of security and cooperation
in Europe. NATO had proposed: adopting agreed principles that should govern
relations between states, including the renunciation of the use of force; and
the development of international relations with a view to contributing to the
freer movement of people, ideas, and information and to developing cooperation
in the cultural, economic, technical, and scientific fields, as well as the field of
human environment.

These two sets of proposals represented substantial but not insurmountable
differences. In response to the repeated US call for the provision of a code of
conduct for state behavior, the Pact issued a Prague Declaration after its January 1972 PCC Meeting that elaborated the "fundamental principles" it thought
the CSCE should address, and thus expanded the scope of the agends. These
principles included:

1. The inviolability of border and the territorial integrity of European States
   must be "unconditionally respected."
2. Force or threats of force must not be used, and all disputes should be solved
   by peaceful means.
3. Differences between socialist and capitalist systems should not constitute
   insurmountable obstacles to the all-round development of relations, which
   should rest on a basis of understanding and cooperation.
4. Good-neighborly relations should develop on the basis of national sovereignty, equality, noninterference, and mutual advantage, so that it will
   "become possible to overcome the division of the continent into military
   and political groupings."
5. Mutually advantageous contacts among European states must develop on
   a broad scale to the economic, scientific, technological, and cultural fields,
   as well as in the fields of tourism and protection of the human environment.
6. European States must assist the solution of questions of general and complete disarmament, and especially of nuclear disarmament, as well as the
   realization of measures aimed at the reduction and termination of the
   arms race.
7. European States should support the United Nations.

8.   A standing body of all participating states should be created to further
     the work of the conference.

   In discussing the conference idea when it was first being seriously considered in the West, US Secretary of State, William Rogers, observed that the
main features of the Soviet proposals were not appropriate issues for a multilateral gathering. The expansion of commercial ties and the extension of
technological know-how and the broadening of cultural contacts were best
handled by existing diplomatic channels. Western agreement to participate in
the CSCE did not change this estimation; it signaled that NATO accepted the
Soviet terms of reference for the Conference—that its main function would be
to provide a political framework for détente in Europe.
   The Soviets hoped that the Conference could serve as a forum for expound-
ing its conceptualization of détente and a means for demonstrating its respectability to NATO countries; a vehicle for projecting an image of constructive
influence in European affairs and gaining Western acceptance that it too was
a positive European power and no longer an outcast. Further, it saw the
Conference as a means of gaining international ratification of the series of
bilateral treaties negotiated with Bonn that recognized the status quo in
Eastern Europe by the principal challenger to the existing political realities.
International recognition of these treaties would serve as a de facto peace
conference, finally terminating World War II and demonstrating Western
acknowledgment of the consequences of this period. Such a de facto peace
settlement would be made largely on Soviet terms and at West Germany's
expense.
   NATO's terms for a peace settlement had changed over time. In the postwar
era the Western Allies had sought the rehabilitation of a reunited Germany that
included a universally accepted solution to the age-old German problem, plus
the resolution of lesser complaints and disputes among the various European
nations. The subsequent acceptance of the division of Germany and the rehabilitation of its own half of the divided nation eased the anxieties of West European
nations about the urgency of solving the general German problem. A durable
settlement had always included, from the Western viewpoint, a solution of the
rights of East European states, for which World War II was initially fought. A
quarter-century of anticommunism campaigning, however, had proven the
futility of the "rollback" or liberation policy. By the 1970s the West had accepted the extension of Soviet hegemony to other Pact nations. Accordingly,
NATO's expectations for a durable settlement were merely to obtain reasonable
assurances that the partition of Europe could be humanized; that the onerous
aspects of the division could become more palatable and less susceptible to
emotional inflammation. Accepting Soviet hegemony and its terms for the
governance of its sphere of influence did not mean formal endorsement of the
political status quo. Indeed, the NATO governments shared a common belief

that change in Eastern Europe was the essential precondition for the attainment of the objectives of the normalization of European relations. In general the NATO partners concurred that their terms for stability and security could best be met through the accelerated modernization of East European nations.

Coincidence of Interests

On this point the aims of the East and West Europeans tended for the first time to coincide. But the projection of their objectives beyond merely resolving political problems and reducing the military confrontations to the broader plane of societal aspirations introduced new complications. Modernization and the anticipated greater degree of societal stability can now best be accelerated through trade and technological inputs from the West. The accompanying relaxation of restrictions are likely to externalize the social conflicts in Eastern Europe, which, in turn, may ferment continued unrest and instability, to the deteriment of Soviet security interests. The technological exchanges necessary for modernization are apt to project to the outside world the scale of societal aspirations and fan Western commercial prognostications. Public expectations in Eastern Europe would be stimulated and local governments would be increasingly challenged by the rise of domestic hopes for improved life styles. Until living standards between Eastern and Western Europe approach rough parity, societal demands will continue to be sources of concern for the Soviet leadership.

A proximity of views is discernible on the issue of change in Eastern Europe. Both sides recognize that change and modernization in this region are vital components of European stability. All parties agree generally that this process must correspond with the Soviets' outer toleration limits. Neither side wants another Czechoslovak crisis, with the agonizing frustrations in human hopes and the crushing reminder of the continuing burden of great-power insecurity. Yet to accept Soviet terms for modernity, which are culturally, economically, and intellectually incongruent with those of most East European societies, merely reinforces the prospects for instability. Thus, the process of modernization has to be skillfully managed if it is not to endanger the priority goals of Soviet security and legitimization of East European regimes. The West can not accept the Soviets' terms for adjustment unchallenged, but can no longer demand conditions beyond those terms. This joint awareness reduces the mutual focus of both sides to the finer problems of modernization, which, in turn, increases the Pact countries' sensitivities about inherent dangers of ideological challenge. The West concentrated its main thrust in the CSCE on the question of freer flow of ideas, people, and information, and the East for the first time attempted to organize a concerted counter to the West's intellectual challenge.

Chief Obstacle

The substance of the Western position was rather standard fare; for years NATO countries have attempted to use the vehicle of cultural exchanges to advance the general aim of gaining freer flow of information across national frontiers. The discretion and circumspection with which the subject was treated was the distinguishing new feature about the Western approach. On the Pact's side, important new innovations were made in both substance and treatment of ideological competition. Pact countries shared an increasing need for "ideological integration." For the first time, the East European members assumed a leadership role and were not the normally passive partners to Soviet machinations in ideological work. The general theme of the new campaign was: "The significance of coordinating the Communist parties' ideological work is greater under the conditions of relaxed international tensions."[5]

East European analysts began to sound the alarm.

It is obvious that imperialism will intensify its attempt to take advantage of the opportunities, to increase ideological *subversion* offered by the struggle for détente and peaceful coexistence; all the more so since this stage of development is accompanied by a number of specific events which, in the final stages are *propitious* to capitalism, namely:

a. socialist countries are developing the struggle for détente on a wide front under the conditions where capitalism is somewhat more advanced in scientific and technological revolution than the world socialist system. As a result, it has managed to obtain, in some areas of technology, a passive—it is true—but currently effective advantage;

b. at the same time, the socialist states have tackled on a wide front the problems created by the scientific and technological revolution, and this involves a basic change in their economic strategy, resulting in a number of complications;

c. the advantage gained by capitalism in the scientific revolution tends to produce—and will probably continue to do so in the immediate future—a temporary reduction of contradictions within the capitalist system and lessens class tensions. This will offer advantages to the trend toward social democracy within the worker movements of highly developed socialist countries;

d. by taking advantage of reserves created by the scientific revolution, at the moment, capitalism is capable of extending so-called aid to developing countries and using it to subjugate them and this to a degree much greater than heretofore;

e. this stage in the struggle for détente has not been accompanied by unity within the international communist and worker movement.

Under these circumstances the Marxist core of the revolutionary
forces is forced to fight on two fronts—and this not only in the
ideological field but in the political one as well.[6]

Other commentators pointed out that new attitudinal problems were
emerging in the ideological competition.

1. Increasing relaxation will bring with it a new, gentler style in international
    relations, especially in East-West relations. Spectacular diplomatic *démarches,*
    characterized by readiness to negotiate and sign agreements, will come to
    the fore. Greater emphasis will be laid on questions which bring the two
    sociopolitical systems closer together, rather than on those which cause
    violent antagonism between them. Moreover, a foreign policy adapted to
    the strategy of peaceful coexistence will demand a greater use of compro-
    mise in various forms of political bargaining involving concessions on both
    sides.
2. This atmosphere in international relations may tempt the Socialist aide
    to lower its guard, especially in the sphere of ideological work. It may
    accelerate the emergence of "supraclass" illusions which depict the
    possibilities of a permanent and all-inclusive understanding between the
    two systems that would insure the disappearance of social and political
    differences between them. This attitude could promote "softness"
    and weaken social vigilance. Slackening vigilance could be accompanied by
    the temptation to extend compromises from the political to the ideological
    sphere.
3. In practice, political détente will create improved conditions for the
    exchange of people and ideas between the two systems. Tourism has a
    number of psychological reefs. A tourist, by the very nature of his visit,
    lays himself open to a greater degree to the external and frequently
    attractive aspects of capitalism.
4. As Western goods and technology become more widespread in the Pact
    countries, they will appear better than those presently available, which
    will contribute to the legendary belief in the superiority of capitalism.[7]

The main thrust of this mounting literature on the subject of ideological
competition is that in the new situation propaganda is going to have to be more
open and direct in "spreading the ideas and truth about socialism and social
construction, malevolently deformed by bourgeois propaganda."[8] To this end,
ideological integration had now become indispensable. The means for implementing this scheme were discussed at the highest level during the annual PCC
Crimean meeting in August 1973. "A number of practical issues suitable for
closer cooperation among the ideological sections and institutions of the fraternal
parties and mass communications media were on the agenda."[9]

Preparation for these discussions was apparently thorough. Since the early 1970s the number of intrabloc ideological and cultural conferences— both bilateral and multilateral—sharply increased. Three research institutions were commissioned to examine in detail the ideological complexities of East-West relations and to "unmask the truth" behind the "modernization of capitalism." In the year preceding the Crimean meeting nine bilateral agreements on ideological matters were signed between five East European countries.[10] In the six months before the meeting three major gatherings on this issue were convened. On 21–22 February 1973 a conference was held in Moscow, attended by representatives of Communist organizations in twenty-seven European countries on the general theme of the role of Communist youth in a period of international détente. A second conference was held in East Berlin on 15–16 March, attended by forty-five delegations from fraternal parties to discuss the importance of contemporary ideological competition on the 125th anniversary of the Communist Manifesto. A third meeting, billed as "an International Theoretical Conference on the Working Class and Its Party in the Modern Socialist Society," took place in May in Warsaw.

The contents of the bilateral agreements have not been released and the proceedings of the conferences have not been published. But several observations can be made about this rather frenetic attention paid to ideological matters. First, the USSR did not participate in the matrix of bilateral accords. Apparently the series were to deal with problems unique to Eastern Europe. If so, this is one of the first acknowledgments that different levels of intellectual sophistication exist between the USSR and its allies, which warrant separate ideological tools. Second, Rumania's nonconformity is due to its concern that a web of bilateral agreements designed to extend Pact integration could ultimately become an additional instrument of Soviet hegemony. It is not a reflection of disinterest in ideological matters; Rumania exercises probably the most stringent cultural controls of any Pact country. Finally, the general impression is unavoidable that the ruling élites in Eastern Europe are seriously alarmed by the prospects of increased intellectual challenge that is inherent in the détente process. They seem concerned about the relevance of earlier experience in coping with the new threat. The precedents afforded them by Soviet cultural policy are not germane to societies that formerly enjoyed greater participation in Europe's cultural heritage. A separate East European solution to Western intellectual competition may now slowly materialize as an important by-product of the CSCE.

Prospects for CSCE

What concrete results can be expected from the CSCE? During the Pre-paratory Consultations and first Foreign Ministers' session in July 1973, the

Pact countries understandably attempted to steer the deliberations toward
issues that would contribute to solutions of their security and legitimacy problems: i.e., acceptance of the political and territorial status quo, East German
sovereignty, the concepts of noninterference in domestic affairs of other
states and the renunciation of the use of force, trade expansion, and technological exchange. In the July session, Gromyko surprised the Western delegations
by unmistakably stressing these points and calling for an adoption of an earlier
Soviet proposal embodying these issues *in toto.* He played down the principle
that sovereignty and noninterference should be applied to "all states irrespective
of their political, economic and social systems," a concept laboriously hammered
out during the Consultation stage. He stressed the importance of applying the
concepts of peaceful coexistence and cooperation among states with different
social systems. He insisted that Western delegates recognize that peaceful
coexistence must be "fully applied in Europe, crossed as it is from north to
south by a visible boundary between the two social worlds." Gromyko called
for unrestricted commercial relations, provided that such contacts remain subject
to "strict observance of the laws, customs and traditions" of the states concerned.
Under questioning by the press, neither he nor official Soviet spokesmen would
accept the possibility of peaceful changes of frontiers, even by mutual consent.
The return to these hardline features of Soviet policy indicated that while
Moscow was prepared to negotiate about the nature of détente, the precise
utility of the concept for the West would remain vague until it could be tested
over time. This harder line was also probably an accurate reflection of the growing apprehension throughout the Pact about the impact of détente.

After the July session it became apparent that the Soviet aims for the
CSCE had not basically changed. It sought a prompt termination of the formal
portion of the Conference, sealed with a Declaration of Intent by the conferees,
and the establishment of some institutional arrangement for ongoing consultations on selected issues. The codification of its security and legitimacy interests
in Eastern Europe was seen as the first dimension of a general political documentation of the parameters of détente in Europe. Such a quasi-peace treaty would
provide the framework for ongoing cooperation and the limits of ideological
competition. With these perimeters more firmly identified and mutually accepted,
a more concrete basis would be erected for military reductions. The United
States supported this logic and joined the USSR in seeking an early closure of
the formal proceedings and a shift of emphasis to the deliberations on military
reductions.

The West Europeans, however, strongly opposed this strategy. In general
they held that the CSCE was more important to the Pact than the MFR talks
and should be used as leverage to insure Pact malleability at the latter forum,
to which the West attached greater priority. Further, the wording of the
Declaration was proving to be a major obstacle. Traditional positions were being
reversed. Historically, Western conventions tend to yield loose statements,

principles, and concepts, allowing broad interpretation for the most efficient application. On the other hand, the Soviets usually seek precise wording of intentions that prescribes the limits of action. The compromise between these two approaches is that the Soviets gain legal prescriptions in binding documents and the West files letters of interpretation with them, which include the terms of reference or the Western understanding of its commitments. The Soviets were now seeking incorporation of broad general principles in the CSCE Declaration and the NATO allies became increasingly concerned with the importance in gaining precise wording. Therefore, the West Europeans attempted to prolong the proceedings, but at the time of writing it appears that they will not gain acceptance of their joint position.

Then what has been the influence of the smaller states over the course of the CSCE developments? In the period from 1966-68 Poland and Hungary mounted an active campaign to gain Western support for a security conference. Their objectives seem to have been not only to gain greater national security through international forums, but also to widen the latitude of East European maneuverability in East-West relations. After 1969 and the Soviet endorsement of a bilateral approach to security problems in the West, East European states, led by the GDR, developed a growing apprehension about the implications of normalization of relations with the West. The East Europeans concluded that their national interests were endangered by ideological competition, and the West Europeans continued arguing that their physical security was still imperiled.

In the period of 1966-68 Denmark, Belgium, and the Netherlands were highly energetic in probing the nature and scope of a possible adjustment among European states on security matters. Indeed, NATO's Harmel Report recommended that NATO institutionalize policy coordination on the issue of European security, because the interests of individual NATO countries had proliferated to the point that single efforts might overrun the common interest. The motives of these smaller NATO states were to gain an agreed formula for reducing European tensions and thereby induce cuts in defense expenditures. After the Prague crisis, however, the reservations of the larger NATO powers gained ascendancy.

By the beginning of the Helsinki session of Foreign Ministers it was apparent that NATO had not been able to reach a unified position on the utility of CSCE or on a strategy for achieving its ambivalent aims. Danish Foreign Minister K. B. Anderson set the tone for the Scandinavian countries by calling for a "basket of three" proposal for the improvement of human relations in Europe. France participated in the CSCE reluctantly. Foreign Minister Jobert's speech gave the impression that his attendance was more "to be there at the conception" than to provide concrete contributions to the formulation of European security. This position was possibly due to France's refusal to participate in the MFR and the awareness in Helsinki that the action was shifting to Vienna.

British Foreign Minister Sir Alec Douglas-Hume presented the firmest
stand of the NATO states. London had consistently maintained that unless
there was progress toward military disengagement, conferences on political
themes were likely to boil down to only propaganda exercises. The UK participated partly because of concern that Congressional pressure in the US was
reaching proportions that to do otherwise might result in precipitous decisions.
London was also anxious to develop its new-found commitment to West
European integration, which required solidarity with its partners, however
disparate their views were on the issue. The tough British position emphasized the
degree to which the Pact had been forced onto the defensive. If the Communist
governments are not prepared for the consequences of détente "they have no
business talking about cooperation and coexistence."[11] The Pact advocated
cooperation first between institutions, then organizations, and finally people.
Lord Hume reversed the priorities to include people first. Yet a tone of
pessimism was apparent throughout the British argumentation that tended to
reflect the rather skeptical opinion of the West Europeans about the durable
contributions of the CSCE.

Of the multilateral negotiations on détente, the smaller states have
probably exercised less influence on the CSCE than any other forum. The
CSCE was largely of Soviet conception and execution; the results are tailored
mainly to their measurements. Their allies have been compelled to develop
unprecedented alternatives to shore up their defenses not on security matters,
as they energetically sought, but on ideological competition, where their
armor is weakest. The West Europeans finally acquiesced that CSCE had
become a quasi-peace conference, but this acknowledgment reinforced their
stakes in MFR. European détente, after all, was still a function of military
disengagement.

16 Multilateral Negotiations on Military Détente: Mutual Force Reductions Talks

One of the key contributing factors to the Cold War tensions was the mutual sense of insecurity shared by both alliances resulting from the perceived threat posed by the opposing side. However graphic these adversary perceptions may be,[1] it is safe to presume that the Soviet perspective of NATO strength is that it is superior in many categories to that of the Pact. The Pact is superior in quantity of conventional arms, but the East European forces are generally not as well equipped as their NATO counterparts. From the Soviet viewpoint, Pact forces are largely defense oriented, particularly the fighter aircraft. While the West has concentrated on procuring self-propelled artillery, the Pact has relied on the more static towed artillery. Tank forces in the Forward Area do have an offensive capability but do not have the indigenous logistic support for sustained operations. Finally, in tactical nuclear weapons the Pact has access to a relatively smaller number of warheads, but larger yield, that are stored only in the USSR; the FRG alone has more than nine hundred artillery pieces that are nuclear capable with warheads available within helicopter flight range.

The physical security of the USSR is compounded by an additional factor not shared to the same extent by Western nations. The Soviets insist that the 400- to 600-mile-wide glacis of Eastern Europe is vital to the security of Russia proper. This buffer zone is relatively small and insignificant in the nuclear age (it can be crossed by a missile in less than five minutes' flight time), but the Soviets are keenly aware that the Eurasian heartland cannot be invaded and conquered by any contemporary global power, unless these Western approaches are first occupied or secured, either through diplomacy or force. Thus, the Soviet military presence along the Elbe River has been justified by the threat posed by NATO and German revanchism and the necessity to insure the political reliability of the Pact members. Both alliances now agree that their respective defense postures have become an undue burden and that means for reducing these forces should be explored.

Opening Exchanges

The Pact nations did not respond to NATO's 1968 signal from Reykjavík until Brezhnev's Tiblisi speech in May 1970 and the June 1970 PCC Budapest Communiqué. The Pact remained silent on the subject of force reductions, however, for the next eighteen months, until the January 1972 PCC Communiqué

253

endorsed agreement in principle to participation in talks on the issue. During this interval Moscow refused to receive the retiring NATO Secretary General Manlio Brosio, who had been commissioned in May 1971 to explore personally the Pact's position on force reductions. Not until 17 September 1972 was agreement reached on the timing for opening multilateral discussions. Presidential Advisor Henry Kissinger reported to newsmen on his return from Moscow that the USSR had offered an acceptable formula whereby the talks on force reductions would begin after the Preparatory Consultations for the CSCE were under way.

The lukewarm-to-cool Soviet attitude toward MBFR may be explained by several reasons. MFR was not a high priority issue; Moscow placed far greater importance on CSCE. As a result, the Pact had probably not studied the issue and its implications in sufficient detail to warrant early discussions. When it became apparent that West European capitals were becoming increasingly responsive to CSCE, but that they were still demanding progress on MFR *before* the Conference, some movement had to be made. MFR is infinitely more complex than SALT, and the Western Allies had been studying the problem since 1969; but they had only reached the first level of understanding about the scope of the problem, and had established no consensus about objectives or criteria for measuring asymmetries. It appeared that the Soviets were much further behind in their preparatory analyses, especially since they had to incorporate the uncertainties of the political mission of their forces in Eastern Europe in their overall estimates of preferred force strengths.

It is now apparent that the timing of Brezhnev's Tiblisi speech, one week before the Senate vote on the proposed Mansfield unilateral US troop cut, was probably intended to forestall early US actions that might have created new uncertainties. Brezhnev clearly demonstrated serious Soviet interest in checking the possibility of enhanced cohesion within NATO that might result from precipitous US actions. Soviet interests could be protected by gaining time to insure deliberation in troop reductions in Europe and in studying the all-important questions of new weapons sytems and strategies for both a "SALT-ed" and "MFR-ed" Europe. Any Western move that would have forced the Soviet hand at that time on these issues or presented Moscow with a *fait accompli* would have been regarded as detrimental. Pressure for Moscow to follow a US unilateral cut would probably have had a destabilizing impact in Eastern Europe, especially in East Germany, where the number of Soviet troops is seen as a measure of Soviet political support. Likewise, a sharp Soviet reduction would have eroded the present tenuous relations with Peking, which could be expected to denounce the action as anti-Chinese. Until there had been at least some discussion with the West on the issue, unilateral moves would have been regarded by both some friends and adversaries as ill-conceived, sporadic decisions that would complicate matters and expose Eastern Europe to Western influence without insuring greater Soviet diplomatic flexibility. Thus, Moscow

moved cautiously until it had assessed the probable effect the MFR talks
were likely to have on the security and cohesion of the Pact.

Initial Problems

The formulation of policy positions by both sides was complicated by
several uncertainties. First, there is no magic formula for determining the
appropriate number of stationed troops in both Eastern and Western Europe,
and there is no precise ratio for the number of stationed to indiginous forces.
Equally important, there is no clear understanding about the relationship of
physical force to political influence; it is even more difficult to predict how
many troops, and what kind, are necessary to protect a nation's and an Alliance's
interests against a political, not a military, challenge. Thus, the most valid argument for preserving the present Soviet troops strengths is that they are the force
levels that have successfully deterred the expansion of the adversary's political
influence; a lower posture may simulate assertiveness.

Yet there is evidence that military drawdowns can take place without
adverse results for either side. In the 1950s the Soviets withdrew one corps from
the Group of Soviet Forces Germany and later consolidated and reduced the
number of Commendantura in the Soviet Zone, cutting an estimated 50,000
troops. At the same time, the US began thinning its forces. Both sides were then
participating in commandant exchanges between the East-West zones and
encouraging the exchanges of military observers for field maneuvers (the
Soviets actually attended several British tank exercises at Pembroke before these
exchanges were discontinued). In another example, the US reduced its forces
in Germany between 1965 and 1968 by nearly 20 percent without creating a
crisis in the Alliance or an enhanced threat from the USSR. Reductions of
stationed forces on both sides did not create a failure of confidence among
Europeans in either camp.

Second, the nature of the European confrontation has changed. Formerly,
it was firmly grounded in the context of ideological challenge and military threat.
But this context has now been superseded by influence competition and political
rivalry. There is still a valid requirement for military security, but it is now
primarily a function of reassurance and stability rather than assured destruction.
In this light, did the intervention in Czechoslovakia increase the threat against
NATO, or improve regional stability? However one argues the point and the
justification for permanently garrisoning five additional Soviet divisions in
Eastern Europe, the intervention unquestionably established Moscow's vital
interests and alleged legal rights to preserve stability within its strategic perimeters. With the clear precedents of 1956 and 1968 of the Soviets' intentions
to use force if necessary to protect their interests in Eastern Europe, the size of
their physical presence becomes less critical. They can move as quickly and
decisively with three divisions as five divisions around Prague.

Third, the above individual actions were one-sided moves, subject to reversal or acceleration without undue reference to adversary reactions. Therefore, at least theoretically unilateral actions may be less durable and subject to more vagaries than multilateral or negotiated decisions. The mere negotiation process increases the interests and influence of both sides in the defensive matters of the other and, accordingly, enhances their stake in responsible actions and long-term undertakings. This aspect of the multilateral approach will be an important contribution to NATO's demands for "undiminished security" and to Soviet insistence on "equal security," concepts which presuppose the continuation of the two security systems in something like the present power configuration.

The main parties concerned held widely varying views about the utility of the talks and were divided about the envisioned objectives for the exercise: should it promote political détente, accelerate change in the East or fragmentation in the West, consolidate the respective spheres, or merely engineer military disengagement? The parties were also undecided about the conceptual basis for proposing reductions. For example, when assuming that military disengagement is the goal, there are two basic schools of thought among Western analysts about preferred means for achieving troop reductions—percentage reductions and cuts that reflect existing asymmetries.

The percentage-cut school argues that whether or not one questions the criteria for force strengths, they have attained the aura of historic validation. Clearly neither side has consulted the other in establishing its standards, and each has attempted to exploit its comparative advantages to the adversaries' detriment whenever possible. Asymmetries exist in intentions, interests, and capabilities, and each has institutionalized definitions of these terms that would economize resources while maximizing deterrence. Three fundamental asymmetries have emerged and been incorporated into the deterrence posture of both sides:

1. Geographic proximity—the USSR is a European power by virtue of geography, while the US is present on the continent only because of policy.
2. Strategic interests—Moscow has demonstrated that it considers the Elbe River its strategic borders, while the US may defend only the United States.
3. Political aims—as a means of legitimizing the Soviet model for Communist development, political stability reinforced by Soviet troops is essential in Eastern Europe; yet the US holds only very limited ambitions of political hegemony over NATO.

The percentage-reduction school maintains that no cuts are conceivable until the West accepts the implications of the Soviet rationale on these asymmetries, especially the political mission of Soviet garrisons in Eastern Europe. The only way, therefore, to insure both Soviet security interests and stability requirements is to reduce troop strengths on each side by fixed percentages—first 10 percent as a sign of good faith, then 20 percent to reflect mutually attractive budgetary economies, and finally by 30 percent to insure mutual security.[2]

The asymmetry-reductions school argues that the advantages and disadvantages inherent in the postures of both sides are so severe that percentage cuts risk a disproportionate loss of advantages and accordingly contribute to insecurity and instability. (The asymmetries cited most often have been discussed in chapter 11.) If just the single factor of weapons and equipment inventories is considered, using only each side's respective assessment of effectiveness, reliability, and serviceability, the complexity can be surmised in establishing agreed standards for evaluating asymmetrical advantages and appropriate cuts. When all inputs in the present military postures are calculated, the exercise becomes infinitely more complicated than the SALT proceedings. The difficulty of defining a precise mutually acceptable formula for reduction is the strongest argument for seeking alternative means.

Great Powers' Positions

The Soviet reaction to these two approaches is instructive. In the first comment in any Soviet periodical on MRF, the authoritative Academy of Sciences published in June 1972 a detailed rejection of asymmetric reductions.[3] The article argued that the 1:3, 1:4 or 1:6 variants in troop cuts were based on erroneous Western assumptions about the impact of geography. First, the reduced units should be disbanded, not merely withdrawn from forward positions. In emergencies, Western Europe would be able to mobilize and deploy reserves at least as easily as the USSR, which would have to call up men from, say, Central Asia. Second, geography would be as detrimental for the USSR as the US in case of emergencies. The USSR has extensive borders to defend and reinforcing Eastern Europe is not merely a matter of dispatching troops from Western Russian military districts, but of moving units over six thousand miles from the Far Eastern districts. (The USSR presently has 31 divisions deployed in Eastern Europe, 60 in European USSR, 8 between the Volga and Baikal, 21 in the Caucasus, and 49 along the Chinese border—54 including those near Baikal.)[4] Third, since any outbreak of hostilities would probably escalate rapidly to a full-scale conflict, the overall global balance between NATO and Pact forces must be calculated. When total forces are included, NATO has a substantial advantage. Finally, both nuclear and conventional forces must be included in any reductions.

The article concludes,

> In our opinion, if we approach the question of reducing armed forces and arms in Central Europe from a realistic position, the only

possible principle is the principle of equal reduction. Precisely this
approach would accord with the main condition laid down, in particular,
at the time of the Oreanda meeting between Secretary General of the
CC CPSU, L.I. Brezhnev, and Chancellor of the FRG, W. Brandt—that
no harm should be done to the countries taking part in such a reduction
(the principle of equal security).

These are strong reservations, and if the experience of SALT remains a
valid precedent, the Soviets can be expected to insist on a rejection of asymmetric reductions. And from the West's viewpoint, the percentage-cut formula
is too simplistic and would enhance the Pact's existing advantages on the Central
Front. Cutting both sides by equal slices would weaken the West more than the
East because of the offensive capabilities, centralized geographic dispositions,
and reserve mobilization advantages the Pact enjoys. Therefore, equal percentage
cuts would reduce the West's position by a factor greater than the specified
slice.

In President Nixon's Foreign Policy Report delivered to the US Congress
on 3 May 1973, he pointed out the complexities of the MFR process regarding
the definition of types of troops to be cut:

> Reductions provide an inherent advantage for the side that has
> postured its forces along offensive lines. Offensive forces would retain
> the initiative to concentrate and attack, while the defense must con-
> tinue to defend the same geographical front with fewer forces. Major
> deployments of equipment, especially those with offensive capabilities,
> are therefore an important element in the reduction process. How can
> equivalence be established between different categories of equipment?
> What ratios would be equitable? . . . Mixed, asymmetrical reductions?
> This means reductions would be made by different amounts in various
> categories of weapons or man-power. It could prove extremely complex
> to define equivalence between different weapon systems.[5]

Clearly a solution is elusive.

Preparatory Consultations

Despite the failure of the two sides to establish a mutually acceptable conceptual framework for their discussions or agreed standards for reductions, it
was decided to convene preliminary talks to tackle the more pressing issues
regarding cuts. The Preparatory Consultations began on 22 November in Vienna,
but were quickly adjourned until 31 January. Protracted informal consultations
precluded convening a plenary session for over fourteen weeks, until 14 May.
The preliminary talks were noteworthy because of the manner in which they

were conducted. No bargaining was conducted between the two sides in formal plenary sessions. Discussions were held privately and decisions on key points were reached between the great powers and then sold to their respective partners. These techniques were better suited to handling quickly a wide assortment of complex issues. The Preparatory Consultations produced agreement on a lengthy list of issues.

The first and perhaps easiest problem was whose troops should be included in the initial cuts: the great powers only, all station forces (including Britain, Belgium, France, etc.), or indigenous national forces as well. The delegates finally concurred that only great-power troops should be involved in the first cut because of several factors: US Congressional pressures; the symbolic effect this would have on the commitment of the great powers to the détente process; and the fact that the great-power forces comprise the core of each side's offensive capability.

The second issue was membership and participation. The West sought to restrict participation at the working level in order to focus deliberations first on the most dangerous area of the East-West confrontation—Central Europe— without the inclusion of a variety of national issues from other regions. This group would include seven nations from the West—the United States, Britain, Canada, West Germany, Holland, Belgium, and Luxembourg—and five from the East—the Soviet Union, Poland, East Germany, Czechoslovakia, and Hungary (those states that could directly threaten or support operations against the Federal Republic). The Pact was caught off guard because of the known demands of Rumania for an open conference in which any member could raise any issue of national importance. To insure that such privileges did not impair progress, a compromise was developed for the final communiqué which provided for two categories of members: full participants with decision-making powers, and states with special status and the right to raise any topic relevant to the subject matter.

To achieve this formula, the Soviets changed tactics sometime in March by abandoning the neutrals (whom they had earlier courted), understandably sacrificing Rumania without much hesitation, and insisting that Italy be included in full status to balance Hungary. The Soviets argued, unconvincingly, that the inclusion of 165,000 Hungarian and 40,000 Soviet troops in Hungary would create a structural imbalance in the talks without bringing in the 300,000 Italian and 10,000 American troops in Italy. More to the point, they reasoned that the inclusion of forces in Hungary would cover all Soviet troops abroad while the talks would affect only a portion of the US forces overseas, creating dissimilar incentives for the two powers during the next round of cuts. Finally, and squarely on the mark, a Soviet official commented informally that the reason for not including the four Soviet divisions in Hungary was because of the "political-geographical" mission they still performed.

From the military perspective there are both tactical and strategic advantages for exempting the Soviet forces in Hungary from reductions.

1. Relative to any potential aggressor in the area, they comprise powerful armor and tactical air units which can be employed offensively as well as to protect vital communications links and the headquarters of the Southern Forces Front.
2. They also serve political functions of guaranteeing the reliability of the Hungarian regime.
3. They are strategically located to exert coercive pressure, along with the Soviet Navy, in the possible political succession crises in Yugoslavia, Albania and Rumania.
4. Should military action ever be required in the Balkans, the undiminished strength of the Soviet involvement could secure communications with the Ukraine, serve as spearhead for combined Hungarian, Bulgarian, and Soviet operations against Yugoslavia, or lend military weight to a Pact encirclement of Rumania.

The United States accepted this stand, but its allies strongly objected: Hungary served as an additional axis through the Danube Valley to Bavaria, along which there would be virtually no resistance; it would continue to act as a pivotal resource reserve from which men and materiale could be shifted north or south; and finally there was no assurance that Soviet troops withdrawn from the Northern Tier would not be transferred to Hungary. Under reportedly strong combined US-USSR pressure, the NATO allies adopted a compromise whereby Hungary would be classified as a special-status nation and the West would reserve the right to question its status or issues relevant to Hungary at a later time—a clear concession to the Soviets.[6]

The Hungarian question introduced the problem of verification before the substance of reductions was raised. The SALT negotiations progressed in part because of the effectiveness of satellite surveillance. Reconnaissance of ground units by national means is far more difficult. In the Second World War, the Czechoslovak operation, and the Suez Canal build-up, the Soviets demonstrated a high degree of professionalism in conducting clandestine troop movements. Their skill in these operations, presumably superior to that of the West, is precisely the reason for their refusal to accept any form of on-site inspection to verify troop reductions.

The verification problem in MFR deals not only with troop withdrawals but with the final disposition of the forces and their equipment. West German Defense Minister Leber claims that there has been an addition of 1500 T-62 Soviet tanks in East Germany alone since 1966, and that the replaced T-55 and T-54 tanks have not been scrapped but stored in forward depots, where they can be rehabilitated on short notice and issued to reinforcement units.

Further, in the annual Pact exercise "Shield 72," the Soviets introduced a massive airlift, similar to the US Reforger and Crested Cap exercises, where dual-based units are airlifted from the US to Germany. But the Soviets employed a significant innovation of mobilizing a major segment of their civilian airline fleet for this purpose. This is the first evidence that the USSR has developed and exercised a concept of dual-basing as possible compensation for withdrawal of combat units from the Forward Area.[7] But the numbers, types, and locations of such units, if they exist, remain to be verified before they can be credibly accepted by the West. This single example illustrates the complexity of the verification question, which was left unresolved during the Preparatory Consultations, and NATO's reservations about Hungary's claim to sanctuary rights.

The types of weapons and equipment to be cut was also raised. It was the Soviet side that introduced the additional term "and arms" into the MFR title for the conference. It was generally presumed that the Pact would use this rubric to introduce its traditional demand that tactical nuclear weapons be included along with manpower cuts. Nuclear weapons are always a delicate question and especially in this context. As Nixon pointed out in his May 3, 1973, report, "How do we reconcile reductions in roughly balanced conventional forces with the fact that the strategic balance is no longer clearly favorable to the Alliance?"[8] The change in the theater confrontation increased substantially the relevance of tactical nuclear weapons in Western defenses, and NATO had not yet determined a precise formula for their employment. The Soviets tentatively decided not to tamper with this delicate balance and agreed to confine MFR to only conventional weapons. In November 1973, however, the Soviet delegation introduced the inclusion of tactical nuclear warheads in a proposed package settlement. The Soviets made it clear that despite earlier understandings, they remained committed to their long-standing claim that equal security requires a reduction in NATO's advantages in nuclear weapons.

The size of the initial cut in great power conventional forces stationed in Central Europe was also discussed. The Soviets reportedly rejected out of hand any consideration of asymmetrical compromises, pointing to their concessions on confining the reductions to Central Europe. (According to the latest figures, there are 310,000 US troops in Europe, 350,000 Soviet troops in Eastern Europe, but only 190,000 US troops in West Germany. The all-European balance in ground forces is 1,410,000 for NATO versus 1,350,000 for the Pace.) These figures indicate that percentage cuts would work to the Soviet disadvantage: a 10-percent reduction would cost 35,000 troops against half that for the US, 19,000, unless they were conducted at the all-European level. Thus, the Soviets could counter the popular Western argument that percentage cuts in Central Europe down to a fixed point would preserve the existing asymmetries intact, without impairing either side's security.

Accordingly, the Soviets devoted the bulk of their efforts during the Consultations to refuting the term and principle of "balanced reductions" and to gaining acceptance of the necessity for "mutual reductions." This was the most divisive issue of the Consultations—first between East and West and then, when the US sided with the Soviet position, within NATO ranks. (In the long run, however, it had the positive effect of forcing NATO to decide finally upon a common objective for MFR and a unified Western stand on the issue of reduction.) It was not until Brezhnev's visit to the FRG and then to the US in June 1973 that the term "balance" was dropped from the title of the Conference and the substitute wording agreed upon for the final 19 June communiqué:

> [The participants] agreed that, in the negotiations, an understanding should be reached to conduct them in such a way as to ensure the most effective and thorough approach to the consideration of the subject matter, with due regard to its complexity. They also agreed that specific arrangements will have to be carefully worked out in scope and timing in such a way that they will in all respects and at every point conform to the principle of undiminished security for each party.[9]

NATO spokesmen argued that the inclusion of the West's terminology "undiminished security" was indeed accepting the underlying principle in the West's meaning of balanced reductions. The trick was to find a formula upon which all can agree that their security would not be impaired. But this explanation brought the Consultations around full cycle: there was no perceptible difference between the Western understanding of undiminished security and the Soviets' original term "equal security."[10]

Alternative Proposals

After the largely informal, unrecorded Preparatory Consultations, what can be expected from the equally informal Working Groups that got underway on 31 October 1973? What alternatives are there to those already presented, and what form are accords likely to take? Nixon apparently postulated the minimum and maximum US expectations in his May 1973 Report to Congress. He rejected percentage cuts as affording advantages to the Soviets and preferred instead "mixed, asymmetrical" cuts, meaning reductions by different amounts in various categories of weapons or manpower, if equivalence can be found between different kinds of weapons. As a maximum goal he will presumably seek reductions to equal levels, whereby common ceilings would be imposed on both sides.[11] Both approaches are unrealistic—the first because of difficulties in equating, for example, tanks and artillery, and the second because it does not accept the political mission of Soviet garrison, which adds an extra quantitative dimension.

In contrast, in November 1973 the Soviets introduced their first detailed package proposal. It called for a numerical cut of twenty thousand in both Soviet and American forces by 1974, to be followed by two successive percentage cuts in 1975 and 1976 of all national forces along the Central Front. This combination of first numerical and then percentage cuts probably approaches an acceptable compromise for the West on force strengths. The Soviet plan also calls for a reduction of tactical nuclear weapons and their delivery vehicles, i.e. tactical aircraft. No mention was made of armored forces or an appropriate armament mix for ground forces. Apparently the Soviets would like to meet the NATO position on personnel cuts and neutralize the West's main deterrent (nuclear weapons), while allowing both sides a free hand in determining future mixes between offensive and defensive systems. The latter proposals are clearly contrary to the US position and will undoubtedly be the subject of hard bargaining.

Of the many alternative proposals offered, two are noteworthy. To compensate for the asymmetries involved, a formula should be devised for establishing fixed ceilings on only offensive capabilities in the Central Front. The ceilings should roughly equate the offensive capability of both sides and should include conventional armor and tactical nuclear weapons and interdiction aircraft. (It is assumed that medium-range delivery vehicles will remain the subject at SALT II negotiations.) The ceilings should be equated to a minimal threat posture for each of a series of incremental reductions. By incorporating only the most destabilizing factor for the overall equation, offensive capabilities, the formula can then more readily accommodate relatively large percentage cuts in manpower. This alternative would allow both sides unrestrained freedom of action in devising appropriate defenses for theater-level hostilities. Thus percentage reductions in in-being forces (stationed and indigenous) and fixed cuts in offensive weapons should be the best check against the hostile intentions of an opponent. Finally, this formula reduces both susceptibility to launch a surprise attack, without impairing either mobilization and defensive capabilities, or, that is, the ability to absorb unexpected attacks. It would also complement the development of a Maximum Defense strategy, discussed above.

The second alternative is a function of the normalization process. Rather than a model for disengagement, it is itself a result of adjustment. In the event that both sides are unable to surmount the complexities involved in agreed reductions, it may be possible and preferable for both sides to introduce unilateral actions that could complement the normalization process and foster efforts toward mutual agreement on ultimate force levels. In the interim, the multilateral discussions could focus on functional aspects of disengagement, as several NATO delegations have already advocated. A wide selection of military tension-reducing efforts might be submitted for consideration by the MFR talks, such as exchange of observers for military maneuvers; removal of travel restrictions on accredited military attachés; notification prior to large-scale maneuvers; construction of "hot-line" communications at the tactical level to cope with inadvertant border penetrations; emplacement of unmanned electronic sensors along frontiers and presumed penetration routes; and creation of a joint standing committee to establish criteria for *provocative* and *precautionary* activities. These and similar functional undertakings would both further military disengagement and foster greater understanding of the nature of political normalization. Furthermore, they would lower the necessity for verification or would rely on unilateral surveillance procedures and thereby improve the political acceptability of a functional approach. Thus, this second alternative would seek interim solutions: making the military status quo cheaper and the political status quo more viable, without substantially altering either. At this early juncture, it seems possible that both alternatives will eventually come under review at the multilateral level, perhaps simultaneously.

If the proposal for fixed ceilings on offensive forces and percentage manpower cuts are rejected, and the US continues insisting on some form of asymmetrical cuts, several general negotiating techniques may be appropriate for achieving these types of accords. First, "correlated systems trade-offs" is a variation on the zero-sum bargaining principle, where a loss for one is equated as a gain for the other side, e.g., an equal number of F-4s and TU-16s, F-111s, and TU-22s could be cut. The difficulty with the correlation technique is that it tends to oversimplify weapons characteristics and cannot be used to tackle the chief source of threat to both sides—their differing offensive capabilities, tanks and aircraft. While the roles may be similar, their respective characteristics are so dissimilar that policing a reduction would be very difficult.

Second, noncorrelated systems trade-offs is an equitable reduction in differing categories in offensive capabilities of theater forces, e.g., one wing of F-4s is withdrawn in exchange for the withdrawal of one tank division. The problem with this technique is that theater forces cannot be satisfactorily correlated on a military basis alone. For example, forthcoming advances in antitank defenses are likely to sharply curtail tank effectiveness, reducing their value as a bargaining counter to the flexible F-4 aircraft. Thus, reductions of noncorrelated weapons would tend to be largely the product of political decisions.

Finally, unilateral concessions or reductions by mutual example pertains to cuts where no corresponding military trade is feasible and the payoff is largely political. The difficulty with unilateral concessions is not merely the problem of determining their military impact, but ascertaining the political risks involved and the rewards that may serve as incentives for reciprocity. In descending order from purely correlated trade-offs to unilateral concessions, the degree of political implication and associated uncertainty increases at least in an inverse proportion. At the outset of the working group talks in Vienna, it seems unlikely that unilateral concessions will receive much attention. But if the technical problems connected with establishing agreed-upon criteria for correlations lead to frustration and stalemate, a gradual increase in the political stakes for reaching agreement may occur, raising the prospects for consideration of unilateral concessions—provided mutual interest in accord remain undiminished.

Prospects for Success

The prospects for a successful outcome of the MFR talks will depend in large part on the degree to which each side can accept the other's peculiar security requirements. This is a statement of the obvious, but needs to be underlined in light of the long history of mutual misperceptions that have distorted earlier relations. Both sides can be expected to seek reductions in the opponent's systems regarded as most threatening to its security and that will not incur major structural adjustments or instability in either alliance. In general, the outer limits of Soviet agreement on measures related to military disengagement in Europe will be those concepts, reductions, or policies that impart no risk of altering the present structure and stability of its alliance and security system. This line of reasoning underscores the political overtones of the MFR talks and highlights the necessity for NATO to accept the political function of Soviet garrisons in Eastern Europe. No long-term success can be expected from these talks unless NATO fully accepts this dimension of the Soviet posture and is able to discount it because of progress in political normalization or compensates for it by adopting a more credible military posture, such as a Maximum Defense strategy.

The political overtones of the MFR talks also bring into relief the lack of consensus among the NATO partners about the utility of the exercise. France strongly opposes the talks and has refused to participate because negotiated reductions would compromise the stature of its independent military stance. Britain is apprehensive about the value of talks, arguing that the psychological side effects likely to accompany any agreement could be far more disarming for the West than the size of the actual cuts. NATO defenses have been reduced to minimum levels because of domestic pressures; they should not be reduced further, even through mutual accord, while the course of political developments in Pact countries remains so unpredictable. West Germany is most anxious to achieve a rapid reduction of forces as a means of further cutting its defense expenditures. Indeed, the FRG held out during the Preparatory Consultations for a cut in its military manning during the first round of reductions. And the US views reductions largely in terms of domestic pressures. The influence of the smaller Western states is likely to be greater in the MFR than in the CSCE (but the reverse will hold for the smaller Pact nations). Indeed, the NATO partners and their lack of unity may act as serious constraint on US options, refocusing attention on the political ramifications of any cuts.

While both sides have had difficulty in assessing accurately the potential impact of military disengagement, they have had greater problems weighing the consequences of failure. The dangers of disenchantment in Western Europe and of resignation in Eastern Europe may be far more crippling for the normalization process than the risks of miscalculations about specific arms limitations measures. The fear of failure alone is likely to produce some positive results. But the negotiation of even minor reductions is likely to be protracted, possibly generating both euphoria and disillusionment before a durable product is achieved.

17

Bilateral Negotiations on Military
Détente: Strategic Arms
Limitations Talks

The US and USSR initially agreed in March 1967 to open talks on strategic
arms limitations, but progress was halted because of the Middle East crisis. Interest was renewed the following year; in July 1968 it was agreed to begin talks
at the earliest possible time. The United States suspended further consideration
of the matter after the invasion of Czechoslovakia, but restated its desire for
formal talks in January 1969. The Soviet Union delayed making a final commitment until the following October, insisting as a precondition that the US
disclaim any intentions to deal from a position of strength. After the US officials
made several public statements to this effect, the discussions finally opened in
Helsinki on 17 November 1969. The preparations and conduct of the talks were
unique in the history of US-USSR negotiations and the détente process. The
negotiations themselves and their implications will be assessed in this chapter.[1]

Previously, formal negotiations were only conducted after the meticulous
preparation of an agreed agenda, identifying specific issues, and often accompanied by draft accords. In the SALT deliberations the great powers agreed to
open formal talks without the sanctity of an endorsed agenda, with no agreement on objectives, scope of interests, or established rules of procedure, and
with no draft proposals or treaties. Furthermore, there was no precedent since
the 1922 Washington Naval Disarmament Conference for a major arms limitation
accord, whereby quotas of specific arms could be established, possibly even
requiring destruction of a proportion of selected systems. Arms accords since
1945 have succeeded in the less difficult task of prohibiting certain types of
weapons or activities, rather than defining and enforcing specific limitations or
reductions on existing systems. Thus, the aims and procedures of the SALT
deliberations represent a breakthrough in the conduct of Soviet/American
relations.

Initial Positions

In this perspective, what motivated the great powers to undertake such a
grave task as a major great-power accord on strategic weapons? Former
German Ambassador William Grewe has offered a partial list of aims: maintenance of a stable balance based on guaranteed (partial) vulnerability;

267

prevention of destabilizing weapons developments; cost reduction and the avoidance of new cost escalations; provision of a ceiling in adversary competition while assuring a satisfactory level of superiority over China; preservation of existing technological leads (especially on the American side); codification of strategic parity (particularity important to the Soviets); and a general reduction of great-power tensions to a manageable level, while keeping open options at the theater level.[2]

Specific American aims in the talks were defined by Secretary Rogers as threefold:

(1) To enhance international security by maintaining a stable US-Soviet strategic relationship through limitation on the deployment of strategic weapons; (2) to halt the upward spiral of strategic arms and avoid the tensions, uncertainties, and costs of an unrestrained continuation of the strategic arms race; and (3) to reduce the risk of an outbreak of nuclear war through a dialogue about issues arising from the strategic situation.[3]

Several inferences can be made from these aims. The US estimated that a formula could be found whereby deterrence could be preserved through a quantitative limitation on strategic weapons. This could be mutually beneficial if it could also curtail the qualitative spiral in strategic arms by reducing uncertainties about each other's capabilities and intentions. Finally, the talks were expected to be an ongoing educational process that could provide invaluable insight into the entire spectrum of strategic issues and the concept of deterrence itself.

No precise statement of Soviet goals is available, but presumably they were sufficiently similar to allow the talks to commence. Both powers promptly agreed to make their exchanges as comprehensive as possible but to exclude all extraneous and peripheral matters (the US decision in August 1969 to proceed with its ABM program and in May 1970 to intervene in Cambodia did not alter Soviet determination to conduct the talks in a "businesslike" manner). The initial task of the conference was to define the scope of the talks and the specific weapons systems they should include. The Soviets reportedly wanted the agenda to include all delivery systems capable of striking the other's territory. The US sought a more refined series of optional packages: a total freeze on all weapons, both offensive and defensive, including ICBMs, ABMs, MIRV warheads, strategic bomber aircraft and sea-launched missiles, based upon an agreed on-site verification system; merely a limitation of existing ICBMs and ABMs to an agreed-upon figure that could be verified by national means of detection alone; or a combination of both approaches. The USSR reportedly set the upper limits on the possible systems involved by its steadfast refusal to allow on-site inspections within its territory. Therefore, any limitations would have to be the subject of national detection systems, such as satellite surveillance and communications monitoring.

The Soviet definition of strategic forces as those that can strike the territory of the other added a further dimension by raising the issue of European-based forces. A prohibition of all delivery systems that could strike the USSR would include a large number of the theater forces committed to SACEUR for the defense of Western Europe, including NATO tactical aircraft, carrier aircraft, and Polaris submarines—the Forward Based Systems (FBS). In return, none of the Soviet strike forces targeted against NATO, especially the medium-range ballistic missiles (MRBMs), in Western USSR would be affected. A formula that required an asymmetrical reduction of theater forces was feared by Europeans as an undue temptation to decouple US strategic deterrence from possible reaction to incursions against NATO. (The replacement of older SS-4s and -5s in the MRBM force by one hundred multiranged SS-11 missiles capable of striking both Western Europe, China or the US introduced a new factor. The SS-11 may be regarded as an FBS.)

The refinement of other aspects of "strategic" forces was even more difficult. A central point in the American bargaining position, as stated by one of the delegates, was that a degree of symmetry exists between offensive and defensive forces, whereby a reduction of a specific number of offensive vehicles would allow, and may require, a significant but not necessarily equal cut in defensive forces.[4] The exact equation was imprecise. If bomber aircraft were included in the formula, what proportion of Soviet air-defense facilities must also be reduced, and how could these cuts be monitored to insure that these forces were not merely shifted from the Central Region or their capabilities upgraded and modernized? If missile-equipped submarines were reduced, should antisubmarine-warfare facilities also be curtailed? The US would not accept a Soviet proposal to limit an agreement to the ABM issue, in which the Russians had a superiority, and the Russians in turn rejected Washington's desire to include both offensive and defensive nuclear weapons, including a MIRV limitation, in which they were inferior. As the President later complained, the Soviets were apparently hoping to buy time to achieve parity in delivery vehicles, in which they were approximately 25 percent inferior. The Soviet suggestions, he stated, lack the specificity and detail to permit firm conclusions about their overall impact.[5] On 20 May 1971, he finally admitted that a deadlock had developed.

In a simultaneous announcement in Washington and Moscow, the two sides agreed to move the talks off dead-center, concentrating in 1971 on working out an agreement for the limitation on deployment of antiballistic-missile systems. The President later stated in a press conference that it might be possible to reach separate agreements: a treaty covering ABM limitations and an executive agreement covering offensive systems. Such agreements were signed in May 1972. (Parallel progress on the two related issues was made in September 1971. Agreements were concluded to hold simultaneous talks on the new satellite hot line, and establishment of certain safety measures for the handling of nuclear "accidents.")

Assessing SALT I

The SALT I deliberations were the most important single example of great-power negotiations during the entire détente process. They overshadowed the earlier dialogues in complexity and implication. For the first time, the great powers were discussing issues explicitly bearing on vital national security interests. To what extent, then, were these momentous undertakings successful? Even a qualified answer depends on how success is defined and measured. Did they impose an arms ceiling, reduce the arms race, contribute to strategic stability, reinforce national security requirements, or foster the "spirit" of détente by promoting good will through mutual understanding?[6]

Of the three accords signed under the aegis of SALT I, only the treaty on ABMs has the quality of permanency. The other two, dealing with offensive strategic weapons, are interim in nature. This temporary nature was due to the existing asymmetries in strategic systems and the resulting difficulties in bargaining exclusively on military capabilities. To offset these discrepancies, the political intentions of both parties had to be entered into the overall calculations. The risks inherent in trying to predict adversary intentions in a still potentially unstable political environment, however, were hedged or balanced by the five-year time limits on the accords and the commitment to seek a more durable basis for limiting physical capabilities during the interval.

The US entered SALT I with the explicitly stated aim of seeking to freeze offensive capabilities at the 1969 level. But in three and one half years of negotiating, the USSR corrected its 25-percent inferiority in ICBM launchers and achieved a 60-percent quantitative superiority. The USSR gained a 5 to 1 advantage in megatonnage (MT) for its ICBM and SLBM forces, 2400 MTs for the US versus 11,400 MTs for the USSR. Both sides retain the right to modernize individual systems, but in doing so cannot exceed fixed upper numerical limits: 1710 for the US, with possibly 710 SLBMs, and 2424 maximum for the USSR, with possibly 950 SLBMs.

Such discrepancies in throw-weight and launchers were temporarily acceptable to the United States because of advantages inherent in its more versatile posture. Because of range limitations, the Soviets require a 3:2 ratio in SLBMs: presently the US maintains 60 percent of its SLBM force on-station, while the USSR can maintain only 40 percent. The US enjoys marked advantages in the manned bomber category: 525 aircraft with a 33.4 million pound payload versus 140 aircraft with only 4.8 million pounds delivery capability. Most decisive, the US has a distinct lead in warhead technology: presently it has 5580 warheads against 2510 for the Soviet Union, and by the expiration of the agreement the US will have an expected 7800 warheads, plus over 3500 in its manned bombers, and the USSR will have an estimated 3800 (the US will have 5650 warheads in SLBMs alone, the USSR with MRVs may have 1850). Finally, the Soviets suffer from an immediate disadvantage not yet encountered by the United States.

Because of geographic peculiarities, the USSR must counter the increasing Chinese intermediate-range ballistic missiles targeted against Soviet cities mainly with longer range ICBMs, a requirement demanding a greater number of total launchers than needed for single adversary deterrence. But each one of these reasons for quantitative discrepancies could be overcome with time, and could destabilize the existing rough balance.

Little is known of the official Soviet evaluation of the outcome of SALT I, but several suppositions can be offered. From the technical aspect, Moscow must regard SALT I as highly advantageous. While it entered the talks in a numerically inferior position, it emerged in a superior posture in some categories, e.g., total number of launchers (providing flexibility and redundancy), and total throw-weight and deliverable megatonnage (with authorization to modernize). It is difficult to argue that the Soviets halted at the present level because of the pressures from SALT. It seems more rational to suggest that budgetary and operational imperatives were the constraining factors. Given the advantages in numbers of launchers and throw-weight and the right to introduce any technological improvements, why would the Soviets want even one hundred more costly missiles? Therefore, Moscow achieved its military objectives while attaining important political gains as well.

Politically, SALT I codified strategic parity and downgraded American strategic supremacy. This shattered strategic concepts that had governed Western policy for over a quarter century. The technical aspects of the accords denied the US its original bargaining aims, and therefore contributed to the Soviet image of political equality. Finally, the codification introduced uncertainties in the political arena that were potentially far more dangerous than the new unknowns in the technical sphere. For example, how would the American loss of assured destruction affect domestic pressures, overseas obligations, and Alliance politics? The present evidence suggests that the Soviets' political gains from SALT I are probably more significant than the purely military advantages.[7]

From the US standpoint SALT I was a classical exercise in misperception. The US entered the talks with a totally erroneous assumption of the Soviet intentions. In 1965 Secretary McNamara told the international press that the Soviets had decided they had lost the quantitative race, and they were not seeking to engage us in that contest. The US openly renounced its policy of strength as an incentive for Soviet participation in SALT and thereby freeze Soviet strategic developments at levels that would preserve our diminishing advantages. The Soviets, however, had no interest in dealing with us from a position of inferiority. They used the talks to signal their good faith and allay US suspicions while they accelerated efforts to secure their military objectives.

The US misperception was reinforced by two alternative views. Doves insisted that the dialogue was the "last chance for peace." In a spirit of desperation one concession after another was suggested as an incentive for Soviet participation. The highest priority was placed on merely getting the Soviets to the table, and great faith was attached to the educational process that was bound to emerge from the talks. These hopes were based on the assumption that the Soviets' desire for "peace" was as strong as ours, if for no other reason than that they appeared to have no other options but to opt for stability and normalization.

Defense planners, more realistically, recognized that the US was approaching a strategic crossroads marked with hard choices. Many US strategic systems were nearly obsolete, and even some of the force concepts were wearing thin. If supremacy was to be retained, a quantum jump in the strategic arms race would soon be required, with all the accompanying domestic controversy and alliance politicking. These leaders saw SALT as a *deus ex machina* that could resolve our strategic problems by eliminating the need for their further consideration. Agonizing appraisals over priorities for assured destruction or force survivability could be avoided through SALT without risk to national security interests.

But the Soviets did not share either view of stability and national interests. They achieved such substantial advantages from SALT I that stability has not been assured and the arms race has not been terminated. True, production costs for potential new systems have been cut. But during the five-year interval of the accords, the US may have to allocate at least as many resources for research and development as in the past to preserve its technological lead. Indeed, similar or higher levels of investment may be required for military technology in the 1970s than were spent in the 1960s, a stimulant rather than a tranquilizer for the arms race. Again, the *deus ex machina* that is to save us from spiraling defense costs is the Soviet Union in SALT II. Unless the Soviets ultimately agree to cut their standing strategic forces, the US may be caught in perpetual "technological struggle for survival."

The most glaring weakness of SALT I from the US viewpoint was the emphasis placed on mutual education. Strategy is not based on dialogue or mutual understanding. It is a function of responding to national aims and perceived dangers, and in application is the product of opportunities, resources, and constraints. US strategy at the outset of SALT I was based on the supposition that stability rested on mutually assured destruction, which, in turn, depended upon the degree of vulnerability of forces. Counterforce threats were regarded as incentives for preemption and force survivability was viewed as a product of an assured second-strike capability, not strategic defense.

Soviet policy during SALT indicates that Moscow regards the entire rationale as inadequate, if not indeed superfluous. The USSR has not been content with formulae for "sufficiency" or mutually assured destruction. It has pursued a defense policy that provides a counterforce first-strike capability and a counter-city second-strike capability that negates mutual destruction. For the first time, it is now conceivable that the USSR can ultimately have the theoretical capability to disable the US counterforce capability and deny the US the option of countercity retaliation by the threat of overwhelming destruction.

With this dissimilarity of doctrines, there was little hope that the two sides would reach an understanding on force concepts, even if such an understanding would be desirable. This conceptual incongruity does not preclude selected limitations on marginal matters, but it does not foster stability as expected—it stimulates instability and competition. Here was the source of shock for Western planners. The Soviets were not playing by our rules. The backstop for such irregularities was the conviction that we could educate the Soviets about the "immutable laws" of US strategic thought, an area of intellectualism that the US has long regarded as its exclusive domain. Washington's success in SALT II will depend partly on its ability to modify its cherished suppositions about strategic policy and to adopt the Soviet ground rules for further agreement, namely that the US will not negotiate from an inferior position or from a posture that places credence on good faith rather than assured defense.

Road to SALT II

The US side reportedly entered SALT II intending to seek some level of destruction of existing strategic systems. Partial destruction of current inventories was regarded as both a confirmation of each side's intentions to pursue a détente course and a physical check that quality improvements by either party would not adversely affect the strategic balance. If successful, and the two sides agree to limited destruction of existing arsenals, it would be the first time since the 1922 Washington Naval Disarmament Conference that major components of the great powers' strategic posture would be eliminated by negotiations.

Such expectations, however, soon appeared unrealistic. Chou En-lai with his personal knowledge of Soviet leaders, repeatedly told American visitors that it was illusory to anticipate the physical reductions of Soviet strategic systems. There are no precedents for such cuts: the construction of the present level of forces was made at great sacrifices to other national priorities, and they will not be scrapped unless there are unquestionable advantages to do so. Historic Russian xenophobia and persisting strains of Leninist ideology are likely to remain as constraints on the level of reconciliation. Moscow will reinforce these anxieties with capabilities rather than intentions. Moreover, while the Soviets have to rely on quantitative superiority in launchers to compensate for technological backwardness, they are unlikely to consider seriously reducing this level of redundancy until they have been able to match American qualitative asymmetries.

If the USSR will not accept destruction of existing capabilities, what are the prospects for developing a more durable basis for the continuing competition in offensive systems? Some express hopes for accord on issues of lesser importance. Using the bargaining techniques described in the previous chapter, there appears to be interest in a correlated trade-off on manned bombers. The US B-52s are a survivable, versatile force that can carry over ten independently targeted warheads. It can be deployed to dispersal bases or launched and held aloft until "safe bases" are identified, then relaunched as a follow-on strike force against surviving priority targets and targets of opportunity. The SRAM system, with a range of 35-100 miles, is a high-confidence penetration aid. Moreover, the demonstrated effectiveness of the B-52 in the conventional role in Southeast Asia is an important complement to American global commitments. The US will probably attach a high preference on retaining this flexible system for the lifetime of the aircraft.

The Soviets have a meager force of 140 antique Bears and Bisons that they may agree to retire for a cut of a larger number of B-52s, say 250 aircraft. Long-range bombers are no longer in production, though the US is developing the follow-on B-1, and both sides must phase out these aircraft within several years (the US plans to cut its strength to 250 by 1975, keeping some 237 in storage). Agreement may be reached on a quantitative trade-off, leaving the US with a substantial force until 1980, and a ban of developing follow-on aircraft. The FB-111s could be assigned to the continental United States, where they have only limited utility, and confined to normal retirement. Such a trade-off would not represent the drastic destruction of existing systems, as in ICBMs, but would indicate merely the mutual acceptance of obsolescence and agreement to abandon ultimately this mode of offensive warfare. If no cuts or agreed future limits can be reached, both sides may achieve the same goals by the technique of mutual example. Either a correlated trade-off agreement or mutual example would be readily verifiable by national means.

A correlated trade-off in air defense could augment one for manned bombers and be used as a counter for the retention of a larger US B-52 capability. To assure a symmetry in follow-on strike capabilities, each side could scale down air defenses to the level necessary to counter the opponent's bomber force. The US presently plans to phase out all of its remaining forty-eight Nike Hercules antiaircraft missile batteries, and at least 50 percent of the seven squadrons of F-106 interceptors, by mid-1976. This schedule could be accelerated to give a dwindling number of Soviet bombers a greater likelihood of mission accomplishment. Using the same logic of offensive effectiveness, a proportionately larger number of Soviet air-defense units would be retained in active service until the B-52s were mothballed or scrapped. Air defenses for the USSR include about 3000 aircraft and 10,000 launchers at 1600 sites. Such a disproportionate trade-off in correlated systems could be accompanied by a ban on development of follow-on manned interceptors—after phasing out the present generation of interceptors in the 1980s, the F-14, F-15, and Foxbat. Each side would retain an air-defense missile capability and the right to modernize its as appropriate. The Soviets can be expected to insist upon the right to deploy any air-defense missile capability commensurate to the Chinese bomber threat. Like bomber aircraft, reductions in air defenses would be based largely on acceptance of obsolescence and limitations of future systems developments. Bans, limitations, and deployments of air-defense systems are also readily verifiable by national means.

Over time the weight of both sides' strategic offensive capabilities are likely to be shifted to nuclear submarines. With agreed-upon numerical ceilings on launchers and submarines, antisubmarine warfare will receive greater importance, both in a damage-limiting capacity and as an ingredient in the overall force-reduction schema. The offensive submarine has inherent advantages over defensive submarines that complicate direct correlations. Even if surface and air ASW capabilities are added, SLBM submarines retain marked assets. Improvements in missile ranges, communications, reactor technology, and navigational aids extend defensive perimeters by factors greater than the increase in nautical miles that must be maintained under active surveillance. Because of improved missile ranges both great powers are equally exposed to SLBM attacks, with slight differences in on-station time that are likely to be corrected over time. Thus, the logic of mission accomplishment and assured destruction arising from mutual vulnerability is likely to govern the parameters of any accord.

There appears to be no feasible means for reaching a mutually acceptable limitation on ASW techniques. The US is believed to be at least five years ahead of the USSR in most aspects of ASW, and therefore has little incentive to accept limitations. And the Soviets would no doubt reject any plan that required physical inspection. Thus, both sides may explore a ceiling of hunter-killer submarines. Any curtailment could be verified by national means, and many naval authorities estimate that the hunter-killer is less a threat than the helicopter, providing some mutual incentives for limitations. But any reduction could not be drastic, because of the sizeable Soviet advantages in conventional submarines. In light of the new challenge posed by Soviet naval parity, it would be imprudent for the US to accept any reduction of its existing hunter-killer and broader ASW assets. Thus, it appears that the most that can be expected in limiting ASW capabilities is a quantitative ceiling on future hunter-killer submarine construction. Because of the similarities in construction between nuclear attack and nuclear hunter-killer submarines, however, such an accord would not be feasible unless it included a ban on construction of all nuclear submarines, exclusive of those permitted in SALT I, or was accepted with a degree of mutual confidence about the adversary's intentions.

If such accords could be reached in the above areas, their aggregate impact would not achieve the desired American goal of a durable strategic balance. Indeed, they would probably contribute to instability by increasing constraints on the US without countering Soviet numerical advantages in launchers and throw-weight. Since it is unrealistic to expect the USSR to reduce these advantages, the US has no option but to focus on the problem of quality improvement and warhead proliferation, the imbroglio of MIRV.

Qualitative Constraints

Phase one of SALT II opened on 21 November 1972 and recessed before Christmas. To the surprise of most observers, during this phase the Soviets accepted the US preference for qualitative limitations and agreed to include warhead proliferation on the apparent hope for US acceptance of FBSs. The US was in a difficult position because of the political implications the FBS issue had for its alliance. As late as 1 May 1973, Chancellor Brandt was told in Washington by the chief US negotiator at SALT II, U. Alexis Johnson, that despite Soviet insistence we would not negotiate on FBSs at that time—the US was apparently still asking for negotiations of the Soviet medium-range delivery vehicles as a trade-off. This issue was a major point in the Brandt visit and the US had reached an impasse on that item. On MIRVs, the US had asked for a ban on Soviet flight-testing of its expected MIRV system, as the most plausible check against warhead proliferation. The Soviets reportedly argued that the testing and possible deployment of MIRV warheads were compatible with both the letter and spirit of the SALT I provisions for modernization of existing systems. According to Warsaw Pact sources, a deadlock developed similar to the one in May 1971.[8]

The stalemate was overcome only during the June 1973 Summit Meeting in the United States, when the two powers agreed upon a seven-point declaration of principles to guide their negotiating teams in Geneva. The terms were:

1. The United States and the Soviet Union will continue active negotiations to work out a permanent agreement over the course of the next year, with the aim of signing it in 1974.
2. Neither nation is to seek a unilateral advantage.
3. Restrictions on strategic weapons will apply both to their numbers and to their qualitative improvement.
4. Limitations on strategic weapons must be subject to "adequate verification by national technical means."
5. Some modernization and replacement of strategic weapons will be permitted.
6. Both nations may reach separate measures on disarmament in addition to the hoped-for permanent agreement.
7. Both are to take necessary organizational and technical measures to prevent the accidental outbreak of nuclear war.[9]

Western analysts pointed to several noteworthy features of the Declaration. First, the Soviets committed themselves to the principle of qualitative limitations. But the US accepted the reservation that "some modernization and replacement" should be permitted, leaving the precise formula to the negotiators. At the time, this concession seemed to have removed the US objection to flight-testing the MIRV system, which took place in August. (The USSR would have tested the system anyway, but probably wanted to prevent clouding the negotiating atmosphere by first securing US approval of conditions under which flight-testing was to take place.)

It may have been more than coincidental that just before the Brezhnev visit, the House Appropriations Committee opened deliberations on the pending Air Force budget, which included a request of $23.1 million to keep the US MIRV option open. The US had made its initial flight test of its MIRV in 1968 and had authorized installation of three separate warheads on 550 ICBMs and up to fourteen warheads on sixteen missiles on twenty Poseidon submarines. At the time of the request, installation had been completed on 350 ICBMs and in the submarines. The Air Force wanted the additional funds to be able to maintain production facilities for the additional 450 ICBMs, if qualitative constraints could not be negotiated—total cost for the additional MIRVs would be $1.9 billion. (It was also announced that 11 Polaris submarines were to be converted to Poseidon missiles by 1975, adding about 1300 warheads to the SLBM force, which already had as many as 4500 warheads aboard.)[10] It is not clear whether this show of MIRV force influenced Brezhnev's decision to accept qualitative limitations or stimulated his interest in flight-testing the Soviet system at the earliest date.

The second major point in the Declaration was the US concession accepting the provision that verification of any qualitative limitations would be conducted by national surveillance. This proviso reinforces and extends the requirements for national means of inspection included in the first SALT accords. These provisions may be as important over time to the evolution of international law as the contribution to national security. Until several years ago the sanctity of international law protected the right of nations to prohibit the reconnoitering by a potential adversary of its military capabilities within the area of sovereign jurisdiction. In the SALT I accords, the great powers modified this principle by encouraging surveillance of strategic systems by any means other than physical inspection. The June 1973 Declaration added endorsement of national verification of qualitative improvements or limitations on the chief components in a great power's national defense. The implication of this mutually recognized right of inspection is likely to be one of the most significant developments in the entire SALT exercise.[11] The verification issue is central to the warhead proliferation problem. The Soviets had refused to negotiate on the subject throughout SALT I—because of the implied necessity of on-site inspections. There must have been several critical reasons for the Soviets to reverse themselves on such a key point.

Possible Breakthrough on MIRVs

First, Moscow may have agreed to negotiate on MIRVs in an effort to forestall the US decision to MIRV the remaining ICBMs and to convert Polaris to

Poseidon SLBMs. Warhead redundancy and survivability on that scale would permit the diversion of a portion of these systems to nonintercontinental missions. The MIRV-2 and follow on -3 are low yield (10-50 KTs) highly accurate warheads that can be launched against as many as fourteen separate small scale targets. With this accuracy and yield, they are well suited for use against theater-level interdiction targets. Indeed, a Poseidon MIRV-missile may be as effective in the interdiction role as the equivalent number of aircraft—except against targets of opportunity—because of its superior all-weather capability, delivering redundancy (several warheads per target), and greater range. The Poseidon can be reloaded at sea and remain relatively invulnerable. Finally, the opponent has no theater defense against the MIRV and must destroy the submerged submarine, while air bases and attacking aircraft are likely to sustain heavy losses. While on-station in the mid-Atlantic five or six widely dispersed Poseidon submarines would be virtually immune from a preemptive attack, reducing the opponent's incentive in launching a first strike in Europe.

An additional argument is that five or six Poseidon submarines could assume all of NATO's "Quick Reaction Alert" responsibilities for strike interdiction and counterforce targets throughout Eastern Europe and Western USSR from the mid-Atlantic. By transferring the Army and Air Force alert responsibilities to the Navy, substantial budgetary savings would be made—only six launching facilities rather than perhaps the present one hundred need be on alert. The SLBM would not replace the fighter-bomber entirely; the aircraft still has superior rapid-reaction capability and greater command and control discretion (it can be directed in-flight), and under favorable visibility conditions (only 15 percent of the time for six months of the year in Europe) it can be assigned targets of opportunity.

Thus, the Soviets may have concluded that warhead proliferation would introduce sufficient redundancies at the strategic level that a serious threat to the theater nuclear balance could soon emerge for which they had no effective countermeasures. Moreover, a shift of the interdiction strike mission to naval forces would deflate the FBS issue, in which the Soviets hoped to make substantial political and psychological gains against NATO. Such a force restructuring would result in budgetary savings that could perpetuate the life expectancy of land forces in Europe, and yet allow the US to lower its military profile there. It would also provide NATO for the first time a reasonable certainty that the US could counter the Soviet medium-range bombers and ballistic missiles (MRBM). At levels of violence in Europe below countercities strikes, MRBM sites should not be struck, but all other nuclear storage and maintenance sites in Western USSR and Eastern Europe could be with this restructuring. If the Pact should be denied a large portion of its medium-range delivered nuclear warheads, the MRBM force would be effectively confined to the countervalue role and could be deterred from striking theater targets by the existing Polaris force and British and French FBMSs. This would still leave the remaining

Poseidon submarines as a credible second-strike deterrent at the intercontinental level. Structuring forces along these lines should assuage West European anxieties about the Soviet countervalue nuclear threat, leaving the Pact with a deficit of nonusable missiles and a relatively less efficient theater nuclear posture, plus the handicap of a restored NATO confidence in US credibility.

A second possible Soviet consideration may have been the realization that there was a natural efficiency level for Soviet proliferation. If the negotiated ceiling on launchers was based on the Soviet estimation of the requirements for a counterforce capability, plus a residual countervalue force, the multiplication of US warheads has not increased the number of targets the Soviets need to destroy to insure damage limitation. Sixty-percent superiority in ICBMs is sufficient redundancy to guarantee launch reliability. Since there is a relatively static number of targets worth the expenditure of an ICBM, the multiplication of Soviet warheads does not increase the threat to the US in proportion to the proliferation. Thus, there would be little logic in a policy of "equal proliferation."

Third, if greater deterrence against the US is the motive behind the Soviets' side of the continuing strategic arms competition, this could be achieved better through alternative policies that would insure greater force survivability and defense against SLBMs. At the end of 1973 the USSR already had deployed 1527 ICBMs and was continuing development of the SS-16 (a replacement for the solid-fuel SS-13), the SS-17 (an improved SS-11) and the SS-18 (a follow-on for the SS-9). The last two have been tested with mutiple reentry systems of three MRVs and will probably be capable of carrying MIRVs. The SS-18 was first flight-tested in 1968 and is an obvious candidate for installation in the twenty-five large, but still unfilled, silos begun in 1970, thus bringing the total Soviet "heavy" ICBMs to the permitted 313. The SS-17 may be installed in the remaining sixty-six incomplete silos, bringing the total to the ceiling of 1618 authorized in the Interim Agreement. Flight-testing of the missiles is believed to be completed, and installation has probably been delayed pending a decision on or development of a MIRV capability (first flight-tested only in August 1973). In the SLBM category thirty-one Y-class nuclear submarines were operational in 1973, each with sixteen SSN-6 1750-mile-range missiles and three new D-class boats with sixteen SSN-8 4600-mile-range SLBMs. This range is superior to the 2880-mile Poseidon. Only these boats count against the permitted ceiling of sixty-two "modern" submarines, although thirty SLBMs in older nuclear submarines count against the total of 950 SLBMs. If the Soviets maximize their SLBM option, it will be probably 1977 before both ceilings are reached.[12] Concentration on D-class submarines, not MIRVs, would give the USSR a first-class SLBM capability with sufficient launchers that US ASW defenses would be significantly compounded. (While the US has more warheads, it has fewer boats to be destroyed.)

Finally, the USSR does not have the same incentive as the US to assign MIRV launchers to theater missions. All of its older nuclear and conventional

SLBM submarines are now or will be assigned to theater waters. Armed with the 450-mile-range SSN-3, these boats would be vulnerable to NATO ASW defenses. And accuracy and yield limitations would restrict their use to larger fixed targets, but they would still provide a valuable complement to the present 500 TU-16 Badger and 200 TU-22 Blinder medium-range bomber force, and the 600 MRBMs plus the 100 SS-11s deployed against theater targets. This appears to be ample coverage for the larger nuclear targets, although none of these systems have the efficiency or versatility of the Poseidon at the theater level.

Thus, it would appear that the USSR does not have the same incentive to proliferate warheads as the US. It will insist on perfecting an operational MIRV capability, both to insure parity in warhead technology and to have readily available the refined capabilities MIRVs afford. But it is unlikely to seek a warhead-to-warhead equivalency. This asymmetry in incentives and the desire to block further US proliferation are the most probable reasons for the Soviet agreement to discuss MIRVs in SALT II.

If this assessment is accurate and the Soviets are prepared to negotiate seriously on proliferation constraints, the question of verification must be re-examined. It is impossible at the present state of surveillance capabilities to determine a warhead's composition without physical inspection; yet it is unrealistic to expect either side to allow the other to have access to its ICBM and SLBM forces. To accept open inspections would be a major step toward general strategic disarmament; neither side is prepared presently for moves of such scale. What alternatives, then, are conceivable?[13]

MIRV Verification

The June 1973 Declaration stresses national means of verification. This represents a major gain for the Soviets, since there is no means of verifying a warhead's configuration except by physical inspection. Even periodic on-site inspections are invalid because configurations can be changed in a matter of hours. Thus, *any decision on warhead proliferation will be made on political grounds.* A purely cosmetic agreement might be reached that would have a "picket fence" effect of providing explicit loopholes and retaliatory measures for merely presumed violations. The structure of the picket fence would be grounded on good faith and intentions, and the calculated assumption that a natural ceiling exists beyond which proliferation becomes meaningless. The Soviets could agree to MIRV only the number of those ICBMs that are not already installed in silos and below the fixed figure of 1618. (It is noteworthy that in the spring of 1973 the Soviets began an unprecedented launching of SS-11 missiles from operational sites, leaving an increasing number of unfilled silos. Silos with MIRVed missiles are likely to require a special refurbishing to provide better launching stability for improved accuracy. Thus, the Soviets may free a number of SS-11 silos for replacement with MIRVed SS-17s.) By the end of 1974, the Soviets could have some 200 empty silos that could be filled by the latest MIRVed ICBMs.

It would still be impossible for the US to determine how many reentry vehicles were in each warhead. Following the US technology, as many as 10–15 vehicles could be contained in each SS9 and SS-18 warhead; possibly three could be fitted on the SS-11 and SS-17. There is no reason why the Soviets could not improve on the US technology and miniaturize their warheads even further. But accepting the present US levels of development, such an agreement would give the Soviets a theoretical proliferation level of 4695 vehicles for the "heavy" 313 ICBMs and possible 300 for the refitted SS-11s. This would be nearly triple the present number of US ICBM warheads, and could assuage the Soviets' penchant for superiority. Indeed, for economic reasons, they may seek a maximum of unfilled silos but refrain from installing missiles in every one (to MIRV the remaining 450 US ICBMs will cost an estimated nearly $2 billion; the Soviets would have to expect similar expenditures for follow-on vehicles).

Surveillance of proliferation for SLBMs, also, introduced a complex problem. At present it is impossible to monitor warhead reconfiguration on sea-based missiles. Should the Soviets choose to install MIRVs or even MRV warheads on their present or future SLBM submarines it could not be detected by the United States. But to date, none of the Soviet SLBMs have been flight-tested with multiple-reentry vehicles. With the present state of technology, the Soviets could not transfer a proliferation capability from the land to the sea dimension, and they would have to develop a separate multiple warhead system for their submarines. Flight-testing a multiple-reentry vehicle is verifiable by national means, and at SALT II the US could seek a ban on Soviet tests of such systems. This would be an effective curb on any proliferation of warheads in the SLBM category. If the Soviets refuse, this dimension of proliferation cannot be monitored and the US could reasonably charge that Moscow had violated item two of the Declaration, which provides that neither side will seek a unilateral advantage in strategic weapons.

Noncorrelation with FBSs

What trade-offs can be correlated to a ceiling on Soviet MIRVed ICBMs and a ban on MIRVing SLBMs? Certainly Moscow can be expected to insist upon no further proliferation of the planned programed US systems. This would include, for example, limits on the installation of the SRAM missiles on only the reduced B-52 force of twenty-one squadrons. The United States could live with such constraints without impairing national security. But Moscow is likely to insist also upon a complete withdrawal on all aircraft FBSs from Europe. The US cannot be expected to relegate its interdiction capability in Western Europe to its 250 Pershing missiles that are nearing obsolescence, or to place exclusive relevance on the seventy-mile-range Lance missile. On the other hand, the Soviets, with their experience in air mobility, are not likely to be satisfied with only the rearward redeployment of strike aircraft. The Soviets will probably hold out for the return of the F-4s to the United States. This would not only dismantle the SACEUR Strike Plan and possibly disarm NATO psychologically, but it would also deny the US a conventional air capability. True, a distinction can be made between nuclear and conventionally capable aircraft, but not without physical inspection. Finally, to reduce interdiction capabilities down to the range of Lance would curtail the responsibility for nuclear war from virtually all of Eastern Europe, as well as the USSR, and thereby risk providing an incentive for aggression. Thus, the disposition of US tactical aircraft and the correlation of trade-offs between opposing medium-range delivery vehicles are likely to be the thorniest problems of all at SALT II.[14] Any agreement will depend largely upon perceived intentions and political decisions. At the end of 1973, Nixon's "Year of Europe" appears to be stillborn. Unless there is a major resuscitation of Atlanticism in 1974, Washington could not accept the restructuring of NATO's nuclear posture explicit in the FBS issue without risking permanent damage to the Alliance. Without first gaining genuine allied endorsement and a broad consensus on workable alternatives, the basic utility of the alliance would be undermined by accepting the Soviet position.

The most plausible solution for the FBS question is an agreement to disagree, relegating it to SALT III when all European nuclear forces can be discussed. By that time obsolescence would figure prominently for all parties—the US, USSR, UK, and France. (The MFR talks would be a likely forum for discussion of the FBS issue, but the French boycott would limit the utility of such a transfer of venue. An expanded four-power Salt III appears to be the most preferable solution.) In the interim it is imperative to shore-up the US position by shifting responsibility for the decision to the Soviets. Either US tactical aircraft in Europe remain in place, to be discussed at some future date, or the US will convert eleven Polaris submarines to Poseidon SLBMs and underwrite the sale of Poseidon missiles for the four British FBMS. The latter would be the cheapest and militarily most efficient option for NATO and the Soviets would probably select the former choice. Such a bargaining tactic would slow down the growing crisis within the Atlantic Alliance and ultimately strengthen NATO by broadening discussions on European nuclear postures.

It should be stressed that the central difficulty at SALT II is in large part of American manufacture. The US-imposed nuclear freeze on NATO FBS capabilities technically arrogated the US assets in this category to the level of great-power discussions. But the vital interests at stake are more European than American. Because of different perceptions of threats and security requirements, there is almost as wide a gap between NATO and the US as between the two great powers on the FBS issue. For their own reasons, to date both NATO and the US have been reluctant to explore a consensus and the US has undertaken merely to inform rather than consult with its allies on FBSs. (The Europeans hope that their abstention will preserve the FBSs and the credibility of the US deterrent intact, and the Americans are anxious to accommodate Soviet terms for European détente.) Clearly it is now axiomatic that this issue be negotiated first in the West and then with the East. To reduce the West Europeans to only a consultative status on matters of vital importance to their security, and to expect them to accept risks to their security the Americans have refused to accept for US defense, will confirm fears that an Alliance crisis is imminent. On their side, it is time for the Europeans to examine urgently a common position that will contribute to and not impede the SALT II negotiations. The danger of further delay is that Soviets may be able to exploit the lack of unity in the West as Nixon's self-imposed deadline for agreement draws near.

The history of SALT I and the prospects for SALT II suggest that wide asymmetries in objectives still persists between the two sides. The Soviets have placed a much higher value on the political consequences of the SALT dialogues than the US, which has confined itself largely to the technical results. Moscow has measured SALT not only in terms of the extension of its influence and the contraction of US prestige, but also for the uncertainty it will inject in one form or another into virtually all important US international obligations. Moreover, the seriousness of the US misreading of Soviet intentions compromised the promotional value the "spirit" of SALT I might have had in soothing alliance politics, leaving the US in even further political deficit. Finally, the US must now devise its own political aims for the "advancement of détente" or accept Soviet objectives. It will be difficult to manipulate the CSCE and MFR as political leverage against Moscow, and it will be sometime before sufficient military disengagement is achieved to lower anxiety about political competition.

This analysis suggests there is now a possibility that the political initiative in international strategic discussions may slip to the USSR. The most effective way for the US to restore its political latitude is to first solve its own strategic problems, i.e. adopt a strategy that will insure the survivability and flexibility of sufficient forces to fight a counterforce battle and still be able to inflict greater countercity destruction than the USSR can after launching a preemptive strike. Only such a nuclear clout will induce Soviet agreement to actual disarmament. And only such a posture will allow the US to view further dialogues from a broader perspective, through which political gains can be made.

18

The Changing Nature of the International System and the Nixon Doctrine

For over a quarter of a century after World War II, the policies of both great and smaller powers were predicated on a single, common feature unique to that period—the bipolarity resulting from the Cold War. While there was seldom a mutuality of interest among members of both "camps" on all other issues, the shared sense of threat to physical security provided the cohesion that dominated individual demands in other sectors. The 1970s, on the other hand, are characterized as the evolution of asymmetrical multipolarity: a grouping of powers with varying national interests, capabilities, and objectives whose single point in common is continued participation in the international system. The change from bipolarity to multipolarity has dictated major shifts in policies of the larger members of the system and warrants a brief survey.

Character of the Cold War

The Cold War, as it is now understood, had several discernible characteristics that dictated the format if not the content of the adversary relationship. First, with the advent of nuclear power, the world was promptly polarized for the first time in Western history and America and Russia emerged as great powers. A great power was soon accepted as one which could not be forced to act against its will by any combination of lesser states. Indeed, it became apparent that even one great power with any combination of smaller states could not force the adversary to act contrary to its interests. And, for the first time, Europe was dependent on non-European powers for its protection and prosperity and even survival. Yet the viability of Europe became the chief competitive goal between the great powers. The force of polarization dislocated traditional political, economic, and cultural patterns and pulled Europeans toward alien ideologies and life styles. The result was political and ideological divisions that were the primary source of great-power tensions.

In a bipolar world in which either power could destroy the opponent without imposing its will or forcing the adversary to adopt its ideology, each still viewed the other as a source of imminent danger. The ideologies of both great powers were and remain fundamentally incompatible and were mutually regarded as a permanent challenge to each side's well-being. With a threat of this scope, each opponent sought to organize its natural advantages to support its respective position. In 1948 the USSR attempted to mobilize the world's revolutionary forces into a cohesive, disciplined, effective anti-imperialist instrument, and only belatedly in 1955 resorted to collective security. The US, on the other hand, first attempted to organize the Free World into a collective security containment barrier and then into an international anti-Communist Bund.

The organization of each respective camp had a rationale and momentum of its own. Each saw the other's operations as attempts to construct a world-wide front or conspiracy against its legitimate political interests, and each strove for the perfection of its respective system. The conspiracy thesis also forced each opponent to link all international crises into the adversary's Grand Design or the general confrontation between communism and imperialism. This crisis linkage had a cyclical nature of its own, escalating tensions with each localized confrontation or outbreak of hostilities.

Another characteristic was the lack of permanence in Cold War tensions. Many developments contributed to the relaxation in Cold War frictions, such as the Sino-Soviet dispute, the Cuban missile crisis, polycentrism, strategic parity, Vietnam, the success of Ostpolitik, and the rise of Japan. All these factors contributed to multipolarity and the erosion of the bipolar structure. They also altered the great powers' perceptions of each other's interests and intentions, resulting in the gradual abandonment of the crisis linkage theory and the conspiracy notion. It finally became apparent, for example, that the entire Communist world was not fully supporting Hanoi, and that the domino theory was largely irrelevant to the realities of effective resistance and the long-term interests of Southeast Asia. These new understandings led to reverse tendencies, the localization rather than internationalization of regional crises. The eclipse of the crisis linkage theory led to a sharper awareness of the segregation of great-power interests into political, strategic, or purely ideological components. Moreover, localization of threats and tensions resulted in a diminution of the emphasis on ideological competition between both powers. This declining primacy of ideology was accelerated by other developments such as the general modernization phenomena, domestic pressures, alliance turmoil, and the growing preference of Third World countries for local brands of nationalism rather than alien philosophies of any stripe. Great-power relations were gradually viewed as a function of competition for political influence, strategic advantage, and physical security, and not as a requirement to guarantee the world against the opponent's values and for one's own. Localization thus tended to minimize the dangers of great power conflict, render competition more manageable, and strengthen regional stability by increasing the prospects of local solutions for local disputes.

A final characteristic centers on the US reaction to the de-escalation of the Cold War and the general questioning of its origins. Was the USSR fundamentally hostile to the West and the US? Assuming the inevitability of Marxist scientific predictions, would a hostile Soviet posture accelerate or retard the forecasted collapse of capitalism and democracy? Assuming that Moscow gained substantially from its wartime cooperation with the West, why did it adopt a more assertive policy, when and for what purposes? Answers to these questions reflect the most delicate and intricate progressions of state interactions yet experienced in the twentieth century. While the ideological questions will remain a subject of personal conviction, political origins of the Cold War can be traced to the attempts at peace in the post-World War II period. The wartime diplomacy reflected the weight of Soviet contribution to the war effort. Moscow demanded and gained, as in 1814 after Napoleon's defeat, recognition of its stature as a great power and the victor over the invader, and the right that its national interests be considered prominently in the structure of the future peace. Consequently, Moscow secured agreement in principle to all its major aims *before* the war ended! It was the implementation of these aims that led to tensions, for the implementation exposed the realities of conflicting national values and perceptions that were only exacerbated by Soviet claims to military prowess which it felt warranted greater global respect. Herein lay the origins of the Cold War.

In sum, the rise and fall of the Cold War was a unique phenomenon in Western political history because of its bipolar structure, the scale of the military imbalance (both nuclear and conventional), the comparative advantages of each adversary that contributed to an exaggerated sense of threat to the opponent's vital interests, and the use of respective advantages assertively that kept suspicions high. The dilution of the bipolar structure, the collapse of the crisis linkage syndrome, and finally the uncertainties about the nature of local crises and adversary intentions, coupled with the consequences of military confrontation, placed upper limits on tensions and a high premium on developing the instruments of crisis management.

Nature of Change in the International System

Are the unique features of the quarter-century-long Cold War tensions offset by the changing nature of adversary relations? Are these changes sufficiently durable to compensate for persisting uncertainties about political intentions? (See chapter 19.) Are there changes outside the context of the adversary relationship that impose enough constraints to bolster confidence and to warrant accepting risks on issues of low predictability? Are there sufficient incentives in the rapidly changing nature of interstate behavior, again outside the framework of great-power relations, to moderate the confrontation? Answers to the latter questions may lead to insights into the others.

Several general observations about the nature of contemporary global changes that have an impact on political behavior are in order. Marshall Shulman has identified several features of change in international politics characteristic of the contemporary international scene:

1. the accelerating pace of technological innovation, notably the rapid intro-duction of qualitative and quantitative changes in strategic weapons systems and the new industrial technology;
2. changes in the structure of the world power system, namely the rise of nationalism and the diffusion of power;
3. the continuing rise of the North-South problem as a source of international tensions, food-population balance, and resource management which cut across classical Soviet-American competition; and
4. the intensification of social and political changes within the industrialized countries, domestic problems resulting from the compromise of traditional values and institutions because of the changing industrial-urban require-ments.[1]

Many of these changes were the result of deliberate policies of one or the other great power; others were the by-products of modernization. The aggregate impact of these changes has eroded many factors viewed after World War II as a potential foundation for a new world order and durable stability. The eclipse of these former influences has introduced new characteristics of contemporary world politics, such as the general decline in the authority of international organizations and the resulting lack of adequate international grievance-solving machinery; the reevaluation by both great powers of issues and interests that are permissive or vital; the gradual constriction of traditional alliances, forcing a reconstitution of collective security without adequate background or exper-ience; the emergence of new theaters of confrontation, such as the Mediterranean, in which great-power rivalry can be expected but without the guidance of tradi-tional interests or precedents; and an increasing great-power concern with domestic problems at the expense of broader international goals. These new properties, however, do not enjoy the sanctity of the common expectations espoused after World War II. The single universal hope was that general war can be averted and that lesser mutual interests will slowly surface.

Global changes have become increasingly important factors in the calculus of national security, influence competition, and détente management. It is generally assumed that the function of reducing international tensions is at least partially dependent upon the degree of international stability and national security that prevails. International stability is hard to prescribe and its ingre-dients illusive. A single factor may be regarded as both a stabilizing component and a destabilizing variable in the same set of circumstances, e.g., the advent of strategic defense (ABM). Furthermore, persisting uncertainties about the aggressiveness of human behavior, the unpredictability of national character, and competitiveness of national political ambitions add question marks to many factors that have been assessed as stabilizing influences. Moreover, those factors that are clearly destabilizing do not directly counterbalance stabilizing phenomena; they seldom measurably outweigh each other. Thus, the term *stability* in international developments must be assessed in a highly dynamic and fluid situation. Stability may be regarded simplistically as the impact of predictable changes on international developments, and instability as the effect of unforeseen, or unalterable changes.

Systemic Stability

The predictability and the distinction between desirable and undesirable changes, plus the prospects for initiating actions that can accelerate the wanted and inhibit the unwanted and thereby preserve stability, is in part a function of the prevailing type of international system. Yet scholars have been unable to agree about which type of system is inherently the most stable and which unstable, even when they are believed to be in equilibrium. Kenneth Waltz, for example, argues that the bipolar model is the most stable, because with only a single opponent adversary actions are relatively more predictable than in other systems. Second, the great powers are less concerned about shifts in allegiance among smaller powers, because in the final analysis no combination of lesser states can force a great power to act contrary to its wishes. Third, both great powers have a mutual fear of nuclear war and act individually or jointly to control small-power conflicts or to impose a ceiling on escalation. Great-power second-strike capabilities have a dampening effect on any confrontation and make it easier to establish a mutually agreed-upon ceiling for local conflicts. Fourth, the great power confrontation is global in scale and rigid in nature, i.e., the respective interests of the great powers are well defined, allowing avoidance of challenges to vital interests. In other words, a strong, compact system in which interests and commitments are known and not subject to sudden or radical changes can absorb destabilizing effects better than a large, loose system which is susceptible to proliferation of interests and demands. Finally, Waltz argues that both great powers are suspicious of each other and sensitive about the responsibility of their respective actions. This attitude insures rational action and a continuing commitment to the preservation of the system. Therefore, great powers cannot be expected to act in a manner that would endanger the system in which they have a perceived mutual investment.[2]

Karl Deutsch and David Singer, on the other hand, argue that a bipolar structure is susceptible to instability because of the narrowness of its base. As the number of essential actors increases or level of organization expands in any system the stability of the structure is improved. They reason that an

increase in the number of actors multiplies the number of interactions between
all members and reduces the attention that any single actor can devote to any
other individual member. Increased number of potential partners also enhances
the constraints against unacceptable behavior. Broadening of interactions reduces
the prospects of misperceptions and misunderstandings that tend to destabilize
a system based on only two actors. Finally, the volume of interactions minimizes
the possibility of unobserved collusion by two or more members of the system,
and thereby reduces the prospects of destabilizing effects. The schema of Deutsch
and Singer relates only to specific situations and intentionally eliminates historical precedents and traditional factors, i.e., the impact of World War II and the
relevance of geography. Largely a behavioral approach to model-building, it is
an attempt to construct a system that can operate in the vacuum of contemporary interactions in which the content of communications determine perceptions and actions.[3]

Morton Kaplan devised a more comprehensive model based on general
systems theory. He presents six models for comparing behavior: balance of
power, loose bipolar, tight bipolar, universal, hierarchal, and unit veto.[4] He
provides values or parameters for each model that are likely to remain constant.
Changes in the overall system will dictate the employment of different models
for analysis, not necessarily the modification of the preferred model.

The balance-of-power system in its ideal form allows for any combination
of actors to organize into alliances, as long as no alliance gains a preponderance
in capabilities. The system tends to be maintained by the fact that any nation
seeking preponderance is compelled to protect its own interests by preventing
any other nation from achieving the same objective. Kaplan outlines six rules
of behavior for the balance of power system:

1. Actors increase their capabilities, but negotiate with each other rather than
   fight.
2. Actors fight rather than pass up the opportunity to increase their capabilities.
3. Actors stop fighting rather than eliminate another essential actor.
4. Actors oppose any coalition or single actor who threatens to assume preponderance within the system.
5. Actors seek to constrain those actors who subscribe to supranational organizational principles.
6. Actors permit defeated or constrained essential actors to reenter the system
   as rehabilitated partners, or bring in a previously nonessential player.

Kaplan's second model, loose bipolar, includes a wide range of actors, both
essential and nonessential, and subscribes to rules that generally allow for expansion of capabilities, a higher frequency and intensity of wars, and joint
efforts to constrain the influence of universal actors. The tight bipolar model

reduces the number and type of actors and resembles the characteristics of Waltz's bipolar system. In Kaplan's fourth model, the universal-international system, all actors strive to gain access to the same facilities and expand the productive base of the international system to accommodate these desires. When conflicts of interest arise, peaceful means are employed for their resolution in accordance with the rules of the international system. The hierarchial model is characterized by a transnational quality, in which individuals are organized into interest groups rather than independent nation-states. The system can be either directive or nondirective, and will have aspirational mechanisms similar to those of the universal model. The final model, the unit veto, negates all universal actors and prescribes military parity to all essential actors. Rivalries are intense and interests are in seeming constant conflict. Hostilities are prevented only by the fear of mutual destruction. Of the six models, the loose bipolarity is potentially the most unstable.

Richard N. Rosecrance has devised another approach to the paradox of equilibrium, competition and instability in a model of bimultipolarity. This is a two-level system in which the great powers reserve for themselves exclusive domains on common interests unrelated to the national interests of other states. The second level, or multipolar system, would expand establishment of common interests. This dualism has the advantages and disadvantages of both the bipolar and multipolar systems. It would provide greater predictability than the chaotic conditions of a truly multipolar system, but less predictability than a mature bipolar environment. Yet it probably provides a greater degree of steering or management than at either individual level. Obviously the success of this model depends on the number of actors incorporated in the multiple level and the intensity and breadth of their common interests, and the degree of interchange between the two levels: the extent to which the great powers could act as regulators of conflict in external areas and the lesser powers can act as mediators or buffers in great-power rivalries.[5]

One of the most enterprising models for stability has been developed by Oran Young. He rejects the numerical emphasis of polarity and combines structural relations of subsystems and functional issues. There is a growing interpenetration of global-wide issues and at the same time the emergence of widely divergent attention on regional or subsystem problems. He develops a "discontinuities model" which encompasses both the global and regional influences in patterns discernible for their congruities and discontinuity. While the congruities at all levels of interaction are important, it is the discontinuities that are the sources of conflict and instability. Therefore, a model for international stability should focus on the discontinuities, the complexities of interpenetration among subsystems, the trade-offs and influence competition across subsystems, the incompability of individual members to systemwide interests, and the relationship of various subsystems and global patterns of political development.[6]

Nixonian Notions of System

The above oversimplified outlines of several models and descriptions of the international system illustrate the complexity of investigating the nature of international relations, the relativity of change, and the value of stability. While these models are designed mainly as methodological tools for research into the "stuff of international politics," they are relevant for a discussion the Nixon Doctrine and the détente process it is intended to foster. Kissinger's early pronouncements resembled the Rosecrance bimultipolarity schema, but this was apparently to be an interim development. A consistent theme in the President's foreign policy reports to Congress is the notion that a safer and better world would emerge if "we have a strong, healthy United States, Europe, Soviet Union, China, and Japan, each balancing the other, not playing one against the other, *an even balance.*" An even balance would introduce the generation of peace he envisions.

Inherent in a balance-of-power system must be sufficient flexibility and potential coercion for any possible disrupter of the status quo to be deterred by the combined authority or force of the other powers. But for this stability to endure, it is imperative first that a high degree of shared interests in the status quo or in mutually agreed-upon changes exists among the contending powers, and second that they can and do exercise sufficient control to correct infractions. Finally, the success of earlier European balances has been the shared stake in legitimacy and ideological precepts. The five members of the nineteenth-century Concert of Europe held joint views about the preservation of traditionalism and orthodoxy, and frequently acted together or agreed to abstain in countering challenges to conservative order. The Metternichian concept of concert is inapplicable where not common basis for legitimacy exists; indeed, the two great powers still pursue differing visions of the preferred world order.

It is quite clear from the above discussion that an "even balance" among the five does not now exist, and is not likely to in the foreseeable future. The US has the greatest stake in the present status quo and the USSR probably the least. Yet only these two have sufficient authority to act coercively against the others. And the US has the least incentive to act punitively against any of the other four potential disrupters. Thus, there is little shared interest in the status quo and little positive contribution that can be made for its preservation. (If the status quo persists it will be more because of mutual lack of interest in its general health.)

This imbalance is due to the uneven development of the five powers. China's global stature is more potential than real; it is likely to remain a military dwarf. Japan lacks political purpose and has even more modest strategic aspirations. Europe remains disunited and disoriented. It is not likely to acquire singularity of purpose or suitable military clout in the near future.

Further, there is an ideological compatibility only among three of the five—the US, Europe, and Japan—which is reinforced by shared interests in perpetuating their industrial supremacy. Until a new public consensus emerges supporting foreign policy, the US will be constrained in the employment of policy options, especially the commitment of military forces.

Probably the most serious criticism of America's role in the proposed balance of power is its lack of public appeal. The era of "bureaucratic politics" and "linkage" between domestic and foreign policy has fundamentally altered the former consensus enjoyed during periods of messianic democracy and anticommunism. Domestic divisions over Vietnam have ended all that. Washington must now be content with merely the external projection of national moods and anxieties. It seems highly dubious that the White House can soon regain the fervent public support that existed for splendid isolationism and later globalism. Clearly a strong element of blind patriotism will be necessary if the US is to act as a true "balancer," shifting its alignments on nebulous issues to protect abstract formulations.

The pentagonal system has several other conceptual shortcomings. In stressing equidistance, it is essential to prohibit closer relations between individual members. The concept of interdependence, upon which American policy rested firmly during the Cold War, must be sacrificed for détente. The Europeanization of Europe will follow as surely as Vietnamization. The Nixon shocks seem to confirm these fears. Demands for equidistance are regarded by many allies as unwarranted scuttling of common principles for which they have taken higher national risks than the Americans because of the greater exposure to Soviet pressure. Moreover, allies concerned with susceptibility to Communist influences remain hypersensitive to signals of American isolationistic tendencies.[7] The shocks generated for the sake of consolidating equidistance have conveyed the impression of a freewheeling, unpredictable government more interested in short-term gains than in contributing to the process of a durable détente. Finally, the concept of lengthening ties with allies in order to shorten them with adversaries is likely to be totally unconvincing to the Soviets and Chinese; a gambit (like Roosevelt's warming up to Stalin at Yalta to Churchill's embarrassment) that could be exploited for whatever tactical advantages arise. Our social system challenges them because of its decadence. Our attempts to gain general recognition of world order based on political symmetry must be regarded in Moscow as confirmation of our desperation. Whatever view we maintain of distance, the Soviets and Chinese will retain a bifocal perspective.

A further problem is that Nixon's description of the pentagonal model strongly suggests a five-legged stool, the stability of which depends upon the symmetrical strength of all legs. Where asymmetries exist the advantaged will contribute to the disadvantaged in order to strengthen stability. This reduces the dynamics of state interactions to mutually agreed-upon cooperative undertakings and precludes influence competition, economic rivalry, and weapons progressions as destabilizing factors. This is far too restrictive. Whereas the equidistance configuration portrays the image of a 1950 US pentagonal army division capable of fighting an omnidirectional threat, the five-legged stool excludes the "stuff of politics" as undesirable. The system must be able to accommodate both the cooperative and competitive aspects of a highly dynamic world.

Many Americans now recognize that our past cannot be our future; values and traditions that were beneficial for earlier generations are no longer universally applicable. Something else is now required. Some agree with Robert Osgood, that to revert to an old order associated with military balances and legal structures in a period without consensus is a permanent invitation to domestic dissent—between those who find such an order too military and those who do not find it military enough, and between those who will deem it too demanding altogether and those who will find it too timid or too selfish in its demands.[8] Stanley Hoffman has elaborated further the pitfalls for Nixon's proposed strategy:

> At a moment when policy-making is more centralized, and in many ways more remote than ever, there is a clamor, born of the Vietnam tragedy, for a "popular" foreign policy, openly arrived at. But some of those who demand one really wish for no foreign policy at all, others expect from it feats of world-good-doing idealism that nothing in the make-up of middle America today allows one to anticipate; others have forgotten that in the absence of a strong consensus, or of the kind of decisive executive leadership which is precisely the opposite of what they wish, the people, the informed public and Congress, are likely to exhibit little more than perplexity. In such a mood, what is more likely to break through the crust of confusion is the kind of protectionism or will to retrenchment that is least likely to help either the new strategy, or, indeed, world order.[9]

A grave danger therefore exists in finding a substitute for the previous consensus. Anticommunism appealed to the entire spectrum of American impatience: realism, evangelism, pacifism, activism, idealism, and indifference. In a period of battle fatigue with the rest of the world, a strong desire has emerged to leave it alone in order to be left alone. These tendencies are antithetical to the cold realism required for a strategy of "flexible alignments."

But probably the most serious shortcoming of the President's conception of a reversed interdependence strategy is that it is not shared by other states. The above discussions provide abundant evidence that the other four entities are busy seeking their own roles and formulae for world order. They also reveal the disappointment we experience when we find out that an opponent has not played by our rules. The most profound error of the proposed strategy, then, is the seeming compulsion to educate others about the virtues of our perception of a new world order and the rules for participating in the new game of nations, regardless of the others' perceptions and strategies, or the weaknesses of the system.

The Soviets in particular do not share our views about policy or the world order. As Kissinger observed many years ago, "To our leaders, policy is a series of discreet problems; to the Soviets it is an aspect of a continuing political process. As a result the contest between us and the Soviet system has had many of the attributes of any contest between a professional and an amateur."[10] The persistent relevance of this parallelism today was underscored by an authoritative Soviet observer:

> Recently the bourgeois press has been making a great hue and cry about the invented question of the direction of change in the contemporary world, whether it be bi-polar (US-USSR), triangular (US-USSR-China), or multipolar. . . . It has become fashionable at present to talk about a pentagonal world . . . This futile approach leads to an obvious misrepresentation of the real picture of the world with its two social poles—socialism and capitalism. The essence of the "bipolar" or "multi-polar" conceptions is that they derive the development of international relations not from the class basis of the participating countries, but from narrow nationalist interests . . . Both "bi-polar" and "multi-polar" conceptions are directed against the foreign policy line of the Soviet Union and the other socialist countries. . . . The principle of peaceful coexistence is first and foremost concerned with the creation of favorable international conditions for the building of socialism and communism, with the strengthening of international unity and cohesion of the socialist commonwealth, with aid to developing countries, with support for all contemporary progressive movements, with the assertion of those principles of international relations which would exclude war as an instrument for solving conflict and which would guarantee non-interference in the internal affairs of other countries, with the development of trade and other economic relations (with other countries) on the basis of mutual interests and with a firm rebuttal of the aggressive forces of imperialism.[11]

This is a harsh reminder that the Soviet model for a new world order and the means for its achievement have not changed substantially since 1956.

While the Soviets retain a totally incompatible perspective of the international system, this does not preclude practical cooperation on a controllable scale.

> There has never been a political doctrine or a government with a keener sense of the realities of power relations than the Soviet. The Soviet system is and always has been distinguished by extreme pragmatism. . . . This being the case, it is groundless to expect that the

Soviet regime will become even more pragmatic. If the Soviet government has agreed to a partial detente with the United States—indeed,
has insisted on it—the reason must be sought not in a growing awareness among its leaders that humanity shares a common destiny, but in
factors having to do with international power relationships [in which
they include economic, social, psychological and political factors].[12]

The incongruities between the great powers' respective models and their
willingness to cooperate on selected issues created confusion among friends
about America's objectives. Was the US making the fatal error of formulating
strategy without calculating the opponent's perceptions and aims? Was the
Nixon Doctrine the prescient identification of the trend toward asymmetrical
multipolarity and the skillful avoidance of domestic retrenchment? Was it
contributing evidence to the 1951 Klingberg Theory of alternating cyclical
developments of US diplomatic history (phases of introversion lasting about
twenty-five years and phases of extroversion lasting about twenty-seven)? Was
the change in American policy prompted in part by the passivity and growing
trends toward isolationism among its main allies; was America's brand of Gaullist
unilateralism of European manufacture?[13] Had commercial and monetary issues
overtaken security and political matters in Atlantic affairs, and was the US
government able and willing to head off a protectionist war with its chief trading
partners and participate conscientiously in resolving international currency problems? Was the US prepared to assume responsibility for precipitating a moral
cirsis with its main allies over the discarding of long-standing, mutually espoused
principles? Finally, what was to be the role of the smaller developed countries
like Australia and the developing nations in the pentagonal system? (Pledges of
continuing aid and friendship were inadequate definitions of future relationships.)

Alternative Models

A more refined prescription for US policy seems preferable; one that would
accommodate both existing realities and the natural systemic quest for order.
To offset the seeming weaknesses of the Kissinger/Nixon world order, a gleaning
from the above-mentioned theorists may provide a more complex systemic structure that could more facilely adjust to functional incongruities. The US is faced
with one tripolar system consisting of itself and its adversaries, China and the
USSR. A second tripolar system is composed of its main allies, Western Europe
and Japan. A third level of organization consists of the regional powers and
developing nations. Thus, three separate, but interrelated, levels of organization
are necessary to accommodate the variety of functions inherent in any nation's
foreign policy.

Over the past several years the diplomatic game has been played increasingly by most states on a horizontal plane rather than a vertical one. Most states of whatever size are concerned first with immediate rivals rather than with greater or lesser states. Common interests can be established below and above, but the chief focus is lateral. A strategy that emphasizes this tendency concentrates attention singularly on priorities by fractioning out secondary interests. By focusing the plane of attention, rivals can be less disturbed about minor shifts and losses. From the American viewpoint such a horizontal leveling of interests on separate planes of engagement might be more receptive to the public and could encourage the degree of activism and identification necessary to counter the pendular swing to protectionism and indifference Hoffman anticipates.

Zbigniew Brzezinski has outlined a new relationship that stresses horizontal activism but negates the grand shifts of a true balance of power.[14] Using the same five political entities, he points out that America-China-Russia form a largely competitive triangle and that America-Europe-Japan form a cooperative triangle. Given the present and foreseeable developments, these competitive and cooperative relationships are likely to dominate the multiple-power game.

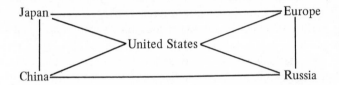

While both competitive and cooperative triangles will remain primary interests for the US, one will be a secondary concern for all other powers. The US has interests in Soviet-Japan, Japanese-Chinese relations, and in Soviet-European affairs. The other four actors also have primary and secondary interests. But the US enjoys the widest freedom of action. It is presently engaged in two major and minor triangular maneuvers, while all the others have only one major and one minor area.

This schematic arrangement stresses several realities of the contemporary relationship. It is not a equitable balance. It stresses the existing imbalance, with the US enjoying a greater variation of interests than any of the others. The central location of the US allows maneuver in a variety of directions. The figure is somewhat artificial and skews slightly Soviet interests in Japan. This slight distortion emphasizes a central point that the US must pursue an activist policy to preserve its present range of interests and maneuverability over the others. The level of activism required raises the question of national priorities.

Should cooperation across the Atlantic and Pacific be made more cooperative, or competition with the Socialists less intensive? Nixon's emphasis on Peking and Moscow summitry has given the impression that he favors the latter;

an impression that has damaged relations with the cooperative nations. This in turn has prompted both Moscow and Peking to play their secondary triangular games more actively. Clearly reconciliation with China and the Soviet Union were necessary preconditions for the development of this favorable multiple triangular arrangement. But there is a clear and present danger that the US may become obsessed with the competitive relations and allow Pacific and Atlantic relations to drift. A natural ceiling has been imposed by both Moscow and Peking on the level to which reconciliation can be raised, beyond which point competition will be intensified. This inevitable level must be recognized, not ignored. No degree of US good will is going to convert the competitive triangle into a cooperative one on the scale now experienced with Japan and Europe, and it is foolish to expect that it will.

The highest US priority, therefore, should be placed on intensifying the natural proclivity of the industrialized nations, in strengthening the sense of common interests, and in reinforcing these bonds with active institutions. Shared political values and common economic prowess should be converted into a stable, viable community of developed nations. A binding community would not only benefit the developed nations but would become a stimulant and reservoir of resources for developing nations. This should be regarded as the absolute minimum of engagement for the American foreign policy. If Japan and Europe become the victims of benign neglect under the guise of limited involvement, the momentum of modernization is likely to convert the existing cooperative triangle into a protectionist, competitive relationship that could reach a level of stand-offishness of the present American-Soviet-Chinese relations. Thus, in the wake of the Nixon Doctrine a paradox has developed whereby the international climate has been distorted from its former prevailing trends. Those countries that have had the highest stakes in cooperating with the US are becoming increasingly reluctant to do so, and those with the least incentive are the most anxious. Rejuvenation of the priority tripolar system is the most problematic because of this paradox, and several recommendations for intensifying US engagement with its traditional allies should be discussed.

Relationships on the Priority Tripolar Plane

There is no reason why Europeanism, Atlanticism, and ties with Japan cannot be strengthened simultaneously, for the problems of one are shared by the others. It should be emphasized that whereas recent differences between the US and its allies have been mainly over economic and monetary problems, effective security and defense policy remain the backbone of the association without which the luxury of disputes on currency questions would be subverted. Further, at this juncture it is essential to stress the cooperation-inspiring aspects of mutual defense rather than the competitive nature of economic rivalries. The US can and should make a bolder contribution to both European and Japanese defenses. Implementation of a Maximum Defense strategy in both regions could be conducted parallel to MFR talks. Provisions could be made for joint production of support equipment for tactical nuclear weapons and for the sale of Poseidon submarines to our allies. (The UK now spends only 4 percent of its defense budget for the operation of its nuclear forces, but France spends 25 percent because it has had to develop an indigenous capability. Yet Britain is now employing a missile system that is going out of service, and must soon find a replacement.) Should Japan ever feel compelled to increase its interest in nuclear weapons the supply of US ballistic and attack nuclear submarines would be ideal for its deterrent and defensive purposes; the US would retain custody of the warheads. Finally, conventional military commitments should be placed on a five-year contractual basis. Force strengths and their offset costs would remain constant factors in national planning for all three partners, with changes subject to mutual agreement. These proposals would both increase American commitments to regional security requirements and also enhance the responsibility of the other partners in local defense. They would reduce reliance on the American strategic umbrella by developing a capability and confidence to perform militarily with greater efficiency. From this posture of stability and credibility, the three partners could negotiate with greater assurance on the various aspects of military détente.

A greater compatibility and standardization in defense procurement would be mutually beneficial to all partners. In the past, national preferences have consistently undermined attempts to rationalize redundancies in weapons procurement. The US has clung tenaciously to its national preference because of economies in prices and troop offset costs from arms sales. Europeans have developed national industries, even when uneconomical, as a stimulant to general economic growth and national recovery. The transition to long-term contractual agreements on troop stationing costs, payable in direct subsidy, could be encouraged if smaller states had greater access to the American market (the German Leopard tank is widely regarded as superior to the American M-6OE, and the British Harrier VTOL aircraft is already operational in the US Marine Corps). Economic imperatives are already forcing greater interest in joint production. The onerous burden-sharing problem that has plagued Atlantic relations could be the least difficult issue if placed on a viable monetary basis. The Japanese-American model is a valid precedent; rental for bases and purchase of arms are strictly financial transactions rather than swaps and trades.

Military institutions should be strengthened, not weakened, during military détente negotiations. The terms of reference for the existing ten-member Eurogroup within NATO should be expanded beyond its present consultative function. Specific responsibilities should be assigned or assumed by the Europeans.[15] For example, the Eurogroup could assume complete responsibility for local infrastructure activities and funding, development of maintenance and logistical interoperability, standardization of reserve training, and rationalization of the myriad supply and logistics networks. Greater European cooperation would improve their relative weight against the US in defense economy matters and would enhance their reputation as a worthy confidant of a superpower. There is ample machinery available for planning and consultation; it remains to be more adequately used. US reservations about NATO have been the chief ob-stacles to date to greater coordination of views and policies. The inability of Western partners to establish a joint purpose or tactics for troop reductions is an illustration of the inadequate utilization of existing facilities for the common benefit.

One of the most urgent tasks of the tripolar group of industrial nations would be to establish a common policy on environmental control and pollution. Technical problems have already been largely addressed. The main obstacles are political agreement on priorities, enforcement of penalties and sanctions, and burden-sharing for remedial measures. (The US Federal budget for pollution control increased from $768 million in fiscal year 1969 to $3 billion in fiscal year 1972, indicating the scope of the global problem in budgeting pollution control.) Major questions must be tackled. For example, what can be done when pollution created in one nation affects the environment of another? What are the trade and investment implications of one nation's antipollution policies as op-posed to another's? What recourse is there when a nation requires its industries to bear the costs of abating industrial pollution—which might translate into higher product prices and results in serious trade disadvantages with countries that do not adopt this policy? From an agreed-upon position, the partners could then seek endorsement from the developing nations. Indeed, many of the more am-bitious proposals submitted to the 1972 Stockholm Conference on Environment could then be addressed.

Despite the emphasis on defense matters, reforms in economic relations are imperative. The industrial nations must undertake a bold reform of the world monetary system. These nations still cling to three irreconcilable proper-ties of the present system, shifting emphasis from one crisis to the next. These contradictory properties are: independent national monetary policies; free capital movements; and a dollar convertible into reserve assets at a fixed rate of exchange. The contending industrial nations are not likely to jettison any one of the three principles, but will probably attempt to salvage desirable aspects of each. A viable solution might include greater coordination of national mone-tary policies, restrictions on the free movement of short-term funds, and greater freedom for the US to fix dollar-exchange rates, possibly including a qualifica-tion of the unconditional convertibility of the dollar. (This would be an interim solution until Europe converts to a common currency at the end of the decade, which will basically alter the existing system.) This also suggests that the dollar will continue to decline in international importance. During the 1960s the dollar's importance rose while the economic role of the United States in the world declined. Now the dollar is following US economic performance, and it is likely to continue to do so. One of the conditions for full US participation in the tripolar group of industrial states must be an acknowledgment that its currency and fiscal policies will have a more measured impact on world developments; an acknowledgment that would register maturity, not resignation or indignation.

Finally, the failure of adequate coordination on the military level highlights the lack of machinery for consultation at the political level. The need for political coordination among the three partners is intensified by their geographic separation and regional preferences. Surely there would be advantages for coordination between Japan and Germany on their mutual technological and commercial interests in the USSR and China. NATO remains too constrained and security conscious for free political discussions that must include Japan. A new institution should be created with a clean slate and might be called the Commonwealth of Industrial Nations. The organization should have a substantial secretariat appointed on a geographic basis, an executive board bound by majority rule, and a budget derived from nominal taxes on commerical transactions among members. Separate semiannual meetings of defense, economics or commerical, foreign, and scientific or environment ministers should be held. Finally, a major deficiency in NATO must be corrected—annual summit conferences of heads-of-states must be held for the purpose of conducting serious business. NATO has held only one, in 1958, after Sputnik. The Warsaw Pact convenes such conferences on roughly a semiannual basis. Chancellor Brandt has voiced strong support for regular Western summit conferences, but so far has been unable to overcome French objections and US indifference. Besides providing the basic service of policy coordination at the ministerial and working levels, such an institutional approach would afford a symbolic linkage and identification between the three partners that is presently lacking. There must be a commonwealth attitude among the three that is reflected in the willingness of the heads of state to discuss all mutual problems together as equals.

Of the three levels of US commitment to and engagement in the international system, the tripolar interdependence or integrative one with Western Europe and Japan is the most crucial. The competitive tripolar model with the Soviet Union and China is most manipulative because of the discontinuity in interests and objectives and the prevalence of a balance-of-power structuring that permits maneuver among roughly equal adversaries. Only at this level is the détente process feasible. (See chapter 19 for further discussion.)

US Engagement in the Multipolar Subsystems

The third level of involvement, the multipolar subsystem, has probably suffered the most from the Nixon Doctrine. The subject of relations with Third

World countries was specifically omitted in the pentagonal schema, and no
provisions have been made for its incorporation or association in the new order.
True summaries of relations on a regional basis have been included in each
presidential report to Congress on foreign policy, but the roles of regions or
individual countries have not been charted for the projected international system, a serious omission.

Plotting the parameters for US engagement in the multipolar subsystem is
particularly hazardous because approval of the announced drawdown in US
commitments to all Third World countries is probably the only foreign-policy
issue on which there is public consensus in America. But the terms for US involvement under the Nixon Doctrine resounded like an indiscriminate withdrawal from all Third World countries, despite previous and continuing interests
or shared principles. At Guam, President Nixon stressed that the United States
would continue to honor its existing commitments, would use its nuclear power
to deter nuclear threats against its allies, but would refrain from committing its
conventional forces for the defense of the interests of friendly Asian states. The
retreat from Southeast Asia, leaving the enemy in control of large portions of
the battlefield and in a position to continue fighting and to establish a third
Vietnamese state, is convincing evidence of how the doctrine is to be implemented. Denied its strategic nuclear option by parity, the United States has
also had its conventional alternative eroded by its own public opinion. Under
these circumstances, some degree of disengagement is imperative.

But the formula for disengagement cannot be universal; Third World countries should not and need not be written off as summarily as we enlisted their
unanimous support during the anticommunist campaign. What is needed is a
set of parameters for US involvement in this subsystem that will reduce overall
liabilities, especially in the event of destabilization, clarify mutual interests,
strengthen means of association, and minimize military commitments.

> The proper way to proceed would be to make a region-by-region
> reappraisal of American interests, present and future. These interests
> should then be balanced against US military commitments in each
> area. In some cases the opportunity for reducing or eliminating com-
> mitments may become clear, in others it may be necessary to increase
> the level of commitments, and in still other cases the present level
> may be considered the most appropriate. Once the balance of inter-
> ests and commitments is determined, we should examine existing and
> planned US defense capabilities as seems appropriate on the basis of
> the prior analysis. In some cases qualitative changes in capabilities may
> be called for.
>   This conceptual scheme is, of course, nothing but an ideal model.
> Reality will present much more complex choices. It is doubtful that
> agreement will be reached easily, for example, on the true nature of
> American interests vis-à-vis particular countries in the latter half of

decade. Nevertheless, only through this type of analysis can we come to a sound approximate measure of what our alliances and commitments should be.[16]

No such order-ranking of priority interests abroad has ever been made by the Unites States government. For example, the decision in 1969 to reduce US war-waging capabilities from a two-and-one-half-war strategy to a one-and-one-half capability was based on a revised threat estimate, not an assessment of political and economic interests abroad. This sequence was a residue of the Cold War. It is now imperative that a systematic evaluation of US interests in each Third World country be made, and a summary definition of the degree and type of US involvement that can be expected must be announced. Without a statement of interests, the prospects for gaining popular support for any contingency where the US position is jeopardized will be dim. A retreat or abandonment of commitments because of inadequate preparation could appear like a rout. The British and French had a more painful task of identifying foreign interests which contributed to a rather disorderly recessional from their overseas commitments. The US should attempt to be more deliberate.

With self-reliance by other nations now a central tenet of US policy that will not end with a change of administrations, it is not inconsistent to encourage allies to accept a greater role, not just in their own defense, but in organizing and supporting regional security arrangements. Asian states have followed the American example and have made some adjustment with China, but this does not eliminate destabilizing political factors or the use of force to secure political ends. A Pacific security pact, supported mainly by Japan, the Philippines, Indonesia, and Australia, could expect an American contribution, but it could no longer count on a preponderant US injection, except in military aid. Similar arrangements already functioning in Africa and Latin America should be tailored to the new prescription.

The contribution the United States can and should make in military assistance to regional security organizations remains rather unclear. In fiscal year 1972 the United States granted $4.2 billion in military aid, of which about one half was service-funded and directed to Asian recipients. This figure has steadily declined, but the appropriate leveling-off point remains undecided. Most of the developing countries have almost no capability for research and development in any area of human endeavor. In Latin America, for example, it is estimated to be only 0.2 percent of the GNP. Asian countries have set a goal of 1 percent for 1980, while the US invests about 3.2 percent annually.[17] Regional powers cannot economically replace the present sources of arms development and production and the United States will probably remain heavily engaged in arms sales to Third World countries. While the threat of great-power involvement in regional disputes declines, the US is likely to intensify its efforts to secure regional arms ceilings, as in Latin America, stressing local military solutions to localized disturbances, thereby reducing the need for heavy armaments. But economic competition and demands of local military leaders will probably deny Washington complete satisfaction on this point.

A second reason for a lack of clarity on regional self-help versus US aid is the ambiguity among smaller states themselves about the nature of the threat during a period of transition in the international system. With Japan doubling its defense spending between 1971 and 1973 to $3.5 billion, much higher than any other Asian nation, and hostilities continuing in several countries, the future power balance is likely to change. Uncertainty about future sources of threat is illustrated by the fact that no Asian state during the early 1970s has recorded a consistent drop in defense expenditures. Thus, US military assistance will continue to be an important means of association with this subsystem.

In the area of economic aid, America's regional partners are able and in many cases willing to make greater contributions. Since the mid-1960s the US allocations for foreign economic aid have steadily declined, but private investments abroad have increased. More important, a new range of foreign investors have emerged and are already playing dominant roles in this area. Japan and Australia have made important contributions in overseas investments and Arab oil states will soon become important creditor nations. The US role in the economic development of selected regions may soon become that of a senior advisor, interested in general trends but prepared to contribute only to developmental pilot projects that hold the prospects of high returns in countries where the US has important political interests.

Thus, the functional parameters for the American involvement in the Third World need not be substantially altered. What has changed is the need for a systematic approach to this involvement, that will permit judicious use of declining resources or the support of continuing interests. A policy of limited involvement and selected engagement should be tailored to reduce unwanted liabilities, balance potential risks, and preclude unacceptable isolation. A policy of selected involvement will fit both national priorities and public expectations by preserving the credibility of principles for which American sacrifices have been made.

The international system has undergone profound changes, and the Nixon Doctrine has had a fundamental impact on the scope and direction of these changes. The Nixon Administration must be credited with having recognized the inevitability of multipolarity and the urgency of finding a formula that would preserve American interests as the world system entered into a period without adequate policy precedent or historic guidelines. But like the "sufficiency" equation for strategic arms policy, the Nixon Doctrine was an interim measure subject to modification as interests and positions become more sharply · defined. The proposal of a three-tiered model for US engagement in the international system is an extension of the administration's attempt to secure systemic stability.

Three-tiered Model for Engagement
and Controlled Liabilities

The three-tiered model of engagement has several advantages. By dividing the level of engagement into one for interdependence, one for détente and influence competition, and one for limited involvement and controlled liabilities, the existing system is merely better structured, not basically modified. No attempt is made to compel other players to adopt an American prescription for the rules of the game. The present rules have evolved largely by mutual consent and are merely categorized by the interests of the players at three levels of association with the United States. This categorizing of interests and rules permits the US to continue strengthening the principles of interdependence and common heritage with Western Europe and Japan that it would be foolhardy to neglect. It also allows the US to engage in a limited détente with both China and the Soviet Union on whatever terms for the new world order they choose to select, without impairment of our own. Indeed, by refraining from trying to impose our own set, it provides the tactical advantage of being better able to exploit the incongruities that exist between the Soviet and Chinese views of the international system. Finally, fractioning out three separate parameters for engagement is a major step toward abrogating the concept of universalism that has been an albatross for American foreign policy since its inception. A policy of limited involvement and controlled liabilities in its multipolar subsystem would tend to negate former tendencies of prescribing American solutions to local problems without adequate consideration of the immediate political culture. With the demise of these tendencies, the United States could more genuinely endorse development efforts for like-minded nations and furnish support to states in which it had important interests, even on their own terms when necessary.

Such an ordering of the American engagement in the international system on the three separate levels along lines already acceptable to the other participants allows a firmer structuring of boundaries between each level. Because the rules have been mutually acceptable, the prospects are good that all participants will respect these delineations. Both the Soviets and the Chinese will be reluctant and disadvantaged for the time being in participating in the industrial subsystem, and will be content to place primary emphasis on dealing with the United States on the détente subsystem. Likewise, smaller states will have little interest in seeking participation in the great-power détente process. Thus, there should be limited cross-boundary interference. This does not mean that other players will not conduct their own diplomatic relations on a variety of planes, from great to tertiary powers, but it minimizes the adverse impact that such dealing can have on America's respective subsystemic relationships.

Finally, these structural boundaries tend to follow functional interests and needs of both the United States and other players; i.e., interdependence, détente, and development. These functions are largely self-exclusive and cannot be transferred from one subsystem to the other, thereby reinforcing the boundary demarcations. More important, these functions are mutually shared, not always to the same degree, but one's interest in a specific general function cannot easily be transferred by any player. Therefore, without conjuring up a new radical model for the international system, leadership by one player in ordering the existing system will induce other players to follow suit. Each player can retain his respective political philosophy and hopes for the future, but the organization of a more rigid schema for its engagement in the system by a leading player will encourage other players to adopt a similar format.

From the viewpoint of an American administration, the success of a more systemic approach to foreign policy will depend not on the rigidity of its compartmentalization, but rather upon the degree of interface and coordination achieved at the center. While a subsystem can often be most effectively managed operating autonomously, centralized coordination is indispensable for long-range planning. The processes of political life, which Henry Kissinger has lamented we lack, require efficiency at each level, but integration and perspective at the center.

19

Adversary Relations and the
Management of the Détente
Subsystem

While the interdependence and cooperative subsystem or level of diplomatic engagement must remain America's prime concern, and the judicious management of involvement in the Third World should be a high priority, the identification, definition, and application of détente has been the overriding concern of Nixon and the world at large. The détente process has been viewed almost universally as the manifestation of the relaxation of global tensions, the end of the Cold War and the advent of normal relations among former adversaries. In the past, adversary relations have transcended all other levels of diplomatic contact. Therefore, the degree of adjustment between the great powers is likely to be the dominant framework for other nations' understanding of normal relations, whether they are based on a concept of social revolution or peace as codified by international law. One of the prime difficulties in measuring the degree of adjustment that has taken place or that can be anticipated is the diverse diplomatic backgrounds of both great powers. The foreign policies of both have led over time to the development of conceptual notions of preferred international behavior that have proved basically incompatible. The incongruities in the fundamental understanding of the nature and purpose of foreign policy of the two states have been a key source of Cold War tensions and should be examined.

Traditional Soviet Diplomacy

Karl Marx once observed that the policy of the Russians is ageless. Its methods, its tactics, its maneuvers may change, but the polar star of its policy— world domination—is a fixed star. Nearly sixty years of Soviet rule have resulted in few dramatic changes in the USSR's foreign policy aims, but there have been important stylistic changes in the conduct of its diplomacy. In the wake of the October Revolution, Moscow abandoned the classical foreign policy aims of Tsarist Russia that were confined to securing spheres of influence in contiguous regions and pursued the "universalist" objective of world revolution. Tsarist Russia sought the preservation of the existing world order, while the Bolsheviks insisted on a commanding voice in the establishment of a new order. But the firm response of Moscow's multiple adversaries denied it the quick victories it anticipated and forced it to make a more realistic assessment of the "world revolution versus international recognition" dilemma. While the revolutionist school retained important influence over Soviet policy aims, Moscow placed much greater tactical emphasis on realpolitik after its diplomatic break-through at Rapallo and the failure of Comintern policy in Germany and China. Security requirements demanded increasing attention for nations that could physically threaten Soviet national interests, reverting Soviet priority aims back to traditional Russian priorities of establishing spheres of influence.

This revision back to more conventional tactical Russian foreign policy aims and the adoption of the program of socialism in one country were evidence that the USSR was not a bona fide global power, but a regional power with vital interests in both Asia and Europe. It attempted to maintain the image of radicalism through propaganda and the conduct of "revolutionary" diplomacy. Its unconventional diplomatic practices were characterized by the use of recognized institutions and principles, such as the League and international law, not for the lofty purposes espoused by others but for the more immediate and terrestrial end of guaranteeing national security. The preservation of the Revolution justified any manipulations of the conventions of international behavior. While "revolutionary" diplomacy was a new additive, Soviet tactical objectives resembled those of Tsarist Russia: the prevention of hostile coalitions along any of its extended borders. Yet its neighbors remained convinced that world revolutionary ambitions remained just beneath the surface of Soviet diplomatic planning. Their reactions resulted in severe diplomatic depressions in 1920–21, 1927, and especially in 1938. That year was the nadir of Soviet diplomatic history: it was surrounded by two hostile concentric rings, the traditional imperialist alignment and the fascists' Anti-Comintern Axis, its numerous proposals for collective security had been ignored and it was denied a seat at Munich, Europe's most important security conference since 1925, and it was heavily engaged in a corps-size battle with the Japanese in the Far East. In 1939 the world witnessed a brilliant display of revolutionary diplomacy that culminated in the Pact with Germany. When the Pact failed to deter Hitler, the Soviets were convinced they were fighting in part to preclude a return to the diplomatic straight jacket of 1938: confronted with a variety of potential enemies and only high-risk associated options.

After World War II, the USSR was confronted initially with only one adversary—the United States with its strategic supremacy. Moscow sought to minimize US supremacy both by consolidating its newly gained spheres in Eastern Europe and Asia, and by rekindling the universalist challenge of inter-national revolution. But once again, adversary reaction altered Soviet foreign policy. The viability of the containment alliances, the emergence of the Sino-Soviet dispute, the Cuban missile debacle, the eclipse of the national liberation movements, and even the rise of polycentrism forced Moscow to abandon its more adventurous global ambitions. Thus, by the first half of the 1960s Soviet foreign policy had gained only limited successes and had sustained serious setbacks: its overall efforts had been diluted by unsuccessful enterprises con-ducted in Ghana, the Congo, Indonesia, etc. The result was the general exposure of the rough limits of Soviet influence in international affairs.

Soviet Policy Under Stress

In turn, the mid-1960s can be typified as a period of Soviet retrenchment. The USSR abandoned its strategy of rolling back Western influence wherever and whenever an opportunity arose and sought to be more selective and systematic in providing a reliable basis for its own influence. It was no longer as critical that every leftist revolution succeed or that every radical movement be Sovietized. Moreover, Moscow also recognized its inability to support physically such an ambitious strategy.

Consequently, the USSR constricted its horizons to contiguous zones of influence and accepted the losses inflicted on its prestige as a revolutionary center by its reduced support for radical movements. Further, it adopted a program to construct a strategic conventional military capability and pursued a plan for neutralizing the containment barriers, thereby allowing this new strategic capability to be exercised more effectively beyond its continental confinement. Finally, the USSR launched a major construction effort designed to insure nuclear parity with the US, reducing the utility of America's vast strategic resources in the conduct of diplomacy.

After the dual shocks of the Cuban missile crisis and the final break with China, Moscow sought holding actions in Europe and the Far East. Under attack for revisionism, Moscow was on the defensive on most fronts, until Chinese excesses resulted in diplomatic defeats. With Soviet resurgence in the Middle East and intervention in Czechoslovakia, it appeared that Moscow was following the US in becoming overengaged. The year 1969 was a turning point. China emerged from the Cultural Revolution and directed assertive policies against the USSR, not the imperialists. The US began freeing itself from its Vietnam obsession and gained more freedom of maneuver in Europe and the Middle East. Both Germany and Japan were demonstrating increasing independence from Washington. Finally the US accepted Soviet claims to strategic parity.

Moscow's reaction to these developments was to consolidate its position by accelerating emerging trends of negotiating on all fronts simultaneously. This is a signal innovation that deserves closer examination. In the past Russia has exploited its central location to all its enemies. It has been able to move from one periphery to another and to maintain pressure in one direction until checked before facing in another. These tactics yielded a host of enemies and allies in Europe, the Middle East, and Asia and the Far East. They also gave Russia the perspective and stature in the nineteenth century of a global rival to the British Empire. The success of Russia's policy was not only its central location but the singularity of its purpose. It was able to isolate issues and areas with a facility surpassed only by England, in part because British sea communications and territorial holdings were superior to and more diverse than Russian land communications. The Soviets pursued similar strategies. To counter imperialist encirclement, and later the American "conspiracy" they accelerated the rate of change in diplomatic thrusts rather than broadening the areas of contact. During the 1950s, for example, Moscow shifted tensions from Berlin to Korea, to the Middle East, to Yugoslavia, to the Middle East, to Quemoy, to the Middle East, and back to Berlin.

But the turning point in the late 1960s did not indicate immediately a clear new course. The June War, Prague Action Program, and Ussuri River clashes appeared initially to be either diplomatic reversals or renewed demonstrations of Moscow's limitations. They compromised the enhanced prestige it had earned by neutralizing twenty years of American asymmetric destruction. Moscow responded to these new setbacks by attempting to insure greater stability in its immediate security zones and thereby guaranteeing greater predictability in the conduct of its foreign policy. In an effort to be more systematic and flexible, the USSR sought to compartmentalize its foreign interests and issues and to insulate each from related factors. Such sompartmentalization was intended to reduce the adverse spillage or seepage from international problems and crises into domestic affairs, permitting greater latitude for tactical diplomatic maneuvers.

Conceptual Innovations

By the 1970s Moscow had demonstrated a growing desire and capability to maintain diplomatic activities on a variety of important issues with virtually all of its major allies and opponents. The ability to manage a multiple-issue diplomacy rather than a single-issue program became the hallmark of a new look in Soviet foreign policy. This trend toward multiple-issue diplomacy affords more flexibility in playing several issues simultaneously against single opponents. The former rather simplistic structuring of issues and areas has now been broadened by a type of multiplier effect arising from compartmentalization. The Soviets can deal with greater confidence and lower risks on issues that have a generative effect of producing new points of interests.

The implications of this new orientation became apparent first in Europe. By December 1969, Moscow agreed to allow its allies to pursue their respective national grievances against the West on a bilateral basis, rather than the purely multilateral approach previously employed. This decision did not signal the adoption of genuine coalition politics as understood and practiced in the West; Moscow still exercised firm control over the negotiations of each ally. But it did allow more responsibility at the national level for the solution of circumscribed local problems. Moscow successfully inverted national attention to parochial problems, without diminishing its ultimate authority. In return, it demanded a freer hand in the conduct of negotiations reserved for the great powers. The result was the conclusion of normalization treaties between West Germany, Poland, and the USSR, the opening of negotiations between West Germany, Czechoslovakia, and East Germany, and Soviet negotiations over arms limitations and the heart of the German problem.

The success of Moscow's compartmentalization was next seen in its Middle Eastern policy. The scale of the USSR's involvement in the Arabs' 1967 defeat and its subsequent resupply commitments created grave concern throughout Eastern Europe. The ensuing debate contributed directly to Antonin Novotny's demise in Czechoslovakia and less directly to Gomulka's later fall in Poland. It was the cause of the first major purge in the USSR under Brezhnev's rule and became the grounds for accelerated Rumanian autonomy. Yet three years later when the USSR undertook its first active military defense of a non-Communist country—the UAR—at the expense of weapons modernization in the Warsaw Pact, no known instance of public criticism occurred anywhere in Eastern Europe. Moscow's legitimate allies appeared genuinely uninterested in Moscow's Middle Eastern policies, commitments that could have led to a great-power confrontation and a threat to Warsaw Pact interests. This was an impressive display of Moscow's ability to insulate issues, to establish and maintain boundaries within its overall foreign policy.

Compartmentalization has also occurred in party and ideological matters. After years of travail, the Kremlin finally succeeded in 1969 in convening a World Communist Conference, which was noteworthy for its failure. Only one half of the ruling Communist parties participated, and barely one half of the world Communist membership was represented. Moreover, virtually all the Asian Parties boycotted the proceedings. The results of the conference confirmed the de facto split in the Communist world between the Chinese and Soviet blocs and emphasized the preponderant European influence in the Moscow-oriented group. The conference also accelerated the pace of polycentrism: dissident parties, i.e., the Rumanian and Italian, were able to criticize Soviet behavior without censure or discipline.

Moscow belatedly agreed to adopt new guidelines for its conduct of party relations. Rather than attempting to formalize a single set of ideological dogma governing the conduct of all parties, as the Conference attempted, Moscow shifted to a particularist formula, whereby ideological matters would be discussed on a bilateral basis. Furthermore, Moscow gradually accepted the importance of placing a higher priority on purely political differences among the ruling Parties. It has not adopted a live-and-let-live policy à la Rumania, but has agreed to disagree with its ideological adversaries while promoting a more cooperative line on political issues. This formula was first tried with Yugoslavia and later became the basis for a limited political reapprochement between Peiping and Moscow. Thus the compartmentalization of ideological disputes has freed the Kremlin of its former constraining role as the guardian of orthodoxy and allowed greater focus on issues related to realpolitik. (For example, in the wake of the Ussuri River clashes, Moscow succeeded in negotiating bilateral military agreements with its East European allies, binding them to its defenses in Asia, while at the same time it conducted negotiations with Peiping over normalization of relations.)

Probably the more remarkable demonstration of compartmentalization has been in US-USSR relations. After 1965, US involvement in the Vietnam War and its bombing of a member of the Communist commonwealth was a major point of tension between the two countries. The level of tensions was due in part to the inability of the USSR to assist physically North Vietnam or effectively counter US "aggression against a fraternal state." Nonetheless, Moscow agreed to reserve the war issue to the specific plane of polemics and diplomatic pressure, while opening negotiations with the US on a variety of strategic matters and agreeing to cosponsor draft treaties in the UN Disarmament Commission in Geneva. Thus the Soviets have been able to discuss issues appropriate for a great power unimpeded by the interests of smaller states; when confronted with the opposition of smaller states at Geneva, it has been able to close ranks with the rival great power.

Thus a seemingly logical progression has occurred from traditional Russian concepts of spheres of influence in a geographic plane to the inclusion of functional issues, e.g. negotiations with West Germany and on the Seabed Treaty. Boundaries have been established on both areas and issues which have been firmly enforced. This new feature has allowed Moscow to exercise greater control over external matters than ever before by permitting a more facile distinction between high priority and less important issues and a more balanced treatment of each category. Moscow has acknowledged the gradual dilution of its authority over lesser matters, while it has preserved the decisiveness of its control over more crucial problems (it accepted Rumania's deviation in foreign affairs but used force to crush the Prague Spring). This transition in Soviet foreign policy produced impressive results. It has contributed to the solution of important European grievances and to the growing stability in security zones contiguous to the USSR. With benign Soviet neglect, US relations with many of its allies have eroded to the point that distinct separation of interests has occurred. Yet in Eastern Europe Soviet authority rests unshakably on the Brezhnev Doctrine. Thus, the most important feature of the present transformation in Soviet foreign policy is the greater systematization of the USSR's comparative advantages on single international issues as related to the overall diplomatic process. The USSR can be expected in the future to refine this process, while expanding the number of issues on which it will have the capability and interest to act. The number of issues under negotiation or consideration at any given time is likely to increase, but they will remain integrated in the diplomatic process and not treated independently. By emphasizing the integrative nature of the "process," compartmentalization has made foreign challenges relatively more manageable than they were several years ago.

Incongruity of the American Diplomatic Model

In contrast, American foreign policy has become a hybrid of earlier isolation and contemporary global responsibilities. Since its inception, America has generally pursued a policy of isolation that was only gradually modified during the last fifty years. Wilsonian optimistic faith in the fundamental reasonableness and single-mindedness of all peoples characterized American views on international affairs during this period. Americans regarded foreign problems primarily from a moral viewpoint, seeing them in terms of black or white and placing a high degree of confidence in signs of good faith from other nations. The US believed that with good faith, permanent solutions to world difficulties could be found. And so, the US went to war four times during this period, not merely in defense of national interests, but to preserve higher human values it believed other people shared. This expansiveness was due to America's insular perspective, similar to the British historic position, which encouraged isolation and reliance on natural defensive barriers, but facilitated the extension of popular thinking to the global dimension once parochial views were accepted as anachronistic.

These beliefs nurtured the growth of a universalistic concept for the conduct of American foreign policy. It has been devoted primarily to the definition and expansion of common interests among like-minded states. Rather than create dependencies like the Russians, Americans have attempted to form global and regional groupings along various political and functional lines that could ultimately exercise a degree of sovereignty or self-interest. Mutual defense arrangements and international organizations have been sponsored in the expectation that the proportion of common interests and mutually acceptable practices could foster international cooperation and expand normal relations.[1]

By comparison, then the concepts of foreign policy held by the rival great powers have been incompatible. Mutual discussions about singular issues did not resolve the opposing perspectives; they tended to reconfirm the mutual sense of antagonism. In this deadlock the side that could alter its conceptual framework would gain important advantages over its rival. The Soviets have made the most noticeable alteration to date.

There are several reasons for Moscow's greater alacrity, First, it was on the defensive, and needed a model that would permit assertiveness without provocation. Second, the US was tied down in a self-consuming military and emotional anticommunism struggle that permitted the USSR latitude elsewhere. Third, because of the emotions involved in Vietnam, America was unwilling to accept the need for conceptual renovations until faced with the horror of moral defeat. Fourth, although the USSR remained a continental power with vital interests around its geographic periphery, it lacked both conceptual tools and military reach to act as a truly global power. Finally, in the area of greatest mutual interest, Europe, the USSR had successfully forced the US to abandon its universalism and to accept Moscow's notion of sphere of influence. But a different approach would be required to make the same inroads elsewhere.

Regional Applications

The middle East is an example of the difficulties involved in applying archaic stereotyped concepts in noncontiguous regions. Political vagaries and geographic diffusion are in fact incompatible with the concepts of both powers. The lack of any significant advantage by either power and the urgency of regional demands have compelled a partial adjustment of their respective philosophies. For example, the Eisenhower Doctrine of January 1957 was propounded as an extension of the Truman Doctrine and implied firm offers of assistance to any endangered Middle Eastern state that resisted communism. The generosity and universality of the Eisenhower Doctrine was designed to protect the interests of the entire region, by extending the umbrella of ultimate weapons for the defense of human rights. It did not, however, prescribe the limits of the American commitments in any given situation.

Conversely, the doctrine allowed the Soviets the tactical option of expanding their influence without affording any measure of physical protection. The Soviets could not rival the level of the American guarantee, but showed little desire to do so, since their commitments were flexible and no vital interests were involved. With minimal interests and obligations, Moscow had nothing to lose and much to gain by encouraging local authorities to exploit the difference between the upper limits of any crisis, which were always controlled by Washington, and the lower intensity of the actual confrontation. As local leaders perceived this disparity, it was used to gain maneuverability, while the Soviets received credit for advancing the interests of their proteges.

An important point overlooked in the recent debate of spheres of influence is that the USSR employs the concept inconsistently.[2] It is now used as an instrument of consolidation, not expansion—Tsarist Russia used it for both. The USSR no longer seeks regional hegemony as a means of expansion. Rather than dealing on an overall geographic basis, Moscow is more eclectic, selecting individual countries and functional issues for its attention. These tactics have tended to polarize regions rather than consolidate them as viable spheres. While political inroads can be promoted by the tactic of polarization, it does not facilitate consolidation of influence, especially in a heterogeneous region like the Middle East. After gaining a level of local acceptance by selected Arab states, Moscow realized that its authority in regional matters remained highly circumscribed. Achievement of its immediate aim of gaining general recognition of its stature as a major power no longer depended upon Arab endorsement, unless they miraculously spoke in unison. Such recognition could only be secured if the United States acknowledged the Soviet Union as coresponsible for regional stability. The USSR still suffers from the weakness of being a continental power that must gain acceptance in regional matters not from local states but from the rival global power. A modification of the polarization tactics would be needed to ease such an adjustment. The USSR, deliberately or not, achieved a posture of dealing on a variety of issues on multiple levels of contacts with a high degree of boundary discipline. The ability to deal exclusively with selected issues or to switch to a wider assortment gives the impression of responsibility. Thus, the USSR has devised a crude systemic context for its Middle Eastern policy, with subsystem divisions, disciplined boundaries, and centralized control over issue integration.

Impact of Soviet Domestic Politics

Yet both powers are experiencing constraints on their foreign policies that will inhibit sweeping renovations. The most important is the linkage between domestic influences and foreign policy objectives. More than its American rival's, the definition of Soviet foreign policy aims is dependent upon the cohesion and reliability of its power base within the Communist world. Many Western analysts have concluded that the Soviet system is experiencing a political decline. Paradoxically, the country is reportedly stronger militarily but weaker politically than it was under Stalin. The collective system of government is supposed to be inherently unstable and the arbitrary demonstration of Soviet authority over its allies is likely to perpetuate their unreliability. Finally, the Soviet economic model is deemed the source of the continuing East-West technological gap that will doom the Socialist states to permanent economic inferiority. The overall effect of these domestic contradictions on Soviet foreign policy have been summed up by Richard Lowenthal as the outward expansion of an inwardly declining society.[3]

The growing volume of literature on comparative communism, however, has contributed to a reappraisal of the West's perception of the Soviet model of Socialist progress. Most scholars presently agree that the Soviet system is not now totalitarian and probably never was, if one applies Hans Buckheim's definition that totalitarianism is the demand for unlimited control over the world and hence social life which is translated into political action.[4] Benjamin Barber aptly stated the majority position when he concluded, "Totalitarianism is to modern science what reason was to Luther: a conceptual harlot of uncertain parentage, belonging to no one but at the service of all."[5]

It is now widely held that the Soviet form of government is a slightly less onerous "authoritarian" brand, in which a strong one-party system exercises the functions of legitimation of political interests, recruitment of political leadership, and social interest aggregation in policymaking.[6] But its inability to exercise all the instruments of totalitarianism denies it absolute monopoly over these functions at all times. The party's authority is subject to continuous competition both politically, over legitimacy and succession, and socially, from modernity and urbanization. To preserve its monopoly of decision-making, the party attempts to control the pace of modernization through repression and slowing down social change. The Soviet party has successfully imposed a model for social mobilization that transformed the old order into new institutions. It is now moving through a consolidation stage to a more adaptive phase. Ideology as a legitimizing and motivating factor has lost its luster, indicating not decay but growing stability. The former exaltation of the leader over the party has been reversed, with the party enjoying greater prestige and influence. Patronage is likely to remain the hallmark of political success, but as the party moves from mobilization it must become more adaptive to the legal-rational challenges to its authority.

As modernity goals have been gradually achieved, despite the repeated damage inflicted by successive revolutions from above, the Soviet government has been transformed into a conservative bureaucracy. The net result is that as the party moves to the adaptive stage its authority is likely to be challenged more, not less, from competing demands for more authentic political participation, wider latitude for national preferences, accelerated economic productivity, and product diversification. These claims will rise increasingly from continuing reservations about legitimacy, alienation, and the influence of pluralizing elites.[7] In facing these challenges, the party must cope with both the increasing complexity of decision-making in the modernization process and the difficulty of aggregating interests in a system where all organization has been subordinated to a single apparatus. Instead of a general staff, Soviet leaders now require a coordinating staff that can accurately measure and interpret influence and interests. In a model where there is more potential than actual influence and which has no systematic means for aggregating interests, innovative technocrats and critical intellectuals assume a disproportionate weight of influence over informally organized groups.[8] Despite the "pluralism of elites" in the Soviet Union there remains almost no reliable empirical means to ascertain their impact of decisions.[9] And only in East Germany, a nation with a radically different social composition, has a "counterelite" of technocrats been identified as an entrenched, influential faction within the party.[10]

Thus, as Richard Lowenthal has sagely observed, in the early 1960s the USSR at last entered the postrevolutionary stage.[11] The party no longer sought to legitimize its rule by imposing forcible transformations on society, as under Stalin, or even reforming its structure in less violent ways, as under Khrushchev. It simply presented itself as the indispensable guardian of continuing growth in Russian power and prosperity. Yet for the first time since the October Revolution, the initiative for political and social change largely passed from the party and state into the hands of an increasingly modern and mature society. The party now finds itself in an increasingly defensive role, both at home and in the bloc, but it has rejected both experiments in liberalism and Stalinism, and has reverted to older police-state methods of harrassment and persecution. These methods have penalized intellectual independence and cultural development; but they have assured steady yet unspectacular technological progress and expansion of power.

Moreover, while not a motive, ideology remains the Soviets' only frame of analysis. The Soviets will not place high values on revolutionary success anywhere, but they will remain confident that the world will eventually become socialist. To accelerate the successful outcome, socialism must be defended everywhere. Consequently, Moscow will view the future as neither a holocaust nor a reconciliation, but as an indefinite conflict over controlled and limited interests. Therefore, the USSR will probably never become a satisfied power, but merely less assertive— content with limited expansion without risk.[12]

Thus there appears to be insufficient evidence to support the oft-heard contention that Soviet leadership is fumbling and the party edifice is crumbling. True, the party and state hierarchy are more stable than any other modern state— there have been fewer changes in leading personalities and institutions than in any other European society since 1939.[13] But there are signs of modernization within the society proper that have given rise to the new demands and claims. These changes were not anticipated by the entrenched hierarchy of Marxist authorities, but they have effectively coped with these contingencies. However unimaginative their innovations may appear, it would be unwise to accept the predictions of the Soviet dissidents about the corrosion and collapse of the system. The very exposure to protest resulting from timid modernizing changes is likely to be sufficiently alarming to keep the Kremlin sensitive to the realistic elements in public opinion.

Such cautious generalizations about the future development of Soviet society are, of course, conjectural. Brzezinski has speculated about five feasible courses of change and evolution: oligarchic petrification, involving the maintenance of the dominant role of the party and the retention of the essentially dogmatic character of the ideology; pluralist evolution, prescribing the transformation of the party into a more pluralistic body somewhat like that of Yugoslavia, and the ideological erosion of its dogmatic tradition; technological adaptation, involving a transformation of the bureaucratic-dogmatic party into a technologically expert party, emphasizing expertise and efficiency rather than political loyalty and party discipline; militant fundamentalism, nurturing a revivalist effort to rekindle ideological fervor and revolutionary idealism; and political disintegration, resulting in internal paralysis in the ruling elite, the rising self-assertiveness of various key groups within it, splits in the armed forces, restiveness among the youth and intellectuals, and open disaffection among the nationalities.

While there is abundant evidence supporting arguments that the USSR could evolve along each of these courses, Brzezinski concludes that barring an upheaval resulting from internal paralysis—and causing either the dramatic appearance of social democracy or, more likely, the seizure of power by a revivalist dictator—the probable pattern for the 1980s is that of a marginal shift toward the combination of the pluralist evolution and technological adaptation variants: limited economic and political pluralism, intense emphasis on technological competence, within the context of a still authoritarian government representing a coalition of the upper echelons of the principle interest groups. This could be the beginning of the return to the Western Marxist tradition—but, at most, only a slow and cautious beginning.[14] Thus the most accurate picture of Soviet leadership for the next decade would be that of conservative, brutally realistic men, with guarded and cautious attitudes toward the masses, attuned to opportunities to enhance Soviet prestige and authority abroad. The conservativism and constraint of the past ten years are likely to persist in the foreseeable future.

The future developments within the West and the long-term character of

American society are also the subject of mystification for both powers. There are undoubtedly many stabilizing and tranquilizing institutions and common beliefs within the American society, but the unique nature of the present turmoil is not clearly understood by Americans, much less by authoritarian socialists. Without firm historic precedents that might aid in defining how far these pressures might move toward disrupting traditional institutions, the Soviets tend to view the possible future of the US as subject to even more dramatic options than Brezinski outlined for the USSR. Moreover, Soviet uncertainties are reinforced frequently by public speculation from leading US officials about the unknown impact of future social developments on American international objectives. Thus, each great power is experiencing a degree of frustration in determining its adversary's future social aims, foreign policy objectives, and views on international behavior. Furthermore, neither power has a theoretical advantage over its opponent in analyzing the other's posture and limitations.

Great-power Competition, Small-power Relations, Systemic Stability

Thus, it has been problematic for the great powers to sort out the incongruities and contradictions in their respective national interests and foreign policies, and to provide a sufficiently predictable basis for their relations to insure systemic stability. These difficulties were compounded by the projection of their rivalry into the contest for the loyalties of Third World countries. Even greater uncertainties existed in this sphere than in ascertaining the various factors relevant to the adversary confrontation.

There is little relevant experience or precedent, for example, that can guide either rival in relating the use of military force to the complex nature of political influence in the Third World. The atmosphere of strategic parity and multipolarity now pervades the Third World and the nature of political influence has become even more diffuse than under the conditions of pure bipolarity. Traditional sources of influence, such as economic incentives, political coercion, and the threat of military power, can no longer be employed on an either/or basis. Each type of influence has now assumed a variety of forms, applications, and inferences not formerly regarded as germane. Furthermore, the cultivation of a recipient and the intrusion of external pressure have been complicated by the spread of nationalism and the priority now placed on national solutions to local grievances. Nationalism tends to foster isolationism and political inversion that reduce the sense of urgency about establishing a commonality of interests with foreign states. The most significant aspect of this new atmosphere is that it applies equally to both great powers.

The earlier mentioned question marks about the great-power confrontation underscore these uncertainties about regional politics, the changing nature of great-power/small-power relations, and the appropriate innovations necessary to promote the national interests of the respective parties. The basic challenge to both great powers is to devise a formula that acknowledges the changing nature of great-power/small-power relations and provides mutual protection for the interests of both. Military operations in Czechoslovakia and Southeast Asia indicate that while the great powers can act independently to protect vital national interests, they are less likely to act alone to achieve less important goals. Broad multilateral moral and material support is still sought when coercive options are deemed necessary; therefore, the demands of small nations must be considered before combined action can be attempted. Thus, the underlying features of great-power/small-power relations in matters of collective security continue to be the traditional great-power desire for combined action and small-power demands for adequate respect for their interests. The dramatic changes that are occurring in force employment concepts for regional operations center on the accommodation of these persisting security requirements with diverging national interests and new methods for applying and controlling force.

Formal alliances have traditionally served as the bond for satisfying several nations' security needs. Historically, legally binding defensive commitments have been negotiated among like-minded states to preserve or promote common goals. Incongruities in national interests have been partially accommodated by the very framework of formal treaties. But incentives for any nation to join alliances as a security guarantee are declining. Because of the diminishing number of situations in which ultimate weapons can be used, the need for nuclear protection is no longer the prime reason for small powers to join security arrangements. Smaller powers have been correspondingly reluctant to accept the restraints alliances imposed on their sovereignty. On their side, the great powers have often used alliances as a vehicle to assert influence over decisions of their allies that might affect the entire system. Yet now it is becoming increasingly difficult for great powers to translate security guarantees into hegemonic authority. Thus, as parochial interests have increased, incentives to accept formal security obligations have diminished.

The partial dismemberment of contemporary alliances and the preference for extending political assurances, rather than negotiating treaties, does not negate the utility of military pacts. Some agreements still satisfy the most urgent needs of the signatories; however, new approaches are clearly required in the Third World. Future security arrangements should incorporate those attributes of the traditional systems that contributed to the degree of success achieved by more viable arrangements. But the Third World nations have demonstrated little propensity for promoting collective defenses and new improvisations will be necessary if their interest is to be attracted, conceivably of an ad hoc nature with limited membership, scope, and duration.

Political Status Quo, Dynamic Change, Systemic Stability

From the perspective of both great powers, a key factor in their present conceptual reappraisal is the nature of the political status quo, the feasibility of peaceful change, the instruments available to perform mutually agreed-upon operations, and the probable consequences of intransigence. In the past, both great powers identified the status quo with consolidation of exposed or threatened areas of interests (the USSR in Berlin, East Germany, and Eastern Europe, and the US in Berlin, Western Europe, and the Free World), while simultaneously attempting to undermine the opponent's influence in his own sphere. Thus a dualism developed incorporating the extent of political influence abroad and the desire to expand those limits in specific areas at the opponent's expense— What's mine is mine, and what's yours we will negotiate. Both antagonists claimed that global stability was dependent upon the other's acceptance of the legitimacy of his own self-satisfying definition of the status quo.

After the American "victory" during the Cuban crisis, the Western interpretation of the status quo was expanded by some observers to be identical to détente.[15] Identification of the status quo with détente was inadequate, however, since it failed to account for those recent dynamic changes that seriously endangered the West's definition of desirable stability. For example, in the seeming immobile conditions prescribed by the status quo:

1. American leadership in NATO lost the initiative temporarily to France and Soviet leadership was sidetracked by Rumanian assertiveness, West German machinations, and Chinese frontal assaults.
2. Smarting from its reversal in Cuba, Moscow scaled down its global ambitions, sacrificing its goal of conquering the moon for the creation of strategic nuclear preponderance.
3. In regions of lesser importance, each adversary seemingly exploited important interests of the opponent—the US devastated a member of the Socialist commonwealth by its bombing of North Vietnam, compromising the credibility of Soviet protection, and Moscow armed and encouraged the Arabs in a conflict with Israel, resulting in the impairment of American interests in the Middle East.
4. Varied East European responses to Bonn's Ostpolitik created the deepest fissures in Warsaw Pact solidarity to date and forced adoption of an active response by the conservative members demands for consolidation of socialism east of the Elbe.
5. The invasion of Czechoslovakia prompted reconsideration of the entire spectrum of vital interests and the uncertainties and dangers in overlapping important great-power interests.

After the Prague crisis, it was clear that declining tensions and the resulting sense of increased stability were not dependent upon promulgation of either power's understanding of the status quo. By 1968 the principal players in the international scene were dissatisfied with the constraints the existing status quo imposed on their policy options. International anxieties and uncertainties were regarded as a manifestation of the imperfection of the status quo. Even the "enlightened" Gaullists and "revanchist" West Germans were lumped together in opposition to the status quo. At the same time, the status quo was also reinforced. The Soviets saw the Prague crisis as a deterioration of the status quo; a view the US held over the loss of its asymmetrical destruction. Both cautiously introduced measures to redress the erosion of its position; in earlier eras they would have been regarded as sufficiently provocative and threatening to warrant major countermeasures.

The reason for this less alarmist reaction to actions strengthening the status quo was that during the same time both powers were seeking an accommodation on selected issues, weakening other aspects of the political status quo. While the great powers attempted to redefine, advance, or consolidate the status quo in virutally every aspect of joint concern, they were prepared to adjust on specific refined components. Thus, while the status quo was attacked from virtually every quarter and polemics continued over Vietnam and Middle East, both sides refrained from sustained threats of massive reprisals that had nurtured the former suspicions of the Cold War. The dialogues that commenced in 1963 opened an era in which both sides gradually recognized that marginal national gains could be achieved through the joint exploration of problems affording some prospects for adjustment and accommodation of respective policies. Concomitant with these explorations was the recognition of the legitimacy of the opponent's interests connected with these issues. Testing his outer toleration limits and the demarcation between vital and merely important values attached to these given interests were necessary preliminary steps. While no formal agreements were exchanged defining their respective positions on selected issues, tacit understandings emerged that reinforced the confidence of each adversary that the opponent was not determined to exploit a given issue for propaganda purposes or to deliberately provoke increased tensions. Finally, both opponents accepted a degree of constraint on their options by accepting the obligations of discussion.

While this growing adjustment in East-West relations is often regarded as a détente, it should be remembered that during the same period both powers sought reliable security through assured deterrence rather than comforting diplomatic overtures. Such vast investments for a preemptive capability do not connote a détente atmosphere.[16] Thus in the framework of a comprehensive political adjustment the terms *parity, stability, status quo,* and *détente* are often regarded as synonymous. In the present environment, however, they should be considered as separate and distinct concepts.

The degree of adjustment within the status quo that any given set of contestants is likely to make is a product of the degree of security each enjoys before and anticipates from making the change. The level of security usually depends upon the degree of political parity, not just military equivalence, each claims. Political parity is the relative balance in each state's posture composed of political aims, national values, military force, technological prowess, economic prosperity, and geostratic resources. States do not and cannot operate in a systemic vacuum. Their essence can only be conceived within the "cobweb of interstate interactions." A state's stature relative to that of others' may vary according to its position in relation to specific issues or principles. A state's image of itself is its most important one, but the level of its participation in the system will also depend upon the image others have of it. States seem most prone to adjust their policies on controversial issues or to modify the status quo when they can claim and are acknowledged to have sufficient political parity with the other contestants on specific issues for the specified change to impart only minimal risks to the rivals' national interests.

The process of adjusting the status quo can have fluid character. In the classical sense it is related to the political and geographic delineation of interests, commitments, and influence. But some interests and commitments on contentious issues may have only a transitory nature; others may have "this far and no further" values attached to them. Governments may view the former interests as subject to accommodation and mutual understanding that may afford the cumulative effect of encouraging larger adjustments and the gradual extension of areas of understanding and maneuvers. Values attached to the latter interests imply that each nation has specific limits to the status quo beyond which the pursuit of political gains by an adversary would not be regarded as conciliatory but as a threat, and would probably trigger retaliation and reprisals. Thus, the status quo consists of specific interests, commitments, and influences confined to precise political issues and values; it also has a flexible feature, characterized as aspirational, that varies with the issue and the opponent. When all aspects of the status quo are regarded as immutable by a given nation, when it has raised the "this far and no further" price to include all important issues, tensions with other nations are bound to rise. It is the growing flexibility in the present status quo that has led many observers to applaud the accompanying stability between the great powers.

Changes in the status quo may be the result of unilateral decisions (Britain's withdrawal from east of Suez), the product of collective bargaining (the West German-Soviet Union Treaty), the consequence of military hostilities (the two German defeats), or the rise of countervailing nationalistic forces and the decline of great-power influence (the decolonization and desatellization processes). These changes altered regions' total political physiognomy; they also illustrate how interests can overlap. The growing flexibility in the present status quo and the persistence of overlapping interests have lead to efforts to systematize the process of adjustment under the rubric of détente.

Nature of Détente

Probably no other term in contemporary international political life is the subject as of much misunderstanding and confusion. The term is sometimes used to describe a concept, a policy, or a situation. It has entirely different connotations for governments and observers with dissimilar political perspectives and, over time, even these connotations have been subject to frequent change. Thus, does *détente* now imply mutual great-power acceptance of coexistence à la Khrushchev,[17] genuine political reapprochement, as Kennedy envisaged,[18] normalization in relations on Adenauer's terms,[19] involuntary convergence of interest on major contentious issues,[20] mutual acceptance of the responsibilities of bipolarity (and a combined effort against polycentrism),[21] tacit approval of spheres of preponderant influence,[22] joint acceptance of pluralism and limited adoption of instruments for crisis management,[23] pause or decline in the arms race,[24] opportunism combining a hard and soft stand on various issues to gain greater political advantages,[25] fundamental changes in national goals and character allowing either side or both to modify their former views and accommodate the opponent's terms for peace (conversion or capitulation),[26] a new form of moderated hostility since the Prague crisis,[27] a complacent acceptance of the status quo,[28] recognition of a new stability in world order that it is mutually beneficial to preserve,[29] an acknowledgment of an inescapable momentum toward détente, greater maneuverability, and dynamic revisionism propagated mainly by smaller states,[30] or a commitment to great power immobilism by ignoring rather than resolving disputes?[31]

Some of these observers have used *détente* to imply *stability,* and others the *status quo.* It is true that the joint pursuit of a détente policy may reinforce global stability, but it is unlikely to strengthen the status quo. The shift from the era of confrontation to the age of negotiation has as yet had only modest impact on the status quo, though it has significantly improved stability. Both adversaries are competing to extend their influence in selected areas, and have grievances about the constraints some previous commitments have imposed on their policy options; yet both have declined the temptation to exploit continuing international tensions to the permanent detriment of the rival. The great powers have adopted a policy of mutually exploring the opponent's values, tolerance levels, relative priorities, probably constraints, and his calculations of possible profits and losses for given decisions. Accordingly, margins of error, uncertainty, and risk have been cautiously identified on specific issues. This entire process of communication and education has aided in uncovering issues of mutual interest, possible resolutions of conflicting interests, and the parameters of immediate values.

A deliberate mutual decision to explore areas of accommodations during periods of persisting tension and distrust may be defined as a *détente policy.* The purpose of this policy as exercised presently by the great powers is a positive step beyond merely reducing tensions and strengthening stability. It is a conscious effort to seek the resolution of those contentious points in the existing status quo that are in part responsible for the tensions. This may require an alteration of attitudes and priorities, but not of principles and ultimate values. A détente policy, then, is a means, not an end in itself. Initially it requires that both powers identify gradually their respective national interests and aims in terms of reducing opportunities for adversary exploitation and profit, rather than seeking ideological conquests. This understanding of the détente process suggests that its emergence was largely fortuitous; and, as a fortuitous phenomenon, it will require new innovative guidelines for the West. *Détente process,* then, may be defined as an interacting continum in which the participants intend to foster a limited degree of adversary cooperation in a nonbellicose atmosphere that is issue-oriented rather than principle or value-oriented. They also seek normalcy in adversary relations as the pragmatic extension of influence on important national interests, excluding areas regarded respectively as ideological privity. A circumscribing feature of détente process is that it will remain limited to issues only and cannot be channeled to the broader historic processes, because of its inapplicability to values. (It is important to note the similarity of this definition to the Soviet concept of peaceful coexistence. See below.)

Principles for Détente Management: Preservation of Parity

The first guideline for the management of détente is that stability in great-power relations is a function of security, which in turn is a product of strategic parity, and a curtailment of the arms race. It was not initially a change in political goals or values, but the mutually perceived consequences of threats after parity was recognized, that moved the détente process to issues affecting vital interests. Thus there is intrinsic value in parity per se, and every effort should be made to insure its perpetuation. Both great powers can strive to resolve their remaining strategic deficiencies to their satisfaction, especially in defensive systems. But efforts should be made to inhibit actions that would seek decisive advantages, upset the existing degree of stability, or impair the projected level of parity. The SALT I accords explicitly impose ceilings on some strategic weapons. Developments in nonproscribed systems must be carefully calculated to promote the technological state of the art or enhance defensive postures without adverse results on parity.

To insure adequate compliance, important changes will have to be made in American strategic thinking; the impact of general parity must be accepted. It must be recognized that parity includes not merely military deployments and capabilities, but the entire spectrum of battle-waging requirements, from mobilization to societal consensus. The US must also revise the theoretical underpinning of strategic philosophy to accommodate the consequences of parity. In the past, naval supremacy and strategic nuclear superiority were regarded as essential because the US could not positively influence Soviet behavior. Parity has not provided greater control than the US enjoyed when possessing an assured destruction capability, but neither has it decreased it. The nature of the relationship of military power to political influence, however, has been modified.

The theoretical premises of Mahan, Mackinder, Spykman, and Douhet, upon which the strategy of containment was predicated, are no longer valid. A continental land power has now outflanked or outranged the former containment barriers, and has the reach, flexibility, and staying power to insure acceptance of its position as a global power. Traditional concepts have been challenged because the geostrategic advantages of the Western powers have now been converted to advantages for the heartland power also. Theater forces are now the most significant component of both great powers' military capability. New strategic doctrines are now needed to provide a more viable basis for military options in this new situation.[32]

These new strategic doctrines must abandon the former requirement for naval and air supremacy. The integration of all three modes, including ground forces, should now be stressed. Since both great powers can now engage each other militarily at almost any level of intensity and in almost any theater, force deployments of the integrated three services should be calibrated as much as possible to support a compartmentalized diplomacy. Local temporary alignments should emphasize the availability of local national forces and the staying power of great-power participants. Theater strategy should no longer seek total military victory and unconditional surrender, assured destruction, and preponderant asymmetrical advantages against local antagonists. Rather than attempt to gain guaranteed dominant power, à la Israel, military forces should be structured to persuade. Erecting a maximum defensive posture at any level or area of local challenge should be stressed. Force survivability of a battle-winning, not war-winning, basis is now axiomatic. The overriding lesson of the Vietnam War is that despite technology men in battle still walk to victory. The ability to absorb punishment and survive is more crucial than firepower and mobility.

A second guideline for modifying strategic thinking deals with military technology. As the dimensions of the arms race became clearer in the late 1960s, the world showed a new awareness of the vital function of technology in international change. More than in any other age, military force and political power are a function of national technological prowess. Therefore, the rate of technological progression and its impact on the arms race has had profound effects on the durability of military parity, and the extent and direction of its change.

Pierre Gallois, the father of the French *force de frappe,* underlined the growing discrepancies between arms progressions and their projected political application. Formerly, he argues, a degree of stability existed because a relative coincidence in time occurred between political action and the turnover of weapons, the former predicting and preparing the way for applications of the latter. Today there is a growing discrepancy between the lead time needed to develop a new weapon system and the diplomatic and political perspective that gives foreknowledge of the conditions under which these new arms will be used. Thus, as political developments become less predictable and weapons systems more sophisticated, arms should be sufficiently diversified to meet all possible political contingencies, not the reverse—expecting political conditions to accommodate the application of single systems, such as the multipurpose aircraft. Gallois argues further that the durability of weapons systems depends upon the technological state of the art supporting that system. Therefore, political strategy today is conditioned by the current state of weapons turnover. That is why a state of technological warfare among the industrial states has replaced the Cold War. In this confrontation, he concludes, even the uncertainties of technological competition afford the surest guarantees of freedom of action—not weapons stabilization.[33]

The technological revolution has produced unprecedented change and a proportionate degree of uncertainties, but several reassuring factors are surfacing for defense planners on both sides that should be encouraged in détente policy. First, only a major technological breakthrough will provide the type of decisive power initially commanded by nuclear energy, the gunpowder, or crossbow. Even the aggregate technological assets of the most industrialized country can no longer provide sufficient power to permit unilateral or arbitrary change in the political status quo—only temporary, localized advantages can now be expected from technological prowess. Despite the layman's hope that the space age will produce a military panacea, no Doomsday weapon or ultimate device appears that will bestow upon its possessor the same authority the US enjoyed through its monopoly of atomic energy. The extensive international exchange of scientific data, the complexity of each weapon system and its wide assortment of supporting component elements, the high quality of technical surveillance and intelligence, and the difficulties in testing elaborate systems under combat conditions render breakthroughs and panaceas unlikely.[34]

Advances in the state of the art for such complex systems as the ABM, satellite surveillance, over-the-horizon radar, and synchronous, multichannel global communications stretch the technology gap between the super powers and secondary nuclear powers to a virtually unbridgeable width. During this decade the point has been reached that any combination of lesser states cannot amass sufficient combined force to upset the existing strategic balance. Likewise, no combination of lesser states and a single great power can wield enough military might to force the other great power to act against its interests. This distinct imbalance is likely to persist for the foreseeable future, relegating secondary states to perpetual inferiority but assuring the super powers that their common interests cannot be jeopardized by outsiders through technological miracles.[35]

Technology, the seeming source of ultimate force, may have produced its own inhibitions and constraints through uncertainty about future applications and relationships to national values. Rather than explicit adversary agreements, technology itself may gradually induce an equilibrium whereby arms progressions may be the product of more rational use of resources, without the wastage and uncertainties created by overestimation and alarmist political apprehensions. In this sense technology, by its complexity, may introduce a degree of stability into international politics unattainable through normal diplomatic endeavors.

Another guideline for détente management should be to insure the continued decoupling of international crises to the point that linkage does not exacerbate the perceived threat. Local solutions for local problems should be encouraged. Yet the relevance of issues of importance to external powers in the broad negotiating process cannot be ignored. The great powers will continue occasionally to employ the tactic of pressing advantages in one confrontation for benefits in other areas. (See chapter 18.)

Soviet Conceptualization of Détente

Still another guideline for Western planners relates to an assessment of the Soviet perception of détente. With the emerging US-Chinese rapprochement, Moscow must now calculate the impact of any détente measure with the West on its relations with China and Eastern Europe. It no longer enjoys, and will probably never recover, its former unitary posture, whereby any détente move could be carefully couched to prevent an erosion of stability in its primary security zones in Asia and Europe. Now Soviet calculus about stability and détente is likely to be even more deliberate than in the past, both because of the uncertainty of allied reactions and the magnitude of moves now necessary to delineate further the normalization process. This insecurity and uncertainty place specific and absolute limits on the degree of Soviet engagement with the West. As presently constituted, the Soviet model for socialist development cannot accept ideological coexistence or free ideological competition with the West. Until the legitimizing process is complete, ideology will remain the indispensable instrument for justifying continued one party rule and the perpetuation of Communist authority.

The Soviets do not have a word or expression that resembles the Western understanding of the term *détente.* The Soviet conceptualization of this process is known as *peaceful coexistence.* As originally expounded in 1954 and practiced since, the concept of peaceful coexistence is a mandate for the continued advancement of the socialist revolution. The economic, political, and ideological aspects of the struggle are to be aggressively pursued. Only those policies that might lead to a military confrontation are proscribed. The present Soviet leaders no longer insist that war is inevitable between the two systems, and are confident that without the chaos of a general war history will dictate the inevitable domination of socialism. From this basic position two stereotyped interpretations of the present détente atmosphere have been voiced. One consistent theme is that détente is a result of the moral, political, and military decline in the West. The changing nature of the world forces in favor of the Soviet Union is the result of the growing economic and military power of the USSR in comparison with the West.[36]

The second theme is that ideological warfare must be sharpened to preserve the benefits of socialism. Brezhnev, for example, specifically reminded the Soviet people after the 1972 Summit Conference of the importance of ideological vigilance.

> We approached the Soviet-American summit talks . . . from positions affirming the principle of peaceful co-existence of states. . . . In striving for the affirmation of the principle of peaceful coexistence, we realize that successes in this important area in no way signify the possibility of relaxing the ideological struggle. On the contrary, we must be prepared for this struggle to be intensified, for it to become an increasingly crucial form of the confrontation between the two social systems. We have no doubt about the outcome of this confrontation, since the truth of history and objective laws of social development are on our side.[37]

It is shortsighted to expect the Soviets to one day cease behaving either like Russians or like Communists. They will not. And herein lies their greatest vulnerability, and leverage for Western bargainers. Paradoxically, the Russian state system and Soviet Communist model have become the guarantors of traditionalism, not change and progress. Difficulties in adjusting to the requirement of modernization have compounded the Soviets' earlier insecurity within the Socialist world. The Soviet threat to the Free World should no longer be assessed only in terms of military forces and hardware capabilities, but in the ability of the Soviet leadership to deliver a consensus and united front among its allies and supporters; the success of their ability to compartmentalize foreign policy. The search for moral support has been one of the strongest constraints in the post-Stalinist leadership. And it is likely to remain a source of major concern for an insecure ruling elite. The West should capitalize on this weakness. Not by exploiting Soviet hegemony through direct Dullesian assaults. The West should reserve as nonnegotiable those issues that hold out the prospects for inducing change in the Soviet sphere. This change need no longer be defined as the overthrow of the ruling elite, but as an amelioration of human conditions for those who seek higher standards. How this can be achieved without compounding Soviet insecurity will be the most difficult task in the détente process. The degree of success will determine the extent to which the détente leads to a genuine normalization of relations between the great powers. In the foreseeable future, however, the Soviet side will maintain its ideological competition as the absolute boundary of détente beyond which no cooperation will be tolerated. Ideology is probably the most perceptible limit to the détente process.

Détente Diplomacy

A final guideline for the management of the détente process is that the West, especially the US, must rationalize its détente policy. To date this policy has been largely negative, following the path of least resistance. The required greater rationalization should include a Western definition of normalization of relations, not merely the tacit acceptance of Moscow's formula for peaceful coexistence. This rationalization should also include an itemization of general areas where accommodation is most feasible and those aspects of the military confrontation that can be prudently reduced and yet contribute to an improved atmosphere. Further national values and interests should be categorized for specific status quo issues and an attempt should be made to estimate the opponent's. Each categorization then could be coupled with the mode of diplomacy and other bargaining counters best suited for its attainment. The linkage of these issues and interests together into an interconnected strategy would be more systematic and self-protecting. Such a strategy might be called *détente diplomacy,* as opposed to nonspecialized operational diplomacy dealing with more routine problems, and could be wisely institutionalized as a separate division of foreign ministries. The function of such a structure would be to steer and participate in ongoing negotiations, while attempting to oversee and ascertain the dimensions of the normalization process. Such an undertaking would be awesome indeed. For as Adam Ulam has observed, the mechanics of détente as used by the West—attempting to educate the opponent about one's ultimate values, while trying to assess his—is antithetical to the Soviet mentality. From the Soviet view, principles and their parameters are never subject to negotiation. It is desirable for the opponent to reveal his, but what is at stake lies between the two limits.[38] However logical this prescription of sound bargaining appears, it is frequently overlooked in the West. Yet this is the best definition of the outer expanses of détente—and the course of its management:neither side in a position of rough parity can be expected to compromise its higher values or principles.

Stability in an international system, groping for accommodation and a definition of normalization of state relations, prescribes acceptance of both the positive contributions of the détente process and its specific limitations. It is no longer realistic to expect that normal relations between contending states can be predicated upon peace as prescribed by legal documents. Systemic stability and regulated relations (a more accurate term) require adjustment among the participants along lines suggested above for détente management. Accommodation will not be complete and will remain imperfect—it can pertain only to issues and not values. Systemic stability, then, will remain subject to a wide variety of variables. Its precarious nature will persist because the variables relate to the participants' highest priority national interests. Balance can only be maintained by enhancing the cobweb effect of enmeshing participants in an ever widening range of issues.

Implications for US Policy

What do these developments mean for the future of US foreign policy, and how can their implications be translated to more specific policy guidance and directives? How do they relate to the changing global system of state behavior and the American domestic interests and pressures, and how specifically do they effect such tendencies as isolationism? Again to reverse the parallelism, the answers to the latter questions facilitate those of the former.

It seems clear from the subsequent discussion that the term *splendid isolation,* discussed in chapter 1, is no longer applicable or descriptive of the recent examples of US disengagement. As the disengagement process continues, it becomes increasingly urgent to analyze the phenomenon and its policy implications, and to devise a conceptual framework that can provide long-term methodological tools for more systematic assessment. The urgency of the task is intensified because the disengagement process witnessed during the first four years of the Nixon Administration was the result of expedient compromises between contradictory pressures that were not adequately handled. Either domestic considerations or changing international circumstances forced decisions that perpetuated or accelerated the process. The second Nixon four-year term will probably be characterized as a minimal crises era: the post-Vietnam, post-Suez, post-Berlin period, when SALT II and MBFR will be the most complex issues under negotiation and the normalization phenomenon itself will be the subject of general international attention. An improved conceptual framework, plus the systemic reorganization outlined in chapter 18 and the administrative improvements suggested above, together should reduce the prospects of engaging in hasty undertakings and should improve the chances for preserving the initiatives the US already enjoys.

Hans Morganthau has observed that the present public debate over the appropriate US position in the world is as intense and vital as such debates twenty-five years ago and covers generally the same issues.[39] The debate is not characterized as neoisolationism, for which no definition has yet been devised. By implication it is widely understood to mean that the US is now considering cutting its foreign commitments and returning to narrow nationalism; that it is pondering a withdrawal from coalition politics and resurrecting nonengagement; that it is deliberating on whether to scuttle its present respect for the national interests of its allies and to reinstitute messianic democracy. But such assumptions are clearly too simplistic. The nation has felt trapped by its overengagement and has sought both compromises on issues of lesser importance and a limited adjustment with its adversaries, until it can define more succinctly the delineations between overengagement and appropriate involvement. This examination process does not call for a rejection of coalition politics and explicit commitments, it calls for a reassessment of goals and their implementation, as well as a reconsideration of the basic questions that led to the establishment of involvement and coalitions. The results are not likely to be a rejection of special relationships or their aims, but modifications of both that will preserve interests while limiting obligations.

Because of the nature of the American system, these results will probably emerge as a notion, rather than a broad design on a Gaullist scale. The US governmental system has been characterized by Henry Kissinger as consisting mainly of trained lawyers and businessmen who employ case study techniques and precedents or the manipulation of knowledge to achieve this or that answer to highly complex problems. This propensity fosters ad hoc solutions and pragmatic diplomacy, rather than perceptive plans and reflective implementation that acknowledges the nation's role in the historic process.[40]

While no comprehensive solution seems probable, several generalizations have crystallized that are likely to orient further examinations. First, it is now widely accepted that the great powers are likely to remain competitive indefinitely, but the sources of challenge have shifted in the West's view from ideology to influence and strategic advantage. This shift of emphasis does not eliminate the nation's security requirements; it makes them somewhat harder to fulfill in the public's view since they no longer reflect the traditional form of threat. Vietnam and Czechoslovakia have convinced both great powers of the onus of having to act unilaterally to advance their interests; both are likely to increase their efforts to preserve multilateral support for international undertakings. This process has compelled both great powers not merely to limited retrenchment at home, but to an active pursuit of a program to *prevent isolation* on key issues. It is the nature of this accelerated activity to prevent isolation, not the desire to reduce entanglements and increase self-reliance, that has resulted in the diminution of overengagement or reallocation of national priorities. Divergences are likely to persist in the two sides' general techniques for precluding isolation. The USSR will continue to seek agreement on specific issues that will consolidate the status quo in regions where its influence is vulnerable or in those that will contribute to its overall economic prosperity. On more controversial issues, Moscow will probably cling to the Krushchevian concept of peaceful coexistence, which emphasized opportunism and prescribed distance from adversaries in the advancement of socialism and Soviet national interests. For

its part, the West is likely to accept the Soviet agenda on specific issues and overlook the competitive nature of peaceful coexistence, in the hope that solutions
to concrete political and economic problems will contribute to the general improvement in relations. While these are mainly trends and atmospherics, it is
widely believed that they will expand our still nebulous understanding of
normalization of relations.[41] Finally, the US is likely to tailor its anti-isolation
notions to the idea that limited engagement should be designed to encourage an
expansion of mutual interests within the more viable coalitions. Groupings such
as CENTO, SEATO, and to a lesser extent OAS have suffered from a mutual
attrition of interests that were the result of many international factors, not
merely a lack of US interest, and here Washington is likely to seize the opportunity to delineate its obligations more explicitly.

Limited Engagement and
Controlled Liabilities

Based on these assumptions, the concept of limited engagement deserves
further elaboration. The United States has become an integral part of the worldwide changes that created new balances and new patterns of change itself. The
US drawdown in SEA opened an entirely new spectrum of relations with friends
and former enemies. The US acceptance of China's role in the new power constellation was an acknowledgment of the futility of its containment policy
against Peking. The US initiative with China encouraged the latter to assume
a unique role between the "have" and the "have-not" nations, and to contribute
to problems between these nations in a respectable and responsible manner. The
US initiative has forced the USSR onto the defensive in this quarter, which will
require redoubled efforts to assure Soviet national interests in this region. Soviet,
Chinese, and American interests on virtually every international issue are subject
to shift; they are neither consistently parallel, complementary, nor contradictory. Moreover, the Nixon visit to Peiping altered relations with Japan and
changed Tokyo's perception of its own role in Asian affairs. After a period of
psychological adjustment, Japan is likely to recognize the disparity in its security
needs and its dependence upon US strategic protection. It may soon recognize
that it is in a unique position to exploit the discrepancy between economic
strength and modest military posture to erect a political stature commensurate
with its national ambitions.

In the Third World the US has now generally accepted that the modernization process has inherent merits itself, and that modernity should receive higher
priority over unabashed influence competition. Indeed, the commitment to
progress toward the technological revolution, integration of communities, and
efficiency of government may become one of the most important single factors
in overall influence competition, which may offset the paucity of US public
funds allocated for this purpose.

Ostpolitik is the most significant German bid for independence since the Second World War. It has already contributed more to Germany's national stature than de Gaulle's quest for grandeur did for France. On the other hand, Britain's entry into the EEC was a demonstration of interdependency, with far-reaching economic, political, and military implications. Both of these developments had strong US support, yet both indirectly contributed to the dollar crisis and the deterioration of the international monetary situation. These movements in Europe have afforded the US only its minimum demands for regional stability. It has lost, probably irretrievably, its leverage on the question of a European peace settlement, while the Soviets have largely achieved their terms. This discrepancy is not pressing under the present level of détente. But should conditions change, i.e., a more assertive Soviet posture, a restive Eastern Europe, or a Finlandized Western Europe developed, the US will have to devise alternative means for protecting its interests. In the past, the Potsdam Agreement and the pending peace treaty were always available to coerce the Soviets. Now other instruments such as troop strengths will have to be used, and such innovations may be perceived by the other side as provocative and destabilizing.

The main reason for concern in this area is the growing sense of alarm among the West Europeans. During the first six years of the Nixon Administration, US policy became increasing competitive with allies and more cooperative with adversaries. General concern is now experssed that the US government has become unpredictable, detached, and deliberate. For example, the 1972 Summit Conference has been called the most important East-West development since the beginning of containment in 1947.[42] Earlier summit conferences had been largely ceremonial or probes and tests of will. The present vintage of summit meetings, however, are genuine working sessions, as evidenced by the number of "spectacular" announcements and accords, including those, such as the Bilateral Code of Behavior, which aggrieved our allies. The Europeans are aware of this change, and fear deals may be made at their expense in order to keep the working nature alive during periods of otherwise barren productivity. US accommodation of, not indifference to, these sensitivities is essential.

Military détente measures completed or under way to date indicate greatpower confidence in their supremacy over smaller states and a desire to rationalize and economize on security matters. Discussions and negotiations on strategic affairs are rapidly becoming institutionalized, providing an element of stability and dependent interests, if not general security. At the same time most major states are devoting increasing attention to domestic problems. The days when national security was regarded as "high policy" and domestic matters as "low policy" are over; the order has been reversed.

The US must participate actively in the attempts to institutionalize the détente process. At present the West has no agreed understanding of détente or normalized relations, and is in danger of gradually accepting Soviet terms of peaceful coexistence by default. Both sides, however, share the view that modernization of Eastern Europe should increase stability and ultimately the humanization of the partition of Europe. The major dispute is over defining the level and scope of Western involvement in this process. Full Western participation in various institutions created to provide a dialogue on such issues would contribute to a clarification of intentions and constraints in this area. There should be little fear that the Soviets will be able to exploit such a dialogue for the purpose of projecting a positive image as a constructive power in Europe. The Soviets cannot enhance their influence in the West much beyond its present level except on the West's terms e.g., accepting a conventional understanding of normalization, or a deterioration of Western political will and an invitation for Finlandization. On the former terms, the humanization of Europe's partition, growing East European ideological vigilance is likely to check any significant Soviet moves.

The degree of US involvement in these changes is less important than the implications for future policy. Did US participation increase its commitments to the progress or stability on each development? Has the somewhat stronger US foreign policy position emerging from its involvement in these developments enhanced its interests in these selected changes? Are there greater obligations now than before to insure stability and the fruition of these initiatives? Or were US actions in each designed to increase its freedom of action in the international arena? Does the increase in the number of issues under review necessarily expand US commitments to the world community? Did the US become simultaneously more eclectic in the number of countries of primary concern and expansive in the number of issues under advisement with a view to ultimately reducing its total foreign profile and commitments?

It is too early to draw clear conclusions. But this line of questioning suggests that as the détente process began to produce a degree of security and stability, the US was able to contract its attention abroad (as the Soviets did in the early 1960s), and to focus it more sharply on priority topics. This shift was, of course, partly fortuitous. But it afforded opportunities to formulate new initiatives that necessarily imparted new responsibilities for their satisfactory conclusion. This contraction/expansion phenomenon was part of the general anti-isolation notion. It was viewed as a contribution to normalization that would reduce the prospect of rising tensions and the necessity for anti-isolation coalitions. It is also safe to assume that American leaders regarded it as the most facile method of intensifying US involvement on selected issues to the point that a broader disengagement could be safely executed.

This speculation leads to further questions. What should be the criteria for overengagement? When and how can the line be drawn between overengagement and limited involvement? Is it plausible to make such distinctions by countries and issues, between spheres of influence and functional problems? In other words, how does one stake out the perimeters of limited involvement? The first criterion should be that no international problem or issue is now worth nuclear war or the risk of a great-power confrontation. Crises that impart such risks must be avoided. Second, the 1960s indicated that the results of local conflicts were usually determined by the strength and skill of locally engaged forces rather than the external influences of even the most heavily committed great powers. This was true for Indonesia, the Congo, Nigeria, the Sudan, the Yemen, the Arab-Israeli conflicts, and the Indo-Pakistan struggles. Only occasionally has great-power presence on the spot been decisive, i.e., in Czechoslovakia, the Sino-Indian border war, the Dominican Republic intervention. Thus, in a majority of cases, external influence has seldom produced the desired results and often cost substantial treasure and prestige. Physical intervention abroad should now be confined to instances when there is a clear and present danger to vital American interests. And the US if possible should not act alone.

A third criterion stems from the nature of foreign influence itself. As the trend toward multipolarity increases, smaller states have generally been able to increase the number of options available to them on given issues. Even more than in the past, foreign influence is now exercised at the whims and pleasure of the recipient state—Czechoslovakia was a rare exception. In most other cases, foreign influence was encouraged, channeled, or terminated at the discretion of the host government. The now standard forms of influence, economic assistance and military aid, have seldom produced the desired ends and have often created unwanted results, except when strong common grounds existed. Accordingly, involvement should be limited to instances when there is a clear sense of shared interests and mutual benefit. In other words, the US should avoid crises in which it may become more determined and committed than the local ally—an application of limited liability.

A fourth standard relates to the futility of forceful threats. Paradoxically, it is probably as difficult to translate military posturing and threats into effective political influence as any of the other forms of influence. The threat of violence implies punitive coercion, but does not always humble deviant opponents. In gunboat diplomacy a gunboat is exactly as effective as an aircraft carrier, and the relative numbers of warships soon become irrelevant. Further, local compliance usually lasts only until the warship steams away. The USSR is building its naval power on the assumption that its influence abroad will grow proportionately to the credibility of military deterrence and physical presence. Twenty years of experience with the Sixth Fleet in the Mediterranean, however, reveals that the US has greatest influence among those Arab countries not visited by the Fleet, and that a powerful presence has had no impact on a political climate that prohibits US presence in Arab waters. Therefore, involvements that risk the use of "compellence" or coercion should be held to the barest minimum.

A fifth standard is an amplification of the notion of limited liability. In the past the US assumed that effective deterrence stemmed from indivisible collective security, that the US commitment to strategic defense was credible and reliable, and that this commitment itself was decisive. Nowhere, except in its own defense, is the US commitment by itself conclusive. This necessarily imposes an upper limit on the expectations of the involvement/deterrence formula. Even in Japan and Europe, it is now conceivable that the US can safely reduce its commitment to deterrence. It is certain that the US will not set these two entities adrift, but it is uncertain what level of deterrence is now appropriate. This uncertainty alone contributes to deterrence, but it is also subject to miscalculation and is therefore dangerous. New limits of involvement should be predicated upon the recipient's commitment and determination that would permit a complementary US involvement.

A last criterion should center on cooperation and self-help. There has always been a strong tradition in American foreign policy stressing the need for self-help in solving local problems. The Alliance for Progress was but one example. Vietnam tended to negate this factor; the US manifested an imperial will that was contradictory to self-help. The degree of cooperation that can be expected from future commitments is likely to be directly related to the legitimacy of the ally's interests that the US recognizes. If for limited liability reasons the US rejects an ally's national interests, it must also limit its involvement accordingly. It can no longer assume responsibility for interests of another state that it regards as onerous or unacceptable. The best measure of the level of involvement is the degree of mutual and reciprocal cooperation experienced on a pragmatic basis.

It remains then to determine if possible whether the Nixon Doctrine will survive the present administration; whether it will provide a generation of peace, as its proponents argue. After the series of domestic scandals and the constant conflict between the presidency and Congress, a Democratic victory in 1976 seems probable, despite the paucity of charismatic leaders. Middle America now appears disillusioned, and the Democratic party may be able to swing its appeal back to the center of the political spectrum. At the time of writing, however, a change of guards is unlikely to result in radical reorientation in foreign policy; the Kennedy days are over. The détente process is likely to develop a logic of its own that will make sudden alterations difficult. Both great powers are likely to increase their stakes in the stability of the system, and to experience unconscious mutations in their concepts of foreign policy and international behavior that will increasingly resemble the characteristics of each other. Richard Nixon is likely to concede points to the opponent if necessary to insure the firm grounding of his Doctrine while he can still control its development. The détente process will gradually remove the burning foreign policy issues, and the Democrats may focus national attention on domestic affairs. Drift could come to characterize US foreign policy, and the detrimental features of the Doctrine, such as reverse interdependence, could rapidly become counterproductive. If this outline is reasonably accurate, it is clear that the time to tackle the more controversial features of the Doctrine is before, not after, the present Administration leaves office.

A historic turning has taken place: the US has fought its last colonial war and is terminating its hegemonic globalism. The emerging strategies and policies will, as before, reflect public mood and temper. It remains to be seen whether they will register maturity, perspective, responsibility or naiveté, self-centeredness, and indifference. A policy of limited involvement and selected engagement, tailored to reduce unwanted liabilities but to preclude unacceptable isolation, is likely to meet both national priorities and public expectations. This book is intended not as a clarion call for national mobilization, or even a stimulant for greater public awareness. It is offered merely as a modest contribution to the continuing public debate about our national policies—a debate that affects some more than others, and most of all those who are prepared to commit themselves to the debate.

Notes

PART I
Chapter 1
The Crisis in Contemporary American Foreign Policy

1. *US Foreign Policy for the 1970's: A New Strategy for Peace.* A Report to Congress, 18 Feb. 1970, p. 2.
2. *US Foreign Policy for the 1970's: The Emerging Structure of Peace.* A Report to Congress, 9 Feb. 1972, p. 13.
3. Kissinger, Henry A., "Central Issues of American Foriegn Policy," in Kermit Gordon, ed., *Agenda for the Nation,* 1968, pp. 589, 599.
4. Pipes, Richard, "America, Russia and Europe in Light of the Nixon Doctrine," *Survey,* vol. 19, no. 3 (88) Summer 1973, p. 31.
5. *US Foreign Policy Report to Congress,* 1970, p. 3.
6. Kissinger, Henry A., *A World Restored: Metternich, Castlereach and the Problems of Peace 1812-1822,* 1957.
7. *US Foreign Policy Report to Congress,* 1972, pp. 8-9.

Chapter 2
Washington's New Look at Latin America

1. US Department of Commerce, *Survey of Current Business,* October 1970; North American Congress on Latin America, *New Chile,* 1972. The preceding Christian Democratic government of President Frei had already nationalized 51 percent of the largest copper mines and was planning a total takeover. Allende accelerated the process and intensified charges of malpractices as grounds for nonpayment of remunerations.
2. *US Foreign Policy Report for the 1970s,* 3 May 1973, pp. 42-43.

Chapter 3
American Interests in the Middle East

1. See this author's *The Canal War; Four Power Conflict in the Middle East,* MIT Press, 1974.
2. For the most detailed peace proposal yet, see Rafael, Amnon E., "A Proposal for Peace in the Middle East," *Orbis,* Spring 1972.

3. *International Herald Tribune*, 28 July 1972.

Chapter 5
Vietnam: Elbe or Waterloo?

1. See "Responses to National Security Study Memorandum 1, February 1969," *Washington Post*, 25 April 1972.
2. See the debate on this question contained in Summer 1972 issue of *Foreign Policy*.
3. Bundy, McGeorge, "Prospects for the 1970s: The 20th Stevenson Memorial Lecture," *World Today*, February 1972.
4. Interview with *L'Express*, Paris, 7 May 1972.
5. Interview in *International Herald Tribune*, 27 July 1972.
6. TASS, 18 June 1972.

Chapter 6
The Chinese Puzzle: Maelstrom or Utopia?

1. See the entire July 1972 issue of *Annals* "China in the World Today," including Melby, "Maoism as a World Force," p. 26.
2. Mehnert, Klaus, *China nach dem Sturm*, 1972.
3. Ravenal, Earl, "Approaching China: Defending Taiwan," *Foreign Affairs*, October 1971.
4. *New York Times*, 26 May 1972.
5. Press interview, *USIS Bulletin* No. 116, 20 June 1972.
6. Interview, *New York Times*, 7 August 1972. © 1972 by the New York Times Company. Reprinted by permission.

Chapter 7
Japan: Further American Retrenchment?

1. See *US Foreign Policy Report to Congress*, February, 1972.
2. Brzezinski, Zbigniew, *The Fragile Blossom: Crisis and Change in Japan*, 1972.
3. Buchan, Alastair, "Power Relationships in the Far East: A European View," *Survival*, May-June 1972.

Chapter 8
Appraising Ostpolitik and the Political Adjustments in Central Europe

1. Interview in *L'Express*, reprinted in *Bulletin des Presse und Informationsamtes der Bundesregierung* (Bonn) (hereafter cited as *Bulletin*), 15 December 1970.
2. *Die Welt*, 28 January and 18 February; *Telegraf*, 8 March; *Frankfurter Allgemeine Zeitung*, 19 May; *Die Zeit*, 29 May 1970.

3. See Foreign Minister Walter Scheel's extensive argumentation, *Frankfurter Allgemeine Zeitung,* 15 July 1970.
4. *Die Welt,* 12 August;and *Bulletin,* 4 August 1970.
5. *Bulletin,* 10 March 1970.
6. "Perspectives of the Alliance," Speech at the WEU Assembly, *Survival,* February 1970, p. 43.
7. Fritz Ermath, *Internationalism, Security and Legitimacy: The Challenge to Soviet Interests in East Europe, 1964-1968,* The RAND Corporation, RM-5909-PR, March 1969. See also this author's *Germany's Ostpolitik: Relations Between the Federal Republic and the Warsaw Pact Countries,* 1971.

Chapter 9
Western Europe: FRG–EEC–US

1. Brzezinski, Zbigniew, *Alternative to Partition,* 1965, p. 4; also George Ball, *The Discipline of Power,* 1968.
2. The three levels of Ostpolitik negotiations, as outlined by Helmut Schmidt, "Germany in the Era of Negotiations," *Foreign Affairs,* October 1970, p. 46, and Theo Sommer, "Bonn's New *Ostpolitik,"* *Journal of International Affairs,* p. 66, are (1) East Germany, (2) Eastern Europe, and (3) Soviet Union.
3. *Die Welt,* 6 May 1971.
4. Ibid.
5. Interview in *German International,* June 1971, p. 10.
6. Kissinger, Henry A., "A New Atlantic Charter," *Survival,* July/August 1973.
7. Brandt, Willy, "Europe's New Self-Awareness," *New York Times,* 29 April 1973.
8. Kissinger, Henry A., *op. cit.*

PART II
Introduction

1. Coffey, Joseph I., "Deterrence in the 1970s," 1971.

Chapter 10
Strategic Parity: The Impact of the Loss of Assured Destruction on NATO Nuclear Policy

1. For complete texts and accompanying documents see *Atlantic Community Quarterly,* Fall 1972.
2. *US Foreign Policy Report to the US Congress,* 3 May 1973, p. 62.
3. *The Military Balance,* 1972-73, IISS, pp. 84-85.

4. *US Foreign Policy Report,* p. 63.
5. *The Military Balance,* p. 85. (Given a limited MRV capability.)
6. For a layman's discussion of the relationship between yield and accuracy see *Strategic Survey,* 1969, IISS, pp. 30-33.
7. *Strategic Survey,* 1972, p. 18.
8. *Military Balance 1972-73,* p. 6.
9. General Holloway, House Armed Services Committee, 92 Congress, Hearings on Military Posture, Part 71, p. 2922, and General Ryan, *Ibid.,* p. 3537.
10. *Military Manpower Requirements Report for 1973,* Senate Armed Services Committee, 92 Congress, Fiscal Year 1973 Authorization Part 2, p. 1193, and Part 6, pp. 3500-541.
11. Polmer, Norman, "The Soviet Naval Threat: Alarmist versus Realist," *The Atlantic Community Quarterly,* Fall 1972.
12. Newhouse, John, *Cold Dawn: The Story of SALT,* 1973.
13. Victor Louis, a Soviet journalist with close Kremlin contacts, *London Evening News,* 19 June 1973.
14. Gallois, Pierre M., "Power and Paralysis," *Orbis,* Fall 1967, pp. 664-76.
15. Aron, Raymond, "De Gaulle and Kennedy: The Nuclear Debate," *The Atlantic Monthly,* August 1962, p. 37; also General André Beaufré, *Deterrence and Strategy,* 1966, pp. 78-86; and Herbert Luthy, "De Gaulle Pose and Policy," *Foreign Affairs,* July 1965, pp. 561-73; André Fontaine, "What is French Policy," *Foreign Affairs,* October 1966, pp. 58-76; William Pickles, "Making Sense of De Gaulle," *International Affairs,* July 1966, pp. 410-20; Guy de Carmoy, "The Last Year of De Gaulle's Foreign Policy," *International Affairs,* July 1969, pp. 424-35.
16. Coffey, J.I., "Strategy, Alliance Policy, and Nuclear Proliferation," *Orbis,* Winter 1968, pp. 990.
17. Kissinger, Henry, *The Troubled Partnership,* 1965, p. 54.
18. Wohlstetter, Albert, "Strengths, Interest and New Technologies," *The Implications of Military Technology in 1970's,* Adelphi Papers, No. 46, IISS, March 1968, pp. 1-14; and Robert J. Lieber, "The French Nuclear Force," *International Affairs,* July 1966, pp. 421-31.
19. Brown, Neville, "Deterrence from the Sea," *Survival,* June 1970, pp. 194-98.
20. Combaux, Edmond General, "French Military Policy and European Federalism," *Orbis,* Spring 1969, pp. 144-59; and F.O. Mitsche, "Western Europe: Security Through Integration," Ibid., pp. 160-69.
21. *US Foreign Policy Report,* 1973, p. 61.
22. Halperin, Morton H., *Defense Strategies for the Seventies,* 1971, p. 72.
23. Marshall, A.W., *Long-Term Competition with the Soviets: A Framework for Strategic Analysis,* RAND Corp. R-862-PR, April 1972.
24. Wohlstetter, Albert, "Is There a Strategic Arms Race," (manuscript in the author's possession), is a revealing statement of inaccuracies in the action-reaction presumption about arms competitions.
25. Marshall, op. cit.

Chapter 11
Parity in Theater Level Forces

1. Assistant Secretary of Defense, Alain C. Enthoven, "Review of a Systems Analysis Evaluation of NATO vs. Warsaw Pact Conventional Forces," Report of Special Subcommittee on National Defense Posture of the House Committee on Armed Service, 90th Congress, 2nd Session, 1968.
2. Healey, Dennis W., "On European Defense" Address delivered to the Sixth International Wehrkunde Meeting, Munich, 2 February 1969, *Survival,* April 1969, pp. 110-11.
3. *Military Balance,* 1972-73, p. 89.
4. Ibid., p. 88.
5. Enthoven, Alain C., "What Forces for NATO," *Foreign Affairs,* October 1969, p. 87; also Carl Kaysen in *Agenda for the Nation,* Kermit Gordon, ed., 1968, p. 569.
6. Pierre, Andrew J., "Implications of the Western Response to the Soviet Intervention in Czechoslovakia," *The Atlantic Community Quarterly,* Spring 1969, p. 65.
7. Ibid., p. 67.
8. *Military Balance,* p. 72.
9. Whetten, Lawrence L., "Legal Basis for the Soviet Military Presence in Czechoslovakia," *Revue du droit international,* Nov.-Dec. 1969.
10. See *Military Balance,* 1971-1972; and F.R.G. Defense White Paper, 1972, Bonn.
11. Brown, Neville, *European Security, 1972-1980,* RUSI, 1972, p. 67.
12. Mackintosh, Malcom, *The Evolution of the Warsaw Pact,* Adelphi Papers, No. 58, June 1969.
13. See this author's *Germany's Ostpolitik: Relations Between the Federal Republic and the Warsaw Pact Countries,* 1971, Chapter 3.
14. Wohlstetter, Albert, "Is There a Strategic Arms Race" (in the author's possession).
15. Sokolovski, V.C., *Military Strategy,* 1963.
16. Canby, Steven L., "NATO Muscle: More Shadow than Substance," *Foreign Policy,* Fall 1972.

Chapter 12
The Arrival of Naval Parity

1. McGwire, Michael, "Soviet Naval Capabilities and Intentions," in *The Soviet Union in Europe and the Near East,* Royal Union Services Institute (RUSI), London, 1970, p. 35. See also Wolfe, Thomas, *Soviet Strategy at the Crossroads,* Harvard University Press, 1964, pp. 118-29; and Cox, D.R., "Soviet Power and Soviet Foreign Policy," *U.S. Naval Institute Proceedings,* June 1969, pp. 298-99; *Le Monde,* 25 December 1969; and Admiral Moorer's Interview in *US News and World Report,* 1 December 1969.
2. Ibid., p. 37. See also Robert W. Herrick, *Soviet Naval Strategy,* 1968.

3. Coyle, Malcolm W., V. Adm., "Task Force 77 in Action Off Vietnam," *Proceedings US Naval Institute,* May 1972, pp. 128-41.
4. If deficiencies occurred, they were probably improved four months later when the Soviets sucessfully orbited Molniya I, their first communications satellite.
5. *Proceedings US Naval Institute,* May 1971, p. 348; see also B.C. Cuthbertson, "The Significance of the Northern Gap," *Journal of the Royal United Services Institute,* June 1972, pp. 45-48; F.P.U., Croker, "Iceland and the Maritime Threat," Ibid., and *Strategic Survey 1971,* pp. 26-29.
6. Weinland, Robert G., "The Changing Mission of the Soviet Navy," *Survival,* May-June 1972, p. 132.
7. *Proceedings,* May 1971, p. 341.
8. The ratio of on-station to cruise time for the relatively short-range Soviet missile submarines has had a critical impact upon both the SALT deliberations and restrict deployment of advanced systems, and on Soviet determination to develop long-range (4,000+ nm) submerged launched missiles.
9. Brown, Neville. "Soviet Naval Expansion—The Global Scene Assessed," *New Middle East,* March 1971, pp. 19-20; also *Soviet Sea Power,* The Center for Strategic and International Studies, Georgetown University, 1969; see also *UN Statistical Yearbook,* 1969, p. 370; and Geoffrey Jukes's citation of official Soviet statistics in *The Indian Ocean in Soviet Naval Policy,* Adelphi Papers, No. 87, May 1972.
10. Dadant, P.M., *American and Soviet Defense Systems vis-a-vis the Middle East,* Rand Corp. P-4352, July 1970, p. 14; also J.C. Hurewitz, *Changing Military Perspectives in the Middle East,* RAND Corp. RM-6355, September 1970; and Robert E. Athay, "The Sea and Soviet Domestic Transportation," *Proceedings,* May 1972, pp. 159-77.
11. Erickson, John, "The Soviet Naval High Command," *Proceedings,* May 1973, p. 84. Copyright © 1973 U.S. Naval Institute.
12. *A Soviet History of Naval Warfare 1970,* reviewed by P.H. Vigor, RUSI Research Bulletin, RUSI Journal, June 1971, p. 40.
13. Cable, John, *Gunboat Diplomacy: Political Applications of Limited Naval Force,* 1971.

Chapter 13
Toward a NATO Tactical Doctrine for the 1970s

1. Kissinger, Henry A., *The Necessity of Choice,* 1960, pp. 14 and 18; also Marc E. Geneste, "Britain, France and the Defense of Europe," *Orbis,* Spring 1969, p. 183.
2. Cameron, Robert, Vice Air Marshal RCAF, "Options Make Good Propaganda but Poor Defense for NATO," *NATO's Fifteen Nations,* June-July 1970, p. 23.
3. Kissinger, Henry A., "A New Atlantic Charter," *Survival,* July-August 1973, p. 191.

4. For details see Secretary McNamara's speech to the New York Economic Club, 18 November 1963.

5. Weizzecher, Karl Friedrich von, ed., *Kriegsfolgen und Kriegsverhütung*, Munich, 1971.

6. The erroneousness of this assumption is revealed by the fact that most outbreaks of hostilities since 1945 (some 160 or 210, depending upon criteria) have remained subtotal, with the main exceptions of the two Communist invasions of South Korea and South Vietnam. Local and international restraints or limitations on objectives have usually been respected. It can be argued that such constraints would probably be at least as intensive in Europe as elsewhere. Yet the testimony of former Deputy Secretary of Defense Roswell Gilpatric still has a lingering impact: "I, for one, have never believed in a so-called limited nuclear war. I just don't know how you build a limit into it once you start using any kind of a nuclear bang." (Quoted by Henry Kissinger, "NATO's Nuclear Dilemma," *The Reporter*, 28 March 1963, p. 24.) At any rate, the urgency of the West's new security requirements dictates that more convincing evidence be presented to support the danger of automatic escalation.

7. Shreffler, R.G., and W.S. Bennett, *Tactical Nuclear Warfare*, Los Alamos Scientific Laboratory, LA-4467-MS, June 1970.

8. Lawrence, Robert M., "On Tactical Nuclear War," *Revue Militaire Générale*, February 1971, p. 238.

9. Stanley, Timothy W., "A Strategic Doctrine for NATO in the 1970's," *Orbis*, Spring 1970, p. 92.

10. Cleveland, Harlan, "NATO After the Invasion," *Foreign Affairs*, January 1969, pp. 253-55.

11. Cornford, E.C., "Technology and the Battlefield," *The Implications of Military Technology in the 1970's*, Adelphi Papers, No. 46, March 1968, p. 48; also Alastair Buchan, "NATO and European Security," *Orbis*, Spring 1969, p. 74.

12. For more detailed elaboration of these ideas, see Robert M. Lawrence, "On Tactical Nuclear War," *Revue Militaire Générale*, January and February 1971.

13. Cited by Samuel T. Cohen, "Tactical Nuclear Weapons and US Military Strategy," *Orbis*, Spring 1971, p. 186.

14. *Strategic Survey*, 1972, pp. 19-22; see also Neville Brown, *European Security 1972-1980*, Royal United Services Institute, 1972, pp. 12-18 and Appendix B.

15. Brown, loc. cit., pp. 142-49; see also the following IISS Adelphi Papers: Robert R. James, *Defense Technology and the Western Alliance*, No. 43, 1967; *Implications of Military Technology in the 1970's*, No. 46, March 1968; Geoffrey Ashcroft, *Military Logistics Systems in NATO*, No. 62, December 1968 and No. 68, June 1970; Erwin Hackel, *Military Manpower and Political Purpose*, No. 72, December 1970; Raymond Vernon, *Multilateral Enterprise and National Security*, No. 74, January 1971; and John Simpson and Frank Gregory, "West European Collaboration in Weapons Procurement," *Orbis*, Summer 1972, pp. 435-61.

16. Andrew J. Pierre, "Implications of the Western Response to the Soviet Intervention of Czechoslovakia," *The Atlantic Community Quarterly,* Spring 1969, pp. 65-66; Harlan Cleveland, *op. cit.,* pp. 251-65; Roberta Wohlstetter, "Cuba and Pearl Harbor: Hindsight and Foresight," *Foreign Affairs,* July 1965, pp. 691-707. The FRG has officially expressed its skepticism about adequate warning; "It would be a fallacy to believe that one could, promptly and at any time, detect a covert buildup of Warsaw Pact forces vis-a-vis NATO . . . ," *FRG Defense White Paper,* 1969, p. 20.
17. It should be noted that the anticipated reduction of US forces in Europe will correspondingly reduce US intelligence collection efforts. Overall NATO intelligence activities will soon shift to the Europeans, a contingency that has not yet been squarely faced.

PART III
Introduction

1. Huntington, Samuel P., "After Containment: The Function of the Military Establishment," *The Annuals of the American Academy of Political and Social Science,* March 1973.
2. Shulman, Marshall D., "What Does Security Mean Today," *Foreign Affairs,* July 1971.

Chapter 14
Progress Toward Military Détente

1. *Department of State Bulletin,* 9 November 1970, p. 573.
2. *Ibid.,* pp. 572-73.
3. *Aviation Week,* 27 September 1971, p. 22.
4. *Ibid.,* 11 October 1971, p. 17.
5. In a related measure, the US announced in 1964 the closure of selected nuclear weapons plants, reducing plutonium production by 20 percent and enriched uranium by 40 percent. The USSR responded by allegedly canceling production of two plutonium plants and curtailing uranium refinement. But the US Atomic Energy Commission reported in November 1965 that no Soviet cutback had been detected. Albert Wohlstetter has demonstrated that the seeming US generosity then was due to the declining military requirements for fissile materials. Since 1959 there has been a steady and substantial reduction in the megatonnage of the US nuclear stockpile; during the same period there has been a marked increase in Soviet megatonnage. "Is There a Strategic Arms Race" (in the author's possession).
6. UN Doc/A/7721.
7. UN Doc/ENDC/PV 353, 5 December 1967.
8. UN Doc/ENDC/PV 357, 18 January 1968.

9. See Waldemar Bessen, *Die Aussenpolitik der Bundesrepublik,* 1970, pp. 391-95, for a discussion of Bonn's desire to connect their forfeiture of a nuclear potential with a solution to the "German Problem."

10. Nerlich, Uwe, *Constraining the Inactive,* Stiftung für Politik und Wissenschaft, Ebenhausen, published in part in "Vor der Bonner Entscheidung über den Nichtverbreitungvertrag," *Europa Archiv,* No. 21, November 1973.

11. UN Doc. ENDC/225/Rev. 1. According to an estimate by the Secretary General (UN dec. A/7575), the area affected by chemical weapons by a single strategic bomber would be up to 60 km., by nuclear weapons up to 300 km., and by biological weapons up to 100,000 km.

12. *Department of State Bulletin,* 15 December 1969, pp. 541-42; and 2 March 1970, pp. 226-27.

13. UN Doc/CCD/283, *Working Paper on Chemical Warfare Agents and the Commercial Chemical Industry,* 1970. See also Ann Van Wynen Thomas and A.J. Thomas, *The Legal Limits on the Use of Chemical and Biological Weapons,* 1970.

14. *Department of State Bulletin,* 27 April 1970, pp. 552-56. President Nixon acknowledged to complexity of the verification issue but indicated in his 1973 annual to Congress that the US was seeking agreement on "some partial measures [that] can be adopted to facilitate more comprehensive measures." *Foreign Policy Report to Congress,* May 1973.

15. UN Doc/CCD/269/Rev. 3; also *Department of State Bulletin,* 3 November 1969, pp. 365-68; 17 November 1969, pp. 425-29; 1 December 1969, pp. 480-84; 28 September 1970, p. 362; and 16 August 1971, p. 185.

16. *Department of State Bulletin,* 15 June 1970, p. 737.

17. UN Doc A/8421; A/8021 (plus Annexes); and A/AC 138/43 and 46.

Chapter 15
Multilateral Negotiations on Political Détente

1. It is interesting to note that the USSR is faced with identical problems on its opposite flank. The Soviets insist on the resolution of political differences with Peking before curtailing its present military build-up along the Chinese border. China refuses to negotiate on political matters while it is threatened by roughly 40 percent of the USSR's military power.

2. For a recent discussion of these objectives see Malcolm Mackintosh, "Moscow's View of the Balance of Power," *The World Today,* March 1973.

3. Bromke, Adam, "The CSCE and Eastern Europe," *The World Today,* May 1973.

4. Shulman, Marshall D., *Beyond the Cold War,* 1969.

5. See Brezhnev's speech in Alma Ata (15 August 1973): "Participants in the Crimea meeting were unanimous in the opinion that it is essential to improve considerably, at the present stage, the standard of the *ideological co-operation* of the fraternal countries and parties. A profound study must be made of each other's experiences and of the *joint struggle* against bourgeois ideology." Radio Moscow, 15 August 1973.

6. Sokol, J., "Peaceful Coexistence and Ideological Subversion," *Wojsko Ludowe,* May 1972.

7. See the following selected articles as representative of the growing amount of literature on the subject: K. Katuschev, "The Main Direction," *Problemy Mira I Sotsializma* (Moscow), No. 8, 1973; I. Aleksandrov, "In the Interests of Peace and Socialism," *Pravda* (Moscow), 7 August 1973; I. Sidelnikov, "Peaceful Coexistence and the Peoples' Security," *Krasnaya Zvezda* (Moscow), 14 August 1973; Y. Nikolayev, "Co-operation and Ideological Struggle," *International Affairs* (Moscow), No. 4/1973; Y. Kashlev, "Ideas Must Serve Peace and Co-operation," *Novoye Vrema* (Moscow), 4 May 1973; J. Kraszewski, "New Methods, Old Aims," *Sovetskaya Kultura* (Moscow), 31 July 1973; S.S. Vishnevsky, "Communist and Bourgeois Ideologies Are Irreconcilable," Radio Moscow Domestic, 29 August 1973; H. Neubert, "Peaceful Coexistence Aids World Revolutionary Struggle," *Einheit* (East Berlin), May 1973; J. Lukaszewicz, "Some Problems of the Party-Ideological Front," *Nowe Drogi* (Warsaw), April 1973; "Discussion: Problems of International Politics," *Miesiecznik Literacki* (Warsaw), June 1973; Sz. A. Pieniazek, "Trying to Get Out into the Wide World," *Polityka* (Warsaw), 14 July 1973; J. Szydlak, "The Party Program Expresses the Interests, Aspirations, and Aims of the Polish Nation," *Trybuna Ludu* (Warsaw), 10 January 1973; J. Kucera, "Ideological Offensive," *Tribuna* (Prague), No. 25, 20 June 1973; V. Jirasek, "The United Nations Organization and the Ideological Struggle," *Tribuna* (Prague), No. 27, 4 July 1973; V. Ruml, "The Socialist Transformation of the Intelligentsia," *Tvorba* (Prague), No. 32, 8 August 1973; T. Palos, "Ideological Struggle—Class Warfare," *Partelet* (Budapest), April 1973; J. Farago, "Power and Democracy," *Nepszabadsag* (Budapest), 18 August 1973.

8. *Rude Pravo,* 25 August 1973.

9. Ibid.

10. A complete list includes the initial accord. The author wishes to thank Edgar Rafael for aid in obtaining these documents.

1971

February 12:	Bulgaria-GDR

1972

June 28:	Bulgaria-Hungary
October 20:	Czechoslovakia-GDR
November 9:	Bulgaria-Poland
December 19:	Bulgaria-Czechoslovakia

1973

January 13:	GDR-Poland
January 28:	Czechoslovakia-Poland
March 26:	GDR-Hungary
May 31:	Hungary-Poland
June 7:	Czechoslovakia-Hungary

11. *The Times,* 3 July 1973; also Christopher Bertram, "Mutual Force Reductions in Europe," *Adelphi Papers,* No. 84, January 1972.

Chapter 16
Multilateral Negotiations on Military Détente

1. See the general "Threat Estimate" carried in *Neues Deutschland,* 30 May 1973. *Rude Pravo,* 1 June 1973, charged that a far greater concentration of combat-ready troops existed in the FRG than in any comparable East European territory and Bonn had the advantage of quicker mobilization, including the transfer of units to attack positions. On the other side, see West Germany Defense Minister Georg Leber's assertion that he feels "secure" despite recent modernization of Pact forces, *Die Zeit,* 23 June 1973; and the assertion by SACEUR General Goodpaster that the Pact threat is greater than ever.

2. Bertram, Christoph, *Mutual Force Reductions in Europe: The Political Aspects,* Adelphi Papers, No. 84, January 1972; Stanley, Timothy W., and Darnell M. Whitt, *Détente Diplomacy: Unites States and European Diplomacy in the 1970s,* 1970.

3. *Mirovaza, Ekonomika I Mezhdunarodnive Otnosheniga,* June 1972. See also RFE Research Memo, 19 June 1972.

4. *The Military Balance, 1972-1975,* London, p. 7.

5. *US Foreign Policy Report to Congress,* 3 May 1973, p. 68.

6. While the right to raise relevant issues was explicitly stated in the June Communiqué, the West directed its spokesman, the Head of the Dutch Delegation, Ambassador Bryan Quarles, to publicly restate this reservation on the Hungarian question. In particular, it was feared that verification could be circumvented by Hungary's absence.

7. Erickson, John, "Soviet Shield 72," *RUSI Journal,* December 1972.

8. *US Foreign Policy Report to the Congress,* 1973, p. 68.

9. As a trade-off Brezhnev agreed that the formal talks would commence on 31 October 1973 (the Soviets had been insisting that the MFR talks be postponed until *after* the completion of CSCE). He gained, however, a seemingly important Western concession on the format and content of the agenda. NATO has insisted upon a detailed, itemized listing of issues that would both prescribe the dimensions of the conference and allow a systematic point-by-point assessment. This mechanism would provide, built-in brakes against unwanted public euphoria and leverage against obstructionism—if agreement was not reached on one point, progress to the next could be impeded. Moscow sought and gained acceptance on the format used sucessfully in SALT: a statement of guidelines and principles, allowing work to proceed on an ad hoc basis. US concurrence ultimately compelled allied endorsement, but the lack of rigidity may work in the West's favor by reducing built-in obstacles and permitting the "good intentions" of all parties greater scope in influencing the negotiations.

10. As the Polish Army daily pointed out, this concept was much closer to the oft-stated French position that "mutual force reductions" could produce a shared benefit in undiminished individual security and predicted the ultimate participation by France when the premises of the conference would accordingly be changed, *Zolnierz Wolnosci,* 5 June 1973.

11. *US Foreign Policy Report to Congress,* 1973, p. 68.

Chapter 17
Bilateral Negotiations on Military Détente

1. *Military Implications of the Treaty on the Limitations of Anti-Ballistic Missile Systems and the Interim Agreement on Limitation of Strategic Offensive Arms,* Hearing before the Senate Armed Services Committee, 92nd Congress, 6 June-25 July 1972.
2. Grewe, Wilhelm, "The Effect of strategic Agreements on European-American Relations," *Adelphi Papers,* No. 65, London, February 1970, p. 19.
3. *International Herald Tribune,* 14 November 1969.
4. Brown, Harold, "Security Through Limitations," *Foreign Affairs,* April 1969, pp. 422-42.
5. *US Foreign Policy Report to Congress,* February 1971.
6. For a critical evaluation of the SALT accord see William R. Van Cleave, "Implications of Success of Failure of SALT," *Revue Militaire Générale,* June 1972.
7. Caldwell, Lawrence T., *Soviet Attitudes to SALT,* Adelphi Papers, No. 75, London, February 1971, p. 21.
8. Kormendi, Istvan, "World Politics, SALT II, and the Value of the Guarantee," *Maggoroszag,* (Budapest), July 1973.
9. *New York Times,* 22 June 1973.
10. *Military Balance, 1973-74,* p. 1.
11. Scofield, Herbert, "Strategic Forum: The SALT Agreements," *Survival,* October 1972.
12. *Military Balance, 1973-74,* p. 1.
13. The greater the reduction in strategic forces, the greater must be the inspection effort. Small violations are hard to detect, and are relatively insignificant at expanded force levels. At reduced levels, small changes are proportionally more dangerous. For the proposed limitations, existing surveillance methods are adequate and relatively inexpensive. But before drastic cuts can be anticipated new and more expensive systems will have to be developed to provide a higher confidence inspection effort. See Jerome B. Wiesner, "Inspection for Disarmament," in *Arms Control: Issues for the Public,* L. Henkin, ed., American Assembly, Columbia University.
14. Nerlich, Uwe, *The Role of SACEUR's Non-Central Strike Forces in East-West Negotiations,* Monograph published by the Stiftung fuer Politik und Wissenschaft, Ebenhausen, FRG, 1973.

Chapter 18
The Changing Nature of the International System and the Nixon Doctrine

1. Shulman, Marshall, "The Future of Soviet-American Competition," *Soviet-American Relations and World Order,* Adelphi Papers, No. 66., pp. 1-2.
2. Waltz, Kenneth N., "International Structure, National Force and the Balance of World Power," *Journal of International Affairs,* No. 2, 1967.
3. Deutsch, Karl W., and J. David Singer, "Multipolar Power Systems and International Stability," *World Politics,* April 1964.
4. Kaplan, Morton A., *System and Process in International Politics,* 1962.
5. Rosecrance, Richard N., *Action and Reaction in World Politics,* 1963; and "Bipolarity, Multi-polarity and the Future," *Journal of Conflict Resolution,* September 1966.
6. Young, Oran R., *Systems of Political Science,* 1968; and "Political Discontinuities in the International System," *World Politics,* April 1968.
7. Sommer, Theo, "After Vietnamization—Europeanization," *Survival,* May-June 1973.
8. Osgood, Robert E., *Ideals and Self-Interest in America's Foreign Relations,* Univ. of Chicago Press, 1953.
9. Hoffmann, Stanley, "Will the Balance Balance at Home," *Foreign Policy,* Summer 1972, p. 85.
10. Kissinger, Henry A., *Nuclear Weapons and Foreign Policy,* 1957.
11. Kortunow, W., "Peaceful Coexistence and the Ideological Struggle," *Voprosy Istolii,* KPSS. 1, 1972; quote by Leopold Labedz, "The Soviet Union and Western Europe," *Survey,* Vol. 19, no. 3, Summer 1973, p. 16.
12. Pipes, Richard, "America, Russia, and Europe in the Light of the Nixon Doctrine," *Survey,* Vol. 19, no. 3, Summer 1973, pp. 34-35.
13. Ball, George, "America and Europe: The Logic of Unilateralism," *Ibid.*
14. Brzezinski, Zbigniew, "The Balance of Power Delusion," *Foreign Policy,* Summer 1972; see also his *Between Two Ages: America's Role in the Technetronic Era,* Viking Press, 1970; and Buchan Alastair, "Power Relationships in the Far East: A European View," *Survival,* May-June 1972.
15. For the most comprehensive statement of the work of the Eurogroup and its future plans see "Report by the Planning Staff, West German Ministry of Defense," reproduced in *Survival,* Nov./Dec. 1972; see also Andrew J. Pierre, "The Future of America's Commitments and Alliances," *Orbis,* Fall 1972.
16. Pierre, loc. cit.
17. *United States Foreign Policy 1969-1970. A Report of the Secretary of State,* March 1971, p. 168; see also Stephan P. Gibert, "Implications of the Nixon Doctrine for Military Aid Policy," *Orbis,* Fall 1972.

Chapter 19
Adversary Relations and the Management of the Détente Subsystem

1. Hughes, Thomas L., "On the Causes of Our Discontent," *Foreign Affairs,* July 1969, pp. 653-67; Charles Bohlen, *The Transformation of American Foreign Policy,* 1969, passim; Arthur Schlesinger, Jr., "Origins of the Cold War," *Foreign Affaris,* October 1967, p. 30. George Ball argues

that the world is still bipolar and the best hope for relaxation of tensions still lies with the great powers, "Slogans and Realities," *Foreign Affairs,* July 1969, pp. 622-41. Polarization of politics is only feasible, however, when vital interests of great powers are in such jeopardy that world peace is endangered. In all other crises involving less important issues, the interests of other nations must be assessed, producing a multipolar political environment.

2. Steel, Ronald, "A Sphere of Influence Policy," *Foreign Policy,* Winter 1971-72, pp. 107-18; and Pierre Hassner and Ronald Steel, "Spheres of What," Ibid., Spring 1972, pp. 142-49.

3. Lowenthal, Richard, *Soviet-American Relations and World Order: The Two and the Many,* Adelphi Papers, No. 66, March 1970, p. 11.

4. Buchheim, Hans, *Totalitarian Rule: Its Nature and Characteristics,* 1968.

5. Friedrich, Carl J., Michael Curtis, and Benjamin R. Barber, *Totalitarianism in Perspective: Three Views,* 1969, p. 19.

6. Huntington, Samuel, and Clement Moore, *Authoritarian Politics in Modern Society,* 1971.

7. Skilling, Gordon H., and Franklyn Griffith, *Interest Groups in Soviet Politics,* 1970.

8. Steward, Philip D., *Political Power in the Soviet Union: A Study of Decision-Making in Stalingrad,* 1968.

9. Fleron, Frederic J. Jr., *Communist Studies and the Social Sciences,* 1971.

10. Ludz, Peter C., *Parteielite im Wandel,* 1970.

11. Lowenthal, Richard, "Continuity and Change in Soviet Foreign Policy," *Survival,* January-February 1972.

12. Ulam, Adam, *The Rivals,* 1971.

13. Szamuely, Tiber, "Five Years After Khrushchev," *Survey,* Summer 1969.

14. Brzezinski, Zbigniew, "The Soviet Past and Present," *Encounter,* March 1969.

15. Windsor, Philip, "The Boundries of Détente," *The World Today,* June 1969, p. 255.

16. Marshall Shulman has observed, "To begin with the term itself [détente] is imprecise and often misleading. Although in its strict sense détente suggests only some reduction of tensions, it is generally used to connote a political rapprochement. In retrospect, we see that even in periods when 'détente' was on everyone's lips, as in 1959 and again in 1963-64, the word had at best a qualified application, since the reduction of tension was accompanied by strenuous Soviet efforts to gain political and military advantages. It seems probable, for example, that the Soviet decision to increase production of intercontinental missiles was made during the post-Cuban 'détente' of 1963-64." "Europe versus Detente," *Foreign Affairs,* April 1967, p. 398.

17. Bjol, Erline, "The USSR Detente, and the Future of NATO," *Orbis,* Spring 1969, pp. 226-35.

18. Address by President John Kennedy, *Bulletin Department of State,* Vol XLIX, No. 1217, October 1963, p. 695. In his inaugural address Kennedy

presented his axiom on deterrence: "For only when our arms are sufficient
beyond doubt can we be certain beyond doubt that they will never be
used." See Ralph E. Lapp, *Arms Beyond Doubt: The Tyranny of Weapons
Technology,* 1970.

19. Adenauer insisted that détente was dependent upon basic changes within
the USSR, *Erinnerungen, 1945-53, 1953-55, 1955-59, 1965-66*; also
Anatole Shub, "The Lessons of Czechoslovakia," *Foreign Affairs,* January
1969, pp. 272-77.

20. Dougherty, James and J.F. Lehman, Jr., ed., "Arms Control for the Last
Sixties," 1967, p. xxxv.

21. Hassner, Pierre, "The USSR Since Khrushchev," *Survey,* Spring 1969,
p. 49.

22. Bull, Hedley, *The Scope of Soviet-American Relations and the World
Order,* Adelphi Papers, No. 66, pp. 102-20; and Bennett Kovrig, "Spheres
of Influence; A Reassessment," *Survey,* Winter 1969, pp. 102-20.

23. Buchan, Alastair, *Europe's Futures, Europe's Choices,* 1969, pp. 56-71, 154-56.

24. Schlesinger, Arthur M. Jr., *A Thousand Days,* 1967, pp. 831-35. This is the
most common interpretation held by the myriad of "general disarmers"
since the early 1950s.

25. Kolkowicz, Roman, "The Warsaw Pact: The Entangling Alliance," *Survey,*
Winter 1969, pp. 86-101.

26. Hassner, Pierre, "The Implications of Change in Eastern Europe for the
Atlantic Alliance," *Orbis,* Spring 1969, p. 243; also Bjol, *op. cit.,* p. 229.
On the difficulties of East-West convergence on social and ideological
matters see contributions by Melvin Croan and Tibor Szamuely, "The
USSR Since Khrushchev," *Survey,* Spring 1969; and Hassner's observation that
the main form of convergence is the convergence of worries (ibid).

27. Philip Windsor has written, "Whereas the détente was previously identified
with the status quo, the status quo is now (since Prague) identified with
increased hostility. . . . Instead of seeking as far as possible to preserve the
status quo in order 'to give détence a chance,' it has now become necessary
to accommodate change if the détente is to be secured. And yet there are
no indications so far that any government is able, or willing to work for
positive changes in East-West relations. . . . Soviet-American relations might
continue to develop but all that can be expected in Europe for the present
is at best immobilism, at worst hostility." *Op. cit.,* 257-58.

28. From Cuba to Prague, "The détente was generally assumed to be identical
to the status quo." Ibid., p. 255. Hassner argues that the great powers are
presently advocating neither status quo nor revisionist policies at the exclusion of the other, *Change and Security in Europe,* Parts I & II, Adelphi
Papers, No. 45 and 49, London.

29. Winsor, Curtin, Jr., "The Nonproliferation Treaty: A Step Toward Peace,"
Orbis, Winter 1969, p. 1015.

30. Hassner, Pierre, op. cit., *Survey,* pp. 45-50.

31. Windsor, Philip, *Germany and the Management of Détente,* 1971.

32. Academics are now beginning to acknowledge that university studies of

classical strategists and geopolitics were prematurely superseded by adoption of methods to examine and explain the international system as a whole, the characteristics of its components, and the nature of its interactions. The search properties and behavior patterns were launched before the strategic principles relevant to the unprecedented bipolarity were fully mastered. In a dialectical sense, not all the means of inquiry were fully exploited before the subject was discarded.

33. One of the most interesting aspects of the accelerating complexity of the technological revolution is the widening gap in comprehension between technicians and political leaders. National policy-makers are required to cope with an increasing number of domestic problems and are understandably often bewildered and uncertain about the ramifications of decisions related to ultramodern weapons systems. See Michael H. Armacost, *The Politics of Weapons Innovation,* 1968; Ralph E. Lapp, *Arms Beyond: The Tyranny of Weapons Technology,* 1970; Thomas W. Wilson, *The Great Weapons Heresy,* 1970; and Pierre M. Gallois, "Power and Paralysis;" *Orbis,* Fall, 1967, pp. 664-76.

34. George W. Rathjens has convincingly argued that in the present technological environment new weapons systems offer no new political options. *The Future of the International Arms Race,* International Conciliation, 1969.

35. The gap between the technological "have" and "have-not" countries substantially reduces the incentives to acquire national nuclear power, still widely regarded as the source of ultimate strength by nonnuclear states. Yet it no longer provides freedom of action in world politics commensurate with economic costs and heighten regional tensions. Though smaller states would presumably acquire nuclear weapons to threaten regional nonnuclear powers not to penetrate great-power missile defenses, the technological lead of the great powers makes regional nuclear defenses as plausible as the independent acquisition of deliverable nuclear weapons. Thus, the technical realities of missile and nuclear development contribute strongly to the enforcement clauses of the Nuclear Nonproliferation Treaty, the strongest single component of the overall status quo yet established.

36. Svetlov, B., "USSR-USA: Possibilities and Realities," *International Affairs,* February 1972; also V. Osipov, *Izvestia,* 17 February 1973; and F. D. Kulakov, *Pravda,* 22 April 1972.

37. *Pravda,* 28 June 1972. For a typical statement of the increasing number of West Europeans who are expressing apprehensions about the utility of ideological competition see Theo Summer, "Entspannung hat ihren Preis," *Die Zeit,* 21 September 1973.

38. Ulan, Adam, op. cit., p. 178.

39. First acclaimed in "Another Great Debate: The National Interest of the United States," *American Political Science Review,* Dec. 1952, and later reiterated in *Foreign Affairs.*

40. Kissinger, Henry, "Domestic Structure and Foreign Policy," *Daedalus,* Spring 1966.

41. For a contrast with an official tone see Joseph Luns, "The Future of the
    Atlantic Alliance in Light of Present European Developments," *The
    Atlantic Community Quarterly,* Summer 1972.
42. Nerlich, Uwe, "Westeuropa und die Entwicklung des amerikanisch-
    sowjetischen Bilateralismus," *Europa Archiv,* Folge 20, 1972.

Index

About the Author

Lawrence L. Whetten is Resident Director of the University of Southern California German Graduate Program in International Relations, Munich, Germany. He is the author of *Germany's Ostpolitik: Relations Between the Federal Republic and the Warsaw Pact Countries* (Oxford University Press) and *The Canal War: Four Power Conflict in the Middle East* (M.I.T. Press); he is a frequent contributor to professional journals. Dr. Whetten received the Ph. D. in political science from New York University in 1962.

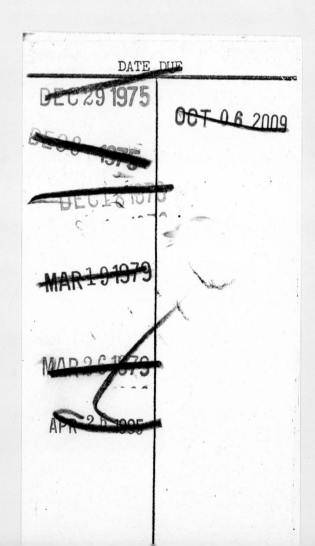